Beware the Great Horned Serpent!

Studies on Culture and Society

Beware the Great Horned Serpent!

Chiapas Under the Threat of Napoleon

Robert M. Laughlin

Studies on Culture and Society
Volume 8

Institute for Mesoamerican Studies
University at Albany
Albany, New York

Distributed by
University of Texas Press

For submission of manuscripts address the publisher:
Institute for Mesoamerican Studies
University at Albany
State University of New York
Albany, New York 12222

For copies address the distributor:
University of Texas Press
Post Office Box 7819
Austin, Texas 78713-7819

Cover: Ambrosio Llano, Bishop of Chiapa

Library of Congress Cataloging-in-Publication Data

Laughlin, Robert M.
   [Gran serpiente cornuda. English]
   Beware the great horned serpent! : Chiapas under the threat of Napoleon /
Robert M. Laughlin.
      p. cm. — (Studies on culture and society ; v. 8)
   Rev. translation of: La gran serpiente cornuda.
   Includes bibliographical references and index.
   ISBN 0-942041-19-4 (paperback)
   1. Tzotzil Indians—History—19th century. 2. Tzotzil Indians—Government
relations. 3. Manuscripts, Tzotzil—Mexico—Chiapas—History—19th century.
4. Tzotzil language—Social aspects. 5. Spain—Colonies—America
Administration. 6. Spain—Foreign relations—Mexico. 7. Mexico—Foreign
relations—Spain. 8. Mexico—Politics and government—1810-1821. 9. Mexico—
History—Wars of Independence, 1810-1821. I. Title. II. Series.

F1221.T9L3813 2003
972'.03—dc21   2003051079

Contents

Illustrations

Maps

Plates

Tables

All this is of purely academic interest.

Michael Glover
Legacy of Glory: The Bonaparte Kingdom of Spain 1808–1813.

The present proclama is one of my "red mark" mss, for all reasons—the scantiness of the material, its translation, and notes, and also its wholly unique character as a Napoleonic document. I know nothing like it in any dialect. It is a translation apparently into that far-off native minor dialect of the appeal for aid against Napoleon issued from Cadiz by the Junta, and throws a most interesting light on the situation at that time. So though my ms. is only a modern copy of the 1813 ms. (where the original is I don't know), it stands also at the very top in interest.

William Gates
Memorandum list #7 sent to Charles Bowditch, 1915?

A very repetitious and pompous proclamation.

Ledlie I. Laughlin

Un precioso manuscrito en lengua tzotzil.

J. Ignacio Dávila Garibi
Datos biográficos del Ilmo. y Rmo. Sr. Dr. y Mtro. D. Francisco Orozco y Jiménez
actual Dignísimo Metropolitano de Guadalajara y Administrador Apostólico de Chiapas.

As the Zapatistas approached town a giant serpent rose up in the sky and a thunderbolt crashed down. They fled to Chamula where a giant serpent rose up in the sky and a thunderbolt crashed down, so they fled to San Andrés Larraínzar, where they are today.

Report from Zinacantán, January, 1994

The shamans prayed for protection in the mountains, so when the Zapatistas approached town a giant serpent rose up and a whirlwind carried off their headgear and they fled. Then the federal soldiers approached town, a giant serpent rose up and a whirlwind chased them away.

Report from Zinacantán, June, 1994

Foreword

Peggy K. Liss

What did it mean that a manifesto issued in Cádiz in 1812 was translated into a Mayan language, Tzotzil? What does it mean to us?

Robert Laughlin is an anthropologist who came across an historical treasure, a transcript in Tzotzil of a manifesto addressed to "the overseas inhabitants" of Spain in the early years of the Spanish American independence movements. Such a document in an indigenous language is extremely rare, and so is a scholar who could make sense of it. Robert Laughlin is also the author of a monumental dictionary of contemporary Tzotzil, and editor of a colonial dictionary of the same language, and so he was well prepared to tackle the manifesto (Laughlin 1975, 1988). Recent events have brought Tzotzil-speakers and other Mayas of Chiapas into world news. This book cannot help but draw some parallels to the situation in Chiapas then and now.

Here an anthropologist focuses on history to understand the cultural meeting-place producing the document.[1] He relates the history of the manifesto, from the circumstances surrounding its origin in Europe to its transformation in America. At the same time, he conveys through narrative tone and style that standard approaches to history are our own cultural artifacts. He writes at a cultural interstice, telling his story soundly, as English-speakers expect, yet also so as to entertain the Maya of Chiapas. It should entertain some other people as well.

Having the texts of the manifesto in both Spanish and Tzotzil versions allows comparison of the terms chosen by Spanish authorities to appeal to creoles with their recasting to win over Mayas. The author's translation of the Tzotzil text provides a glimpse at how one Spanish-speaker, probably a priest, couched an appeal for Maya loyalty. Here is an example of political spin in the early nineteenth century. Interestingly, Spanish language policy for the previous half century had sought to combat native languages and bring Mexico's indigenous population into the Spanish-speaking mainstream. The avowed goals, within operative liberal principles of political economy, had been "to civilize" native speakers and bring them into a single Spanish-speaking nation—as producers and consumers. It was a vision of material progress promising an enhanced life on earth for everyone. This document is a marked departure, its recourse to Tzotzil surely responding to the emergency of Mexican insurgency.

The story of the interplay between events in Spain and Spanish America on the eve of independence is a complicated one.[2] When the French invaded Spain in 1808 and captured the royal family, Spaniards reacted by forming regional juntas claiming to preserve sovereignty for the crown prince, Ferdinand VII. Among Spaniards, Napoleon stirred up hornets' nests of national patriotism. Spain's patriotic fervor, language, and juntas set off a chain reaction—the birth of nationalism—throughout the Western world, including in Spanish America. Surely mindful of what had happened to Britain when that nation excluded Americans from parliament and certainly desirous to keep Spanish America out of Napoleon's camp, the central junta—the governing body that emerged in opposition to Napoleon in Spain— included American deputies when it called a nationwide Cortes. The Cortes met under a successor group, a regency, and in 1812 produced a liberal constitution.

Earlier in Spanish America, the successful American Revolution of 1776, and the more extreme "Liberty, Equality, and Fraternity" of the French Revolution, had nourished desires for greater self-rule. With the Napoleonic invasion of Spain and Spanish resistance, propertied urban men in America, creoles for the most part, seized the opportunity to emulate Spanish patriots in taking charge of their regions by forming juntas. Mexican creoles chose to view their country in traditional terms, as the Kingdom of New Spain—in theory connected to peninsular Spaniards only through the king, who was now absent. They even foresaw that this kingdom might quite possibly become head of the Spanish empire should the regency fall.

By late 1809 Napoleonic agents were using the United States as a base for dispatching agents and pamphlets to revolutionize Spanish America, claiming the United States, Napoleon, and God were on the side of the colonists. The United States, at odds with the British in the Napoleonic Wars, favored the French. Thomas Jefferson in 1808 offered friendship to independence-minded Latin Americans and spoke of commonality of interest and hemispheric solidarity. Spanish Americans wanted no domination by French, English, other Americans, or Spaniards.

American juntas of 1808 emulated their Spanish counterparts in claiming to represent the collective "people" and perceived Spanish weakness. With the royals absent, all of them, claiming to embody the sovereignty returned to the nation, were quick to participate in a general fallback to greater regional autonomy. Creole deputies called to the Cortes in Spain discovered they shared grievances and realized the extent of their fellowship. Proclamations of the regency published in Mexico and Peru, meant to counter French incitement to independence, told Americans they were "raised to the dignity of free men"; their destiny was in their own hands.

Visions of political and economic liberalism, injected with new romantic nationalism, and in the face of Spanish weakness and an avowed fear of French invasion, exploded into armed struggle for independence. Imminence of a joint invasion by the United States and the French was the rationale for the Mexican creole conspiracy from which Miguel Hidalgo emerged to lead an unsuccessful social revolt in 1810. The radical following he attracted dampened creole ardor for militancy and undoubtedly for independence as well.

Among the five members of the new regency formed in 1812 was Joaquín de Mosquera y Figueroa, a Colombian Creole. He had been a judge on the Mexico City Audiencia, then had moved on to rebellious Caracas and was well aware of the temper in America. Mosquera y Figueroa wrote the manifesto of August 30, 1812, directed to overseas inhabitants, promising them the liberal desiderata, protection and prosperity, and urging loyalty to the mother country and the new constitution. Other regency proclamations promised equality and opportunity for indigenous people. The work of liberal American deputies in Cádiz, those manifestos can also be read as attempts to counter Napoleon's inciting Americans to independence, propaganda that was so reminiscent of French revolutionary ideas that had sparked uprisings in South America and the Caribbean. French influence on America in those years was substantial, both through revolutionary concepts and the anti-revolutionary rhetoric that played on fear of an invasion by Napoleon and of Indians rising to join him. Hidalgo's army of 1810 fed those fears.

Chiapa, which lay within the jurisdiction of the Kingdom of Guatemala, was an imperial fringe area, accessible to contraband, including ideas. In Chiapa loyalty to the crown, the far-distant and absent monarch, was much stronger than that to the Captain General of Guatemala. In 1813, local oligarchs, including the civil authorities of Guatemala City, resented being milked by the peninsula, but because they enjoyed relatively free trade and great political autonomy, they tended to espouse liberalism. They, and the Guatemalan deputies to the Cortes, became stalwart foes of the archconservative Captain General and his soul mate, the archbishop. Even so, when the Manifesto arrived in early 1813 and was translated into three Mayan languages, it was conservative rhetoric that was employed to keep native peoples loyal to King and Country.

That Robert Laughlin thinks the anonymous translator or, better, interpreter of the Manifesto was a conservative priest is readily understandable, given the text's highly charged religious language and its nature. The translator converted Mosquera's modern-leaning, neo-classical propensity to speak of tyranny, liberty, and fame into an apocalyptic scenario updated from the Book of Revelation and at times expanding on that book's Old Testament references. In the Tzotzil version, Napoleon is the deceiver, depicted as a latter day Antichrist who falsely claims, "I am the Lord of the Universe." In Revelation the forces of evil are directed on earth by Satan, who is also the Dragon, and his many cohorts— Antichrist, heretics, unbelievers, demons. Among the Maya, as Laughlin points out, the horned serpent too deceives, wears a mask, but the Horned Serpent is not evil. In the Tzotzil manifesto, though, the translator has updated the primordial combat myth, "this cosmic struggle" between good and evil, order and chaos, that figures so prominently in the Book of the Apocalypse.[3] The Spanish nation is the new Israel, favored by heaven, and Spain is the New Jerusalem, the millennial kingdom. Its ruler has departed but will return. He is the desired one, the messianic king, "the substitute for God on earth," the heroic savior. He loves and will protect his (Indian) children, much as in the Book of Revelation the Lord was to seal off the faithful on the Day of Wrath. Spain is also a woman—she will be protected from evil by the power of the Constitution. The role of the Constitution resembles that of the apocalyptic angel (usually identified with St. Michael) who binds the dragon in the pit for 1000 years, and it also recalls the constitutive biblical agreement, the covenant God made with Moses. Napoleon's soldiers want to drink blood, as did the Whore of Babylon. And Christian soldiers, in the Tzotzil version, are willing martyrs, whom God will not let die.

Was this patterned apocalyptic imagery by then a staple of Christianity in Chiapa?[4] Was the translator appealing to concepts that had become real to his target audience? Robert Laughlin finds that the horned serpent figures in Mayan mythology and, I would guess, represents a fusion of earlier Mayan myth with the Christian combat myth, which itself amalgamated older non-Christian traditions.

In the Spanish text, Mosquera also speaks of seducers and of innocents seduced. He grieves for the motherland, the poor nation weak and abandoned, in decidedly non-classic, baroque-cum-prophetic fashion. The wise people in Cádiz, he says, are blessed and have given us "a sign of our salvation." He thereby hallows the Spanish constitution and links its authors and the authorities in Cádiz to the millennial saints, God's chosen people.

The translator of the manifesto into Tzotzil condemns Indian insurgency as upsetting the good order of God, which includes a society composed of those who command and those who obey. He exhorts taking the holy path and embracing God's goodness. He has Spanish Christians promised a great star, portent of the holy day and of "our lives,"—in triple reference, to Christ risen, the Day of Judgment, and immortal life for the faithful. Yet while his imagery is apocalyptic, his message is more earthbound and concerned with the present. Perhaps the difference between the articulate liberal politician and the priest steeped in traditional political theology seems greater than it is. Both oppose the anti-religious French. Both seem to appeal to the presuppositions of their readers and hearers regarding political arrangements. Both demonstrate that political assumptions were fused with religious concepts. Yet the question remains of whether the Tzotzil writer was in fact appealing to Christian presuppositions then existing among the Maya or adapting his own storehouse of rhetoric to the problem at hand. And to what extent was the imagery he drew on syncretic with non-Christian Maya traditions? The case of the great horned serpent indicates that similar imagery had dissimilar meanings. Robert Laughlin has opened avenues of research for both historians and anthropologists, as well as for students of rhetoric and political theory.

When Ferdinand VII returned in 1814, and The Desired One proved to be ultra-conservative and generally obnoxious, the dashing of the hopes that had been raised in and by his name spurred many Spanish Americans to independence. Time, though, seemed to stand still for the Indians of Chiapa, implies Laughlin, much as it did for manifestos addressed to retaining or regaining their adherence.

NOTES

1. As Aaron Gurevich (1992:3), states, conversely: "we [historians] begin to see the new outline of history as historical anthropology."

2. For broader context, see Knight and Liss 1991. For a sampling of views, see Lynch 1994.

3. See Collins 1976

4. For earlier Spanish political use of apocalyptic imagery, see Liss 1992.

Acknowledgments

In "How, Who, and Why" will be seen the varied contributions made to this endeavor by Jane Walsh, Benjamin Bentura and his daughter, by the late Marianito, Eugenio Maurer, S.J., Lawrence Feldman, Terrence Kaufman, Bruce Mannheim, Tziak Tza'pat Tz'it, Samuel Robledo, Tranquilino Moreno Espinosa, William Merrill, Mario Humberto Ruz, and Carter Wilson. To each of them, for posterity, I repeat my thanks. Eugenio Maurer also aided me in identifying and translating Tzeltal vocabulary, in improving my Spanish translation, and comprehending the priest's biblical references. Alfred Bush gave me access to, and a copy of the 1906 "original" *Proclama* document. Angélica Inda as always searched every corner of the San Cristóbal episcopal archives to reveal hidden pieces of the puzzle. Macduff Everton captured in color the portrait of Bishop Llano in those archives, and Oscar Horst tracked down for me a portrait of Archbishop Casaus y Torres. Christopher Lutz provided me with copies of the *Proclama* discovered by Lawrence Feldman. Peggy Liss corrected errors in the manuscript and gave me valuable leads. At the Smithsonion Institution, Victor Krantz and Marcia Bakry promptly prepared the illustrations for this study. When I was confronted by electronic complications Kurt Luginbhyl saved the day. Joyce Sommers. wise as a serpent, pulled me, year after year, through the Smithsonian bureaucratic jungle. Repeated grants from the Smithsonian Research Opportunities Fund permitted the necessary travel to Mexico.

My late father, Ledlie I. Laughlin, whose judgment I always found entirely reasonable, gave me a sobering assessment of the quality of "my" proclamation, but his perennial delight in the absurd renewed my resolve. An unknown review reader asked me to clarify the absurd! "How, Who, and Why" tells of the trans-Atlantic trip shared by my family; my wife, Mimi, my daughter, Liana, and my son, Reese, but it does not hint at the emotional costs of my obsession with this proclamation. Their endurance and encouragement were vital elements. At last Mimi will be delivered from the great horned serpent and all the other nineteenth century characters so that we can live together again alone!

Introduction
How, Who, and Why

On a gloomy winter day nearly thirty years ago my colleague Jane Walsh handed me a batch of papers that she had found in the National Anthropological Archives, three flights down from my office in the Smithsonian Institution's National Museum of Natural History. "Have you seen this?" It was marked *Manuscrito en lengua sotzil* [Manuscript in the Sotzil Language], surprising because of the scarcity of Mexican material in these archives, and astonishing because it had landed in the building that also housed a Tzotzil Mayanist "expert." The manuscript as well as the expert had been moved some years before from the Bureau of American Ethnology in the Smithsonian castle.

This typed document, a Tzotzil translation of a Spanish proclamation dated 1812, had been donated to the Bureau of American Ethnology in 1930 by William Gates, who had added the following note:

> This transcript, together with two others, the large and important Sotzil Dictionary, and the Soque sermons, was presented by Orozco y Jiménez to Dr. Nicolás León, who later sold them to Paul Wilkinson, from whose (second) sale I bought them.
>
> The Bishop's palace was completely looted by the Carranza-Alvarado forces, the brutal leader of which I later encountered as Governor in Oaxaca when I passed through there in 1918. After the looting above, i.e. in the Spring of 1915, my agent, F. J. Smith, was given leave to enter the former library and "help himself." He reported "nothing left."[1]

The original manuscripts had been found nearby in Comitán around the turn of this century by the Bishop of Chiapas, Francisco Orozco y Jiménez (plate 1), who transferred them to his episcopal library in San Cristóbal, and assigned "M. M" in 1906 to make a copy of the dictionary and the proclamation. My assumption that he was a priest cannot be verified, for there is no one with those initials in the list of priests of the diocese shortly thereafter. The next year the Bishop had the copies delivered to the director of the Museo Nacional de Arqueología, Historia y Etnología in Mexico City. It was almost surely the proclamation sent to the museum that was described by the bishop's biographer as "a beautiful manuscript in the Tzotzil language" (Dávila Garibi 1913:8).

Then began a long odyssey for these transcripts as they passed from hand to hand, in Mexico City from the Mexican anthropologist Nicolás León to the American bibliophile Paul Wilkinson, then to the Mayanist William Gates in Point Loma, California, in 1914, then to the bibliophile Robert Garrett in Baltimore in the late 30s. He donated them to the Institute for Advanced Studies in Princeton in 1942, from where they were transferred to the Princeton University Library in 1949. This odyssey is described in detail in *The Great Tzotzil Dictionary of Santo Domingo Zinacantán* (Laughlin 1988). In addition to the Princeton copy, and Gates' typed copy at the National Anthropological Archives, is a photocopy made by Gates, stored in the Wilkinson Collection of Indian Languages at the Library of Congress.

M. M.'s clear hand gave no indication of the identity of the nineteenth-century translator whose task it was to convey to the Indians that they were protected by a new constitution and a new Overseas Ministry that would soon bring prosperity and happiness to all the inhabitants of Spanish America, so long as they remained loyal to the Motherland and did not stray onto the path of Napoleon and the insurgents. But it was clear from the style, the parallel phrases studded with metaphors, the religiosity and moral pronouncements that the original Spanish political proclamation must have read very differently.

Now began the task of locating the Spanish original. In those good old days when the stacks of the Library of Congress were open to scholars, I spent many hours in what turned out to be a fruitless search, despite the discovery of many proclamations dating from that era. The only alternative seemed to be a trip to Spain.

In the summer of 1975, with my family I crossed the Atlantic on one of the last voyages of the Leonardo de Vinci, traveled through France, and then by train from Hendaye across the border to Irun, from where, because our official passports lacked official visas, we were set back on the train and deported to Hendaye where, after a long search, I was able to discover a hospice vacancy so that we could celebrate the annual Basque festival before returning to Spain.

For two weeks I trekked from library to library in Madrid, including the newspaper library. Several times I thought the proclamation would be placed in my hands, but it was never so.

Wondering if a copy had been saved by the family of the Duque del Infantado who, as President of the Regency in Cádiz, had signed the proclamation, I secured a letter of introduction from the American cultural attaché and proceeded to the duke's residence. Repeated rapping on huge wooden doors caused them to be opened a crack. An old woman peered out at me suspiciously. When I asked for the duke she replied, "The duke is on vacation on his yacht," and pushed the door tight shut.

In my library research I happened on Benjamin Bentura's *El Hidalgo Payanes*, a biography of Joaquín de Mosquera y Figueroa, regent and, he claimed, author of the Proclamation, with a paragraph from the Proclamation included in his biography. A search in the phone book produced Bentura's name, but on calling I learned that he, too, was on vacation, but was given his phone number in Zaragosa. Intrigued by my project, he suggested that his daughter could take me to his apartment to search through his library. He promised to phone her and gave me her number and address. At her invitation, I took the elevator up to the eighth floor of a condominium tower, but no, it was not her apartment. With sinking heart I tried another tower and another before I found her. We set off the next morning to her father's apartment behind the bullring. Opening a glass-fronted bookcase, I examined eagerly book after book until finally I discovered a book dated 1820, wherein the author, Joaquín Lorenzo Villanueva, one of the deputies of the Cortes imprisoned by Ferdinand VII, writing from his jail cell, called for justice. He wondered how it was possible that his judge could be Joaquín de Mosquera y Figueroa who had written—then followed quotations (not always correct) from that very same paragraph of the Proclamation cited by Bentura. Here was proof that de Mosquera was indeed the author of the Proclamation, but the jailed deputy offered no further information.

Days spent in the Archive of the Indies in Seville resulted in nothing more than my embarrassment as the archivists watched my clumsy attempts to rebundle the dockets as neatly as they had been before I untied them. No luck either in the library of Cádiz. And so with only a paragraph of the Proclamation in my folder we returned home.

A week later, at summer's end, I made my way back to the stacks of the Library of Congress. Disheartened, I randomly pulled a book off the shelf and opened it up to see *"Proclama del Duque del Infantado a los habitantes de ultramar"* in a collection of documents from the Archives of Guatemala.

The next scene, winter in the episcopal archives of San Cristóbal: a large, dingy room in the back of the cathedral where, for nearly fifty years, bound packets of documents had sat from floor to ceiling, gathering dust and creating a zoo of bookworms.

Marianito, the sacristan, bent double with age, would insert an enormous iron key in the door to let me in. Assuming I was a priest, he asked me to bless his saint pictures! No amount of searching revealed the original Tzotzil document that must have disappeared when the Carranza forces looted the library in 1915.

Who was the translator and what had provoked the Bishop of Chiapa, Ambrosio Llano, to ask for a translation?[2] I pored through the bundles, some ordered in the 1930s by subject, with seventeenth-century parchments nestled between twentieth-century carbon copies in no apparent order. Finally I discovered an enormous collection of the correspondence directed to "my" bishop, Ambrosio Llano. The life and times of don Ambrosio had its own drama when a severe earthquake shook the letters out of my hands. At last I opened the letters of two priests who, protesting their age and their infirmities, declined to do "the difficult interpretation" of translating with such "elevation" the proclamation sent from Spain.[3] But that was all. In dusty bundle after dusty bundle not another word about the Proclamation.

And then one day I snuck upstairs and peeked through a large keyhole: broken pews, pulpits, shelves loaded with ancient tomes, stacks of newspapers and Church missals. A visit from my Jesuit anthropologist friend, Eugenio Maurer, incited me to ask the sacristan's permission to inspect the shelves. In a few moments my companion pulled out a bundle of worm-eaten proclamations, sewn together, including a copy signed by the Duque del Infantado.

Returning to Washington in the spring, I thought, "This is an old man's job, I can do it when I reach that stage of my life." And so the Proclamation was shelved once again.

But several years later I was visited by Lawrence Feldman who, having just returned from Seville, recounted his discovery of four copies of a Spanish proclamation, translated into different Indian languages. One was in Ixil, another in Q'eqchi', a third with the mysterious name "Zeefe," and the fourth unidentified. "Who signed the proclamation?" I asked. "The Duque del Infantado in 1812." Realizing that the passage of time had stripped away any reason for postponement, I began again.

With copies in hand, I phoned Terrence Kaufman, but had great difficulty in reading aloud the Zeefe and the unidentified text. "I thought you had gained experience in reading colonial Mayan manuscripts," he rejoined. "No, apparently not. I'll send them to you," was my lame response. A few days later he called to boost my spirits with the report that Zeefe was the extinct, non-Mayan language Xinka, and that this was the longest surviving text known to date.[4] The other was Quechua from Peru, identified later by Bruce Mannheim as being of the Cuzco dialect.

Once again I returned to the San Cristóbal archives, now carefully ordered by community and housed by Angélica Inda in the upstairs room, under the gaze of every Bishop of Chiapas, their portraits lining the walls in red- and black-robed splendor. More pieces of the historical puzzle were fitted together, but never has there appeared the Archbishop of Guatemala's request for Indian translations, nor the Bishop of Chiapa's request for a Tzotzil version, nor any further reference to the Proclamation.

In an effort to set the stage for the presentation of a Tzotzil proclamation in Chiapa, I gleaned the episcopal archives where, apart from Bishop Llano's correspondence, I found only scattered references to life in the late eighteenth and early nineteenth centuries. But in 1993 I came on a recently discovered and published collection of documents that had disappeared from the episcopal archives (Porrúa 1992). Dating from 1779 to 1782, they chronicle the struggle between Joseph Ordoñez y Aguiar, the "perpetual rector and vicar for His Majesty of the

Town of Chamula," and the Indian caciques of that community (Porrúa 1992:254).
From these 567 pages of manuscript emerges a vivid portrait of Indians caught in
the vise of Church and State, where cruelty, intrigue, and corruption prevailed,
where the determination to maintain Maya Indian identity conflicted absolutely
with the outsiders' attempts to "civilize" and Christianize the community. Looking in this dark mirror, it is startling, disturbing, to recognize a familiar face, that
of the ancestor of today's Chamula.

Though the events chronicled in these documents occurred twenty years
before don Ambrosio's arrival in Ciudad Real (San Cristóbal de las Casas)
and though they occurred in just one town, it was the major Indian community.
The sentiments of the Chamulans were central to the concerns of Church and
State in Chiapa.

Chamula was the focus of the only other proclamation known to be translated into Tzotzil, in two columns, with Spanish on the left and Tzotzil on the
right. This was a broadside signed by two priests in San Cristóbal de las Casas, in
October, 1870, during the War of the Castes, or the War of Saint Rose. In sharp
contrast to the benevolence of the 1812 proclamation, this proclamation assails
the Indians with messages uncannily similar to those offered in the 1990s by the
Mexican government to the Zapatista Army of National Liberation. Titled "For
All the Rebellious Indians to Hear," the 1870 proclamation declaimed:

> The Government of this state is disposed to punish severely Indians
> who have disrupted the public order and to bring them back under the
> rigor of the law.
>
> But because you are so many and because in our fatherly hearts we
> hate to take the full measure against you, and because we consider you
> guided by ignorance and perhaps by terror your leaders instilled in you,
> the Government has given you eight days to surrender yourselves.
>
> And since you may not understand this, we undersigned have sent
> you this letter in your own speech, making the following observations:
>
> 1. If you surrender within eight days, you will be forgiven, and if not
> then you will be persecuted and you will die, either by gunshots or by
> hunger in your flight.
>
> 2. If you do not surrender, not only you but your wives and your
> children will die. Not because the Government would kill *them,* but
> because fleeing into the mountains the poor women and children will
> suffer terrible hunger, and from hunger will follow death.
>
> 3. Pursued, you will be unable to plant, and with no one tending them
> you will lose your stores of corn, so even those who are not shot will
> simply die with nothing at all to eat.

4. What you demand is unjust. God, the Most Holy Virgin of the Rosary, your Patron San Juan, San Mateo and Santa Rosa are angry with you, and have brought about the fall of your religion.

5. You were cheated by your leaders. This Galindo cheated you. Many died in your war, but who has come to bring them back to life?

6. The President of the Republic now knows what you have done and is angry with you, and though there are enough soldiers here, now he is going to send us many more, and then you will be brought to an end. Those who are coming do not know you, they do not love you as we do. The proof of our love is that so far we have sent so few soldiers against you.

Everyone in this city is begging the Government to pardon you, but only if you surrender at once and lay down your arms so we can believe you. (Wilson 1972:282–283)

This proclamation essentially heralded the end of Indian armed resistance in Chiapas until our times.

Turning now to the Tzotzil translation of the Proclamation of 1812, a close examination of the text showed that it was sprinkled with vocabulary from the neighboring language, Tzeltal. In 1994, when I read the Proclamation to my Tzeltal friend Tziak Tza'pat Tz'it from Tenejapa, a crooked smile crossed his face as he heard how his "elder brothers" in Spain cared so for the Indians of America, and when the Proclamation promised a new age with "good teachers in the schools" he shook with laughter. Indeed, the 1812 Proclamation's promises of good roads, good teachers, hospitals, bountiful crops, strengthened industries and increased trade read like every governor's annual report, less the statistics.

Two priests' letters in the church archives, one sent from Simojovel and the other from Huitiupán (then Gueyteupan), together with the linguistic evidence of the Tzotzil translation itself, suggested strongly that the text was penned originally in Huitiupán. This tropical town in the north of Chiapas, today with a population of 12,000 inhabitants, a majority Tzotzil-speaking, is virtually unknown to the Tzotzil Indians of the Highlands. In the seventeenth century, on the Royal Highway from Ciudad Real to Villahermosa, it boasted three large churches and their Franciscan friaries. In the 1860s the priest asked permission to remove everything from the remaining Church of San Pedro because there were only three or four huts left nearby. Today, a small chapel built in the 1920s is dwarfed by the ceiba tree in the main square. A few old men still wear white cotton shirts and pants, their wives' waists wrapped in dyed blue skirts woven in the Barrio de Mexicanos in San Cristóbal.

It is comfortable to assume that Huitiupán, home of the Proclamation of 1812, with the passage of time has witnessed progress in human rights for its Indian population. Alas, this is far from the truth.

Towards the end of the nineteenth century much of the land in the whole area of northern Chiapas was purchased by a handful of San Cristóbal elite who established coffee fincas and cattle ranches. Arriving in the principal town of Simojovel and learning that the giant ceiba tree in the plaza was considered by the Indians to be sacred, they plied the mayor with liquor so that in a drunken state he gave permission for the ceiba to be cut down. The Ladinos promptly had it felled (surely by Indians) and built a new courthouse, a house of justice.

In the 1930s, when Graham Greene in his *The Power and the Glory* chronicled the persecution of the priests and the burning of the saints in the neighboring state of Tabasco under the orders of Governor Garrido, a similar drama was being enacted across the state line: "Following the course of Garrido Canabal in Tabasco, the Governor of Chiapas, Victórico Grajales ordered the burning of the saints in the public squares of each town. He prohibited Indian languages and the use of traditional clothing" (Pérez Castro 1989:76). This is remembered in Huitiupán.

A Mexican anthropologist, Ana Bella Pérez Castro, studying the agrarian movement in the region, interviewed the people of Huitiupán in 1983. Their memories are not easily forgotten: "Don Benjamín Mazón hid the people, his peons; he hid them in the woods, that's why there was a delay in giving them land; he hid them so that it would seem that he had no people, so they wouldn't fight, so they wouldn't take away the land, that's why they remained slaves." (Pérez Castro 1989:79)

A son presents, with no apologies, indeed with pride, the life of his father as feudal *patrón* in the middle of the century, *this* century. With intimate detail he paints a vivid portrait of Indian serfdom in shockingly recent times:

> [His father] had just reached 69 years of age. Some say he had 80 children, and others say no, that there were around 90. What I can tell you for sure is that the late Filemón, my father, was the master and lord of Sacaltic. Many say that the late Filemón raped women, but it's just pure lies. He was good, yes indeed, all the wives of the peons passed through his hands first. When they reached ten or twelve years, he said to their fathers: "Look, now it would be good if you sent me your daughter to work on the finca." And as everyone knew that he was the boss, they sent them. If they did not send them, he ran them off the very same day, but in all those years he only sent one running. One who for sure was nobody's father.
>
> It's true I didn't see it, because the one I'm going to tell you about, who lives now in the ejido La Competencia…is 45 years old now. But they tell me that one day don Filemón got mad, really mad, because he learned that Isidoro Hernández had a wife who hadn't passed through his hands.

He summoned all the peons, struck Isidoro in the face and the stomach and ran him off the finca. And to teach everyone a lesson he took out his knife and cut off Isidoro's left ear, who departed with the blood pouring down.

Don Filemón liked things to be right. That old man who was here began as a child earning 20 cents for a whole day's work. From six to six. And that other one told me he worked one week for don Filemón, and the next on other people's cornfields. The deceased had a shop and sold to us on trust. When someone wanted to leave he said to him, "Very well, you can go, but pay me first."

Those who did not get up early to work he scolded and put them to work on Sundays from six til noon, for nothing. But it's true he never whipped anyone, as many of the bosses used to do here.

He said to those who had plenty of work, but were very lazy; "Now you're going to get it straight, loafers." And he sent them to bring firewood, to pick corn, tobacco and bananas. They say that people used to be stronger. They each carried loads of 50 kilos on their back, from here to Simojovel where the deceased sold his things, because others took them out directly by plane.

On this finca the deceased had about 60 women, but don't think they all lived with him. When they were little they worked in his house and then each one went to their hut and did the best they could. Most of them married other peons (don Filemón himself found husbands for them), and others left. When he was tired of one and wanted to have another join him, he just sent first for the father to advise him of it…Yes, my father, the late don Filemón, was a lecher! (Pérez Castro 1989:68–69)

In 1993, ten years after Pérez Castro's study, I sought the aid of Samuel Robledo, a Ladino of Huitiupán I had met the previous year who knew some Tzotzil. He had led my wife and me through chigger-infested fields (we later learned) to see the ruins of the church and monastery of Santa María Asunción, the patron saint. Hidden in the jungle, fragments of the huge walls were pulled together and apart by tangles of roots and vines. To check on the Tzotzil vocabulary of the Proclamation of 1812 and its possible similarity to the dialect of Huitiupán he took me to interview his old *compadre,* Tranquilino Moreno Espinosa. Together they confirmed my suspicion that the text had been penned in Huitiupán.

Though Sr. Robledo was pink-cheeked, he proved to be entirely fluent in Tzotzil, explaining that he had come as a young child to Huitiupán. I asked if he knew of don Filemón Penagos' reputation as a lecher. Nodding his head, he continued in Tzotzil: "I was brought up in Sacaltic. I saw don Filemón cut off the ear of Guadalupe—his name is Guadalupe, not Isidoro—Hernández, who lives at La Competencia. As a boy I once saw don Filemón stroking the legs of a little girl. Then he ushered her into his room, and when she began to cry I heard him tell her in Tzotzil, 'Shut up and suck your candy!'" I asked about don Filemón's son: "He died recently; same name, same habits."

As I left Huitiupán, I gave a ride to a hitchhiker who turned out to be one of the 150 soldiers encamped at the edge of town, with the duty of protecting the remaining fincas from Indian "invasion." On Oct. 16 [1993] more than 1,000 state police in Chiapas, Mexico, violently evicted a group of indigenous *campesinos* who had been occupying the Huitiupán mayor's office for a week in a local political dispute. More than forty protesters were beaten and wounded in the attack and five were arrested. The *campesinos* were to meet that day with state authorities and release the mayor, who they said had been "arrested by the people" (*La Jornada*, 17 October, 1993). In a 1993 report, the Miguel Agustín Pro Juárez Human Rights Center (CDHPRO) reported that Chiapas accounted for 63.8% of the 3,387 human rights violations against indigenous people recorded in Mexico for 1992 (*Weekly News Update on Nicaragua and the Americas*, #196, October 31, 1993, Courtesy of Carter Wilson.). Great horned serpents of various stripes are still alive in Chiapas!

The "why" for this study generates no easy answers. The Spanish proclamation is a model of conciseness. Sent to all the colonies of America and Asia, it was a valiant effort to restore Spain's hegemony, but shortly after its issuance, absolutism under Ferdinand VII returned with a vengeance. It became an irrelevant, forgotten document. I could find no copy in Spain. I only know of copies in the archives in Seville, Guatemala City, Lima, Mexico City, and San Cristóbal. I know of only five books that give it a mention: two bibliographies, two biographies, and the plea written by the jailed deputy. It is likely that it, just as the 1812 Constitution itself, promoted a demand for liberal government throughout the colonies, establishing a mind-set that would no longer tolerate abuse, contributing to the revolutionary cause, to the irresistible desire for independence.

I could find no edict from Spain calling for the translation of this proclamation into native languages, and yet its existence in four Indian languages of the Captaincy General of Guatemala and in one of Peru implied that such an edict must have been dispatched to the colonies. A tip from Bruce Mannheim provided the missing piece: a bibliography of Peruvian documents revealed that the Quechua translation of the Proclamation had been printed in Lima in 1813 by order of the Archbishop who, in his letter to Spain, referred to "[letter] #121, according to which the Minister of State of Your Excellency requires that as soon as the Proclamation is translated and printed for the inhabitants of these kingdoms, copies of it be sent in triplicate, as I was notified by His Most Serene Highness in the decree of August 30 of the past year. Consequently I enclose a published copy of the best translation of many that were done so that Your Excellency be so kind as to inform His Most Serene Highness" (Rivet 1951:247). The bibliographer, Paul Rivet, commented, "Because of its historical interest and rarity we reproduce in full the text of this proclamation" (Rivet 1951:247).

All pertinent royal decrees were routinely sent to both the civil and religious governments. But the destruction of their archives in the military turmoils of the nineteenth and twentieth centuries, together with the difficulty of penetrating the surviving Church archives, has impeded the discovery of other translations of the proclamation into Indian languages of Mexico and South America, and possibly native languages of the Philippines. With its particular concern for "the Indians, that beautiful portion of mankind, inhabiting America," this proclamation called not only for the colonists' loyalty, but also for a new, national respect for Indians.

These translations emphasize the Regents' intention that Indians be aware of the new political order.

To my knowledge, this is the only Spanish decree ever sent to the colonies with specific instructions that it be translated and printed in the native languages. By the beginning of the nineteenth century, the number of Indians literate in their mother tongue must have been limited, but the elite, both in Peru and in Tlaxcala, did publish texts in their own language. The Viceroy of New Spain issued edicts in Nahuatl that warned of the perils of following the rebel Hidalgo. Although directed primarily to the inhabitants of northwestern Mexico, for whom Nahuatl was not even a first language, their number indicates that the local government considered it appropriate to communicate to the Indians in native languages, not only in Spanish. Perhaps it was under the influence of the Peruvian deputy to the Cortes, Inca Yupanqui, and the Tlaxcalan deputy, José Miguel Guridi y Alcocer, who were the most eloquent spokesmen for the Indian cause, that this order for translation of the Proclamation was promulgated. It may be taken as a reflection of the sincerity of the liberal deputies of the Cortes of Cádiz.

We can dare to surmise about the general historical significance of the Proclamation of 1812, but locally we are without a clue. If the Tzotzil proclamation was read in the churches, if it won the Indian parishioners' loyalty to the Metropolis and gave them a new sense of self-respect, for this we have no evidence.

While there are Tzotzil word lists, grammars, catechisms, and sermons from the 19th century, this is a unique survival of Tzotzil narrative from that period. There are no earlier narratives of any length. The mixture of Tzeltal with the Tzotzil is puzzling. Perhaps it was a deliberate ploy of the anonymous friar so that his translation would reach the speakers of both languages. Huitiupán was situated on one of the main routes from the Chiapas Highlands to the Caribbean Coast and so would have been visited by many speakers of both languages. Today, Indians living along the border area of Tzotzil and Tzeltal are fluent in both languages.

There is no way to judge from the available historical records what the significance of the Proclamation was in the nineteenth century, either nationally or locally, but in company with contemporary decrees and correspondence, it opens a window on the years just prior to independence: a chapter of Spanish,

French, and local Chiapas history that has been allowed to slumber on the shelves. Who of us would dream that for the officials of that time Napoleon and his spies were like the "red scare"? This was a period of high hopes, of dark intrigues, of failed aspirations, when Church and State worked at times in union and at times in great conflict, when the general public in 1812 celebrated in Spain and in America the birth of the Constitution, and two years later, with equal gusto, its premature death. In the foreground strutted Napoleon and Joseph Bonaparte in combat with Lord Wellington; just behind stood Ferdinand VII and his premier, "the Prince of Peace," then Alexander of Russia, the "fanatic insurgents," the "wise men" of Cádiz, archbishops, bishops, captains general, and an anonymous friar all imploding on the lives of the Tzotzil Maya Indians of the Province of Chiapa. Or maybe not.

There is our friar who struggled with "the difficult interpretation" of the Proclamation so that its elevated tone would be conveyed to the Indians and simultaneously reach their hearts—a task he carried out loyally, weaving an elaborate tapestry of metaphor, bedizened with horned serpents, whirlwinds and jaguars, converting a political decree into a moral exhortation, and yet a task that this conservative friar, believing in the divine right of kings, must have performed with deep misgivings.

The pages that follow present a theater of the absurd, a fabulous history with myriads of details as if set in the Milky Way. The reader will not be comforted with an historical "argument." Seldom is there a logical, reasonable explanation for the existence or significance of these realities that time and again warrant the adjective "incredible." Those familiar with Chiapas will be amazed at the parallels with current figures and events. The political-religious strife of the town of Chamula in 1778 reads like today; Indian caciques, supported by the government, refusing that their people be catechized, have run the priest out, and caused many Chamulans to flee to San Cristóbal. In both periods we see a bishop moderating between the conservatives and the liberals (Ambrosio Llano, Samuel Ruíz), a government representative who strives valiantly, but in vain, to gain rights for the Indians (Mariano Robles, Manuel Camacho), a conservative church official who works against the bishop (the archdeacon and the papal nuncio), eloquent revolutionary military leaders (Matamoros and *subcomandante* Marcos) and bands of ill-armed insurgents who lurk in the woods.

In 1993, 181 years after the friar spoke of rights for the Indian population of Chiapas, for the first time since 1527, the Indian merchants of Hidalgo and Oaxaca were prohibited by the mayor of Cholula in the state of Puebla from selling their handicrafts at the patron saint's fiesta because he did not want "*animalitos*" in the streets. Racism in Mexico is not limited to Chiapas.

The historical images that parade through this book lead up to and follow the proclamation that promised all good things for the colonists in return for their loyalty. It was drafted in Tzotzil-Tzeltal by an unknown friar who, attempting to speak for the government and the Indians, embellished his phrases with strings of metaphors. And so Napoleon and his spies and, between the lines, the "fanatical insurgents," become great horned serpents, whirlwinds, and jaguars. And now it is *subcomandante* Marcos, the masked, also non-Indian representative of the Indians who, having absorbed their metaphorical vision, proclaims, "we are the mountain," "we are the people of the night, the Tzotzils, the bats."

It is my hope that this serpentine tale, doubling back on itself again and again, will proceed with fresh surprises. In Mayan style it will entertain, often with levity, the great hardships of the Indians of Chiapas.

Throughout the history of Chiapas, from Napoleonic times until now, the local powers at all levels have proclaimed that they can solve the problems of Chiapas with no outside help. Only their own sovereignty is relevant. Any external influence is an intrusion. The fallacy of this view is obvious; the economic, political and social reality of Chiapas has been, and still is, dictated in large part by mysterious external forces. For this reason, I do not present the "Tzotzil" proclamation at the beginning of this study, but rather focus on the situation from the other side of the ocean, coming closer and closer, through New Spain, to Guatemala, and, finally, to the province of Chiapa where one can see the authentic Chiapanecs at work.

Having set the scene on both continents I will present the regent's Old World proclamation, followed by the friar's New World proclamation. Then I will compare the two documents from a variety of perspectives—historical, philosophical, literary and linguistic—to show how our anonymous friar sought with great style to reach the hearts of his illiterate Indian "younger brothers." I then return to the events in the two continents that rendered the regent's and our friar's efforts exercises in futility, so that their words that I have quoted in full, the products of their lofty designs, are reduced to forgotten scraps of history.

My technique mirrors that described by Hannah Arendt, discussing the contribution of the German historian Walter Benjamin:

"The main work consisted in tearing fragments out of their context and arranging them afresh in such a way that they illustrated one another and were able to prove their *raison d'être* in a free-floating state, as it were. It definitely was a sort of surrealistic montage." (Arendt 1968:47. Courtesy of Carter Wilson.)

In Benjamin's own words:

It is the "attempt to capture the portrait of history in the most insignificant representations of reality, its scraps as it were" (Arendt 1968:11).

"The writing consists largely of quotations—the craziest mosaic imaginable" (Arendt 1968:8).

"Quotations in my works are like robbers by the roadside who make an armed attack and relieve an idler of his convictions" (Arendt 1968:38).

Beware!

NOTES

1. "Manuscrito en lengua sotzil": cover page.
2. The name of the state of Chiapas was invented in the beginning of the past century to replace the term for the colonial provinces of Chiapa y Soconusco. The readers' familiarity with "Chiapas" prompted its use for the title, but throughout the text Chiapas refers to the Mexican state and not the colonial province.
3. Letter: Montes de Oca to de la Barrera, 23 January, 1813, de la Barrera to Llano, 26 January, 1813.
4. More recently, Frauke Sachse has discovered over a dozen Xinka speakers in one community.

I

The World
of the
Proclamations

1

Spain

A FAMILY AFFAIR

In the early nineteenth century, a Spanish family affair dramatically influenced the history of two continents. Charles III, known for his liberal Bourbon reforms, was succeeded by his son, Charles IV, called "The Favorite" (plate 2). Charles IV was wedded to his first cousin, María Luisa of Parma (plate 3), when she was but fourteen years old. He was a pleasant but innocuous ruler, indecisive and afflicted by occasional periods of madness. His major decision was the choice of a prime minister. Charles, a lover of music, happened on Manuel de Godoy, a young, street-singing guitar player, who was blessed with a dashing figure and a keen mind (plate 4). Godoy rose to prominence with the speed of a meteor. He also caught the heart of the queen, and María Luisa soon gained the reputation of a nymphomaniac. A wily and unscrupulous courtier, before long Godoy became commandant of the armies and grand admiral. After Godoy negotiated the end of the war with France, in 1795 at the Treaty of Basel, Charles declared him "The Prince of Peace."

And then there was Charles's son, Ferdinand, Prince of Asturias, who despised his mother and her supposed paramour, and held little respect for his father. He became *"El Deseado"* [The Desired One] because the people were waiting for the death of his father, who was totally blind to the queen's numerous infidelities.

Under the rule of María Luisa and Godoy, the treasury emptied and foreign credit disappeared. Godoy tied Spain to France in a series of disastrous treaties, sacrificing Spain to his personal aims. The Prince of Peace was described by his contemporaries as "flighty, indiscreet, pleasure-seeking, slothful, his principle is to have no principles. Money is his lodestone and falseness is his policy" (Glover 1971:13).

In 1807 the plot thickened. Ferdinand laid plans to poison his mother and Godoy. Condemned to death, he begged pardon and was absolved, but he betrayed all his followers, who were jailed or exiled. He also appealed to Napoleon for a bride from the Bonaparte family. His letter was intercepted and Charles was induced to imprison his son for conspiring to gain the throne.

On October 21, Godoy treacherously signed the Treaty of Fontainebleau permitting Napoleon to bring his armies into Spain to conquer the British army in Portugal. The treaty stipulated that Godoy would become the Prince of Algarves, under Spanish suzerainty.

In November, with two French armies occupying the north of Spain, Charles deemed it wise now to support his son's request for a Bonaparte bride, but, well aware of Ferdinand's conspiratorial nature, Napoleon rejected this second appeal with contempt.

Family discord erupted once again in March 1808, as Napoleon's brother-in-law, General Murat, advanced with his army to the south. In Aranjuez, after denying that the king and queen were about to flee, Godoy was seen loading the royal carriages. Running to his palace, he took refuge from the enraged mob. Accounts differ; some say Godoy was caught rolled up in a carpet on the third floor, others, that after being holed up for a day he ventured out, seeking a loaf of bread, only to be stripped nearly naked and severely beaten. Malcontent nobles loyal to Ferdinand were quick to accuse Godoy, "the Sausage Maker," of treason. Ironically, while Godoy for the first time decided to resist Napoleon and seek safety for the king by removing him to Seville, the crowd believed they were fleeing to America, probably to Mexico.

On March 19, lest the Prince of Peace be executed by Ferdinand and the mob, Charles abdicated in favor of his son, who promptly declared himself Ferdinand VII, King of Spain and the Indies (plate 5).

But not many days passed before Godoy induced Charles to change his mind and reassert his reign. Ferdinand, still pining for a Bonaparte bride, wrote Napoleon that he was going to Bayonne because of "the confidence that Napoleon inspired in him and the desire to convince him that Charles IV's abdication had been made spontaneously." Napoleon, upon reading the letter, exclaimed, "What? He is coming? This is impossible" (De Vadillo 1836:260).

So Napoleon, fed up with the constant intrigues of the Spanish royal family, ordered the ruling political body, the Spanish National Junta, to Bayonne and arranged for a royal family reunion there at the Imperial Palace. In support of her beleaguered husband, María Luisa confided in Napoleon that Ferdinand was not really Charles' son, and so not properly eligible for the throne. On May 9, 1808, Napoleon forced Ferdinand to return the throne to his father, who, unbeknownst to Ferdinand, had the day before ceded it to "my dear friend the Emperor Napoleon" (Boletín del Archivo General del Gobierno 1938:III: 3, 329).

Thus began the French exile of the Spanish royal family and the Prince of Peace. Both Charles and Ferdinand received handsome pensions. Ferdinand fared best as a captive in Talleyrand's chateau in Valençay, while Spain and the Indies awaited the return of "the Beloved" (plate 6). Napoleon, by banishing Ferdinand, had made the king a hero, and won for himself the eternal enmity of the Spanish people in Spain and abroad (plate 7). Ferdinand's abdication was considered void because it was without the consent of the nation. Who would have believed that this devious man, forever courting Napoleon's favor, would become for the Spanish people a national symbol of independence, of freedom from conquest? They looked to him to reestablish the political, social and religious institutions of their country.

A BROTHERLY AFFAIR

Now it was Napoleon's turn to take full command. He quickly drafted a new constitution that pretended to be democratic, but codified a thinly disguised absolute monarchy. He ordered the Spanish National Junta, there in Bayonne, to approve it.

Though Napoleon had little praise for his family—"They are all insanely ambitious, ruinously extravagant and devoid of talent"—on July 7, 1808, he declared his eldest surviving brother Joseph King of Spain and the Indies (Glover 1971:28). At this, Ferdinand VII "cordially congratulated" Joseph (plate 8), adding that "he considered himself to be a member of the august family of Napoleon, because he had asked the Emperor for one of his nieces to be his wife and he hoped to gain her" (Fernández Hall 1928:129). Joseph made a grand entry into Madrid, but "it was a melancholy scene. The silence and disdainful looks of the inhabitants were all the more significant since so much solemnity was given to the ceremonial" (Glover 1971:43). Joseph was despondent as he viewed the populace and confronted the arrogance of the Spanish officials. Without informing his brother, Napoleon gave specific military orders to scattered generals, a policy he continued throughout the Peninsular War, to Joseph's exasperation (plate 9).

Joseph had been a popular king in Italy.

> During his brief reign at Naples, Joseph effected many improvements; he abolished the relics of feudalism, reformed the monastic orders, reorganized the judicial, financial and educational systems, and initiated several public works. In everything he showed his desire to carry out the aims which he expressed to his consort in April, 1806: "Justice demands that I should make this people as happy as the scourge of war will permit." (Encyclopedia Britannica 1910:4, 193)

The author of a romantic novel, he was kindly and ambitious, charming but totally ineffective. Again and again he urged sensible, appropriate courses of action on his brother, four times threatening abdication if his voice was not heard, but Napoleon consistently overruled or ignored the man he had chosen to be king.

Joseph arrived in Spain with a vision, to establish a constitutional monarchy that would constitute an independent country, a good neighbor to France. A genuine reformer, "half philosopher, half king," he attempted to appeal to the national past by encouraging national theater and setting up a commission to exhume Cervantes' remains (Encyclopedia Britannica 1910:151). He patronized a national museum of painting.

Joseph was better housed in Madrid than was the Emperor in the Tuilleries. He staged grand dinners for sixty to eighty guests with ladies in court dress and men in uniform with silk stockings. He brought Italian opera and also ballet to Madrid. In 1809 he celebrated his brother's birthday with a procession, *Te Deum*, an opera and fireworks.

Joseph, who never had gained a reputation as a military leader, sought to vindicate himself by opposing Lord Wellington at Talavera, July 27–28, but before he was able to reach his armies they had been defeated. For this he earned a continuation of his brother's scorn.

Napoleon, wishing only a satellite state, ignored Joseph's "constitutional monarchy." To strip the nobility and the Church of power, he abolished all feudal rights and dues, and gave orders to suppress the Inquisition and to close one third of the monasteries.

In February of 1810, Joseph, at the head of his army, traveled south to Seville, where he was acclaimed by the whole city; the despised local junta promptly fled. In eastern Andalusia, he was welcomed by those who hoped he would stop the French generals from looting their treasures and sending wagonloads of art back to France. He visited archeological sites and attended bullfights. In Ronda he met a descendant of Moctezuma, who became his courtier and was rewarded with a key, the badge of a vice-chamberlain.

But Joseph's welcome was short-lived. From the beginning he had been dubbed "The Intruder King." Others called him *"Pepe Botellas"* [Joe Bottles], though in fact he was not a heavy drinker, and mocked him mercilessly in numerous caricatures: one shows him kneeling in prayer within a bottle (plate 10), another riding a *pepino* or cucumber (plate 11). A play was produced in Madrid in 1808 entitled *"El sueño del Tio José, que quiso ser primero y quedó cola"* [The Dream of Uncle Joseph, Who Wished to Be First and Became the Tail End].

In the winter of 1810–1811 in Madrid, fifteen hundred people died of hunger, even though Joseph had bread baked in the palace and distributed to the needy. Tax collectors were being murdered, so that collections of tax money required a troop escort. Joseph lost the sympathy of the Sevillanos as Napoleon gave orders to the individual generals who ravished the countryside, while Joseph's protests were ignored by one and all. He complained bitterly to his brother, "How long can public opinion go on supporting a man who has no money, no territory, no troops, and no authority?" (Encyclopedia Britannica 1910;211).

On March 16, 1812, as Lord Wellington advanced through Spain, Napoleon finally gave Joseph supreme command, but the generals either did not know or did not care. The people's "indignation rumbled hoarsely for a time, like a volcano in labor, and then burst forth in an explosion of fury" (Rydjord 1972:259). On August 12, Joseph, with five thousand infantry and thousands of minor Spanish officials, fled Madrid for Valencia with two thousand carriages, carts, and wagons. Wellington entered the capital city in triumph. In November and again in December, Joseph returned to the capital for a few days. His final departure on March 17, 1813, was at Napoleon's orders. On June 21 the French retreated to France. Napoleon blamed his brother and stripped him of his command of the armies. On April 18, Joseph abdicated.

Joseph journeyed to America, where he fathered a child by a Quaker girl, returned to Europe, and died in 1844, "at his request buried with the Golden Fleece, Spain's highest order of chivalry, about his neck. He had awarded it to himself" (Glover 1971:328).

THE PENINSULAR WAR

In 1807, when Napoleon sent his armies into Spain, he thought the troops would only be necessary to maintain public order and to man the forts. Once the Spanish armies were defeated he expected the people to become passive and anticipated the withdrawal of the British. On May 2, 1808, the city of Madrid rose up against Napoleon's brother-in-law, Joachim Murat, who quelled the rebellion with such viciousness that May 2 became a symbol of national resistance, provoking the local juntas in province after province to revolt and, on May 5, to declare war. In November, Napoleon's army outnumbered the Spanish by five to three. He expected an easy victory, but the Spanish armies, despite their ill-trained troops and ramshackle equipment, had an extraordinary ability to recover strength. Although scorned also by Wellington, by their very persistence they became Napoleon's most dangerous opponents.

Nobles, clergy, and soldiers united with the people and calmed disorder, but many from the propertied class in occupied Spain cooperated with French authorities, while others crossed the border into France. Essentially it was the "little people" of the provinces who provided the principal opposition. Peasants and university students pillaged rifles and demanded that the juntas represent them forcefully. The local juntas became the center of the civilian war effort, taxing, organizing guerrillas, chasing deserters, and countering defeatist propaganda, but the generals were perpetually in conflict with them. This was, indeed, when the term *"guerrilla"* was coined.

The Central Junta of Seville promptly assumed the title of majesty. Its members engaged in personal controversies, issuing "endless decrees with empty professions and visionary reforms" (Walton 1837:1, 142). Despite its follies and perversions, its attention to nonessentials, the Junta was bitterly anti-French and called on the people to cause the French soldiers as much harm as possible.

On January 22, 1809, the colonies were recognized "as an essential and integral part of the Spanish monarchy," for the tribute of the Indies and the voluntary contributions from America were absolutely essential to the cause (Salvatierra 1939:282). Bewailing the capture of Madrid, the Junta urged the fidelity of the Americans. "There is not a single American who wishes the Metropolis to be in danger, but they could be tricked, seduced by appearances."[1] On May 10, the Secretary General of the Junta sent a second plea for support from the colonies: "As it is difficult to decide if the French are more fecund in the arts of evildoing, than in their search for all the means to seduce and deceive, it would not be surprising if they follow the iniquitous plan of usurpation that their Emperor has proposed, trying to extend their machinations to the Americas, as they have done in all Europe."[2] After a lengthy description of the latest military events, the Secretary General returns to the purpose of this royal order: "so that making it public in those Dominions their natives guard against the sinister impressions that could be caused by the machinations and intrigues that our ferocious enemies are employing now more skillfully than ever, exaggerating their might and their triumphs to intimidate the Powers, who, like us, have to avenge the insufferable outrages, and defend their just rights."[3] Spain was falling away from America; its authority was collapsing. There were revolts in Argentina and Venezuela.

Communication within Spain was so difficult then that opposing armies spent days locating each other in the mountains, and generals who called for reinforcements often received no aid, because their cohorts could not find them! With the failures of the regular armies the guerrilla tradition became central to Spanish patriotism. Guerrilla warfare was a rural phenomenon that sanctified violent individual action.

At the Siege of Zaragoza, February 1809, ten thousand French troops were killed, while the Spanish military casualties were only six thousand; however, disease and starvation carried off forty-eight thousand civilians!

The various armies were not so stellar as their generals would have wished. Arthur Wellesley, Lord Wellington, the man most responsible for winning the Peninsular War, felt quite alone (plate 12). His Iberian allies were not at all of the quality that he deemed necessary for the enterprise of conquering Napoleon. He is reported to have made the following judgments: (1) "There exists in the people of Portugal an unconquerable love of their ease, which is superior even to their fear and detestation of the enemy" (Glover 1971:268); (2) "I have never known the Spaniards *do anything*, much less, do anything well" (Carr 1966:106); (3) regarding Spanish generals and government, "It is impossible for any rational man to talk to any of them. ... Examine any transaction in which they have been concerned and it will be found characterized by delay, weakness, folly or treachery" (Glover 1971:269).

When Wellington's British soldiers re-entered northern Spain they discovered a town where every cellar was stocked with casks of wine. Stoving in the barrels, "they literally floated in the lakes of wine" (Glover 1971:82). After the battle of Vitoria, a captured French officer confessed to Wellington, "the fact is, my lord, that you have an army, while we are a walking bordello" (Stanhope 1888:144). And the junta of Valencia complained in a proclamation of June 7, 1809, that the French "have behaved worse than a horde of Hottentots. They have profaned our temples, insulted our religion and raped our women" (Carr 1966:107).

The Peninsular War has been called "the first total war" in modern history (Anna 1983:116). "It created for European romantics the image of a nation *sui generis,* a natural force uncontaminated by Europe" (Carr 1966:105).

Though the country had been reduced to a "skeleton"—with all of Spain, except the port of Cádiz, under the French since 1811—Spanish resistance continued unabated. The Spanish lion had the French eagle in its teeth (plate 13). Lasting five-and-a-half years, from November 1807 to June 1813, Napoleon's adventure into Spain cost the lives of 300,000 of his countrymen. If we believe his words spoken in St. Helena years later the figure could be raised to 300,001: "It was that miserable Spanish affair...which killed me" (Connelly 1985:385).

PROCLAMATIONS (1808–1809)

Napoleon's outrageous deception of the Spanish people, aided and abetted by Godoy, and followed by his invasion, was proclaimed to the world and to America by individuals and juntas in a chorus of pompous protest.

In 1808, a proclamation appeared, addressed to Spaniards and all of Europe, "translated from vulgar Arabic," and supposedly penned in Tangiers by one Abunnumeya Rasis:

> Ah Spaniards, though I am African and barbarian, raised in the burning climate of Numidia...[I speak of the] armed invasion under the appearance of friendship and good faith...The greedy monster who gloried himself with the title of the Prince of Peace reduced the Spanish nation

> to a fatal state of inertia regarding France, and on the other hand commit-
> ted it to an endless and destructive war against England...With the
> pompous names of independence, regeneration, liberty and happiness
> you had lulled the souls of the Spaniards. (Abennumeya Rasis 1808:19,
> 3, 7, 22).

This, as he remarks, until May 2.

Rasis points out that the constitution brought by Joseph lasted but two days.
He called for the establishment of a central junta in Madrid and the creation of a
mature constitution, possibly modeled after the English constitution.

Perhaps in this same year appeared a proclamation addressed to Spanish
Americans, from the "Sevillians:"

> The frenetic and ambitious conqueror, the cursed and declared enemy of
> humanity, a man without morality or character, an incomparable mon-
> ster of perfidy and ingratitude, the audacious and sacrilegious profaner
> of laws, rights, and religion, in a word, Napoleon Bonaparte... Was not
> France our ally? ... This despot cannot be an inhabitant of cultivated
> Europe, nor can he be a man like us. The fierce lions of Libya and the
> horrible serpents of Persia have fed on blood more human than his.[4]

After describing the abdication and invasion, the Sevillanos speak up hope-
fully:

> Even the climate is fighting with us. The spirited Andalucian, the in-
> domitable Catalan, the audacious Vizcaíno, the noble Asturian, the
> suffering Galician, the valiant Estremeño, the loyal Castillian, all run [to
> defend] the cold Pyrennees.
> An American is a true Spaniard... You are now warned if there are
> venal and bastard Spaniards trying to seduce and trick you, swear to
> Ferdinand VII in your vast hemisphere. Loyalty, obedience and fidelity
> should be the distinctions that decorate you.[5]

On January 1, 1809, the Supreme Junta of Seville published a lengthy "Manifesto of the Spanish Nation to the Other Nations of Europe":

> Nations! People of Europe! Princes who are at their head! Good men of
> every degree, of all states! The Spanish Nation, and in its name the Junta
> of Government, to whom the unjust and atrocious captivity of its King
> has entrusted the authority, is about to hold up to the light before you the
> series of misfortunes and injuries which it has suffered; and presenting
> to you a faithful picture of its actual situation and of its intentions,

confidently claims your compassion for its woes and your concern for its fate.[6]

The Junta speaks of "a disgraceful peace," and "a ruinous and unequal alliance."[7] After the Tumult of Aránjuez, "'The Favorite' [Charles IV] was precipitated to the insignificance whence he ought never to have emerged."[8] The Junta laments that initial Spanish victories were followed by defeats, "But the provinces have redoubled their efforts... Let the Tyrant undeceive himself how many soever intrigues he may plot, however many advantages he may obtain, he will never take from us, either the hatred to French domination, which animates every Spaniard, nor the indefatigable constancy, with which we will rush to repair the caprices of fortune."[9]

Describing the suppression of Madrid by Murat on May 2, 1808, the Proclamation states: "the children were transfixed on the bayonets, and carried in triumph as military trophies; the sanctuary of the temple sacrilegiously despoiled and sprinkled with the blood of the defenseless priests, whom even there they slaughtered."[10]

It speaks of the ruination by Napoleon of Italy, Switzerland, Holland, Germany, Austria. "If Spain should fall, Austria will perish!"[11] It warns Emperor Alexander to beware of Napoleon's promises and treaties.

It concludes, "Imitate us, therefore, in our constancy and our efforts, Oh Monarchs and Peoples of the Continent, and the world, threatened with being the spoil of a monster, will at last recover its independence, and its tranquility."[12]

To this proclamation were appended documents from General Murat. He informs General Dupont that on May 2, twelve hundred of the populace were killed and that on the following day the junta, "dreading a repetition of the 2nd of May," begged him to be their president.[13] In a circular to the Spanish Captains-General he informs them, "Order now has everywhere returned: the past is entirely forgotten."[14] He exhorts the Captains-General to adhere to the government and to aid in "hindering the shock of the affairs of Madrid from being felt in your province."[15]

The same junta, on January 22, 1809, sent a decree to America, "proclaiming that creoles should be considered as people, not things, citizens, not exploitable material, that colonies are not factories, but an integral part of the Spanish monarchy" (Salazar 1928:117).

Frustrated with the incapacity of the Supreme Junta of Seville, the English ambassador to Spain, Henry Wellesley, declared that he would leave Cádiz and tell the English government to stop all aid unless a government were formed in Cádiz. To show respect for the king, he advised them to name their government body a regency. And so the members of the junta headed south for a tumultuous reception in Cádiz.

NOTES

1. Decree: Suprema Junta de Sevilla, January ?, 1809.
2. Decree: Suprema Junta de Sevilla, May 10, 1809.
3. Decree: Suprema Junta de Sevilla, May 10, 1809.
4. Proclama a los españoles americanos, Los Sevillanos, 1808?:1.
5. Proclama a los españoles americanos, Los Sevillanos, 1808?:3–4.
6. Manifesto of the Spanish Nation, to the Other Nations of Europe 1809?:2.
7. Manifesto of the Spanish Nation, to the Other Nations of Europe 1809?:3
8. Manifesto of the Spanish Nation, to the Other Nations of Europe 1809?:7–8.
9. Manifesto of the Spanish Nation, to the Other Nations of Europe 1809?:17–18.
10. Manifesto of the Spanish Nation, to the Other Nations of Europe 1809?:18–19.
11. Manifesto of the Spanish Nation, to the Other Nations of Europe 1809?:26.
12. Manifesto of the Spanish Nation, to the Other Nations of Europe 1809?:29.
13. Manifesto of the Spanish Nation, to the Other Nations of Europe 1809?:35
14. Manifesto of the Spanish Nation, to the Other Nations of Europe 1809?:37.
15. Manifesto of the Spanish Nation, to the Other Nations of Europe 1809?:37.

2

Cádiz, the Cortes, and the Constitution

CÁDIZ

The dark scenes of imperial and royal intrigue in northern Spain have an operatic tone. In Cádiz darkness turns to light as the city becomes the center and symbol of Spanish popular invincibility and enlightenment.

The port of Cádiz is seated on the tip of a narrow, sandy island, difficult of access (plate 14). It was from here that Christopher Columbus set sail on his second and fourth voyages. It was to here that the treasure ships returned with their cargoes of gold and silver. In the nineteenth century, the town was defended by walls with four gates. The narrow streets were lined by tall, flat-roofed buildings, with their backs to the land, facing the sea. The seventeen *barrios* had but three plazas.

In 1810 Cádiz had trade goods from all of Europe, from America, the Philippines, and Africa, but with Spain under siege, these far-flung commercial activities declined generally while trade with the United States increased.

The people of Cádiz, perhaps because of the large number of resident foreigners, were known for their hospitality, generosity, and tolerance. The regents and deputies were loath even to execute spies. The kindness of the people of Cádiz extended to animals, for there were no bullfights. Class distinctions were muted in this port where the nobles became bourgeois merchants, liberal and nationalistic.

In Cádiz resided the English ambassador, the Papal Nuncio, the Minister of the Two Sicilies, and the Minister of Portugal. The people of Cádiz felt closer to America than to the rest of Spain. Cádiz was, indeed, the only Spanish town that lived close to the American problem. From the beginning the populace looked on America with comprehension and sympathy, asking for equal rights for Americans. The large population of resident Americans and the constant business contacts fostered a romantic sympathy for liberty among the merchants of Cádiz, even though it went against their own interests. Cádiz did not favor insurrection, but it was understanding about it. Many spoke with an objective tone, trying to find reasons for keeping America united to Spain.

While there is no census available, the population rose precipitously in 1810 as Spanish soldiers arrived from all over the country to defend the last bastion of Spain. They were followed by the American deputies to the Cortes. In 1802 there were 42 rooming houses; the number multiplied greatly in 1810. The deputies lodged in private homes or rented houses.

The cultural life of Cádiz was remarkably active considering that Cádiz was under unremitting siege and constant bombardment for three years—a bombardment with few mortal victims, but one which battered the nerves.

There were 20 bookstores, many book collections, seven presses. Here was born the café society of Spain. In 1802 there were 23 cafés and 29 sweetshops. The cafés became the seat of intellectual debate. Here the people flocked to get the latest news of the insurrections in America and to discuss the proceedings of the Cortes. When the deputies arrived there was but one newspaper, with business news. Overnight the newspapers multiplied. The best newspaper, *El Conciso,* was a fervent defender of the Cortes, with an edition of 2,000, astonishing in a town where most of the population was illiterate. The *Censo General* was the newspaper of the *serviles* or conservatives. Poorly written, an enemy of the Cortes, it specialized in virulent insults. Daily the *servile*-liberal polemics were broadcast in the newspapers. One journalist reported that he and a pretty girl were in love and wanted to marry, but her father refused, not because he was of bad blood or poor, but because her father was a servile and he a liberal!

With freedom of the press declared in 1812, the number of newspapers grew from 11 to 17. For the first time, newspapers represented public opinion, (1) because the new conception of the State involved popular intervention in the destiny of the nation, and (2) there was now freedom of the press. This freedom permitted people to oppose the notion of a free press, but only those who had something to hide attacked the press.

But this right was severely tried by the publication of two "dictionaries." The *Diccionario razonado manual para inteligencia de ciertos escritores que por equivocación han nacido en España,* published in 1811, was a satiric attack on political and religious reformers, which inspired the Librarian of the Cortes, Bartolomé José Gallardo, to write his *Diccionario crítico burlesco* in 1812. This second "dictionary" caused a great scandal for being anti-church, calling down the wrath and insults of the bishops. Gallardo was imprisoned for being a subversive, but later he was freed and deported. The first dictionary was also banned as being provocative of arguments. There was a fear that the Inquisition would be reinstated.

In addition to the café society, there was what has been called a "cultural matriarchy," for Cádiz was the home of many educated women interested in learning languages, acting as interpreters, secretaries, journalists, writers, and doctors (Solís1969:364). One famous salon was led by a conservative, and one by a liberal.

No less important in the cultural life of the people of Cádiz was the theater, which became a center of patriotic expression. Of course there was debate about the morality of conducting theater, especially in wartime. There were two theaters, staffed with 97 actors: 76 men and 21 women. In the period of 1811 and 1812, they performed 117 comedies and 91 burlesques. No tragedies are mentioned! Puppet theater was also popular. Cádiz also had a School of Fine Arts and many merchants owned art collections.

Lest spirits be palled by the French bombardment and by the scourge of yellow fever in 1811 that took 264 lives, including those of deputies and a president, there were horse shows, popular concerts, dances, illumination of the city, and fireworks. Reports of victorious battles were celebrated by elaborate firework *castillos,* topped by a barrel and *Pepe Botellas* hoisting a glass of wine.

But perhaps the most notable creations of the citizens of Cádiz while under fire were the endless jokes and poems penned at the cafés. To celebrate Wellington's victory at Salamanca, a hymn was composed:

> *"Ya ¿qué importa que á la España*
> *turbe un mónstruo su sosiego*
> *si en Wellingtón tiene luego*
> *por defensa un Semi-Dios?"* (de Castro y Rossi 1862:141)

> [Now, what does it matter to Spain,
> If a monster disturbs her peace,
> If she has right away in Wellington,
> A semi-God for her defense?]

Or the patriotic verses:

> *Váyanse los franceses*
> *en hora mala*
> *que Cádiz no se rinde*
> *ni sus murallas.*

> [May the French be gone,
> At this evil hour,
> Cádiz will not surrender,
> Not even its walls.]

Con las bombas que tienen
los fanfarrones
hacen las gaditanas
tirabuzones." (Solís 1969:231)

[With the bombs,
Of the show-offs,
The women of Cádiz,
Make corkscrews.]

To this chorus was added the voice of the Countess of Chinchón, who, psychologically broken by the infidelities of her husband, Manuel de Godoy, fled with other aristocrats from Madrid to Cádiz and, standing on her balcony, sang the popular Spanish song, "Death to Napoleon!" (Schickel 1968:71).

But the defense of Cádiz was assured not only in verse, but by the unity of the people. Priests and monks formed "brigades of honor." Together the rich and the poor, nobles and peasants, citizens and foreigners pulled down balconies, banisters, and window grilles to add to the fortifications as they raised them ever higher. Watchmen were stationed in the monastery towers to watch for the puff of smoke from the French cannons and to quickly ring the alarm on the monastery bells. From 1810 to 1812 there cascaded on the city 472 grenades, but so few exploded that their major effect was to provide a source for mockery in the songs of Cádiz.

Although many English sailors, merchants, politicians, and writers were living in Cádiz, the Regency's call for aid for Lord Wellington was not received with joy. Only five years before, the Spanish fleet had sailed from Cádiz to be shattered at Trafalgar. Only three years before, Spain had signed peace with England, on January 14, 1809. The English had been considered throughout Spain as heretics and hateful foreigners, so their arrival was met with suspicious silence. And yet the British ambassador, Henry Wellesley, had endeared himself to the people by providing a triumphal reception on August 1, 1809, after the victory of Talavera. Indeed, it was his policy to mark Spanish military successes with dances until, in 1812, when it became too dangerous, he offered fireworks displays. Nor could the populace ignore the fact that it was the British galleons in the harbor that were bringing bullion from the Spanish colonies and munitions. From 1808 to 1810 the contributions from America amounted to 71,616,268 pesos.

In 1810 the Duke of Albuquerque and 11,000 exhausted troops sought refuge in Cádiz. But the Spanish army was reinforced by the arrival on English frigates of many sunburnt Portuguese and 1,000 "gigantic Scotsmen in kilts" (de Castro y Rossi 1862:70).

When Lord Wellington arrived in December 1812, he was offered a banquet and a tragedy recently written by a Cádiz playwright, despite the Spaniards' fears that he would be an adversary of the Constitution and would press to abolish liberal reforms.

To the defense of Cádiz came Manuel Jiménez Guazo, a former official of the Supreme Junta of Seville, who marshaled a band of troops under the name and banner of the Crusades. Bishops and priests exhorted the people to join. His followers fought tenaciously, led by their general, wearing the insignia of the Crusades on his chest, an enormous sword at his belt, bearing a Crusades banner, and endowed with a large "dragon-like" moustache (de Castro y Rossi 1862:100). Here was a figure embodying the human and the divine, uniting war and religion, indignant that the young people sarcastically called him Don Quijote.

But he was not unique, for there was also the Marqués de Palacio, who, on May 30, 1810, arrived at the Cortes for festivities in honor of captive King Ferdinand. He entered with 100 soldiers dressed in ancient style with doublets, britches and short capes, followed by six officials. "As if in masquerade,. the Marqués also in old style clothing with a modern general's sash …peers through his glasses, bares and points his sword, and in a loud, harsh voice reads some disordered verses exhorting everyone to follow his example and lead a life as of old, scorn the modern ways and continue struggling for the good cause. He accompanied his reading wielding his sword, striking the air to right and left. His outlandish costume, his tall, burly figure, his bad verses caused muffled laughter" (de Castro y Rossi 1862:70). He returned to the island proud of having convinced the people of Cádiz to abandon modern ways. This extravagance later won him interim appointment to the regency.

But most valiant in the defense of Cádiz and Spain was the Scotsman Juan Downie, who created the *Legión de Leales Estremeños*, all dressed in the garb of the armies of Phillip II: scarlet and white doublets, breeches, scarlet capes, scarlet and white caps, carrying lances with scarlet and white trim. Infantry and cavalry were equipped with swords and pistols. (Downie believed this clothing was specific to Spain, but in fact it had been worn throughout Europe.) But Juan Downie bore Francisco de Pizarro's huge sword.

As Downie led his battalion into action, a French bullet pierced one eye, and as he felt himself falling from his mount and surely into captivity, with a mighty effort he heaved Pizarro's sword back to his troops. Abandoned by the French army on the roadside, he made his way back to his battalion and recovered his sword. Returning for the glory of Spain, he rode into Seville, tall, lean, with his long, drooping moustache, and a black patch covering the left side of his face, causing such an uproar among the populace waving banners of welcome from their balconies that the French soldiers abandoned the city in haste. While he, too, was the subject of jokes, he was also highly esteemed as a brave cavalryman of the Middle Ages.

THE CORTES

When the members of the Seville Junta arrived in Cádiz, they were met with insults and condemnation for having wasted national funds. "The patriots" quickly imprisoned them. The Cortes were meeting in the theater at the Isla de León, next to Cádiz. From the windows they could see the French sentinels. Their discussions were interrupted by military trumpets and drums. Their voices were drowned out by cannon fire. But no sooner had the Junta fled to Cádiz than, on February 5, 1810, a French general sent a message to the undefeated Cádiz, calling for allegiance. Their proud answer, "Cádiz, faithful to its word, recognizes no king but Ferdinand VII" (Glover 1971:158).

Two days later three Spanish generals under Joseph's command and forty thousand troops demanded Cádiz' recognition and again were refused. On February 16, King Joseph I, himself, arrived at the city gates, promising an end to all taxes if they would swear allegiance to him. He was refused allegiance and entry into the city.

The first regency, formed on January 31 at the insistence of the Marqués of Wellesley, and composed of five members, one for America (from Mexico), had been in operation only two weeks. During its brief tenure it issued many important decrees, the majority of which were focused on the colonies. The first, addressed to the Spanish Americans, was signed just two days before Joseph's arrival. It gave a catalogue of Spain's military defeats, informed the colonists of the flight of the Junta of Seville, the capture of Seville, the resignation of the Junta, and the arrival of the Duke of Albuquerque with the army of Extremadura. Then, "Thanks to our magnanimous, sublime resolution, thanks to your loyal and generous following [the Despot of France] could not subjugate us in the beginning and never will subjugate us" (*Gazeta de Guatemala,* 14 June 1810:XIV(149), 36). This is followed by an earnest declaration of the fraternity and equality of the Spanish Americans:

> From this moment, Spanish Americans, you see yourselves elevated to
> the dignity of free men, you are no longer the same men as before,
> bowed down by a yoke much heavier since you lived further from the
> center of power, regarded with indifference, vexed by greed, and de-
> stroyed by ignorance ...Your destinies are no longer dependent upon
> Ministers, Viceroys, or Governors, they are in your hands. (Rodríguez
> 1978:28)

The colonists were instructed to send deputies to the new Cortes from the four viceroyships and seven captaincy-generals of America and the captaincy-general of the Philippines. One deputy was to be chosen from three candidates in each capital. After election the deputy was to travel to Mallorca to await the convocation of the Cortes. The deputies from the colonies were promised a stipend equal to that of the Spanish deputies.

On May 5 the Regency sent an appeal to the generosity of "Americans, loyal Indians, to the diocesan prelate, to the best-thinking people of the Cortes, government, military chiefs, consulates, literary bodies, colleges, titled persons and reputable merchants, and parochial priests" to aid in the defeat of the "Monster Napoleon."[1] It declares, "Your gold and silver are as necessary to the state as the blood and the arms of the Spaniards"(*Gazeta de Guatemala,* 26 September 1810:XIV(176), 247). The Regency informed the colonists of the defeat of Austria and the forty battles waged in Spain, stating that "no nation, no prince of Europe, has resisted this tyrant for so long a time"(*Gazeta de Guatemala,* 26 September 1810:XIV(176), 244). On May 26, the Regency declared that Indians, but not the "castes" (including mestizos and Africans), were free from paying tribute. One third of the land was to be distributed among Indians for prompt cultivation.

On June 26, the Regency informed the colonists that because of the critical circumstances the Cortes must convene before the arrival of the 28 American deputies. The Regency urged the immediate departure of all of America of America deputies for Cádiz. In their absence, substitutes would be chosen from Americans residing in Cádiz. Afterwards, when Venezuela, Argentina, New Grenada and Chile had revolutionary juntas, Americans residing in Cádiz were elected in their place. On August 20, an edict was issued clarifying the February 14 decree that had meant to include Indians and mestizos as possible deputies to the Cortes. A plea for the renewed loyalty of the colonists was made on September 6.

To celebrate the opening of the Cortes on September 24, a Mass was given by Spain's highest prelate, the Archbishop of Toledo, uncle of Ferdinand VII. Indeed, every session of the Cortes was preceded by Mass.

There was concern in the Cortes that the sixteen million inhabitants overseas would dominate the ten to eleven million Spaniards on the Peninsula. The Peninsulars did not want the two to three million overseas whites to have overweening power. And so, by giving no rights to Africans they effected an approximate equilibrium in their edict of October 15, whereby it was made clear once again that not only, as stated on February 14, were the Spanish Americans equal to the Peninsulars, but that this included the Indian population. Attempting to win back the hearts of those colonists in revolt, they declared a general amnesty for everyone who had been involved in past disturbances.

Freedom of the press was declared November 10.

On January 2, 1811, it was decided that two days a week the proceedings of the Cortes should be devoted to America.

The Regency issued a decree on January 5 calling for the protection of "the Indians, primitive natives of America and Asia" (Comenge 1909:445).

Once again, on February 9, the Regency returned to the issue of equality, declaring that the Americans would have equal representation in the Cortes and that Americans, whether Spanish or Indian, should have equal opportunities for employment in the court, church, politics or military professions. Furthermore, all Americans could plant and manufacture whatever they wished, with equal access to public services.

The following day the Cortes focused on the well-being of the Indians:

> Having called specifically to the sovereign attention of the General and Extraordinary Cortes the scandalous abuses that have been observed and the innumerable vexations that are imposed on the primitive Indians, natives of America and Asia, those worthy subjects deserve from the Cortes a particular consideration of all their circumstances. [All civil officials must] dedicate themselves with special conscientiousness and attention to cut at the roots such abuses condemned by Religion, reason and justice ...[There should be no pretext for action which] afflicts the Indian in person, or which causes him the slightest harm to his property.[2]

All infractions should meet with the severest punishment.

The above decree was to be read throughout the Spanish Empire for three days consecutively at Mass, then distributed to each town government, "Letting it be known by this means to those worthy subjects, the paternal concern and solicitude with which the entire Nation, represented by the General and Extraordinary Cortes, shows for the happiness and well-being of each and every one of them."[3]

Freedom of the press was reasserted on February 20.

Deeming the Isla de León too fraught with danger, the Cortes moved on February 24 to the Church of San Felipe Neri within the city walls. Here the deputies sat for their deliberations. On the wall over their heads was inscribed in bold lettering, *Paraíso*. But Paradise it was not, for although it was more secure from French bombardment its central location invited public attendance. Here could be witnessed the shouting of the crowds, the histrionics of the participants, the frayed nerves of the deputies, combined with the government's financial troubles, the cramped quarters and the French siege. In all of this the American representatives figured prominently.

With the opening of the Cortes in Cádiz came a near moratorium on decrees as the deputies became deeply engaged in the heady business of writing the Constitution. On April 22 the Cortes prohibited torture, shackles, handcuffs, chains, etc. On November 8 they asserted anew the equality of Spanish Americans and promised as before an amnesty for rebellious colonists.

To qualify for election as a deputy of the Cortes the individual was required to be a male householder of good character, at least 25 years of age. If competent native Indians were found, they were to be seated.

While four deputies per province were chosen in Spain, one per province represented America. While one deputy represented fifty thousand people in Spain, in America he represented seventy thousand. According to William Walton, a U.S. patriot based in London, 154 deputies represented a population of

14 million in Spain, while 54 represented 17 million in America (Walton 1837:182). Another author gives the total number of deputies as 303, while both he and Ramón Solís give the American representation as 63 or 21% (de Armellada 1959:11; Solis 1969:525). This figure pertains to 1812.

The majority of the members of the Cortes was composed of *liberales,* the first time the term "liberal" was used in politics. Within the Cortes the Spanish liberal "brain trust" became a brilliant, arrogant clique that exiled one of the first regents, the patriotic Bishop Orense, and also the Mexican, Miguel Lardizabal y Uribe, because the bishop and his cohort felt that sovereignty rested in the people *and* the monarch. They censored anti-liberal texts and promoted anti-clericalism in seeking to abolish the Inquisition. These liberals were vindictive toward the *afrancesados,* who had joined Napoleon in France. Many of these exiles had been leaders of their provinces and later fought against the liberal cause with a vengeance. At the same time, "the liberals did little to win colonial opinion; they restricted the number of American deputies in the new constitution lest American opinion should 'swamp' the Cortes; they neglected the protests that the 'American' deputies already in Cádiz had no claim to represent American opinion; they refused any substantial concession of free trade" (Carr 1966:103–104).

The substitutes chosen for America were largely young, liberal patriots. Because America was so under-represented, and because the regents demanded a quashing of sympathy for the Caracas rebellion, as the Cortes began, the American contingent formed a compact, extremely active and combative political group. Equal representation was promised for the future, but not the present. Minority representation meant that America lost every opposition vote. For example, the American substitutes presented the colonists' main grievances in eleven propositions on December 16, 1810, including the demand that "American Spaniards and Indians should have equal opportunity for all positions in the Cortes as well as any place in the monarchy, be it political, ecclesiastical or military" (Anderson 1966:189). Most were voted down. Perhaps in compensation, the Peninsulars regularly elected the Americans to Court positions. Of the 37 presidents, 10 were Americans; of the 14 members of the Constitutional Commission, five were American. As early as 1811 a Mexican, Juan José Gureña, was elected President of the Cortes, the first time in history that an American would be in charge. His vice-president, Joaquín Maniau, was also Mexican.

The deputies were primarily middle-aged, middle-class intellectuals. A selection of 263 deputies was composed of 90 religious (6 bishops), 56 lawyers, 49 bureaucrats, 39 military officers, 15 professors, and 14 nobles (Solis 1969:250).

The British statesman William Walton, upon visiting Cádiz, observed that the Cortes resembled the French States-General in 1791, as most members were unknown. He found much to criticize in the nature of these Cortes. They "did not meet to supply the want of a regal power, to provide means of defence, obtain the redress of grievances, or reconcile opposite and jarring interests." The delegates "were ambitious of being the founders of a new code; whereas their countrymen beyond the precincts of Cádiz were fighting for their independence, their religion, and their laws, as they stood" (Walton 1837:165–169). He commented that many decrees seldom reached beyond Cádiz and that their authors labored with literary and philosophical exertions both for the Cortes and the periodicals while calling for a scorched-earth policy in the provinces. Even so, as their first act, they defined the responsibility of the regents, who, having no precedents, were perplexed about the range of their duties and their authority.

Although the members of the Junta of Seville had a harsh reception on their arrival in Cádiz, they brought many ideas to the Cortes, for they had investigated education, religious issues, economic problems and projects, medieval parliaments and legal systems.

There were three major issues that alienated the Peninsular liberals from the Americans. First, they did not appreciate any reference to the "Black Legend" of colonial Spanish domination or negative characterizations of New World inhabitants. When the representative of the Consulado Europeo de México, speaking in the name of all its European members on behalf of the Spanish merchant oligarchs in Mexico City, addressed the Cortes on September 15, 1811, he gave a speech so offensive to the Americans that the next day they attempted to walk out, but were blocked at the door by the guards of the Cortes on the order of the President, with no interference from their liberal allies. This is what the representative had said:

> [Indians] are brutish from the beginning, drunken by instinct, lascivious in every kind of vice, lazy, robbers, uneducated, even in the Christian doctrine. The castes have the same vices, and are worse because of the money they acquire to enjoy them; nevertheless they feel no shame in their nudity, they are lazy and unworthy of compassion. The creoles are irreligious, hypocrites ...The American deputies, painting their fellows as men, have tricked the Cortes. (de Mier Noriega y Guerra 1922:241–242)

Second, insurrections in the New World hung over the Cortes like a dark cloud, prejudicing for the Peninsulars, even the liberals, the expressions of the American deputies. On the second day of the Cortes the Americans demanded discussion of the insurrections, but they were refused. They tried twice more in 1810, twice more in 1811. Finally, on August 1, 1811, all 33 American deputies united and spoke with one voice, protesting the misconduct of the governing body. They argued that neither Napoleon nor the British nor the Americans were the cause of the rebellions, that each and every rebellion, though occurring independently, was in response to local misgovernment. They confessed that, "Here, here, is the place of the difficulty" (Salvatierra 1939:315). The Consulate of Cádiz financed 32 military expeditions to America involving more than forty-seven thousand men. Of the ten thousand sent to New Spain eight thousand died in battle or from disease. When Viceroy Venegas, with the aid of three thousand Spanish troops, defeated Hidalgo, the Cortes honored him, comparing him to Cortés.

The third major difference was the matter of free trade. Again and again the Peninsular liberals from Cádiz supported their merchant colleagues in Spain, defeating any proposal for free trade.

"By mid-1811 American loyalists advocated free foreign trade, abolition of internal hindrances to production, parity of career opportunity in army, state, church, provincial autonomy—a middle position between absolutism and separation" (Anna 1983:85). And yet the Americans complained of the scorn that was directed at them. "Spain has told you: 'You are free, despotism has ended.' Yes, sir, you have said so, but have deeds corresponded to words? ...Look at the scorn with which they treat their own brothers. And what can the remedy be for such evil? The equal rights that the Spaniards enjoy, the same favors, the same liberty" (Salvatierra 1939:335).

A final concern of the Americans was the Courts' decision to delay for eight years any possible revision of the Constitution, but they were outvoted on this issue.

The Americans were counting on British support, yet the messages were contradictory. The British Foreign Office authorized the purchase of arms and equipment by revolutionary agents, but in a letter to the Spanish government, the British War Minister promised to aid in restoring rebelling colonies to Spain and to defend their independence if Spain should fall to France. He explained that the rebellion in Venezuela was caused by the belief that Spain had fallen or would surely fall. On September 27, 1810, Wellington declared that England would not aid in the suppression of Latin American revolts. When the Regency became bankrupt in 1811, it was bailed out temporarily by Wellington. But the British, too, were in dire economic straits, so Ambassador Wellesley suggested to the Cortes that England be allowed to trade with Latin America. The Cádiz merchants, wanting to hold on to their monopoly, refused. British efforts to mediate with the Cortes and the rebels on July 16, 1812, were rejected two to one by the Cortes even though strongly supported by the Americans. A second attempt in June 1813 was also refused. "Wellington discovered in the Regency and the *Cortes* self-willed bodies perhaps even more determined to retain their imperial dominions than to rid themselves of the Napoleonic scourge" (Kaufmann 1951:63).

In addition to England's diplomatic ventures in Cádiz, there was the secret society *Lautanos,* composed of Spanish Americans in Cádiz, whose four hundred members received funds and inspiration from London. English, American, and French money was sent to Latin America to inspire rebellion. Masons in Cádiz, with money from the United States, tried to bribe officials not to go to the colonies. Another secret society, the *Caballeros Racionales*, had many American members who favored independence.

The *serviles* or conservatives formed the third contingent of the Cortes. Allied with the regents, they fought the attempts to reduce the Church to socially useful functions and to separate the Church from civil administration and government. They opposed the restriction of noble privileges and the limitations on the authority of the monarch. Quite naturally they were unsympathetic to attempts to diminish the Empire. They were defeated in their efforts to have the clergy continue to serve as deputies to the Cortes. Supporting the bishops, they defended the discipline, doctrine, privileges, and property of the Church. The Constitution began with, "In the name of the Omnipotent God, Father, Son, and Holy Ghost," but this was not considered sufficiently pious. "Some deputies ...want a fuller demonstration of the the profound religious sentiments of the Spanish people ...[One bishop] was so bold as to propose ...inclusion of the Christian doctrine in the preamble of the Constitution" (Bentura 1971:235).

Although the Inquisition was arrogant towards the people and the government, the *serviles* fought for two years to prevent its abolition, finally losing in a vote of 90 to 60 on February 22, 1812.

Despite their differences, the three groups all agreed that change was necessary, that the Indian was the forgotten American. They all accepted the Constitution with joy.

THE CONSTITUTION

Many Spaniards assumed that the Constitution would answer Americans' demands and end revolts. Many Americans claimed that it was a European constitution for a European Spain.

Although the Constitution's political principles conferred no material benefits on the colonists of Latin America, they did afford them a large measure of spiritual consolation. Indeed, the Spanish Cortes had a significant and largely overlooked influence on instructing democratic processes in the New World. In the later struggles with Ferdinand VII the importance of the Constitution within Spain grew to mythic proportions. The Constitution, as a synthesis of traditional thought and new ideologies, exerted great influence also in Naples, Portugal, and Greece.

By exploring the parliamentary institutions of medieval Spain, the deputies were able to find precedent for the tenets of Rousseau and Locke, to present a constitution based on the constitution of Revolutionary France, so that radicalism became respectable. From Rousseau they adopted (1) the social contract as the base of political order and national sovereignty, (2) civil and political equality,

(3) law as the expression of general will—all ideas expressed in medieval times. From the French Constitution they adopted unicamerality, in the knowledge that the Spanish medieval Cortes represented the clergy, the nobility, and the people. From Locke they adopted (1) sovereignty residing in the nation, (2) the separation of executive and legislative powers, (3) free press—also supported by traditionalists. Tradition and revolution were superimposed on each other.

The Constitution severely limited the King's functions, condemning it to destruction on the King's return. While the Constitution abolished all privileges of the nobility, local Cortes nevertheless favored the nobles. Slavery seems to have been too intractable an issue for the Constitution to abolish it.

The deputies, representing the intellectual bourgeoisie, had been influenced in all economic matters by the Bourbon reforms of the eighteenth century. The guilds were abolished, replaced by a free market. Uniform income taxes proportional to wealth were established. These features, combined with civil equality, personal liberty, the rights of property, and freedom of contract, presented the legal framework of a bourgeois society.

Public education was a foremost concern in Cádiz. The deputies called for a corporation of intellectuals to supervise the national educational establishment with a uniform policy in "the sciences, literature, and the fine arts" (Rodríguez 1978:84). On June 8, 1813, the Cortes called for the creation of economic chairs in all universities and courses on individualism and the United States Constitution.

In sum, the Constitution of 1812 declared "popular sovereignty, division of power, equal representation of all male citizens, creation of social classes to replace legal estates, a unicameral Cortes, complete centralization of government, society led by the bourgeoisie, government directed by legislative branch" (Kern 1990:164). But all of this was in a country where Catholicism continued to be the state religion and where the King was still a sacred figure.

Prior to the signing of the Constitution on March 19, 1812, the Cortes issued a series of decrees, especially in the month of January. The first, on January 7, abolished the New Year's procession of the Royal Standard in the colonies, for it was felt that it was a monument to the conquest of those provinces. In recognition of the colonists' loyalty, the procession in Spain and in the colonies was now restricted to the proclamation of a new king.

On January 22, came the announcement that a new regency had been formed, headed by the Duque del Infantado (plate 15) and four others, including Joaquín de Mosquera y Figueroa. De Mosquera y Figueroa was a native of Popayán, Colombia, member of a distinguished family, recipient of degrees in the humanities and law. He was named Deputy Assessor in Cartagena, where he displayed a talent for careful, honest administration, but in that capacity he was to witness his brothers and brothers-in-law join the rebel cause. A firm if moderate royalist, in 1795 he was named to be *Alcalde de Crimen de la Real Audiencia* of Mexico City, where he acted with restraint in the judging of creole conspirators. The Viceroy of New Spain, Miguel José de Azanza, was so incompetent that de Mosquera y Figueroa essentially became acting Viceroy. In 1804 he received orders to depart for Caracas as a *Visitador* and *Regente* of the local *Audiencia*, with high recommendations from Viceroy José de Iturrigaray, who spoke of his literary abilities, constancy and probity. In Caracas, which had been in the throes of rebellion, it was his task to set the government back in order. As a foreigner confronted with the extraordinary mismanagement of the local officials, it was a painfully disagreeable assignment that he carried out with his accustomed tact and thoroughness. In 1809, he was elected to be a representative of the Cortes and, in 1810, minister of the *Consejo de Indias*.

The first act of the new regency was to send an appeal to the Americans, signed by de Mosquera y Figueroa on January 23. The Americans are reminded that this is the fifth year of "your heroic struggle." "Americans and Spaniards are members of the same family ...Remember your Mother Country *[Madre Patria]*...Don't forget us, Americans." The Regency calls for war and vengeance against Napoleon and swears to rigid observance of the Constitution. "One day [Spain] will be the refuge of the sciences and the arts ...Do not give your ear to the suggestions of our enemies, whose impure mouths fan the fire of discord among you ...May the sweet ideas of brotherhood and unity that have fashioned our common happiness for three hundred years be reborn."[4]

On January 24, hanging was replaced by the garotte, and on January 31, three edicts were issued. The first was a plea to all ministers of justice to be active, honest executors of the law and to send frequent reports on their activities lest people be seduced by the "furious, vengeful Despot."[5] The second was a request for support. "The General and Extraordinary Cortes, after giving the Constitution to the Spaniards of both hemispheres," asks all religious and public officials of America for a contribution to continue the war to defeat the "modern Attila."[6] The third grants to Africans the right to take holy orders and to attend universities.

In January and again in February, de Mosquera y Figueroa, as acting President, urged his countrymen to defeat the French armies. First, the Castillians, "descendants of many heroes," were exhorted "to exterminate the infamous race of the barbarians of the Seine."[7] Second, the *Estremeños*, "Brave sons of Cortés and Pizarro, *vengeance* and *war* to exterminate your enemies."[8]

During the final writing of the Constitution, the Duque del Infantado was frequently leading his troops in combat, replaced as president by de Mosquera y Figueroa. This was the first and only time that an American was supreme sovereign of the Spanish Empire.

It took eighteen months to frame a constitution for 30 million people, signed by 184 members of the Cortes, of whom 51 were Americans (plate 16). The publication of the Constitution was scheduled for Saint Joseph's Day, March 19, so that while throughout Spain everyone was expected to celebrate the "Intruder," King Joseph's festive day, in Cádiz they were celebrating the birth of their own Spanish Constitution. Just a few days before, the French cannonaded Cádiz, but of 103 grenades only 17 landed within the city walls!

The birth of the Constitution was celebrated by having "the Regency Palace, the Chapter Houses, the Cortes, the English and Portuguese Embassies magnificently decorated with figures of Hercules with a mace clearing the earth from devils and tyrants."[9]

The Constitution was signed by de Mosquera y Figueroa, accompanied by a committee composed of Spanish nobility, ambassadors, generals, and men of science and letters. Then followed a triumphant procession, with bands, to the church of El Carmen (believed safer than the Cathedral). A Mass and *Te Deum* were celebrated while the rain poured down in sheets, the thunder crashed, and the French batteries cannonaded Cádiz. A reception and banquet were offered in the Regency Palace.

The Constitution, bound in Moroccan leather, was borne in a procession of civil officials and cavalry escort to a tablet where an image of Ferdinand VII was unveiled, and the Constitution was proclaimed aloud by the oldest king of arms, or herald. The entourage proceeded through the streets, in the downpour, to three more tablets, where the Constitution was again proclaimed. The crowd, playing on the Spanish nickname for Joseph, *Pepe*, shouted, *"Viva la Pepa!"* honoring the Constitution on this St. Joseph's Day. But a tree was felled by the howling wind, so people wondered if this were a bad omen.

In these days, *"Roma libre: tragedia en cinco actos,"* "Free Rome: A tragedy in five acts," by Antonio Saviñon was performed. On the title page is inscribed: *Representada en el Teatro de Cádiz en ocasión de celebrar los profesores cómicos la publicación de la nueva Constitución de la Monarquía Española,* "Performed at the Theater of Cádiz on the occasion when the comic professors celebrated the publication of the new Constitution of the Spanish Monarchy" (Savinon 1812).

Bronze medals commemorating the Constitution were issued.

THE CORTES, 1812–1813

While the Cortes were in session during the month of May, the French troops, encamped in front of the city walls, were seen deserting. A blockade of the ports had prevented any food from reaching the French army, whichwas starving. But from June to August the French renewed their siege—three months of constant bombardment until August 24, when the army finally abandoned its campaign after inflicting on Cádiz a total of 14 deaths. On Sunday, August 30, a celebratory Mass and *Te Deum* were given.

The Regency recommended on June 2 that the presidents of the *Audiencia* and the captains-general take the proper means to avoid the penetration of Napoleonic agents who could provoke rebellion.

On July 20, Alexander of Russia recognized the Cortes and the Constitution. On August 14, the Cortes decreed that Santa Teresa de Jesús was now the patron saint of Spain, as decreed by the Cortes of 1617 and 1626. They further announced that all city and town squares where the Constitution was sworn to and promulgated should be named Plaza de la Constitución.

On August 30, a proclamation, written by de Mosquera y Figueroa and signed by the Duque del Infantado, was issued. It was "a call to the inhabitants overseas with the consoling hope of being able to attract them and shelter them benignly on their breast," promising the observation of the Constitution under a program of prosperity (Vela 1956:62). It was a Tzotzil translation of this proclamation that has engendered the present book.

The Regency declared on October 6 the "need for exact knowledge of the different castes of Indians, their customs, languages, inclinations, industry and belief."[10] Consultations were to be made by the civil and religious authorities. A detailed questionnaire was appended.

Of great importance for the colonies was the decree of November 9, wherein forced labor *(mitas* and *repartimiento)* was abolished, as was the payment of church taxes *(obvenciones)*. Indians were freed of personal service to public officials and priests. Communal labor was to be assigned regardless of class. Half the communal land was to be distributed among married Indians or those 25 years old or older. Indian scholarships were promised. This decree was to be read three times at Mass.

On September 8, 1813, the flogging of prisoners was replaced by public works. The Cortes closed on September 14.

NOTES

1. Regency Decree: May 5, 1810:1.
2. Regency Decree: February 10, 1811.
3. Regency Decree: February 10, 1811.
4. Regency Decree: January 23, 1812.
5. Regency Decree: January 31, 1812a.
6. Regency Decree: January 31, 1812b.
7. Regency Decree: January ?, 1812.
8. Regency Decree: February ?, 1812.
9. Bentura 1971:236. "Hercules, incidentally, was considered by many Spaniards as Spain's founding father, Spain's Aeneas, also from Troy. Old histories and myth placed the royal line in direct descent from his nephew, Hispanus or Hispalis," Peggy Liss, personal communication.
10. Regency Decree: October 6, 1812.

3

Peru

The remoteness of Spain from her American colonies is exemplified by Peru. News reached Peru in five or six months, usually second or third hand. In 1790 the Canichanas Indians of San Pedro (now Bolivia) composed and sang songs honoring Charles IV and María Luisa: "Let us sing before the portrait of King Charles IV with contentment, for he is our King, honoring also our Queen, María Luisa." (Lemmon 1987) Little did they know!

Peru was very peaceful, but in 1810 rebels in Buenos Aires, Argentina, intending to send troops to the neighboring province, were printing leaflets in Spanish and Quechua and distributing them in Peru, urging the Indians to join their cause. An example of this revolutionary bilingual propaganda is the proclamation by Francisco Xavier Iturrí Patiño, *Proclama del mas perseguido americano a sus paysanos de la noble, leal, y valerosa ciudad de Cochabamba,* "Proclamation of the most persecuted American to his countrymen of the noble, loyal, and worthy city of Cochabamba." He pleads here for Indian support, ending, *"viva la patria, viva la unión"* (Garcia Rosell 1960:492–493).

The following year, the Bishop of Arequipa extolled the extraordinary resistance of Spain even though it had been reduced to a "skeleton" (Bermejo 1960:363). He pointed out, "if thousands of Spaniards have died, Spain has also been the grave of three or four thousand Frenchmen" (Bermejo 1960:364).

But even in Peru there was concern over Napoleon's role in the Americas. The Bishop of Arequipa speaks of him as a "fraudulent robber," playing "tricks to divide brothers, fathers and sons" (Bermejo 1960:370,365). "He poses as a messenger of God, but uses intrigues, money, lies" (Bermejo 1960:371). The bishop urges his clergy to speak to their parishioners about "his execrable, seditious ideas that are opposed to all justice…advising them ever more firmly to love our Father and Sovereign Ferdinand VII" (Bermejo 1960:378).

One of the most eloquent proponents of the American cause in the Cortes was Dionisio Inca Yupanqui, from Cuzco, educated in Madrid. On December 16, 1810, he spoke up: "I have not come to be one of those individuals who composes the ruin of the glorious and afflicted Spain, nor to sanction the slavery of virtuous America...The majority of the deputies and of the nation scarcely have any knowledge of this vast continent" (Fernández Almagro 1944:64). It was his plea that stirred the Cortes, moving them to declare their edict of January 5, 1811, insisting that Indians should be properly treated and their personal liberty assured, that they would have equal access to public services and the freedom to choose their crops, industries and crafts. There was no mention of the abolition of Indian slavery. Six days later he complained that Americans were "tired of hearing brilliant and pompous decrees in their favor" that amounted to nothing (Lafuente 1869:210). "Truth and justice, harassed and trampled by the general corruption, have abandoned the earth and returned to their peaceful mansion in the skies...The religious, political and civil institutions of Peru, the moral virtues of this great people, were in no way surpassed by those of the celebrated Egyptians, Greeks, and Romans" (Comenge 1909:504). He pointed out that there had been a "scandalous reduction of population from 8 million to 900,000" (Comenge 1909:504). He spoke of "the large number of inept and hateful officials who have affected a vain and puerile superiority....You feel greatly the suffering of 20 years of clumsy despotism, but why do you forget that *we* have tolerated this for the period of three hundred years, giving a miraculous example of subordination and loyalty" (Comenge 1909:506–507). Free men were citizens, but were Indians slaves? The Constitution, despite Inca Yupanqui, did not answer.

The Viceroy of Peru established the freedom of the press on October 2, 1812, but he thought it very dangerous and impractical. Nevertheless, the Constitution, reaching Peru in September and October, six and seven months after its signing in Cádiz, had been received joyfully by the officials and eventually became a model for the constitutions of both Bolivia and Peru.

On an unmarked day in what must have been the year of 1813, a scribe, almost surely a priest, translated into the contemporary Cuzco dialect of Quechua the Duque del Infantado's proclamation to the overseas inhabitants, announcing under the Constitution a new Ministry of Foreign Affairs that would assure their prosperity in return for their loyalty in the struggle against "the Monster Napoleon" (Rivet and de Créqui-Montfort 1951:247) and the insurgents. This proclamation would have been directed to the elite, to the landed nobility who were bilingual sponsors of Quechua and of Inca traditions that they appropriated for their own ends. The translator faithfully copied Spanish rhetorical structure with a very limited use of Quechua couplets and triplets to clarify ambiguous passages.

This same translation was printed in Lima under the orders of the archbishop, in two columns, Spanish and Quechua, with brief notes at the end explaining the alphabet used and the manner of pronunciation. The archbishop, on December

20, 1813, sent a copy to Spain with a heartfelt discussion of the problems of translation:

> As the perfection of a language in relation to another is dictated by the civilization and culture of the nation that uses it, Quechua cannot equal the richness and gracefulness of Spanish; so that the ideas that one expresses with simple and particular words, the other gives the same meaning with compound expressions and long circumlocutions. I know well that a paraphrase is not translation but commentary; but the translator has no other recourse for explaining the meaning when the vocabulary is not equally abundant. This is evident in the accompanying proclamation: full of sublime thoughts, of abstract ideas unknown to the Indian language so that it has been necessary to sacrifice the fire of imagination for meaning and the elegance for intelligence; nevertheless those in the know will surely confess that the second column demonstrates all the beauty of which the language of the Quechua empire is capable. (Rivet and de Créqui-Montfort 1951:247)

The archbishop's sensitive, if patronizing, commentary on the translation of this very proclamation forecasts the commentary of the friars in Chiapas. It was this archbishop's correspondence with the metropolis that reveals that "our" proclamation was sent with specific instructions that it be translated and printed in the languages of the realm, becoming the only known Spanish decree with such a distinction.

4

New Spain

MEXICO CITY

In 1808, news of the plight of Spain reached a Mexico ill-prepared to respond effectively.[1] At this distance it was not clear who was in charge in the homeland, the Junta of Seville or a similar junta in Oviedo. While the Mexicans refused to recognize the juntas, they did send aid, but by 1809 there was decreasing success in the efforts to raise money for Spain; the people were unable to spare more.

The church was rife with corruption. The Inquisition was an intolerant institution that attempted to keep liberal ideas out of Mexico. Four fifths of the native clergy, i.e., Creoles, hated the peninsular Spaniards. The lower clergy was dreaming of independence.

New Spain was the most prosperous of Spain's colonies in the Americas. There were nine Spanish and nine Creole millionaires. "Not every nobleman was rich, but almost every millionaire was noble. The Mexican plutocracy included old Creole aristocrats who made their money from the domestic economy, new immigrant merchants who speculated in the import-export trade, and Creole and Spanish miners, who, after enormous expenditures, made fortunes in silver" (Ladd 1976:25).

The councilmen of the *Cabildo* of Mexico City were propertied and professional elements of Creole society, who compounded their pride in the Spanish heritage with their sense of belonging to Mexican soil (and of it belonging to them). They were semi-feudal lords, seldom well-educated and of questionable pedigree, pleased to invoke a golden past. An exception was the great-nephew of Sor Juana Inés de la Cruz, José Antonio Alzate y Ramírez, editor of the *Gazeta de Literatura*, "who looked to an idyllic future employing useful knowledge...He eulogized ancient Indian civilization and considered Indians capable of being educated" (Pike 1969:104–105).

The viceroys were overworked, often weak, strangers to Mexico. Iturriguray, who had been appointed by the Prince of Peace (a man hated by the Spaniards in Mexico), was ambitious and dishonest. Seeing the confused political situation in Spain, Iturriguray informed the Junta of Oviedo that there were sentiments in Mexico for an independent and republican government. The Spanish residents, believing that the Viceroy was attempting to become King of New Spain, deposed and imprisoned him. This action spread hatred against the Spaniards and brought forth protests from the provinces about the right of the *Cabildo* in Mexico City to be speaking for them. The following viceroy, Lizana, was old and weak, with no understanding of how to govern. At this time an Indian claiming direct descent from Moctezuma considered himself a suitable candidate for the crown of Mexico. The *Infante* Don Pedro in Brazil was suggested. On February 13, 1811, the Tlaxcalan priest Guridi y Alcocer, one of the most eloquent American deputies in the Cortes, spoke with great bitterness at how, after the Godoy era had ended, they thought things would improve, but that the Regency, overlooking "celebrated and worthy men there [in Mexico] gave the sinecure to a youth [Francisco Javier de Venegas] who still plays with tops and kites" (Comenge, 1909:540). It was Guridi y Alcocer who, on January 9, 1811, at the opening of the Cortes, had warned the deputies of the revolution in Mexico, "that fire which is spreading like a flood and burning up entire provinces" (Anderson 1966:189).

The Spaniards in the civil government were outraged that the Cortes had granted Indians and castes the right to represent them in the Cortes. The merchant guild protested vehemently, tarring not only the Indians and castes, but also the Spanish Americans. Here are a few selections from the speech that caused the Americans in Cádiz to attempt a walkout:

> [The Indians] were preoccupied with the most rabid superstition, with rites and ceremonies insulting to reason and to nature, with laws malevolent, absurd, mad, and with practices adding up to an abominable composite of all the errors and atrocities committed by peoples in every land and time...In vain do some foreigners, infatuated with the fanatic and hypocrite Las Casas, emulate him slavishly and bitterly accuse us of brutality in the conquest. By the most marvelous metamorphosis that the centuries have known, the orangutan settlers [Indians] of America were suddenly transformed, Sire, into domesticated men, subject to a mild government...[The Indian] is gifted with laziness and languor that cannot be described...Stupid by constitution, without inventive talent or force of thought, abhorring the arts and trades, he does not lack a way of life. A drunkard by instinct, he satisfies this

passion at little cost with very cheap beverages and this depravity takes up a third of his life. Carnal, with a vice-ridden imagination, devoid of pure ideas about continence, chastity or incest, he provides for his fleeting desires with the women he encounters closest to hand. He is as uncaring in Christian virtue as he is insensible to religious truths, so remorse does not disturb his soul or restrain his sinful appetites...The Indian does not at present carry his ideas, thought, interests, and will beyond his own reach or the range of his eyes. Disinterested in patriotic sentiments and in all social activity, he asks of public authority only an indulgent priest and a lazy sub-delegate...[The castes] are of the same condition, character, temperament, and negligence as the Indian, in spite of being reared and living in the shade of cities where they form the lowest class of the populace....Incontinent inebriates, indolent, without shame, pleasantness, or fidelity, without notions of religion, morality, luxury, cleanliness, or decency, they appear more mechanical and slovenly than even the Indian himself...Their clothing is rags and the sun...A million whites, called Spanish Americans, show their superiority to the other five million natives more by their hereditary wealth, their careers, their luxury, their manner, and their refinement in vices than by substantial differences of temperament, sentiments, and propensities. According to experience, the multitude of whites sink themselves into the populace by squandering their patrimony...They swell the professions and arts and console themselves, in the absence of wealth, with dreams and schemes of independence that would give them domination of the Americas...[But] the European Spaniard [has earned] the reputation of a loyal vassal inseparably united to the metropolis by chains of nature, of recognition, and even of egoism. Yes, Sire, egoism is part of this noble fidelity, because the European Spaniard runs the risk of losing his life at the first cry of American insubordination...[New Spain] is the abode of five million automatons, a million intractable vassals, and a hundred thousand citizens addicted to order. (Pike 1969:125–127)

The representative concludes his harangue with this inversion: "Would not the parallel between the Spaniard and the Indian be a comparison between a crowd of gibbon monkeys and an association or republic of urbane men" (Pike 1969:128).

New economic ideas entered Mexico at the same time as French philosophic ideas. People recognized their lack of economic progress. There was a general feeling of exasperation with the local government and the chaos in Spain. Even so, Napoleon found it more difficult to extend his domain over the colonies than he had expected.

NAPOLEON BONAPARTE

In 1808 the Bishop of Michoacán, Manuel Abad Quiepo, sent a proclamation to the French, "in which they are shown the shocking contradiction between the doctrines and servile conduct of the ferocious despotism of Bonaparte, and the character of this monster is described" (Hernández y Dávalos 1877:2, 874). The Bishop points out that France was in anarchy after the revolution and that "no Washington, no Franklin appeared" (Hernández y Dávalos 1877:875).

> Yes, Frenchmen, this is the happy moment to break your chains...Five hundred thousand volunteers enlisted in two weeks; and in their first attempts have destroyed one third of the invincible French army...[The people] will raise in the Pyrenees a wall of China to separate perpetually degraded France from ennobled Spain. (Hernández y Dávalos 1877:878–879)

Another proclamation was sent to the Supreme Central Junta in Spain by Antonio de Aguirre Arza y Sanpelayo from Havana on December 16, 1808. He offered 500 pesos for the construction of a prison in Spain to jail Napoleon and Godoy and their families and all other traitors. He refers to Godoy and Napoleon as Cerberus, the three-headed Hellhound and son of the giant Typhon, asserting that they should be placed as porters at the entrance to the prison.

Napoleon addressed a letter to the viceroys and captains-general, signed by his Foreign Secretary and dated May 17, 1808, but not sent until June 25, informing them of the abdications and promising a new prosperity. He wrote, "The dynasty has changed, but the monarchy exists" (Villanueva 1911:175). He promised them a wider field for trade, and instructed them that news would be sent by means other than Spanish ships in Cádiz so it would arrive faster. In August 1808 a French brig docked in Vera Cruz with papers for the viceroy. The papers were angrily burned and allegiance was sworn to Ferdinand.

The Central Junta in Seville, on May 10, 1809, warned the colonists of Napoleon's designs. Loyalty to Ferdinand was pledged throughout the colonies.

In 1809 Baltimore became the seat of Napoleonic intrigue in the Americas, staffed with 50 agents, "Apostles of Bonaparte" or "Disciples of Bonaparte." The agents were headed by a Mr. Desmolard, who lived with great ostentation, decorated livery and a tricolored cockade. But a Spanish merchant in New Orleans, Luis de Onis, kept a close watch on the agents and sent their names to frontier officials. In 1810, ten agents were known to be working in Mexico and four in Central America. The mission of these agents was to spread the word to the Creoles of the United States, progress in commerce, agriculture, navigation, freedom, and "comforts." Assemblies of notables were called to exercise "the will of the community." In the words of Joseph Bonaparte to his envoy:

The object which these agents are to aim at, for the present, is no other, than that of manifesting to, and persuading the Creoles of Spanish America, that the noble and royal highness has solely in view, the giving of liberty to a people, enslaved for so many years, without expecting any return for so great a boon, other than the friendship of the natives, and the commerce with the harbors of both Americas...[Referring specifically to the Indians, he adds]: They will also remind the Indians, circumstantially, of the cruelties which the Spaniards employed in their conquests, and the infamies which they committed towards their legitimate sovereigns, by dethroning them; by taking away their lives or enslaving them...They will, moreover, make the Indians observe, how happy they will be, when they become, once more, masters of their country, and free from the tyrannical tribute which they pay to a foreign monarch. And lastly, they will tell the people, that their said monarch does not so much as exist in his own government, but is in the power of the restorer of liberty and the universal legislator, Napoleon. (Walton 1814:ii–v)

In April and June, Viceroy Garibay forbade the landing of Frenchmen or other foreigners in New Spain. If they landed in Vera Cruz they were to be arrested and taken to San Juan de Ulúa prison.

There was great consternation over rumors that Napoleon planned to install Charles IV as King of New Spain.

In the name of Joseph, "King of Spain and of the Continent of America," a Baltimore agent wrote and sent a proclamation on October 2, 1809, "instructing the agents to foment revolution. Creoles were to be reminded of their shameful treatment by Peninsular Spaniards, while Indians were to be told of the dreadful cruelties of the Spanish conquest" (Robertson 1939:68). Joseph urged the clergy to make their flocks faithful to him, assuring them Napoleon had rescued the Church in Europe from atheism.

On December 12, 1809, Napoleon, upset that funding for the Spanish resistance and the English came from America, decided to ignore his brother and to foment independence in America, declaring he would never oppose emancipation of the Spanish colonies (this despite his brother Joseph's reign over them).

The Bonapartes' declarations spawned a whole series of indignant proclamations. First is José de Iturriguray, "Your Viceroy speaks, listen to him! And with what confidence you must hear him, well-accustomed to the style and sweetness of a father he cannot speak to you in another way!... Two things bring misfortune to towns, fear and disunion. Fear makes cowards and slaves, disunion, weakness and victims of oppression."[2] Opposing "the rapacious eagle of Corsica... Our brothers after two years still fight without being defeated, while the tyrant has destroyed republics, kingdoms and powerful empires in a few days."[3] "The Machiavellian politics" [to disunite Creoles and Spaniards must be blocked, for]

Creoles and Spaniards are like brothers or like uncles and nephew."[4] They have *"the same religion, the same laws, the same sovereign."*[5]

On April 22, 1810, the Inquisition declared that edict of October 2, 1809 "as detestable for Napoleon's impiety as for his ignorance even of the Spanish language in which he speaks to us" (Hernández y Dávalos 1877:2,445) With outrage the Inquisitors relate how Joseph urges priests in confession to persuade penitents to follow Napoleon. They promise excommunication for anyone who does not submit to the Holy Court copies of the proclamations or any other seditious literature.

Two days later the Viceroy gave his opinion: "Their proclamations are ridiculous and impolitic, whose barbarisms and solecisms of the language would make you laugh if you read them."[6]

Commenting on how Joseph threatens severe punishments to those who do not submit to his rule, the Viceroy asks, "How does it seem to you, noble and generous Mexicans, the sweetness with which your new Sultan treats you, and with which he tries to gain your affection?"[7] He asks of Joseph, "What do you plan to do with *this country you call a slave*, and which you consider *immersed* in *ignorance* and *brutality*?" He comments on "the ignorance of this intrusive protector who does not even know of the countless olive trees that cover our fields."[8] He insists that the "Indians will resist the race of Napoleon that is crueler than that of the Montezumas."[9] He reports how "the infamous brother of Napoleon" urges servants to poison his enemies and how he has sent his force to the New World, "And with what soldiers? *Ten* fatuous, hare-brained, miserable Spaniards, unworthy of such a name, that he has sent to the Kingdom of Mexico and *four* to Guatemala that will be reinforced by up to five hundred others."[10]

> He believes you are as stupid as the Mohammedans of Egypt, and as cold and frigid as the Hottentot...Happy land that won't be trod on by the black eagle who has terrified Europe...If you believe Joseph you will be sent to Russia for "your *regeneration*...He wishes to trick you under the astute and perfidious name of the peaceful king and tame sheep, being in reality a carnivorous wolf, a monster from Hell who wants to devour you.[11]

Quite a different image of Joseph than that painted in Cádiz!

Not to be outdone by the Inquisition and the Viceroy, on April 26 the Governor of the Sacred Miter (custodian of the archbishop's miter) sends a circular "directed to the parish priests and clergymen of the Archbishopric of Mexico, recalling the obedience and fidelity to God and to Our Captive King Ferdinand VII," wherein he refers to the "infamous," the "false," and the "irreligious" Napoleon, and finally to "the prince of darkness, the Caiaphas, the Herod, the Judas, and the infernal dragon of our times, Napoleon."[12]

Joseph's proclamation is burned by the hangman in front of the Viceregal Palace. Citizens are urged to notify officials of any "seductive and incendiary papers" (Hernández y Dávalos 1877:2,447).). A ten-peso reward is offered for apprehending any spy.

When the Viceroy's proclamation reached Tlaxcala on May 16, the civil authorities responded in kind:

> Tlaxcala has not forgotten and will never forget the happy day, September 23, 1519, on which, giving to the whole world evident testimony of its fidelity to the august crown of Spain, it had the incomparable joy of receiving the splendor in its wide territory of the sacred light of the Holy Gospel...The whole valiant nation of Tlaxcala is happy to spill all its blood in defense of our beloved monarch Sr. Don Ferdinand VII...or for the royal Council of the Regency...This bright man [Joseph], whose title I [Juan Tomas de Altamirano] contemplate with indignation, for his hateful lasciviousness, better suited to a beast, tries unhappily by his bold and ridiculous proclamations to treat us as if we were Iroquois and Hottentots...[The civil authorities of] Tlaxcala, which is to say, the first city of this new world, [deplore how Napoleon's followers] belittle the rationality of the Indians...regarding them as ignorant...the Tlaxcaltecs take it as a point of honor and boast of being the exact imitators of the customs, honor, and conduct of the beloved Spaniards...They incite the whole Indian nation of this western America to accompany them in their firm resolutions and propositions. (Hernández y Dávalos 1877:51–53)

Napoleon continued his campaign with a declaration issued on March 20, 1810, that spoke of the benefits of independence, such as agriculture freed of restrictions. He urged priests to preach independence and to instruct their flock that Napoleon was sent by God to punish the pride and tyranny of monarchs. He told of the difference between the United States and Spanish America, stressing the great freedom and wealth of the former.

On June 20, 1810, the Count del Peñasco sent a letter to Captain Juan N. Oviedo, warning him against Napoleonic emissaries that had stirred up common people against the privileged Spanish in Zacatecas. "This discord of tongues, more powerful than that of arms, is what has facilitated their conquests, their tricks wage greater war than their bullets" (Hernández y Dávalos 1877:2,54)

On September 16, 1811, Napoleon offered to supply arms for independence, so long as the colonists did not establish relations with England. He expects a shipment of arms from the United States, for "on a former occasion France promoted the independence of the U.S." (Robertson 1939:93).

But in a proclamation from "Mother Spain to her American Children," addressed to "Spanish Americans and to loyal and Christian Indians," printed in

Mexico in 1811, comes the consoling news that "the fires of disorder that the Emissaries of Napoloen lit in our soil have been extinguished."[13]

Indeed, while Mexicans envied the freedom and prosperity of their neighbors to the north, they feared that "Big Brother" might descend on them in force at any moment. Even Napoleon had his doubts: "I embarked very badly on the Spanish affair, I confess: the immorality of it was too patent, the injustice too cynical" (Rydjord 1972:290). Although the Hidalgo insurgents were described by the government as agents of Bonaparte, this accusation was based more on political aims than reality.

HIDALGO AND MORELOS

In 1808 the French general Gaëtan d'Alvimart entered Mexico to incite rebellion among the Creoles. After his capture he spent "an entire night talking secretly behind a closed door" with Miguel Hidalgo y Costilla (Hamill 1966:103). In his trunk the general was found to have some French uniforms, a copy of Machiavelli, and a treatise on the art of war. And yet Hidalgo shouted to his troops, *"Viva Fernando Séptimo, guerra a muerte a los gachupines!"* "Viva Ferdinand VII, war to the death to the Spaniards!" (Comenje 1909:436). It is said that the revolutionaries proclaimed both independence and allegiance to Ferdinand simultaneously, sure that he would never return.

One day before the *Grito*, Hidalgo's rallying cry to his troops, Francisco Javier de Venegas became Viceroy. He was honest and hard working. As a general he had distinguished himself in Spain's first military victory, defeating the French army at Bailén. To oppose Hidalgo he created the elite corps of "Distinguished Patriots for Ferdinand VII." On September 2, 1808, the President of the *Audiencia* of Guadalajara called for volunteers to defend that section of Mexico. Four thousand volunteered including "Indians who offered themselves armed with bows and arrows and even promised that their wives and daughters would sally forth to fight" (Robertson 1939:58).

"A Manifesto of the Faculty of the University of Mexico," on October 5, 1810, appeals to the citizens to reject Hidalgo's rebellious troops in Dolores, remarking that, as Napoleon's ships cannot reach America because of the "generous English," he must rely on sedition (Hernández y Dávalos 1877:2, 147). Arguing that the Spanish conquerors brought civilization and "innumerable exemptions and privileges" protected by the Cortes, there should be no need for rebellion (Hernández y Dávalos 1877:148).

The manifesto is seconded by the "Proclamation of an Indian priest of the bishopric of Valladolid, to all the Indian priests and vicars, and to our sons, the chiefs, governors, and other Indians of this America." In Valladolid, now Morelia, a plot had been fostered among the intellectuals, including some clergy, to establish a junta to protect New Spain against the United States. and France. Later, members of this group joined the forces of Hidalgo. The priest asserts, "Hidalgo talked to us and our children, sometimes saying, 'poor little things, how sad to see you like this,' but suddenly, too, the scene would change, and then we were just 'beasts of burden, stupid animals, a race that must be exterminated, trunks and limbs for the bonfire.'"[14] Referring to Hidalgo as the "Lucifer of New Spain," he urges his fellow priests "to inspire peace, submission, obedience, loyalty and solid piety in our beloved children, the Indians…so that the desolation begun in Dolores will not extend further."[15]

The manifesto is seconded again by a proclamation of the Tlaxcaltecs:

> The war provoked by Hidalgo and his companions is not, and cannot be, directed solely against the Europeans, it must be against everyone regardless of class and condition…The Indians of Tlaxcala do not have in their hearts nor on their lips anything but Viva our religion, our well-beloved King Don Ferdinand VII, and death to the enemies of the country. (Hernández y Dávalos 1877:2,172–173)

Viceroy Venegas, on December 4, 1810, proclaimed that the Supreme Government had "inexplicable satisfaction" in its loyal colonists, but great sorrow over those who have created commotions "as if they were not sons of the same mother" (Hernández y Dávalos 1877:252). He implored Caracas and Buenos Aires to "imitate us in moderation and confidence!" (Hernández y Dávalos 1877:253). Citing a loss of 200,000 French soldiers in Spain, he exclaims, "This union, like a stalwart cliff, is what [Napoleon] fears in Spain and wishes will be undone in America" (Hernández y Dávalos 1877:254). He pleads with his subjects to remain loyal.

Initially many of the nobility, including Creoles, admired Hidalgo, but soon they refused to support him, partly because of their confidence in the Cortes, but mainly because of their fear of the destructive horde that had been unleashed. After Hidalgo and his three generals had been executed on July 31, 1811, their heads were placed in four metal cages and were hung at the four corners of Guanajuato's granary for ten years!

Undeterred by this gruesome example of the possible fate of revolutionary leaders, José María Morelos to the south was capturing town after town. On December 23, 1812, he sent a manifesto to the inhabitants of Oaxaca, expressing his disillusionment with the current relations with Spain:

> The Cortes of Cádiz have claimed more than once that the Americans are equal to the Europeans, and to flatter us more, they have treated us as

brothers; but if they had proceeded with sincerity and good faith, it would have followed that at the same time that they declared their independence, they had declared ours and had left us the liberty to establish our government, just as they established theirs. Moreover, they were so far from doing it that way that scarcely had they established their first councils when they imposed laws on us, demanding from us oaths of loyalty, one after another, while over there they dissolved some and created new ones at the whim of the merchants of Cádiz in agreement with those of Veracruz and Mexico City. (Lemoine Villicaña 1965:243)

Morelos declared that no sooner had the Cortes been established than they demanded many oaths of loyalty, while at the same time, swayed by the merchants of Cádiz, Vera Cruz, and Mexico City, they imposed new laws to the detriment of the common man.

NEW SPAIN AND THE CORTES

The pioneer North American interpreters of Mexican history Hubert Howe Bancroft, Henry Bamford Parkes and Herbert Ingram Priestley argued that the Cortes, the Constitution of 1812 and the laws subsequent to it had little impact on institutional and political developments in Mexico. And yet the Cortes' and the Constitution's primary revolutionary concepts, *"popular or national* sovereignty, the separation of powers, equal representation, equality of rights and privileges, and *semi-autonomous* local governments," subsequently were all adopted by the Mexican constitution (Garza 1966:45).

Mexicans, repelled by the looting and bloodshed of Hidalgo's followers, looked to the Cortes and the Constitution to formulate a Mexican congress and constitution. Seventeen Mexican deputies were elected to the Cortes in 1810; eleven priests, two bureaucrats, one professor, one lawyer, one soldier, and one miner.

Viceroy Venegas on October 5, 1810, four-and-a-half months after its publication, announced the Cortes' decree declaring Indians free of tribute. He extended those rights to the castes and ordered that his decree "be translated into all the languages of these countries" (Hernández y Dávalos 1877:2,139). On the very same day the decree was published in Nahuatl in the name of *"Totlatocatzin Rey D[on] Fernando VII"* (Hernández y Dávalos 1877:140).

The decrees of February 9 and November 8, 1811, granting (1) equal representation for Americans in the Cortes, the equality of Indians and castes, and (2) amnesty for revolutionaries, were not published until April 3, 1812. This extraordinary delay of 13 months for the first and 6 months for the second angered the colonists. The Morelos insurgents believed these were concessions made in response to necessity that would be abandoned as soon as the insurgents surrendered. It had been the failure of the Cortes to apply the right of equality to Indians and the castes in the first decree that had so enraged Inca Yupanqui and the Tlaxcalan priest Guridi y Alcocer.

At this time no news reached Mexico City from Vera Cruz for three months. The fourth expedition of Spanish troops arrived in August, but in September poor communication and banditry still reigned throughout Mexico. The Viceroy maintained relative quiet through fear rather than violence. The United States Constitution was published secretly in Mexico City and distributed there.

On June 25, 1812, the Viceroy decreed that all revolutionary leaders would be shot, giving them time only to die a Christian death.

The Constitution reached Mexico City on September 6, 1812. It was sworn to by the Viceroy and the bishops on September 30. Copies of the Constitution received by the Archbishop were to be distributed to the priests to be read in the churches.

> There seems to have been no hesitation on the part of New Spain's clergy, either high or low, in taking the oath to uphold the document...A Mass was celebrated in the cathedral by Archdeacon Beristáin, who preached a sermon exhorting the faithful to support the Constitution. After the mass a *Te Deum* was sung. In the next few days the oath was administered in all the parishes, convents, and monasteries of the city...the kings had never been sworn to with such solemnity, especially by all the corporations. (Breedlove 1966:122–123)

The Constitution was celebrated in Mexico City by a local college, the *Colegio Mayor de Santos,* with statues of Spain and America joined by a huge banner declaring, "Although the ocean separates them, the Constitution unites them" (de Alba 1912:53).

An important feature of the Constitution was the establishment of a *Consejo de Estado* (State Council) comprised of 40 members, with at least 12 from overseas, together with a new system of local government in the provinces. The American deputies in the Cortes were enraged that the council would be headed by a *jefe político,* but even the Spanish liberal leader Agustín Arguelles approved it. At least the Americans won the concession that the chief must be a statesman and a native of the province.

Of equal importance was a provision introduced by the priest Miguel Ramos Arizpe, "the so-called father of Mexican federalism,...probably the most ardent defender of local autonomy," who proposed a new system of local government in the provinces, whereby the chief of each Provincial Deputation was to be appointed by the king, with seven locally elected members (Garza 1966:56–57).

Popularly elected town governments *(ayuntamientos)* replaced *ayuntamientos* of *regidores* whose posts had been perpetual and which formerly could be renounced or sold.

Freedom of the press was not sworn to in Mexico City until October 5, 1812, thirteen months after the decree's appearance in Cádiz, because it was opposed by the *Audiencia*, the *Cabildo*, five *Intendentes*, and all the bishops but one. Exactly two months later, Viceroy Venegas suspended freedom of the press, and on October 30 decreed that no press could publish the Constitution without government approval, lest it be modified.

It would have been around this time that there arrived in New Spain a three-and-a-half-page proclamation from the Duque del Infantado addressed to the overseas inhabitants, advising them of the Constitution and the good prospects for prosperity. On the very day of its publication, August 30, ten copies had been sent to New Spain. But a parallel six-and-a-half-page proclamation addressed to the European Spaniards, dated August 28, was not sent until September 17. This "magnificent edict" assured the Spaniards of the value of the Constitution that "removes the relics of feudalism... You see yourselves reinstated in the condition of free men," no longer the prey to corrupt courtiers, "All you Spaniards of both worlds look with respect and veneration at the sacred deposition of your [property and judicial] rights."[16] The term "Indian" does not happen to appear in this proclamation!

Carrying out the provisions of the Constitution, elections for the provincial governments were held on November 29. Not a single Spaniard was elected. In disgust, Venegas suspended the municipal elections and once again abolished freedom of the press.

The choice of a successor to Venegas centered on Félix María Calleja, the general who had been most prominent in pursuing Morelos (Timmons 1963:91). "Should that come about, despotism and tyranny will ascend to the greatest height, for in cruelty, ability, skill, and influence, Calleja surpasses Venegas," said the followers of Morelos. On February 28, 1813, Calleja became Viceroy of New Spain. He reestablished the Constitution, holding a magnificent fiesta in its honor on its first anniversary, March 19, and reinstating municipal elections—a victory for the Americans. But freedom of the press was not permitted. Indeed, realizing that the Constitution reduced the viceroy to being a mere political chief, Calleja depended on his advisors to confirm his authority.

Calleja declared on April 27 that citizens of France and of countries under French rule must leave the country unless they proved to be loyal to the king. On May 24, citizens of the United States were forbidden entry.

In the election of deputies for the Cortes, fourteen Creole deputies and four substitutes were elected; there were no Spaniards nor Indians. The Mexican deputy, Guridi y Alcocer, pointed out that there were 21 languages in the bishopric of Oaxaca, but that there were always bilingual Indians who could come to the

Cortes. Another deputy, Pérez de Castro, added, "I know very well that Indians are not in the state of civilization of the Europeans, but I know that there are Indians with enlightenment, property and culture, and it would not be too much to expect that there would be one in 50,000 who could come to Congress" (Armellada 1959:20). Alas, as Calleja declared that there were insufficient funds for the transportation to and support of the 14 elected deputies in Cádiz, only two were sent to Spain.

VERA CRUZ, TABASCO, AND THE YUCATAN

It was perhaps in 1808 that the widow of Don Manuel Comes Esquinas de Porriño published in Cádiz a proclamation "From Vera Cruz to the American Spaniards":

> The unhappy inhabitants of the usurped kingdoms have only been left with eyes to look at their misfortune, to cry over their misery…Generous Americans, [Napoleon is] a monster of Iniquity who knows no other god than his ambition…Americans…aid your kings. Lift your hands to the sky, implore the justice of God to carry out revenge, arm yourselves like strong men and never bend your back under the insupportable yoke of France…Americans: you, too, are menaced by the same fate as Europe…Look at him as a monster of pride, ambition and tyranny, as a chief enemy of all humankind, as a Giant Pirate.[17]

On February 14, 1812, two weeks after the Constitution was sworn to in Mexico City, the same was done in Vera Cruz. On November 3, a new government was elected there.

In Yucatan, Gustavo de Witt, an elegant and monied gentleman, reported variously to be a Dane and a Dutchman, arrived from the United States. In Mérida he became a popular member of the high society, until he was so bold as to reveal that he was a Napoleonic emissary. He was sentenced to hang on November 12, 1810. Conflicting historical reports state that for lack of a public hangman he met his death either by a firing squad or by crossbow. His incriminating documents were burned publicly.

In 1811 the deputy from Tabasco, Dr. José Eduardo de Cárdenas y Romero, accompanied the deputy from Chiapas to the Cortes, Manuel de Llano. A cavalry escort was provided to honor the illustrious travelers for a league and a half out of the city of Villa Hermosa. Dr. Cárdenas wrote a lengthy report describing the mismanagement of the government of Tabasco. He had further remarks about the condition of the Indians in his province:

> The Indians very much love knowledge, and as they are equipped with
> the natural light of reason, are aroused by the same sweetness of the arts
> and the sciences...After a weary day in the sun, in a hot climate, they try
> to teach the doctrine to their children, and excel in giving instruction in
> reading and writing... and they try to place themselves in the houses of
> European and American Spaniards so that they can learn...But if there
> are no capable teachers, nor even elementary books for the task? To
> learn without books is to draw water with a sieve. (Lacroix 1985:89)

The capture of Ferdinand VII caused great pain and confusion in Mérida because, "Señor Capitan General, these loyal Yucatecs love their adored Ferdinand to such a degree that one has neither the strength to explain it to you, nor are there tongues to persuade you. As if he were their father, everyone holds him in their hearts" (Rubio Mañé 1968:147).

In 1811 an infantry body in Yucatan was named *"Fieles de Fernando VII,"* "Ferdinand VII's Faithful." Miguel González y Lastiri, a deputy to the Cortes, returned to Mérida in July, 1812, with seven copies of the Constitution, but Governor Manuel Artazo Torre de Mer, an absolutist, delayed its proclamation three months, until October 14, Ferdinand VII's birthday; the announcement was followed by six days of festivities. On that day, the Bishop of Yucatan wrote to the Bishop of Chiapa that "the wisdom and holiness of the Constitution" was celebrated by a military salute, the ringing of bells, and a *Te Deum.*[18] A plaque with letters in gold was erected; the *"C"* of *Constitución* was encrusted with diamonds, the gift of the mother of Andrés Quintana Róo. The Governor tried to prevent the Constitution from reaching Campeche by claiming a lack of copies. The Constitution was finally sworn to there on December 8. The President of the city government kissed the Constitution and, following the customary gesture of respect, placed it on his head, and after reading it, shouted, *"Patria, Constitución, Rey, Cortes, y Religión"* (Lanz 1905:111). The Constitution was not sworn to in Villa Hermosa until March 25, 1813, when an obelisk was planted in its honor. From 1812 to 1925 the main square was named the *Plaza de la Constitución.*

The first newspaper of Yucatan, *"El Misceláneo,"* published a "Dialogue between the Indians Juan and Pascual," where the two Indians debate the value of the Constitution. They are sad because "before that thing came we were surely slaves, but we did not realize it" (Echánove 1947:5, 23).

In Yucatan the absolutist governor was opposed by a group of liberal priests, the *Sanjuanistas,* led by the Chaplain of the *Ermita de San Juan Bautista,* Fr. Velásquez, who circulated copies of Bishop Las Casas' *"Destrucción de los indios* [sic] *por los españoles"* and demanded extreme reforms in benefit of the Indians: "These poor Indians constitute the immense majority of the Yucatecs, descended from the primitive lords of the land, our fathers usurped all their rights and enslaved them, under the pretext of religion. So they can and must provide the laws in this country" (Rubio Mañé 1967:1226).

Under the Constitution the *"repúblicas de indios,"* that had been established years before, "violated the liberal ideas of freedom and equality; the *repúblicas* were therefore abolished in favor of municipalities to be governed by 'constitutional' town councils that would be elected by all the local residents regardless of caste. (Farriss 1984:376)

This well-intentioned action destroyed the last vestige of Indian autonomy as it was the conservative Creoles who were elected to the Provincial Deputations, or town governments, and promptly sold the communal lands. For the Indians, a positive effect of the Constitution was the annulment of tributes, personal service, and whipping. The *Sanjuanistas* persuaded the governor to free the Indians from forced labor service for the clergy as well as the special contributions. The priests declared, "It has been all destruction, nothing built!" (Rubio Mañé 1968:438). The Bishop complained that the priests had to ring the church bells and even sweep the floors of the churches. The Maya refused to pay tithes or to serve the priests even for pay.

But before long the conservatives would again have their way!

NOTES

1. Although Vera Cruz, Tabasco and Yucatan were entities of New Spain, for geographical reasons, their closeness to Chiapa, I am considering them at the end of the chapter.

2. Proclama del Arzobispo Virrey de Nueva España a los fieles vasallos de Fernando VII, January 23, 1810:3.

3. Proclama del Arzobispo Virrey de Nueva España a los fieles vasallos de Fernando VII, January 23, 1810:4–5.

4. Proclama del Arzobispo Virrey de Nueva España a los fieles vasallos de Fernando VII, January 23, 1810:8–9.

5. Proclama del Arzobispo Virrey de Nueva España a los fieles vasallos de Fernando VII, January 23, 1810:11.

6. Proclama del Arzobispo Virrey de Mexico, contra los engaños pérfidos de los Bonapartes, April 24, 1810:4.

7. Proclama del Arzobispo Virrey de Mexico, contra los engaños pérfidos de los Bonapartes, April 24, 1810:5.

8. Proclama del Arzobispo Virrey de Mexico, contra los engaños pérfidos de los Bonapartes, April 24, 1810:7–8.

9. Proclama del Arzobispo Virrey de Mexico, contra los engaños pérfidos de los Bonapartes, April 24, 1810:9.

10. Proclama del Arzobispo Virrey de Mexico, contra los engaños pérfidos de los Bonapartes, April 24, 1810:10–11.

11. Proclama del Arzobispo Virrey de Mexico, contra los engaños pérfidos de los Bonapartes, April 24, 1810:13, 15, 16, 19–20.

12. Circular que el Señor Gobernador de la Sagrada Mitra dirige a los Parrocos y Eclesiasticos del Arzobispo de Mexico, recordando la obediencia y fidelidad a Dios y a Nuestro Cautivo Rey Fernando VII, April 26, 1810:82, 87, 89, 96.

13. Proclama de la Madre España a sus hijos los americanos 1811:1.

14. Proclama de un cura del obispado de Valladolid, a todos los padres curas y vicarios indios y a nuestro hijos los caziques gobernadores y demas indios de esta America 1811[?]:2.

15. Proclama de un cura del obispado de Valladolid, a todos los padres curas y vicarios indios y a nuestro hijos los caziques gobernadores y demas indios de esta America 1811[?].

16. Proclama a los Españoles Europeos, August 28, 1812:10.

17. Proclama de Veracruz a los Españoles Americanos, 1808[?]:2–3, 5

18. Letter: Estéves to Llano, October 22, 1812.

5

Guatemala

BEFORE THE CORTES OF CÁDIZ

The Captaincy General of Guatemala, which included Chiapa, Soconusco and what are now all the Central American countries north of Panama, was in a serious depression during the quarter century preceding independence. Exports, money transactions, and roads pulled the Indians into the world economy. *Ladinos* (mestizos) encroached on their lands for the indigo trade, etc., but even that was in a severe decline. Malnutrition and dependence on food imports marked the economy. But as early as 1799 the importance of primary school education for Indians was decreed because "first impressions received in early life are generally preserved for one's whole life, and most of them receive Christian and political instruction only in the schools" (Bartes Jáuregui 1920:2, 552).

In 1801 there appeared an article in the *Gazeta de Guatemala* entitled, "An Illustrious *Ladino* Defends the Indians Against Those Who Believe That They are Lazy and Drunk by Nature." After describing the Indians' industry and humility, he comments on a report he has seen that claims that the best way to make Indians industrious is to have them wear shoes and Western clothes. This report, attracting much attention in Guatemala, was written by Fray Matías de Córdoba, later the prime figure in declaring Chiapa's independence. The illustrious *Ladino* objects:

> This author forgot the most important fact. He forgot that among us the Indians are the only ones who water the land with the sweat of their brows to guarantee us the bread they do not eat. He forgot that if they did not work, we would have to do so ourselves lest we die of hunger…In conclusion, the arms of the Indians are the horns of plenty of Guatemala. (De Vos 1994:246–247)

Governor González issued a decree on January 25, 1805, with minute instructions on how to carry out smallpox vaccinations, citing the outbreak of the disease in Chiapa "not three years before."[1] In each province a smallpox board was to be established, composed of the bishop, the governor, a member of the ecclesiastical government, a member of the civil government and a secretary. The priests were to keep records of the individuals who had not yet been vaccinated.

> It is the duty of the Priests and the Judges to explain to their parishioners
> and subjects, whether from the pulpit or in conversations and discourses,
> the marvelous effectiveness of the vaccine in providing protection against
> pestilent smallpox, and the imponderable benefits of this inoculation.
> The priests will confront the Indians' rusticity with all the power of their
> sacred ministry.[2]

The priests and the judges would be held responsible for any rebellious attitudes.

Aggressive Peninsular immigrants married into Creole families and played a major role in commercial growth. Several decades before independence, the social and economic oppression of the royal court spawned the wish for it. Already in 1808–1809, there were court cases against people accused of being disloyal.

Communication was so minimal that in 1807 mail from Guatemala to Oaxaca was shipped once a month. On June 30, 1808, the captain general published a copy of the royal decree of March 19 in which, in Alajuelas, Charles IV abdicates "my Crown to my heir and very dear Prince of Asturias."[3] News from the Viceroy of New Spain, informing the captain general of the abdications in Bayonne of Charles IV and Ferdinand VII, was brought, again three months after the fact, on August 13, 1808, by "two muddy, tall-hatted Mexican Indians" (Zamora 1935:35). On September 5, declaration of war against France was announced with drumbeats in Nueva Goatemala (Guatemala City). The General Council (advisors to the captain general) rejected as invalid Ferdinand's abdication and recognized him as their lawful monarch on September 9. On September 26, a letter from Ferdinand VII advising his subjects of his abdication was received by the members of the city government, who took it, read it, and placed it on their heads. For Guadalupe Day there were three days of illumination of the city, fireworks, and a bust of the king was placed on a pedestal of hearts.

In the 1790s the Franciscan friar José Antonio Goicochea taught at the University of San Carlos in Guatemala City, where he introduced French encyclopedist thought into Creole society, contributing to the establishment of the *Gazeta de Guatemala* and the *Sociedad Económica de Amigos del País de Guatemala*. This experimentation, progress, economic growth, and new currents of thought were limited to Nueva Guatemala (Guatemala City), despite the efforts of the members of the Economic Society who urged all city governments to send correspondents to Guatemala City to strengthen "the bonds that unite the capital with her provinces," and permitting "us to take advantage of the enlightenment and knowledge of its individuals" (Rodríguez 1978:42). A professor of philosophy at the university, Father Mariano López Rayón, with great success taught the Indians of the Highlands to improve their crops. Seventeen artisan guilds were reformed and a school of painting founded.

The Creole elite became a liberal and national force, while engaged in contraband trade and commerce with England. In 1808 the mayor urged the biennial election of aldermen (positions that would not be bought). Captain General Antonio González was angered, but gave in to the mayor's demands. Guatemala City had municipal reform long before the orders from the Cortes of Cádiz. The Creoles in Guatemala City tried to form a junta and asked González to be president. He refused and strengthened the troops in the city.

Loyalty to the crown was strong. When Charles IV abdicated his throne to his son, the Guatemalan merchant guild hailed Ferdinand VII as not only "King of Spain," but also as "Restorer of Europe"! The board of trade and other local institutions struck medals to commemorate the captive monarch, while prominent citizens swore oaths of loyalty to him (Woodward 1965b:452).

But the economic and political woes of Guatemala were intensified by the "Voluntary Patriotic Donations" that began as early as 1780 when Indians and castes were asked to give one peso apiece, and the Spaniards two pesos, to defray the costs of the war with England. In September and October of 1808, after the declaration of war against France, priests were ordered locally to collect donations even before the request was made by Spain. Huge amounts were collected. On September 3, 1809, "Ferdinand" gave thanks to the "loyal and generous caciques, governors, mayors, principal judges and other natives of the reign," for giving 100,000 pesos to sustain "the just cause against the perfidy of Napoleon Bonaparte and his iniquitous followers." In the name of the King, "Protector of Indians," the Treasury of Guatemala gave thanks to the Indian judges for the generous Indian contribution and "will in peacetime recompense you, and in the meantime wear these medals with the royal bust."[4] But in response to the latest demand for a donation there was a brief rebellion south of Guatemala City in the town of Chiquimula in this year.

Measures were taken to minimize the danger of Napoleonic intrigues. On September 5, 1808, the Captain General and the local government decreed that the property of all Frenchmen who had not been naturalized be impounded and that its owners be seized. Foreign vessels should be excluded from Central American ports and Spanish and British vessels searched. The captain general modified this decree on May 6, 1809, such that it asked only for inspection of the papers on ships from Spain and Latin America, lest trade be diminished, but on June 27 he warned the people that King Joseph had sent spies to America.

GUATEMALA IN 1810

Were it not for the *Gazeta* little would be known about Guatemala in this year, but the metropolitan newspaper kept the citizens of the capital abreast of all the latest political and social developments, often with vivid commentary.

The liberal government of Guatemala spoke of:

> the unhappy state of Indians due to their ignorance and lack of care for bettering their customs. Despite the beautiful dispositions with which the aborigines are graced, one sees them with pain, lowered by stupidity, degraded and knocked down to the extent that they drag their chains of slavery without repugnance and perhaps bless the sacrilegious hand that usurps from them the beautiful prerogative of free men. They are the ones who sustain all of us, they are the principal farmers who irrigate our lands with the sweat of their brows. It is they who handle the plow that cultivates and benefits these lands. They carry our food on their shoulders, they sustain us all and pay tribute. (Salazar 1928:142)

But the Captain General was far more concerned about the menace of Napoleon, who seemed to become an obsession for him. On April 22 he issued a decree reminding the citizens that the "Machiavellian French Government" had sent spies to the United States to infiltrate Central America (*Gazeta de Guatemala,* 25 May 1810: XIV(149), 1). For this reason foreigners would only be able to enter port for reasons of safety. Since there were no interpreters in the ports and it was difficult to distinguish between English and Anglo-American ships, both would be forbidden. Papers received from foreign ships should not be read, but sealed and submitted to the officials. Papers of passengers on Spanish ships must be inspected. As spies may come as sailors, servants, and naval officers there was a need for careful observation of their actions, conversations, friendships and connections.

González took further precautions. Those who received guests or passengers in their houses must show papers to a judge. There should be a list of recent foreign residents and all subsequent visitors. There would be a reward for denouncing a spy. Anyone who failed to inform the government of a spy would be considered his accomplice. And watch out for muleteers, they may be spies too!

On May 15, the *Audiencia* of Guatemala warned officials to beware of spies or emissaries of King Joseph's government. González formed a Vigilance Tribunal to which he appointed three Spaniards, no Americans. The city government objected, to no effect, and sent a formal complaint to Spain, where the tribunal was finally disbanded on February 20, 1811. On May 17 the *Real Acuerdo* approved the Captain General's attempt to discover French spies. Two were reported to be in the Petén.

In a manifesto on May 22, González analyzes the political situation. "There are Spanish bastards, there have been and there always will be" (Boletín del Archivo General de la Nación 3:3:355). Commenting on the latest news from Vera Cruz regarding the United States' recent disagreements with England, whereupon the United States broke neutrality and allowed French ships in its ports, González remarks,

> The states that are said to be united, are only so in the titles and headings of their records...If their Government were so crazy as to wage war on England, the signs of civil war are manifest in their public documents and in their speeches before Congress...Even if they unite with our abominable enemies in the black design to enslave us, it will still be useless. (Boletín del Archivo General de la Nación 3:3:357)

The *Gazeta's* editors provide a new perspective: "To know what is thought of the Bonaparte bulletins in France, it is enough to say that in Paris when the fruit or vegetable sellers doubt a person's veracity, they say, 'he lies like a bulletin!'" (*Gazeta de Guatemala*, 3 July 1810: XIV(155), 75).

The Captain General is at it again on July 6 with his review of "three barbarous papers": the October 2 proclamation of Joseph Bonaparte addressed to those whom he "in his delirium calls vassals of *his possessions* in America"; another to the high clergy in the same hand; and "The Advice and Exhortation of a Spanish Creole to His Fellow Citizens of America." González outdoes the members of the Holy Court in his condemnation of King Joseph's literary style:

> All three writings have a French author. Their half-breed, vile language demonstrates that without doubt. They do not have Spanish paper, nor printing, and only some words clumsily taken out of some bad dictionary. He uses the verbs *learn* for *teach*, *hesitate* for vacillate or waver, useless articles and prepositions, or disused in our elegant language, and Gallic locutions that no pure Spaniard would understand, unworthy even of the indecent translators, corrupters of our beautiful language .(*Gazeta de Guatemala,* 7 July 1810: XIV(157), 93)

These "barbarous papers" were duly burned in the main square.

A few days later, the editors of the *Gazeta* comment: "There is not in the world a *finca* as productive as the *lie* in the hands of Bonaparte; and it is amusing how everyone helps him to fertilize it...The first words that our children utter next to their mothers' breasts are curses against the French" (*Gazeta de Guatemala,* 27 July 1810:XIV(162), 135, 137–138).

In November they inform the citizens of Guatemala City that in Grenada, Nicaragua, there was discovered skirt material that had at one end "the odious figure of the abominable tyrant of Europe, and its inscription lest there be any doubt, that said, 'Bonaparte'" (*Gazeta de Guatemala,* 6 November 1810: XIV(183), 306).

That same month the editors publish a "Patriotic Dialogue," sent from Mexico City, reputedly reporting the conversation of three men, sitting and drinking their chocolate. They discuss Hidalgo and the hinterland, naming the revolutionary as "a flustered rake," "a Don Quijote de la Mancha," "a General of Comedy" (*Gazeta de Guatemala,* 10 November 1810:XIV(184), 317). His aide, Allende, is a "harebrained youth" (*Gazeta de Guatemala,* 10 November 1810:XIV(184), 316).

> Yes, it is a horrible thing, a clergyman as a swashbuckling swordsman, a priest laden with arms, a priest leading bandits, looting homes and killing innocent men. And the most simple Indians and the poorest artisans are scandalized by such a monstrosity...Upon hearing from the opposite side a couple of cannon rounds, they will say "This isn't for us, let's go home." And this can be understood if the poor fellows are used as bait for the first volleys. (*Gazeta de Guatemala,* 10 November 1810:XIV(184), 319)

The cause of the war is described by the chocolate drinkers as a result of rivalry between the Spaniards and the Creoles:

> But look at the Moors and the Christians, [and here] those who have the same Religion, the same King, the same laws, and basically the same customs—it is not only a ridiculous situation, but unjust and criminal...The European who makes a fortune is richer because he conceives, works, and operates with honesty and economy...Because he doesn't like [to eat] *chirimoyas*, because he is revolted by black zapotes, passion fruit and pulque, must we consider him our enemy? (*Gazeta de Guatemala,* 10 November 1810:XIV(186), 321, 323)

There follows a long list of officials of church and state who are Creoles. "Spain never has been *systematically unjust* to the Americans." The reader is asked to remember all the cities, buildings, churches, hospitals, roads, carriages, stores, etc. that have been built in the colonies. "Napoleon says he is sent by God, but he comes to extinguish the Catholic Religion" (*Gazeta de Guatemala,* 10 November 1810:XIV(187), 334).

While the government and the press were stewing over Hidalgo and Napoleon, other men were preparing for Guatemala's entry into the Cortes of Cádiz. These were members of "the family," related to the Marqués de Aycinena, the only holder of noble title in the colony. It was an aristocratic oligarchy composed essentially of twelve families related to the Aycinenas, all planters and/or merchants of indigo.

One of their own, José María Peynado, a distinguished politician, prepared a 79-page book of instructions for the Constitution, entitled, *"Instrucciones para la Constitución fundamental de la monarquía española y su gobierno."* Beginning with a quotation from Tacitus, the introduction deplores the past administrative and colonial policies, and declares the need for a constitution when the King is "a father and a citizen" (Salvatierra 1939:293). Peynado expresses the need for "philosophy" and "enlightenment" to promote "the general welfare." His instructions fuse the current "enlightened" thoughts with Bourbon reforms and the French Revolution. They called for "[1] diversified agricultural enterprise and free labor. [2]…supported the right of Spain to monopolize commerce in those products she could supply. [3]…recognized the Catholic Church as absolute. [4]… replicated the Declaration of the Rights of Man and spoke of natural law. [5] In addition, they suggested that a head tax be imposed on all" (Wortman 1982:200). Peynado gave the Provincial Deputations power over finance, judiciary, royal patronage, and public affairs.

He calls for free trade, free movement, mutual preference for exports between Spain and America, freedom of the press (except in respect to religious subjects). Peynado's progressive notions on economic, social, and political matters and his advocation of local autonomy and laissez-faire, buttressed by quotations from Sully, Zoroaster, Demosthenes and Confucius, were in step with the ideology and spirit of the Cortes, though much more conservative.

In retrospect they have been judged as "aristocratic,…monarchical, with all those instructions they represent an historical monument, in which liberty and equality are recognized for the first time in Guatemala" (Salazar 1928: 130–131). The book was "revolutionary in its treatment of the problem of government, finance, taxes, and justice…a remarkable document conceived and written in a land that had never known political freedom" (Rosenthal 1962:90). The "Instructions" were well received in Guatemala City and praised in Mexico City.

The Creole-dominated city government, afraid of the menace of hostilities, sought to convince the Peninsular-oriented merchants to purchase arms, but the latter showed their colors by suggesting that this be financed by taxing the Church and Indigo Growers Association, i.e., "the family!"

The city government had been very upset at the establishment of the Regency in Cádiz without their voice, but finally conceded on sending deputies to the Cortes. Their first vote was for the canon of the cathedral, Antonio de Larrazábal, born in Antigua and educated at the university (plate 17). He had been a village priest and was considered to be a rustic deputy. It was his duty to carry the "Las Instrucciones" to the Cortes in Cádiz. Larrazábal's election was celebrated by a *Te Deum*, illuminations, music, and street decorations.

A manifesto dated December 3, 1810, arrived in Guatemala City shortly before Larrazábal's departure for Spain: *"El Dr. D. Agustin Pomposo Fernandez de San Salvador da una idea de lo que son los diputados en las Cortes."* With great relief the writer exclaims how the Spanish world has been saved in 39 days from Hidalgo and his generals, Allende, Aldama, and Abasolo.

> Now we Spaniards, Indians, castes, white men are one nation, one religion, one society, one family governed by one scepter. [The writer speaks of the Virgin Mary who freed Indians from the] diabolical power [of tyrants], reducing you to such slavery that lifting your eyes to those who were your kings, emperors or senators, was a crime that was punished most cruelly, those who did to you what tigers, bears, serpents and scorpions do not do to their offspring, because some false priest of the idols said so...Rational Indians who had to eat serpents and snakes, worms, mice, dogs, cats and plant grubs. [He exhorts the Indians to read the royal decree of August 20] of this year that declares that it is the wish of His Majesty that Indians and *mestizos* can be Deputies in the Cortes...You can sit on the throne, handle the scepter, have on your shoulders the royal crown that girds the temples of Ferdinand VII, to dictate laws and do the same as European and American Spaniards for the benefit of yourselves and of all our brothers who are the sons and inhabitants of these lands...Say to those who try to deceive you, 'The *loyal Indian subjects* of Ferdinand VII, *now we are men, now we are Spaniards. There is no honor too high to be awarded a loyal Indian, and even the son of an Indian man and a Spanish woman, or of a Spanish man and an Indian woman.'* (Hernández y Dávalos 1878:249–251)

Loyalty to the Cortes was sworn to in Guatemala City on December 24 with a *Te Deum*, military salutes, and visits to the prisons.

During 1810 there were a number of economic, political, and cultural events not mentioned above that were of importance. There was strong opposition to Spain's tobacco monopoly. The economy was further damaged by New Spain's suspension of its annual subsidy to Guatemala of 100,000 pesos to help pay civil and military expenses.

"The King," i.e., the Regency, thanks the *Regidor* of Comayagua for his patriotism, loyalty, and love for distributing an engraving of himself to the inhabitants of the province (what is now Honduras), and especially to the Indian leaders. In October, after learning that the Cortes of Cádiz have declared a blockade of Venezuela, Guatemala breaks off all communication with Venezuela. On October 31, after civil discord in El Salvador, San Salvador pledges continued allegiance to Guatemala. In September, Antonio González regrets the delay in receipt of the decree of May 5, but urges the people to provide a contribution to Spain. In November, the President of Guatemala receives thanks from the Regency for sending 207,289 pesos and a half *real*.

GUATEMALA IN 1811

As Antonio Gonzáles was ill in Antigua, he was replaced as Captain General by José de Bustamante (plate 18) on July 16, 1811. Bustamante presents himself in his decrees as D. JOSE DE BUSTAMANTE GUERRA DE LA VEGA, RUEDA, COBO, ESTRADA, Y ZORLADO, CABALLERO DE LA ORDEN DE SANTIAGO, TENIENTE GENERAL DE LA REAL ARMADA, DEL CONSEJO DE S.M., GOBERNADOR Y CAPITAN GENERAL DEL REYNO DE GUATEMALA, PRESIDENTE DE SU REAL AUDIENCIA, SUPERINTENDENTE GENERAL SUBDELEGADO DEL COBRO Y DISTRIBUCION DE LA REAL HACIENDA, JUEZ PRIVATIVO DE TIERRAS Y PAPEL SELLADO, CONSERVADOR DE LA RENTA DEL TABACO, SUBDELEGADO DE LA DE CORREOS, DE LOS RAMOS DE MINAS Y AZOGUES &c.[5] His predecessor, González, subsequently traveled to Oaxaca where he was captured and executed by the insurgents. The new Captain General was a man of considerable distinction. At the age of seventeen he became a Brigadier. From 1789 to 1794 he was second in command of a "political-scientific voyage around the world." Admiral Alessandro Malaspina, captain of the corvette *Descubierta*, and Vice Admiral Bustamante, captain of the corvette *Atrevida,* departed from Cádiz, sailing around Cape Horn, up to the Northwest Coast, then to Macao, the Philippines, Tonga and back to Cádiz. Their ships were veritable laboratories. Their voluminous report is replete with anthropological observations, principally of Argentina, "Russian America," California, the Philippines, and Tonga, with word lists from Tonga and an atoll of the Marshall Islands (Malaspina 1885).

Malaspina, who, "was in fact a Spanish spy, instructed to look over military installations and reinforce the Spanish claim to Nootka Sound," (Peggy Liss, personal communication) was commended by the Marine Minister, D. Antonio Valdés, as being "the leader of the Spanish Armada, and unique in that position, with the soul of the cultured and distinguished society that our sailors should represent in the American countries, to influence favorably the spirit of the creoles" (Malaspina 1885:viii). This was the most ambitious, well-documented scientific expedition ever carried out by Spain. But on their return, Bustamante fared better than his cohort, Admiral Malaspina, who, according to the historian Joaquín Villanueva (whose own misfortunes will be disclosed later), was found to have entrusted a letter to Queen María Luisa regarding his trip—a letter kept in a drawer and discovered by one of her ladies, who slipped it to the Prince of Peace. Godoy, construing it as a sign of María Luisa's infidelity, notified King Charles IV, and had Malaspina jailed and then deported to his native Lombardy, under pain of death should he return. Broken in health, he died shortly thereafter.

Bustamante was remembered for his honest, progressive rule in Montevideo (capital now of Uruguay), in 1803, which was terminated by the British in 1804 when he was wounded, captured and sent as a prisoner to England. When

Vice Admiral Bustamante entered office he asked for suggestions from all municipalities to help the region to prosper. For the capital he proposed many enlightened measures: street lighting, restriction of pubs, more night watchmen, the establishment of a College of Surgery. But when he asked the city government to inform him about the decadence in the city, hoping to receive advice, the members of the city council asked for no material improvements and insisted on the need for a constitution, equality between Creoles and Spaniards, liberty, and protection of property.

> In Central America it would not be seen until the 1820's that most of [the constitution's] supporters were not guided by true liberal or progressive spirit, but by self-interest. For the moment, however, it meant political liberalism, including elective and representative offices, relaxation of the commercial restrictions, a conscious effort to stimulate production and to develop intellectual as well as economic resources, and the emergence of incipient political parties. The aristocrats maintained their control of the municipal government and [later] of the newly elected provincial deputation, but other elements of the society challenged this control. (Woodward 1965:557)

The major challenge was to be provided by the new captain general. With hindsight, Bustamante was described as an "absolutist, sailor, and professional soldier, despotic aboard his ship, the same as on land, with an imposing figure and a proud personality" (Salazar 1928:151).

The first year of Bustamante's reign gave few hints of what was to come. On January 17, he sent a circular calling for three days of public prayers to celebrate the establishment of the Cortes. Then the Cortes's decree of February 9, 1811, arrived in Guatemala. It gave equality to Indians as representatives to the Cortes and in their choice of occupation, as well as amnesty for those previously involved in civil disturbances. On November 25, the production of cane liquor was restricted, as there was increasing drunkenness among "the beautiful class of Indians..."[6] But Bustamante went to the heart of the matter first: "Considering that this infamous vice is more rooted in this capital than in the provinces, and being the agent of all kinds of crimes, there is the need for stronger correctives, and a more effective vigilance than in other places where the common people are not so bloody."[7] Accordingly the liquor stores in the capital were reduced from thirty-six to twelve. In the Indian towns, Indians were prohibited from both the production and sale of hard liquor, but *chicha*, being "healthy and refreshing," could be made and consumed by Indians in their houses, but not sold nor mixed with spirits.[8]

A royal plea for donations for the defense of Spain was circulated on December 30.

But Napoleon's evil designs were not limited to Europe, for Bustamante, on November 8, had warned the populace of the presence of a spy in the capital. Six days later he repeated the warning, advising that even the face can be disguised. All foreigners travelling without passports should be regarded with suspicion. "Delinquents are those who spread news in favor of the French in Spain, Mexican insurgents, whoever speaks ill of the Supreme Government, the Congress of the Cortes, who stirs discord between American Spaniards and Europeans, as all are brothers. Whoever stirs up the people…is a public enemy" (Boletín del Archivo General del Gobierno 3:3:368). A list of four Spaniards who were operating in Guatemala as French spies was published.

Responding to this threat, Bustamante called for the establishment of the *Voluntarios Distinguidos de Fernando VII*. These civil patrols, whose officers were required to be Spaniards, were to maintain tranquillity and faithfulness. They were to be armed with muskets, swords, machetes and lances.

Civil unrest was beginning to emerge in the Captaincy General of Guatemala, provoked by economic depression, centralized government and regionalism. A lawyer from the capital was imprisoned for urging independence. The imprisonment of three brothers, all priests, in San Salvador caused the people on November 5 to depose the governor. There were also uprisings in the towns of León and Granada in Nicaragua, and in Honduras, where demands were made for the abolition of slavery, the deposition of European officials, the reduction of taxes, and the suppression of cane liquor. Only Costa Rica, the poorest province of Guatemala, was loyal.

Deputy Larrazábal, who had reported with satisfaction his arrival in Oaxaca on December 7, 1810, was forced to wait many months in Mexico for a transatlantic vessel. Finally he travelled on a British frigate to Portsmouth where he waited another month and a half for a Spanish warship to take him to Cádiz, where he arrived on September 17.

LARRAZÁBAL IN THE CORTES

Antonio de Larrazábal, despite a speech impediment, captured the imagination of the galleries with his liberal views. His decisions were noted for their judiciousness and equity. Together with Miguel Ramos Arizpe of Mexico and Florencio de Castillo of Costa Rica, he denounced the oppression of the Indians and pleaded that mulattos be given citizenship. These deputies provided strong voices for American rights and social and economic justice. In the humanitarian spirit of Bishop Las Casas, the Guatemalan deputy urged successfully that royal lands be distributed among the Indians, that work levies be abolished and that measures be taken to help Indians advance, such as scholarships, community resources for Indians who received land and enforcement of laws to prevent officials from pilfering community chests. Regarding the number of deputies assigned to the Cortes from America he shouted that it was a "monstrous inequality" to give overseas territories only one third of the deputations (Rodríguez 1978:67). With his fellow Americans, he complained that the Provincial Deputations were only consultative bodies rather than political units. He was bolstered by the government of Guatemala which, quoting Locke, sent pleas to the Cortes to establish effective regional governments. Larrazábal's and the other Americans' passionate defense of free trade was ignored by the Cádiz merchants in the Cortes.

GUATEMALA IN 1812

Beginning to show his colors, Bustamante demanded on April 13 a contribution to establish an army. The leftover money would be sent to Spain. Indians were reminded that as they remained "under the debt of being vassals...they must contribute to the maintenance of the religion, the return of the adored King Ferdinand VII, and the sustenance of the war in Spain" (Wortman 1982:210). He required that Indians contribute donations of the same size as the tributes had been, providing "that which they voluntarily want for the expenses of the present war so that in this manner they can prove they are good children" (Wortman 1982:210).

Responding to Bustamante's request, the Archbishop Elect of Guatemala, Ramón Casaus y Torres, penned a circular letter for distribution to his flock (plate 19). Casaus had been in Mexico City at the time of Hidalgo's rebellion and hated him with a passion. In his letter he catalogues scenes of disorder in Latin America: Quito, Santa Fé de Bogotá, Buenos Aires, and Michoacán. He claims that the revolution could have been speedily suppressed—with 50 soldiers led by an active chief the heads of Hidalgo and Allende could have been hung up in front of the church in Dolores rather than later in Chihuahua. References to the "carnivorous wolves" are followed by condemnations of the revolutionary and anti-Christian pamphlets of that "Lucifer" Napoleon.[9] The Archbishop hopes that Viceroy Venegas in Mexico can suppress "the hordes of savage cannibals" (Wortman 1982:210:10). He concludes his letter explaining that he has catalogued these disorders to convince people of the need to be able to maintain an army. Later he will speak of the obligation to contribute to the defense of Spain.

In May, the continued resistance of the Grenadians of Nicaragua convinced Bustamante that Americans were insincere and disloyal to Spain. Now began a mailed fist policy. "Hard, inflexible, suspicious, absolute, vigilant and reserved, his plans of government were a perfect reflection of his character" (Wortman 1982:201).

It was probably September when a lengthy decree arrived from the Regency, dated June 2:

> Illustrious Sir—to the Captain General, President of this reign, I tell of the royal order of this date in what follows: Although the Regency of the Kingdom is intimately persuaded that the zeal of your Excellency and other superior authorities of this Kingdom, aided by the favorable disposition of its inhabitants, will never permit ideas subversive to public order be propagated in this happy country, [ideas] that have been and still are the affliction of the bordering provinces of New Spain, still the desire that the inalterable tranquillity and inner calm of this Kingdom be maintained and the predilection which your loyal natives so justly deserve, places your Excellency in the obligation of remembering the necessity of taking all prudent means that may be indispensable in the present critical circumstances in these dominions, in agreement with what is anticipated in the laws of the Indian Digest, in order to avoid on the orders of your Excellency that suspicious people enter or reside in these Provinces, with the depraved design of involving [the people] in the horrors of anarchy, making them take part in the plans of subversion that the tyrant of Europe would like to spread throughout America, where fortunately it is not possible for him to take his devastating armies. Certainly nothing could contribute so to the concept of your supreme Authority to which are consigned such wholesome ends, as the vigilance of all the superior authorities, to whom is confided principally the public administration of this Kingdom in its various branches, and their uniform and concerted cooperation in the agreement to and execution of the appropriate rulings. It is hoped that your Excellence will have the accredited zeal and enlightenment together with that of the Archbishop and the Royal Audience, maintaining that unity and good harmony that as is known has been conserved until now, with such well-known advantages. You will form an irresistible force against the evilly inspired projects of those who wish to introduce into this happy Kingdom mourning and desolation, the only fruit that has been picked by the unwary Americans who have let themselves be deluded by the impractical plans of emancipation of the Metropolis and of independence. This is transferred to Your Excellence for your understanding, not doubting in the pastoral zeal that Your Excellence has shown in the performance of your Ministry since your entry in this Kingdom. Penetrating the spirit of the Royal Order which precedes this, you will contribute with all your authority and influence so that the rulings designed for the indicated goals will be fulfilled and executed with the greatest exactness, requiring the reverend bishops, priests and Religious Communities of this Kingdom, that in the functions of their respective ministries and in the pulpit and confessional they exhort the faithful to show the proper obedience to the legitimate authorities, letting them know what the truth is, that the happiness and security of

Spanish America depends absolutely on their intimate union with the
Metropolis, and that in the plan for emancipation or separation from it,
designed by its true enemies, their perdition and ruin is maliciously
involved. Fortunately the illustrious clergy of the Kingdom of Guatemala is convinced of these truths. Your zealous conduct has assured
this on the few occasions that public tranquillity has been slightly men-
aced in several provinces, a circumstance which united to the good
administration that Your Excellence knows how to provide opportunely
in such a favorable way, gives hope for the happiest results and this is
promised by Your Excellence.[10]

With this robust support from the Metropolis, the Captain General and the
Archbishop are free to do what they know is right!

On June 8, 1812, three months after its publication, the Regency sends one
hundred copies of the Constitution to Guatemala. On September 12, Bustamante
orders that the Constitution be circulated and sworn to in the various municipalities. On September 24 and 25, following a formula prescribed by the National
Congress, Bustamante and his officials swear to the Constitution. With their
right hand on the Bible, and kneeling, each is asked, "Do you swear by God and
by the Holy Gospel to respect and obey the Political Constitution of the Spanish
Monarchy, sanctioned by the General and Extraordinary Cortes, and be faithful
to the King?" "Yes, I swear it." (Boletín del Archivo General del Gobierno 1938,
3:3:517–518).

A witness to the scene reported:

The presence of such a brilliant entourage, the stately airs of the march-
ers, the happiness that beamed on their faces, the gaiety of the large
crowd, the adornments of the horses, the general pealing of bells, the
din of the artillery, and the pleasant harmony of the military bands,
produced a grandiose effect, a sublime picture, that charmed spirits and
brought tender tears to all eyes. (Rodríguez 1978:101)

The presence of all the religious and military officials was complemented by
a group of Indian justices, bearing the insignias of their respective villages. They
played simple tunes in honor of the Constitution. Pictures of Ferdinand VII could
be seen everywhere. The reading of the Constitution "seemed more like a religious act than a civil ceremony" (Rodríguez 1978:102). Five hundred pesos of
memorial coins were thrown to the crowds. But this grand event was controlled
entirely by the Captain General, causing the city government to send a protest to
Spain. The city fathers were soon disillusioned by Bustamante's support in Cádiz.
On October 1, Bustamante circulated the May 24 decree of the Cortes regarding
the election of deputies and the establishment of Provincial Deputations. On
October 17 the Royal Audience congratulated the Cortes for the creation of the

Constitution. Both Bustamante and Casaus gave the impression at first that they supported the Cortes, both sending medals to Cádiz.

The African slaves of Omoa, Honduras, the "most miserable of all the inhabitants in the Kingdom of Guatemala," had contributed 1,280 pesos to the Spanish cause, so Bustamante gave them their freedom (Rodríguez 1978:70).

GUATEMALA IN 1813

The resources of Guatemala were drained by the contribution of nearly a million gold pesos for Spain. Despite the Constitution, Indians were forced to pay equal taxes and, in certain areas, contributions for parish priests. Some Indian villages pleaded for restitution of the tribute since it had been a less onerous tax! Tribute reform generated Indian resentment and led to instability throughout Central America. The royal officials also preferred the tribute as it was easier to collect. The Constitution gave Indians the right to sell their land. This became a means to transfer Indian and public lands to agrarian entrepreneurs for plantation development.

The Cortes called for the election of deputies every two years: one each for Costa Rica, El Salvador, Nicaragua, Honduras, and Chiapa, with seven from the other parts of Guatemala. This stirred opposition to the Guatemalan dominance by those to the south.

1813 was a year of great public unrest in Guatemala City, with the liberal city government and later the Provincial Deputation in endless confrontation with the Captain General, the Archbishop and the Religious Audience. On January 3 the local government, as its first act, sent a condemnation of Bustamante to the Regency for not holding elections for the Provincial Deputations and for despotism. He clearly did not wish to relinquish his power over finance, judiciary matters, royal patronage, and public affairs, as ordered by the Cortes. On March 16 Bustamante again ordered the formation of the *Voluntarios Distinguidos de Fernando VII*, the civil patrols he had called for two years earlier.

When the Captain General learned from Ciudad Real (now San Cristóbal de las Casas) that Morelos had captured Oaxaca, he decided to move mulatto troops from Omoa, Honduras, through the city, to the north. The city government protested:

> Your Excellency has not dealt with this municipality with the union and harmony that one would expect from its chief. Ever since you assumed office, you have not related to the citizenry of this city, principally those most esteemed by the indigenous population of the country; you work for only yourself without consulting the most respected subjects. (Wortman 1982:205)

Bustamante ignored the city government's protests, housing the troops within the city limits before sending them on to Chiapa with orders for them not to cross the border into Mexico.

Another dispute arose over the inauguration of a church. The members of the city government had ordered chairs and cushions for their seating at the ceremony. Bustamante replaced them with benches, inciting the rage of the authorities who now, together with their fellow citizens, referred privately to the Captain General as *"El Sonto,"* "One Ear."

The *Gazeta* now only told Bustamante's lies about insurrections and Napoleonic defeats. Freedom of the press was a farce. Just two presses were in existence, and they were under his control. The local government could not convince a press to publish one of their proclamations because both publishers feared Bustamante's authority. The municipal leaders insisted on the immediate publication and announcement of decrees from Spain in order to keep the public informed on the latest innovations. The government pressured Bustamante to keep them informed on news from Mexico.

The city leaders were supported by the dean of the university, Antonio Juarros, who was "a veritable Don Quixote in his defense of the Constitution and of the American cause" (Rodríguez 1978:120). They engaged in experiments in the urban educational system, offering mathematics and science at the primary level, with open competition for teaching posts. They proposed an examination for comprehension of the Constitution. They also proposed public city council meetings, but were refused by Bustamante. They were staunch supporters of economic development and laissez-faire. Jails were in a terrible condition as were their inmates. The city government deplored Bustamante's constant obstructionism: (1) no money for deputies to the Cortes, (2) censorship, (3) withholding decrees, (4) preventing jail reform, and (5) the Granadian prisoners. The leaders of the rebellion in Nicaragua had been forced to walk in chains to Guatemala in the rainy season, departing in July and arriving in August. The city government requested moderation. Bustamante did not respond, ignoring the popularity of the city officials who had developed an unequivocal affirmation of civic conscience among the citizens. But their efforts to reach a humane settlement were in vain.

The Provincial Deputation was installed in Guatemala City on September 3. Of the seven elected members, four were religious. It was an outstanding body whose young members later became liberal leaders. Not surprisingly, Bustamante, who saw that he would simply be an eighth member in a nest of liberals, was enraged when the city government held a big celebration with a *Te Deum*, illuminations, and so forth, in honor of the Deputation's installation.

Bustamante, sharing the Archbishop's hatred for liberals, referred to "suspicious" priests and friars as "silkworms" (Zamora 1935:33). There is a report of five priests being indecently dressed, and one who pulled a bottle out from under his stole, saying, "This is my Breviary." Bustamante was convinced that all the Creoles took off their hats to the name of Ferdinand VII, while they winked with hypocrisy. Bustamante's suspicions were soon justified. On the night of December 21, Cleric Ruíz, met with a group of fellow conspirators in the church of Belén, planning to free the prisoners of Granada, proclaim independence, and send Bustamante back to Spain. But with the aid of "One Ear's" nephew, a Carmelite friar, who had been installed in the post office to read all the mail of suspects, the plotters were discovered. Many were sentenced to death, but the sentence was never carried out.

The city government composed a list of all Bustamante's despotic actions and sent it to the Cortes, where it was read a few days before the Courts' annulment.

The *Audiencia*, composed of Spaniards, routinely slighted and insulted the city government. Archbishop Casaus was enraged by the city's attempt to discover whether indeed, despite his denials, he had confined two priests as political prisoners in a monastery. The city government sent a complaint to Spain, reporting the Archbishop's lies.

THE PROCLAMATION ARRIVES

Circulars, including proclamations, were routinely sent to 42 archbishops and bishops of the New World, including the Archbishop of Manila and three bishops of the Philippines, and to 14 viceroys, captains-general, governors and commanders of America, including the captain general and governor of Guatemala.

Four copies of the proclamation of the Duque del Infantado, sent to Guatemala on August 30, 1812, arrived on February 19, 1813.

> With your letter of August 30 this government has received the proclamation accompanying it with the same date, that the most serene Regency directs to the inhabitants of these provinces and others overseas. And wishing as a body to make it public in the whole capital, has passed for this purpose an example to each of the parishes so that its contents excite more, if it be possible, the loyalty of the people it represents.[11]

Nearly a year later the Archbishop sends to the Office of the Colonies, *Ministro de la Gobernación de Ultramar,* in Spain, translations of the proclamation into the two Mayan languages Q'eqchi' and Ixil, and the unrelated, now extinct language Xinka (this is the longest surviving text in that language).

> The most reverend Archbishop of that capital submits the Proclamation of the Regency of the 30th of August, 1812, that he had translated in the

three languages that those Indians use so that they may know about it, limited to showing them the state in which Spain was then, the alliance with England, the defeat of the French in Salamanca, the recognition of Yourself by the Emperor of Russia, and that they remain faithful to the King and to the Country.[12]

Knowing the Archbishop's sentiments, it is not surprising to see that he fails to mention the primary subject of this proclamation, the Constitution of 1812. Casaus continues:

Fulfilling the Royal Order of August 30, 1812, I had the Proclamation of the Regency translated in three languages, of which I enclose the corresponding example as it was prepared. It has not been possible to translate it into the other Indian languages that are spoken in this diocese, for lack of people knowledgeable in them, nor have these been published, for lack of characters, and knowledge about verifying them in the two printing presses of the capital. But I have managed to circulate the Proclamation and inform the Indians of all the towns about it. The zealous priests explain in my name the love, goodness and zeal with which His Majesty and the Regency attend to their true happiness. I am still waiting for the submission of translations in two more languages of the country, which I have commissioned.[13]

NOTES

1. Decree: González, January 25, 1805:1.
2. Decree: González January 25, 1805:1.
3. Decree: González, June 30, 1808:1
4. Manifiesto que el Asesor General del Reino, dirigió a los Justicias Indígenas del Reino de Guatemala, September 3, 1809:1.
5. Decree: Bustamante April 10, 1812.
6. Decree: Bustamante November 25, 1811.
7. Decree: Bustamante November 25, 1811.
8. Decree: Bustamante November 25, 1811.
9. Circular: Casaus y Torres April 20, 1812:2.
10. Regency Decree: June 2, 1812
11. Letter: Sala Capitular de Guatemala to Ministro de la Gobernación de Ultramar February 19, 1813.
12. Letter: Casaus y Torres to Ministro de la Gobernación de Ultramar, ?, 1813.
13. Letter: Casaus y Torres to Ministro de la Gobernación de Ultramar, ?, 1813.

6

Chiapa

THE EIGHTEENTH CENTURY

The eighteenth century was a tale of woe for most of the inhabitants of the Province of Chiapa, but most especially for the Indians. A document from the first decade reports that the official daily wage for labor was one and a half *reales*, but that the actual salary was only one half *real*. There is a plea for the lowering of tribute because so many have died. The town officials, *alcaldes* and *regidores*, must sell their horses and their possessions and go to the haciendas to pay back the town's debts, but generally they only meet their death there. The town of Zapaluta in 1808 had 273 tributaries, but a few years later the number had been reduced to 127, yet they were required to pay the tributes of the dead!

The news from the last quarter of the century was hardly better. Church and State were primary controlling factors in the economy. The Spaniards had small wheat, cotton, sugarcane and cattle ranches in the lowlands, but after 1700 they became heavily indebted to the religious orders, which acquired capital from the Indian *cofradías* or brotherhoods, from donations, and their own investments. They granted mortgages at 5 percent interest. The Jesuits and the Mercedarians of the capital, Ciudad Real, by the end of the century had lent out nearly 30,000 pesos. At this same time the Dominicans were beginning to expand their land-holdings tremendously.

The Indians were still abandoning their villages in large numbers to escape the tribute. There were a multitude of interlocking arrangements between the hacienda owner and his Indian debt peons and sharecroppers whereby he would pay their tribute.

The intendant (royal provincial governor) of Chiapa controlled the *repartimiento* system, whereby the caciques and Indian town officials compelled the people to weave and dye cotton textiles. In exchange for a paltry sum, the cloth was prepared and transported to New Spain. High quality material was exported to Europe. The *alcaldes* of Ciudad Real also profited from trade. English textiles were smuggled into Villa Hermosa, the port of Tabasco, and those textiles together with Spanish wines were purchased with the sale there of hides, cotton, and dyes that had been brought from the Highlands to the port by indentured Indian muleteers. In 1784 an *alcalde* bought cacao at 10 pesos a load and sold it in Guatemala for 75 pesos.

In 1778 the Church in Chiapa was comprised of five chapter members in the cathedral government—archdeacon, dean, canon, choirmaster, and schoolmaster—who had administrative, consultive, and judicial responsibilities. There were also 66 secular or diocesan priests, 66 Dominicans, 15 Franciscans, 8 Mercedarians, 3 Juaninos, and 28 Franciscan nuns. The number of friars had doubled though they served only one-third of the curates.

The diocese was divided into vicarages, each with its own subdivisions. The highland vicarages were those of Chamula and San Bartholomé (both Tzotzil), and Oxchuc (Tzeltal). Each priest was served by a steward; a doctrinal teacher (who at least knew how to sign his name); sacristans; cantors; solicitors (or *fiscales*), who maintained order and meted out punishments; two porters, who carried out domestic duties; and two stablemen, who cared for the priest's two horses. The porters and stablemen worked alternate weeks. Priests received from the community 15 pesos monthly, payment for certain sermons and Masses, and their daily ration of food or funds for such. The priest of Chamula was traditionally assigned on All Souls' Day "the first fruits" or 60 sheep. His daily ration of food consisted of a half *almud* of corn, a small box of lard and another of salt, a box of beans, a box of tomatoes, some chilies, one hen, one pullet, 20 eggs, 25 potatoes, 10 onions and 5 cloves of garlic. In addition to these costs were the annual tribute of 24 *reales,* the tithe of 3 *reales,* and the sheep tax of 8 *reales.*

The Dominicans had organized community chests to provide money for tribute and other costs, but by 1771 most of these chests had been removed to the residence of the *alcalde mayor* in Ciudad Real. Religious fiestas were now paid for by the individual Indian stewards or *mayordomos* because the cofraternities had had to borrow money from the priests at 5 percent interest.

The political government consisted of the Governor of Chiapa and his lieutenant or *alcalde mayor* in Ciudad Real, who bought his five-year salaried position. The lieutenant was administrator, judge, and military chief. He was also in charge of the officially contraband tobacco monopoly. He appointed annually a governor for each town whose primary duty was to administer his *repartimientos* or work levies as well as any other of his commercial deals. The Indians elected annually the other members of their town government: two *alcaldes*, four *regidores*, one *alguacil*, one *fiscal* and one scribe. Under them there served one *mayordomo* and several *mandadores* to collect tributes and taxes, joined by *patancopes* (*patan* was the word for tribute in Tzotzil, while *k'op* is affair or matter) and one horticulturalist. In addition to the appointed and elected officials were the elders, both male and female, who clearly exercised some degree of authority.

The inability of the Church to "civilize" the Indians was decried by Governor Juan Hurtado in a decree of January 2, 1788, where he prohibits wakes and festivities in private houses.

> They are the most serious injuries caused in the meetings which the Indians are accustomed to hold in private houses, motivated by their festivities. Which in some towns are called *Flowers,* and the *Wakes* for dead babies and similar other events where they commit horrible excesses, drunkenness. Therefore I prohibit all such wakes and I order the governors to never permit them, and that they punish severely all who violate this law. And I order that no meeting such as those mentioned above be held without the necessary presence of the governors, or at least with permission. And in those that are held in the houses of those called *confreres* the governor or an *alcalde* must be present to supervise and avoid the above mentioned disorders, which, should they occur, punish with suitable moderation.[1]

The governor spoke of festivities called *guancos*, where towns accompany the saints for 30 to 40 leagues. Masked dances, called *historias*, were prohibited unless performed in the sponsors' own towns.

Bishop Francisco Polanco, viewing "a pile of old and indecent Saints" in San Andrés, wished to bury them, but the Indians protested that the old saints favored them most in their necessities. And in San Pedro their patron saint on the altar was also "ugly and indecent," but they refused to have him replaced, claiming he was "young and white" (Porrúa 1992:114). Bishop Polanco despaired over their insistence that the priests of long ago had taught them that the Sun was the third person of the Trinity, and over their use of caves as sanctuaries, but he dared not destroy their shrines.

Letters to the King from the bishop and the succeeding governor give an intimate view of the deplorable condition of the Church, the State, and the Indians. On May 20, 1778, Bishop Polanco wrote,

> The vexations, nudity and idiocy of the Indians is caused principally by the excessive work levies on cacao, cotton, corn, cochineal, dyes, indigo, horses, mules…meat, wax, iron, steel, cloth for skirts, hats, jackets, and straw mats. Two solutions are required…The first is to entirely remove the work levies…The second solution is to form Patrician or Native Societies in these Provinces. Tariffs…on work levies have neither been seen nor heard of in this City. They could have reached the hands of the *Alcaldes* who, acting as Scribes, and keeping the Archives in their homes, store them there in perpetual silence.[2]

On November 28 of the same year, the bishop reported that half the population was unfaithful and idolatrous, and that the Indians were fleeing from the *alcaldes*. He paints a picture of total misery, complaining about the great distances between towns and the nearly impassable rivers. The Tridentine Seminary (formed in 1650) has few students, and the Dominicans, unlike the Jesuits, who had been banished, refused to teach Latin. There were very few priests, because most bright people became merchants or contrabandists. It was thought that the priests profited, but "They have no bread, they have to eat corn ground between two stones, the way chocolate is ground...The Indians are exempt from paying tithes, first fruits, and church fees."[3] The cofraternities were penniless. The *alcaldes mayores* had moved the communal chests to their houses. The money that had been stored in these chests, formerly to pay tributes, provide loans for the members of the community, host visiting officials, and feed the priests, was removed by the *alcaldes* when the Indians could not provide the labor draft of spun cotton or cloth. Some churches were in ruins.

After cataloguing the desperate state of the Church, the bishop turns to the Indians. The Indians are poorly fed and clothed. "I have not yet seen an Indian man or woman with shoes, but I have seen many naked."[4] The population of the town of Chiapa had dropped from 20,000 to 253. He argues that the population drop, despite early marriage and great fecundity, must be due to inhuman treatment. The Indians are worked like beasts of burden. The authorities are paid what they want for Indian produce. The Indians' principal food is ground corn and chile. Many Indians have fled the despotic officials and joined the "barbarous" Lacandon Indians in the jungle. He remarks that the Indians would be happy to have *alcaldes* of their own race and that they are loyal to the King. The bishop ends with a plea for support for the Indians.

On May 2, 1792, Governor Agustín de las Quentas Zayas tells the monarch how he had to use his own salary to pay for bridges and other public works. He complains that not even the main streets of Ciudad Real are paved, and that despite the presence of springs of sweet water, the fountains in the center are horrible because there is no money for underground pipes. Women beggars abound who should be taught to weave and sew. The men are drunk. Tributes are paid with much delay. There are no schools in half the towns and there is no money in the towns to pay the teachers. There is no money to build churches. There is only decadence and poverty.

> The Indian is an animal of habits who could properly take his position between monkey and man, for one observes in him actions common to both species; he does nothing unless he is ordered to do so by the *alcalde* or the priest; since he is content with little and has no ambition, he is not motivated to work...The means is to apply an agent to him who will move his machinery.[5]

The governor complains that the *alcalde*, his general deputy and three or four inspectors make Indians, ladinos [creoles] and mestizos work for them. Since abolition of the work levies "Indians are no longer planting much cotton, therefore tributes are not paid, nor cacao, nor anything, but corn."[6] There is so little money that the churches are in ruins, the priests suffering, the fiestas cancelled, and there are no more voluntary payments. The governor calls for better roads to Palenque and Playa de Catazajá, and the cultivation of cochineal.

In 1794 Bishop Polanco established a weaving school in Teopisca, confident that it would aid the Indian women. He brought a master weaver from Ciudad Real and female teachers to teach the girls Spanish. Forty girls attended and eighty widows from Amatenango and Aguacatenango. The school was closed after eight months because the bishop distributed the cloth but failed to pay the weavers. Some of the weavers pretended to be sick, others were taken by their families to the lowlands, "for a piece of cloth they did not have to have their daughters become slaves to weave for the bishop."[7]

In 1799, seven years after Governor De las Quentas Zayas had complained that half the communities lacked schools, there were 37 towns with teachers and 43 without.

The town of Chamula, with a population of 6,000 Tzotzil Indians, reveals in sharp focus the prevailing misery of the Province of Chiapa. Here, in 1763, the Dominican friar was replaced by a diocesan priest, Joseph Ordóñez y Aguiar. Don Joseph was a member of a prominent Ladino family in Ciudad Real, highly educated, well-versed in canonical law. But for 13 years he carried on the harshest governance in Chamula which, according to the allegations, resulted in the deaths of three of his parishioners. Two were reported to have died from their public whipping. One was given a hundred lashes on three consecutive Sundays before the church door and then was jailed in stocks. One of his assistants was given a hundred lashes for stepping on the tail of the priest's dog and creating an uproar during Mass. Another of his parishioners was sent to work on the ranch of don Joseph's elder brother, Fr. Ramón (who figures importantly later). "He was not paid. He was not given a tortilla nor even a little *posol* [corn gruel] and to no purpose he died of starvation" (Porrúa 1992:314). Further accusations made later apparently date back to this period. They include whippings when tied to the pillory, the use of stocks and shackles, and "the frequent whipping of women on their *narcas* or bottoms" (Porrúa 1992:136).[8] "The women are toiling (for the priest), making tunics without being paid a half *real*" (Porrúa 1992:320). It was claimed that don Joseph for his payment of "first fruits" demanded 400 sheep instead of the traditional 60! Not only was he accused of cruelty and greed, but of denying Indians burial in the church.

As a result of many accusations the religious chapter initiated cases against this priest in 1766, 1770, and 1775. In the final case he was found guilty and removed briefly from his post as "perpetual rector and vicar by His Majesty of the

Town of Chamula" (Porrúa 1992:254). Bishop Polanco found the chapter's action extreme and rescinded it, but urged don Joseph to be moderate in his punishments. After his reinstatement, don Joseph mended his ways considerably, but this was not enough to satisfy the caciques of Chamula, who continued their campaign to have him ousted. The 567 pages of documents written during the three-year period of 1779 to 1782 demonstrate the persistence of the caciques to prove the priest's guilt and the priest's determination to establish his innocence. On one side are the caciques, the lieutenant of Ciudad Real, and the religious chapter of the cathedral. On the other, the priest, supported with judicious restraint by the Bishop of Chiapa. The people of Chamula are caught in the middle.

Don Joseph's personality was surely a contributing factor in this religious-political contest. He was haughty, irritable and probably hot tempered, vengeful, "not greedy, but a fanatic, obsessive evangelist, made desperate by the Indian resistance...and the obstinate survival of ancient beliefs" (Porrúa 1992:37). Assailed by the Indians' "impertinent writings" and "unjust complaints," don Joseph initiated a series of interrogations under the direction of outside individuals to show beyond a doubt that the accusations were false (Porrúa 1992:254, 282). The responses of many Chamulans actually support his innocence. He protests that he is in fact a defender of his parishioners, and for that very reason the victim of a combined Ladino and Indian conspiracy. Indeed, he offers refuge, food and medicine to the poor of his diocese. This and so much more he does despite the fact that "the Indians of Chamula are perverse, irreprehensible, and disobedient" (Porrúa 1992:118).

His trials are many. Commenting on the service provided by his porters:

> For we priests it is a serious business to have to treat familiarly with these rustic boys, and their wild customs, endure their petty thefts, and other impertinences, that would become tolerable by the end of the week if these were not substituted by others who take their place who are so barbarous because they have just been pulled out of the woods,...the service and familiar company of the porters is one of the insufferable jobs that we Priests of the Indians have...Those whom I civilized, indoctrinated and taught to read and write for the utility of the Town have used and continue to use this skill to copy Petitions against me. (Porrúa 1992:834, 836)

As for the accusations of excessive punishment, don Joseph had only had two Indians whipped that year, one for disobedience and one for drunkenness—12 lashes apiece. This was confirmed by everyone's answer to the legal inquiries. The right of a priest to mete out punishment, short of capital punishment, was established by the Third Mexican Council of 1585, followed also in the Captaincy General of Guatemala, though proper punishments are not specified. Bishop

Polanco advised don Joseph to consult the formulas presented in the Synods of the Archbishopric of Lima and the Bishopric of Quito. Representative of these punishments is that assigned for eating meat on Friday—for the first time, 24 lashes in public, and for the second, 50. The Bishop suggested that, for a general policy, don Joseph administer no fewer than six lashes and no more than 50.

The lieutenant is his enemy because don Joseph criticized him for his notorious corruption. Investigating the reason for so little attendance at church, he learned that great numbers of his male parishioners were sick or exhausted, having returned from one of their three to five compulsory annual trips carrying the lieutenant's tobacco and *petates* (straw mats) on journeys to and from Huitiupán, Simojovel, and San Bartholomé. Men were forced to carry the loads of two men, for which they were paid a mere half *real*. "I cannot persuade myself that it is the wish of Our Lord the King (whom God protect) that the Indians be treated with such inhumanity, that in prejudice to their health, and known risk to their lives, they be obligated to do themselves what could very easily be done by a muletrain" (Porrúa 1992:862). Don Joseph claims that the Indians want to flee Chamula because of the lieutenant's "terrible extortions" (Porrúa 1992:366). He is convinced that the Indians' petitions are being written by a Ladino trying (unsuccessfully) to imitate the language of the Indians. Though he names no names, it is apparent that he is pointing the finger at the lieutenant. And to rub salt in the priest's wounds, the lieutenant is promoting "pagan" rites by his extravagant sale of candles (Porrúa 1992:50)!

The chapter members, headed by *don* Joseph's "capital enemy," the choirmaster and later archdeacon José de la Barrera (who later is intimately involved with the Proclamation), initiated cases against don Joseph, he thinks because he refused to demand more money from the Chamulans for the Church (Porrúa 1992:700). The chapter requested that the Bishop install an interim vicar because of "the present urgency to reestablish the peace and tranquillity of these Indians, no less necessary for their spiritual advantage, than for their improved temporal and civil prosperity" (Porrúa 1992:264).

But far more troublesome, and even fearsome, was the faction of Chamulan caciques, around 27 members, or 5 percent of the population, present and former political officials who, in that capacity, with the aid of the lieutenant, had become the only wealthy members of the community. Under the lieutenant's guidance they organized four trips to Nueva Goathemala carrying petitions to the *Audiencia Real de Guatemala*. After waiting in vain for four years for a decision by that august body, the only body with the authority to act on their demands, they initiated a reign of terror against members of Chamula and the priest himself.

They renewed all their accusations of the priest's greed and cruelty. Why, he only paid a *"micería de mierta,"* a trifle, to the *alcaldes* (Porrúa 1992:128). At first there were only threats: the threat to take all Chamulans, young and old, to Nueva Goathemala, the threat to move the whole population of Chamula to Barrio Mexicanos and Barrio Tlaxcala in Ciudad Real if the priest does not leave, the threat of whipping, exile, hanging or beheading for anyone who supported the priest or refused to contribute his share to the expenses of the trips to Nueva Goathemala.

These threats were followed by action. First, the civil officials denied the priest his daily ration of food, except on Sundays, a kindness he refused, pointing out that his Dominican predecessor had received a far grander ration. He also pointed out that the very fathers of the present officials had tormented his predecessor with unjust accusations. The civil officials then denied the priest his tithe, a procedure that don Joseph cites with great erudition as having been in Guatemala a typical retaliation by civil officials when priests denounced them for their exploitation of the people. Don Joseph reminds the bishop that the right to a tithe, dating back to 1529, was reaffirmed for the "*Obispado de Chiappa*" in 1678 and again in 1692 (Porrúa 1992:380).

Chamulans were forbidden by the civil officials to attend Mass or learn the doctrine. The church was boycotted so they would not have to answer religious questions. Then, in nearby Theopisca the vicar discovered two families of Chamulans living in the woods. When they confessed that they were refugees, the vicar advised them that they would have to leave as he had no authority to tend to their spiritual needs. A Chamulan who had fled for three years returned, but had to take refuge in the priest's house, where he remained with the priest under house arrest. Two Chamulans who favored the priest were attacked on the road and beaten. When they registered a complaint to the lieutenant in Ciudad Real he had the assailants whipped and fined, but when the civil officials of Chamula spoke to him he turned the victims over to the officials, who whipped them and placed them in the stocks. An ex-steward was reportedly killed by the officials.

Actions were taken directly against don Joseph. The Governor of Chenalho admitted receiving pay from the Governor of Chamula to kill the priest by witchcraft. The priest's helper was not allowed to buy food for him, and his mail was censored. Finally, under further threats of murder, don Joseph fled to Ciudad Real. The faction appointed new *fiscales* to the church. In the words of *don* Joseph there occurred "the extinction of the Law of God in the parish" (Porrúa 1992:1088). Chamulans, with fear in their hearts, sought his religious services in the city.

Looking to the future, don Joseph urged the Bishop to take a number of corrective steps. He advised that *alcaldes* and *gobernadores* be elected with the approval of the priest. *Alcaldes* should not carry out cases, collect tributes, and so on, during the hour of Mass. The *alcaldes* should not carry out their duties at night, for frequently they are drunk and punish people brutally. There is an urgent need for a new count of tributaries, for the *alcaldes,* shielded by the lack of a correct count, are pocketing vast sums.

But don Joseph's outrage over civil improprieties was nothing compared to his concern for the spiritual well being of his parishioners. He speaks of the "labor in separating the Indians from their Idolatries, and instructing them in the Christian Doctrine" (Porrúa 1992:348). "The Indian is no less devoted in the Church, pouring out his tears at the feet of a holy Christ, than when he joyfully offers Incense in a cave to the demons" (Porrúa 1992:350). He allows that the Indians can have their milpas in the countryside, but they must not live there (as they still do), or they will practice idolatry, not learn the doctrine, and not be buried in holy ground.

There were three major religious issues where the political faction and don Joseph were always at odds. The first was the accusation by the faction that the priest refused to bury the Indians in the church. Don Joseph protested that the only bodies that he had not buried in the church were those of people who, though they had been sick long prior to their death, had never made confession, or of those who had for years abstained from the Easter season examination of their beliefs. Another body he had insisted be buried in the cemetery and not the church had been accompanied by a basket containing a rabbit's head and legs. On this issue he was supported by Bishop Polanco, who stated that "the insolence, lack of respect, and small degree of fear" justified the priest's action (Porrúa 1992:110).

The second issue was that of a *rancho* or *Calvario* that had been erected on a mountaintop next to a cave. Bishop Polanco agreed again with don Joseph that this shrine should be destroyed and rebuilt with its crosses at a location chosen by the priest.

The third issue was the most important. The faction wished that don Joseph be replaced by a "bland" priest who would simply hear general confessions (Porrúa 1992:63). Don Joseph, however, was convinced that "evil weeds always flourish...the earth tends to breed thorns or furze, which must be carefully cut so that they do not overshadow and infest the good fruits" (Porrúa 1992:122). Accordingly, he believed it to be the first order of business to ensure that his parishioners were true Christians and did not believe in some sort of syncretic mix of paganism and Christianity. Every Easter it was his obligation to test their beliefs. For this purpose he was equipped with a Tzotzil catechism abbreviated for Indians, printed in Mexico in 1560. Bishop Polanco every Lent assigned presbyteries, fluent in Tzotzil, to Chamula to interrogate the people about the doctrine and to hear their confessions so they "would be saved" (Porrúa 1992:118). In 1780, with the exile of don Joseph and the boycott of all church activities, his assistants instructed the civil officials repeatedly to ring the church bells to bring the inhabitants out of the countryside. Only 188 adults appeared to be asked about the Christian doctrine, i.e., the creed, Our Father, and the commandments of God and the Church. Forty-one men and 78 women responded, with a number of errors. Seventy-seven others "told such clear and repeated heresies that you would want to shut your ears" (Porrúa 1992:756). In this situation don Joseph protests with a deep sense of inadequacy and perhaps fear that with smallpox assailing his flock and numerous demands for Last Rites there is no way he can save the souls of those who have never been converted and who lie prostrate before him.

A final issue can serve as a postscript. Don Joseph prohibited the traditional blowing of trumpets before the church doors on the *novena* before St. John's Day, the fiesta of the patron saint of Chamula. Bishop Polanco complained that three hundred Chamulans had come to Ciudad Real to protest. Why did they not, in a reasonable and orderly way, send their *justicias* to present their complaint?

No documents have been found to reveal whether the *Audiencia* ever decided don Joseph's guilt or innocence or what his fate was. Surely this difficult case was uppermost in the mind of the new bishop when he arrived to replace Bishop Polanco.

BEFORE THE CORTES OF CÁDIZ

The last earthquake left the cathedral in ruins for the twenty-second Bishop of Ciudad Real de Chiapa, who arrived on September 23, 1802. Ambrosio Llano, born in the town of Rueda, Valladolid, Spain, had been a distinguished student at the University of Valladolid. For three years he studied philosophy, another three years scholastic theology, and then two years of law, to receive bachelor degrees in Arts, Law, and Canonical Law. After further study at the *Gimnasio,* he became its Secretary. As a newly ordained priest he accompanied the Bishop-elect of Guatemala to America, where he served as Treasurer of the Cathedral. Among his first achievements was the construction of the Tridentine College. In a letter to the King of Spain recommending the treasurer's elevation to Archdeacon, the Archbishop states:

> Despite the laboriousness in confronting the general upheaval that is seen in that Capital [Antigua], he has acted and acts with the greatest skill, purity, and integrity...one must admire the manner and the ease with which he unites precision and mildness in the administration of justice, and he conserves and foments harmony between the two Governments [Church and State] with the satisfaction of the President and Ministers of that Reign.[9]

Subsequently, as Vicar General, it became Llano's responsibility to move the Church from earthquake-ridden Antigua to the new capital of Nueva

Goathemala, founded in 1782. For 22 years he served as Vicar General, bring-ing order out of chaos. No sooner had don Ambrosio entered the province of Chiapa than he set about to restore the cathedral with the aid of architects brought from Nueva Goathemala. This was an enterprise, together with his support of the Hospital de San Juan, that engaged his efforts and his treasury during the rest of his lifetime. In 1803 he was instrumental in launching a smallpox vaccination campaign.

Apparently there was still concern that the priests be able to carry out their services in the native languages, for in 1804 José Miguel Correa wrote his "*Breve esplicacion de la lengua tzotzil para los pueblos de la provincia de Chiapas,*" a 102-page manuscript with nine pages devoted to grammar, 17 to lexicon, and the remainder to translations of the manuals for administering the sacraments. In that same year, Mariano Guzmán y Solorzano, who was later to become don Ambrosio's right hand man, was appointed *examinador de los Idiomas Zendal, y Sozil*, entrusted with the task of testing the priests' fluency in the two Mayan languages Tzeltal and Tzotzil.

Don Ambrosio was met not only by a cathedral in ruins but also by a treasury emptied by the cathedral personnel. The diocese was virtually abandoned. The tally of clergymen of the *Intendencia de Ciudad Real* in 1806 records only 39 priests for 110 towns and 15,664 tributaries. But these low-level figures give no hint of the lofty ambitions of his clergy, one of whom, Fr. Juan Bautista Redón, on May 11, 1806, sent up his balloon and was "the first in Ciudad Real who has been seen to rise to the upper regions and [who] fell a league and a half from where he departed."[10]

On October 19, 1808, don Ambrosio distributed the request for a contribu-tion to the war effort in Spain. The bishop's care as an administrator, for which he was reknowned, is exemplified by his letter of December 20, in which he tells a priest that he must know the name of the collector of the national contribution in Teopisca. The next day (how rapidly mail arrived then), the priest explained that he was suffering a very painful toothache and so had not noticed the collector's name. In another report it appears that on the day of collection throughout Chiapa, November 23, only priests gave a contribution.

The government of Ciudad Real commented in 1805 that the Indians "have the planted fields which even with their seeds that are a first necessity are in so deplorable a state, that they are worthier of tears than of praise and as much as one exaggerates, never could one do a painting true to life of the miserable state of the natives of the country."[11] Idleness and drunkenness, as always, are reported. In 1809 Juan Bartolomé Tosso of Tuxtla complains of "the sad situa-tion, and evident danger that I have seen on the Royal Highway from Zinacantán to this town." He names "practical commissioners" to see that "the Indians [who] are sunken in idleness and drunkenness" be engaged in work, and he prohibits the sale of liquor to Indians.[12] To add to the Indians' misery are the locust plagues such as the one that afflicted Gueiteupan (Huitiupán) and Tila in 1808, and a six-year locust plague reported from Ocosingo in 1809, which prompted public petitions, a penitential procession, and a continuous issuance of proclamations.

The government of Ciudad Real requested one thousand pesos from Guatemala, to swear a proper oath of loyalty to the deposed king, on January 16, 1809, but it was informed that no such sum was available, nor were the coins on hand that should be distributed. In the hopes of receiving support from the Royal Audience, the city fathers proceeded to hold a grand celebration lasting five days, from January 16 to 20. Three tablets were erected. A portrait of the "Well-Beloved" was hung in the corridor of the Conventual Houses "with the pomp appropriate for the joy and sorrow of the circumstances of the day."[13] The preceding night there had been fireworks and illumination in the park. An effigy of the king was carried in a triumphal carriage, accompanied by the Royal Standard, with Spaniards, Ladinos and Indians arriving at the freshly whitewashed town hall. A sermon was given by one of the best orators of the city, and a Thanksgiving Mass was celebrated. The civil officials swore an oath of loyalty to Ferdinand in the presence of his bust, which was placed on a crimson velvet mantle and a pillow of the same color furnished with braided gold galloons. The oath was sworn holding Christ on the Cross in the right hand and with the left hand placed on the Bible. Of course there were musical orchestras, and "refreshments in the capitular foreroom for the decorated and distinguished inhabitants and their consorts."[14]

Once again, in 1809, a contribution was requested to aid in the defeat of Napoleon. The Captaincy General of Guatemala gave an astonishing 100,000 pesos, but of that, Chiapa contributed only 6,284 pesos. There are a number of sorrowful letters directed from the priests to their bishop. On February 10, 1809, the priest of Ixtapa offered 25 pesos because his faithful were "his poor ones." On May 17, the priest of Zinacantán, Juan Nepomuceno Chávez, gave six pesos, "and no one else in this town because of the great poverty of the natives, and the two Ladinos themselves, who say the same."[15] The importance of these donations to the cause was underscored by the priest of Tonalá, Luciano Figueroa, who wrote to the bishop:

> Ferdinand VII, that model of virtue, meekness and fear of God, the David for whom we cry, not only persecuted, but in the sad chains of the usurper tyrant. We must all exert ourselves, understanding that in such a just war we ecclesiastics can also be soldiers able to take up arms to restore the Religion injured by those highwaymen…That Mother Country where the holy Religion is maintained without evil and with all the purity and splendor that characterizes it. Spain, Sire, that center of Religion and Heavenly Garden is greatly injured.[16]

The Regency, in the name of Ferdinand VII, gave its thanks to Guatemala on September 5. Bishop Llano received 23 gold medals on October 31, and distributed them to the Indian communities on December 5.

The first revolt in Central America occurred in Ciudad Real on September 21, when the city government deposed and arrested the governor, José Mariano Valero y Ortega, for disloyalty and sympathy to French ideas. While Valero was accused of being an antimonarchist it was in fact his venality that had aroused the city fathers, the rent chiefs and the commander of arms. When Governor González in Guatemala City heard of this, even though he must have thought Valero was a traitor, he considered the act to be "scandalous," for who said that a city government would have such authority (Moreno 1927:12)! Bishop Llano pleaded for Valero's release from prison on October 14, but Valero was sent in chains to Spain. The government offered the post to Bishop Llano, who declined, saying that the first *alcalde* should assume the position. He must have reconsidered, for in a later letter (February 12, 1813) he commented that the insurrection began in Ciudad Real, so he took control of the Government and the Intendancy while the Governor of Guatemala was settling the matter, and "everything calmed down" (Anaya y Diez de Bonilla 1934?:3,33). Don Ambrosio is the only Bishop of Chiapa to have served, too, as its political leader.

The *Gazeta de Guatemala* informed its readers in its July 6, 1810, issue that the official of Ciudad Real (presumably Valero's secular successor) promised "to maintain at all costs his responsibilities, and especially that of preserving public tranquillity, blindly obeying his orders" (*Gazeta de Guatemala,* 6 July 1810: XIV(156), 89). In their August 14 issue, the editors add that Ciudad Real has decided to celebrate annually the installation of the *Suprema Junta Central* in Spain as if it were the king's birthday. But earlier, on June 5, they had received a copy of the royal decree establishing the *Consejo de Regencia* on the Isla de León on February 2 with its five members, one of whom was to represent the Americas.

Governor González' concern about Napoleonic spies, expressed in his circular of May 15, is not noted in Chiapa until July 16. The Governor advises the public to inspect all foreigners, especially those who may be spies "in the clothing and disguise of muleteers."[17]

Once again Spain sends a plea for financial support to defeat Napoleon. Sent May 9, it does not arrive until October 6, five months later..

But the dangers are closer than the Governor suspects and surely nearer to home than had been imagined by the Intendant of Chiapa who had sworn to blindly obey González' orders. For on October 16 the latter is presented with an anonymous manifesto from "The Patriotic Citizens." They propose independence, attack monarchy, and complain of the taxes and the preference for Europeans. They present a catalogue of wrongs:

> We will know how to imitate Quito, Santa Fé, Caracas, Cartagena
> …Guatemala will count among the nations. For the first time in this
> climate human rights, arts, agriculture, business will be recognized.
> [The Spaniards wish to have] the Cortes be a farce, obliging America in
> its name to make all the sacrifices that are willed by its caprice. [The
> solution will be in the deputies to the Cortes], *in this way we can
> organize a free Constitution* analogous to our customs, to our climate
> and character. (García Laguardia 1971:278–279)

Guatemala sends its news of Hidalgo's excommunication, published October 13, but not noted in Chiapa until December 2 in Comitán.

CHIAPA IN 1811

Don Ambrosio, learning on December 22, 1810, of the establishment of the Cortes, three days later had the Regency edict read from the pulpit and attached to the church doors. He outlined what celebrations should follow: On January 6, with the presence of Governor Junguito and all civil and religious officials, a Mass and *Te Deum* were to be sung in the cathedral. For the next three days Masses were sung accompanied by Litany processions that were also sung to celebrate the good news and to pray for divine aid against "the Tyrant Napoleon." On January 7, the Mass was dedicated to the Immaculate Conception, "patron saint of Spain and the Indies," on the eighth to Santiago, and on the ninth to the "Reknowned Martyr San Xtoval [Cristóbal] who is particular to Our Holy Church, city, and Diocese."[18] A circular was sent to the priests on January 17 directing them to read and explain, on the first religious holiday following receipt of the circular, the establishment of the Cortes—this to be preceded by a Thanksgiving Mass and *Te Deum*. Three days were to be assigned for public orations offered to God.

But there were problems at home, for the subdelegate of Simojovel informed the governor that the Indians of Amatán refused to pay the tribute because they knew of its abolition, having heard of it from travellers journeying between Ciudad Real and Tabasco. He asked that an edict be made calling for the punishment of those who "suggest to and stir up the Indians with such conversations."[19] The governor informed Bustamante. He requested that tributes be lowered in Chicoasén because of the virtual extinction of the population. Requests for exoneration from the tribute were made by the towns of Amatenango, Chiapilla, Zapaluta, and Acala.

The Cortes' decree of February 10, calling for special consideration for the Indians on the part of the officials, arrived in Ciudad Real on June 22.

Bustamante, on March 29, had asked for information about the loyalty of every priest. Receiving no response, he repeated his request on July 3. Finally, on July 30, the Bishop asked Matías de Córdoba (later an agent for the independence of Chiapa) to investigate the matter. Córdoba replied with a each priest itemized by age, provenience, ability, and patriotism. All were generous patriots, who give explanations of the Cortes' decrees in the Indian languages.

Bustamante sent out a circular encouraging the propagation of cattle, especially among Indians: "In the hands of good priests is the prosperity of the towns."[20]

Perhaps it was Bustamante's obsession with spies that caused the Governor of Chiapa, Manuel Junguito Baqueiro, to request permission from him to have a personal guard. In the months of October and November circulars warning of the danger of spies were the commonest item. So, on October 20 a local circular advised priests to inform travelers from their diocese that they must carry passports. Priests were warned of enemies who disguised themselves as priests. A circular sent by Bustamante on October 22 arrived in Ciudad Real on November 2. It informed the public that two suspicious people had arrived from Mexico, that all foreigners should have passports, that all should be required to show them whether they were white or dark-skinned. Priests should instruct Indian *alcaldes,* telling them of 500 pesos reward for the detention of anyone who brings to justice persons accused of "the execrable crimes of insinuation and disturbance of public order."[21]

Bustamante became almost lyrical in his description of the latest intruder that arrived in Ciudad Real on November 11:

> He is tall, sturdy, full-faced, red-faced, hair trimmed at the forehead, large and long-nosed, big blue eyes, sideburns to the beard. Aged thirty to thirty-five years, [he wears] a frock coat, or dress coat of light blue cloth and a high crowned cap, a shiny, black belt with silverwork. [He rides] a grayish skinny horse, with the four hoofs shod, low saddle and long stirrups, hind cloth with yellow fringe, silver stirrups.[22]

Priests along the Royal Highway from the Guatemalan border to New Spain and Tabasco were advised to alert the people, and there was promised a reward of 500 pesos for the denunciation and 1,000 pesos for the capture of "the Emissary of the abominable Napoleon."[23]

Regarding the national donations by Spaniards, Bustamante specified that, "Jewels, fruits, and whatever other articles of value may be given." The gifts that had been received were to be listed in column 1, while in column 2 would be listed promised gifts by month or year, "to be obligatory, but not demanded rigorously."[24]

Lest anyone forget the Napoleonic menace, a circular was issued locally, telling the priests to apprehend

> the impious and irreligious men and all those who, as Ministers of the Tyrant of the World…have come only to disturb and upset God's order among us, with seduction, disunion, discord and with the iniquitous pretensions that we should disobey and fail to recognize our legitimate King and the Cortes and the Regency which hold and exercise the sovereign and supreme power of the Government of Spain and the Indies. This kingdom has endured and suffered desolation, sadness, orphanhood, misery and the horrors of Death. They have experimented with grief and great offenses against God, Our Lord in the Provinces of Mexico and in others of the Indies, as in Spain by the same means of perversity, impiety and the tricks of that tyrant and of his cruel and cursed emissaries and satellites, and of the Devil, his legitimate Father.[25]

Indeed, a decree from the Regency, July 8, 1811, stipulated that all French citizens without naturalization papers should be deported and their possessions seized. Even those who had papers, including those who may have served in the royal army, should be deported with no recourse if there were "the least motive for suspicion."[26] An unfortunate French merchant, Manuel Texedor, a resident of Ciudad Real, his loyalty to the Spanish crown suspected, was taken to court again and again for the next five years on charges of unpaid debts, but at least was not sent into exile.

A final circular, sent by Bustamante in November, prohibited the sale of cane liquor to Indians, since "the detestable vice of drunkenness…has increased, especially in the towns and among the beautiful class of Indians."[27] Cane liquor must not be sold to Indians, nor could they make it, but they were permitted to make *chicha*.

Back to his favorite subject, Bustamante sent a decree informing the populace of the need to establish "Honorary Volunteers." In the Indian towns its members should be those who are industrious and can explain matters in Spanish. They should wear a crimson ribbon on their left shoulder and a hat band with V.H. *(Voluntario Honorario)* and the initial of their town. They must pay for their own arms and uniforms. "Day and night patrols should disperse meetings of suspicious and vice-ridden persons, confiscate their arms and offensive material. Seditious fliers, etc., should be turned over to authorities without reading or copying them."[28]

Presumably the above decree reached Ciudad Real on January 1, since mail took one week from Guatemala City, arriving on the first, eleventh, and twenty-first of every month. Mail sent from Ciudad Real to Mérida would reach that city in a week's time. The intellectuals of the capital, however, were most anxious to receive the incoming mail from Spain, to hear about the latest battles in the defense of the nation and the latest news from Cádiz—all, of course, three months old. As there was widespread circulation of the *Diario de Cortes,* and detailed coverage of the constitutional debates in the newspapers, the intellectuals were well aware of the Americans' attempts at achieving reform.

CHIAPA IN THE CORTES OF CÁDIZ 1810–1811

When the Cortes opened in 1810, Chiapa was represented by two American substitute deputies: Andrés de Llano y Nájera, a sea captain and merchant, and his brother Manuel, an artillery colonel. The first was a progressive deputy who supported freedom of the press and was against exclusion of the castes; the second concentrated his efforts on the liberalization of the army. They were replaced by Manuel de Llano, from Chiapas. There is no record of when the Chiapa deputy, after being accompanied by the Tabasco deputy and a cavalry escort out of Villa Hermosa, arrived in Cádiz. Once at the Cortes he argued that "the insurrectional movements were not a desire on the part of the Americans to separate themselves, but born of the anxiety to recover their rights as Spaniards" (Anderson 1966:189). It was he who signed the Constitution in the name of Chiapa.

On November 4, 1811, a vote was taken in Guatemala City to elect a successor to de Llano. Following the proper protocol, three names were enclosed in little balls and given to a "decent" child of nine years to select. The chosen one was Mariano Robles Domínguez de Mazariegos, descendant of the founder of Ciudad Real and secretary to Ambrosio Llano, Bishop of Chiapa. Robles, then, was one of the six deputies from Guatemala.

CHIAPA IN 1812

The still deplorable state of the Church is described in reports to don Ambrosio by his *Promotor Fiscal* (cathedral treasurer), Fernando Antonio Dávila, who was later to accompany Mariano Robles in the Cortes. Apparently acting on the bishop's order, Dávila assures Llano that guitars are no longer being played in the churches. Don Ambrosio responds with satisfaction, "the guitar will be banished from the Church forever."[29] But there are other unseemly customs. On January 14, Dávila speaks of the bishop's edict of March 11, 1809, that has not been enforced. It forbade the presence in Lenten processions of individuals (one or two) wearing horse masks, accompanied by shield bearers and arms bearers. This custom could still be seen in Ciudad Real, Comitán and Tuxtla, disturbing the solemnity of the occasion. Equally distracting were the hundred or so Indians from neighboring towns who would lead the procession "half drunk," their faces covered, carrying banners, and "privately playing a drum and a hoarse trumpet," provoking much laughter from the "louts and plebeians."[30] Just as bad were the boys, also with their faces covered, who, awarded with a half *real*, would carry a candle in the procession, but with constant noisy behavior. Dávila is going to forbid anyone covering their face from joining the procession.

But even more annoying is the custom of having young boys act the part of angels for the Lenten processions. First they are fortified with chocolate and various kinds of pastry made with eggs and with other material not "licit" during Lent (i.e. lard). Worse yet, their female custodians insist on sticking right next to them during the procession, getting in the way. Their one interest, in fact "their mania," is to see "which angel is the best dressed, which angel has the most gold, silver, and jewelry."[31]

Dávila is equally disturbed by the Indians who also play flutes before the church altars: "the most contemptible and dreadful sounding noise, disturbing the devotion of the congregation."[32] On January 22 he complains about the Indian *cofrades* marching at the head of processions swirling clouds of incense in every direction. He has just learned that they celebrate some wakes with "clarinets, trumpets, violins and other instruments."[33]

But don Ambrosio has more to think about than these minor disturbances of the peace, for in January Archbishop Casaus warned Bishop Llano to be very vigilant in catching the emissaries of the insurgents. He speaks of the rebels in León and San Salvador, and "the band of rogues in Buenos Aires."[34] With relief, he mentions the peaceful, orderly state of Peru:

> May God wish that we enjoy the tranquillity that has existed up until now in this kingdom, despite the pamphlets of half a dozen drugsters and ambitious ones who for some time have been trying to excite the emotions and turmoil for their twisted goals, and who have the sagacity to conceal themselves (although they are well known), disguising handwriting, but they will fall.[35]

A circular is sent to the priests in January, telling them to inform the Indians that the tribute has been ended. "The unequal, compulsory donation" should be replaced by voluntary exhibitions that demonstrate their love and loyalty to the King.[36]

The Archbishop penned another letter to the Bishop, informing him that he had offered 200 pesos for the arrest of one Francisco Cordon who had stolen guns and had tried to stir up the people of Acasahuastlán de los Indios. When he was apprehended, Cordon begged mercy, saying he had heard that Frenchmen had disembarked, some dressed as monks, and he had intercepted a letter in Catalán and thought it was French. Casaus concludes, "If he is not crazy, *Cordon* will pay with a rope *[cordón]* around his neck."[37]

In April the Church agreed to celebrate the anniversary of the national day of resistance, May 2, as called for in a decree of May 30 of the previous year:

> The General and Extraordinary Cortes, are penetrated vitally by the sad and glorious memories that will at the very least renew this day for every good patriot…as long as there is a single village of free Spaniards in these two worlds, the hymns of gratitude and compassion that are owed to the first martyrs of national liberty will resound in it.[38]

It was not long before the Indians were asked once again to demonstrate their love and loyalty to the king, for on May 19, Bustamante's decree of April 10 was distributed. The Governor calls for resistance to Napoleon's "fatuous brother Joseph, who greatly insults all Americans by titling himself King of the Indies."[39] He explains that a contribution "is not a purely voluntary act, it is an obligation of conscience and justice."[40] Because the exemption of tribute for Indians severely affected the treasury he had asked for a donation on January 3. Every priest accompanied by an *alcalde* or a secular neighbor is required to see that everyone "by spontaneous deeds" contributes.

> Indians are relieved of tribute, but not of the debt of vassals…It is a very great difference that they give voluntarily, what before was demanded rigorously, but it should not be less, rather more, if possible, for the great need, in thanksgiving for such a singular benefit and since the quota of two pesos is so moderate…In other parts Ladinos were tributaries like the Indians. They never have been in this district.[41]

Despite the abolition of tributes, the people of San Lucas in 1812 were still begging exoneration from them. On the same day as Bustamante's decree was received, Bishop Llano sent a circular to the priests asking them to carry out the subscription, collection, and annotation of each donor of a contribution. He, himself, offered 500 pesos as the first donor. A priest responded to the plea for a three-peso donation, saying, "They are all poor who hardly have enough to eat. I am sick, but I will give it."[42]

In the spring and summer several Indian towns established their brigades of Honorary Volunteers: San Bartolomé, Socoltenango, and Soyatitán with 110 soldiers each, and Teopisca with 92. The Archbishop, on June 2, exhorted his bishops to do all in their power to strengthen their parishioners' loyalty to the Metropolis. On July 18 Captain Tiburcio José Farrera asked the Bishop for a priest to accompany the troops, "who will console and inspire those who are subordinate to me and attract those who have been seduced by the perversity or who are targets of this seduction."[43] Two days later he informed the Bishop that "all the exemplary priests, residents of this City, are disposed to accompany the troops, for in every conversation among them they describe how they would be glad to go if Your Excellency would be kind enough to name them."[44] On July 29 the Bishop received a letter from Urbano Aguilar, the priest of Pueblo Nuevo Ixtacomitán, who had been trying there unsuccessfully to recruit troops. Although insurgents had overrun the town of Acayucan, Veracruz, the month before, and it was feared that they would head for Tabasco and penetrate Chiapa via the nearby towns of Plátanos and Ixtacomitán, the hacienda owners were more afraid of the Indians than of the insurgents. The day after the priest's letter, the mayor of Pueblo Nuevo wrote the Bishop, saying that they were trying desperately to raise funds for their defense and that one of the priests had contributed his own silver service "as he had nothing of greater value."[45]

The Archbishop sent his views to the Bishop: "It seems as if some of those insects have approached the border of Tabasco...The best cure is to exterminate the first bunch of bandits, before they begin to stir up one town after another."[46] The Archbishop advised Ambrosio Llano that if governmental boards are set up in Ciudad Real and Ixtacomitán he should see that they are disbanded because "[all members] will want to become domineering."[47] In September the cantor of Plátanos, Martin Robles, informed the Bishop that the insurgents who had appeared "like a malign cloud" had been defeated by the King's army in Acayucan and were begging pardon.[48]

Guatemalan deputy Larrazábal sent a copy of the Constitution to Ciudad Real on May 12. If one estimates that it took about three months for most correspondence to cross the Atlantic, it was probably August before it arrived. Here this new, liberal Constitution must have seemed sandwiched in between public strife and poverty.

Don Ambrosio, clearly concerned about the lack of ability to collect the last national contribution, remarked on September 17, "The poverty of this bishopric is notorious."[49] Two days before, the priest of Tila had offered four *reales* apiece from his parishoners, but he could not assure that amount for they still owed the tribute from previous years "because of the extreme poverty in which they are submerged." He protested that the "loyal vassalage" was anxious to aid "our bewailed and beloved monarch."[50]

On September 15, Antonio Bergosa y Jordan, Bishop of Antequera (Oaxaca), informed don Ambrosio that no mail had arrived from Mexico City, Puebla, and Vera Cruz for five months, "and now I am rightfully afraid of Morelos. He has the most diabolical intentions to authorize and dignify his evil deeds under my name, and that gives me more cause to tremble than death."[51]

Finally, five months after the May 24 publication of the Regency's decrees, under the presidency of Joaquín de Mosquera y Figueroa, regarding the election of deputies to the Cortes and to the Provincial Deputations, Bustamante, on October 1, sent them to Ciudad Real. On October 16 arrived an official copy of the Constitution, delayed for seven months. A circular was sent to the rural priests on the 19th, telling them to read and swear to the Constitution in their towns on the next fiesta. The Constitution was read and sworn to in the cathedral of Ciudad Real on the 22nd, and on the following day a Thanksgiving Mass and *Te Deum* were sung. Three days later the Constitution was read before the *"Noble Ayuntamiento"* and the Governor in the main Plaza before a large public. Everyone was asked, "Do you swear by God and the Holy Gospel to protect the political constitution of the Spanish Monarchy, sanctioned by the General and Extraordinary Cortes of the Nation, and to be faithful to the King?" To which all responded, "Yes, we swear it."[52] This was followed by the Bishop's blessing. A letter to don Ambrosio arrived from Yucatan, written on October 22, describing the celebration and swearing in of the Constitution in Mérida on the 14th. "The wisdom and holiness of the Constitution" was proclaimed by the Bishop, with a military salute, the ringing of bells, and a *Te Deum*.[53]

Contrasting darkly with the celebration of the Constitution is a letter of December 14 from the three chapter members of the Church, addressed to don Ambrosio:

> We have seen with our own eyes the anguished sheep of Your Excellency leave this city not as ferocious lions, inspired by the echoes of war trumpets, but rather like tame sheep being pulled to the slaughterhouse ...We have placed at the service of this government, for the urgent defense of the Crown and the Country in the invasion which threatens it, the wealth of the Church, its jewels, our income and our own persons.[54]

The Bishop, on December 21, praised them for being

> moved by charity, humanity and Patriotism, and using their right as citizens, so honored by the new constitution. In one voice, spontaneously and unanimously they resolved to make known the dismay, fears and bitterness which this most faithful and peaceful Town suffers, [by offering the government the wealth of the Church] of which I am the unworthy husband, excusing themselves for not having received my blessing, and permission beforehand.[55]

Nearly a year-and-a-half passed before the Church agreed, on November 18, 1812, to respond to a Regency decree calling for the establishment of a fund to provide for an annual pittance for the "meritorious," i.e., the families of prisoners of war and war dead to be paid until ten years after the end of hostilities.

As if the Governor had forgotten his dispatch of the Constitution to Ciudad Real in October, he sent six copies on December 27 with similar instructions for its publication.

CHIAPA IN 1813 "IN THESE MISERABLE TIMES"

It must have been in January when the Regency's decree of October 6, 1812, reached Ciudad Real, expressing "the need for exact knowledge of the different castes of Indians, their customs, languages, inclinations, industry and belief."[56] Consultation by the civil and religious authorities was required. To this decree is appended a questionnaire, parts of which display such anthropological sophistication that it seems a wonder.

Questionnaire

(1) They will tell how many castes the population is divided into: that is, Americans, Europeans, Indians, *Mestizos, Negros,* etc., etc., without omitting any.

(2) What is the origin of these castes, except for the first two? This is because the origin of the *Negros* is not the same everywhere, because although generally it is Africans who have come to America, in the Philippines there are natives of the same country who have taken refuge in the mountains since the Malayans dominated those islands.

(3) What languages do they generally speak, the number of them, and if they understand Spanish?

(4) If they love their wives and their children? What kind of education do they give to them, and if they apply them to agriculture or mechanical arts?

(5) If they show friendship to the Europeans and Americans, or do they hold complaints or hatred against them, and what [complaints] are they?

(6) Considering the causes that could contribute to this, what can be done to attract them and reconcile them?

(7) If they know how to read and write in their respective languages? If they do it on our paper, or on leaves or the bark of trees or plants, telling them by their names?

(8) What simple, easy means can be employed so that they dedicate themselves to speak and understand Spanish, and what has prevented them from doing so up until now?

(9) What are their most dominant virtues? If they are charitable, generous and merciful, noting both sexes?

(10) If they possess certain superstitions; what are they, and what methods could be employed to destroy them?

(11) If in the diverse and various languages which abound in the Americas and the Islands there are catechisms of the Christian Doctrine approved by the Bishops?

(12) If they still lean towards idolatry, explaining what it is, and the means that can be used to depose it.

(13) Comparing the moral and political state of the Indians twenty or more years after the pacification, according to the various contemporary historians, with that which they have now, is there an advantage or a disadvantage and if the latter what could have been the causes?

(14) What pacts or conditions do they celebrate among themselves in their matrimonial agreements? What kind of service does the groom provide for the parents of the bride, and for how long?

(15) Since they do not have doctors in their towns, what remedial cures do they use for their sicknesses? If they have plants, roots, bark or tree leaves which they use; their names and means of application? If they use bloodletting, purges or emetics; what herbs or mixtures are they composed of? Do they use thermal waters that abound so in the Americas, and for what sicknesses? Of these, what are the commonest ones and are they seasonal or not? Does the death rate correspond to the birth rate and what is the difference?

(16) How do they recognize the seasons of the year? If they have particular calendars for these, and if these are the same as they had in their paganism, explaining this, with an accompanying copy. How do they regulate the hours of the day for the distribution of rest, meals, and work?

(17) How many meals do they prepare for the day, and what kind of food, and the cost per person?

(18) What kind of fermented drinks do they use, and if they are useful or harmful, explaining their composition and their contents?

(19) In their paganism in many places they worshipped the sun and the moon, tell whether they have any memory of this, bad habits or leanings.

(20) Do they still conserve some customs of their primitive fathers; and if they have any news or tradition of the place or direction from where they came?

(21) If in their burials and wakes they use some strange ceremony, describing what it is simply and properly.

(22) If they are honest in their dealings and carry out their word or their promises?

(23) If they are inclined to lie; and if they have erroneous opinions about this, whatever they may be?

(24) What vices are the commonest in either sex?

(25) If they are quick to borrow money, seeds or fruits from each other, and under what pacts and conditions this is done, describing the various kinds of contracts they have and also their names.

(26) What kinds of contracts do they make for their seed plots, whether on their own or rented land, among themselves, as among Spaniards and castes that prepare them, pointing out what they pay for the land, the seed, for the plow and yoke of oxen, and how much money is administered and advanced in various seasons, and if in some places they supply them with goods and fruits and at what price?

(27) If they are angry and cruel? What kinds of punishment do they use among themselves?

(28) If they observe or recognize still any inclination to immolate human victims to their gods in cases of idolatry that may occur and of which there are examples?

(29) If among savage Indians they still make sacrifices to their Gods? If they offer human victims? What ceremonies do they observe with the bodies they bury, and if in some places they put meals with them, or cremate them?

(30) If there are well-to-do and rich Indians and other castes and with what kind of industry they have gained their wealth?

(31) What kind of life is led by the chief Indian Caciques and past Governors? How do they behave towards the other Indians? Do they pay their laborers and how? How do they bother them and what kind of services do they demand from them?

(32) Do they offer some personal service, the Indian men and women?

(33) Do they like music? What kinds of instruments do they know, string or wind? Are these the same as they have always used? Do they know ours and do they use them? Do they have some songs in their language, and are they sweet, merry, or sad? Do they prefer moving, melodious music or martial music? If they have some songs of their own, the tones they use and if possible a description and note of these.

(34) What illustrious men in warfare and letters have they had? To what kind of literary work have they dedicated themselves the most, describing them, and the names of one or another, pointing out the era in which they flourished, and a brief description of their works, and if the first ones are still in print.

(35) What ideas do they have of Eternity, of rewards and punishments, of the Final Judgment, Heaven, Purgatory, and Hell?

(36) Finally, what kind of clothing do the Indian men and women use in their towns, the same for the common people of the large cities, accompanied by, if possible, pictures or drawings of the costumes, informing at the same time the means that can be employed for avoiding nakedness where it occurs.[57]

In this same month of January must have arrived in Ciudad Real the *Proclama a los Habitantes de Ultramar,* signed by the Duque del Infantado on August 30, 1812, for there are two letters regarding the Bishop's request for its translation into Tzotzil. The first, dated January 23, was sent by the Loyal Executor of Huitiupán, Marcos Montes de Oca, to Father José de la Barrera in nearby Simojovel:

> Dear Esteemed Sir: I have carefully looked at the published Proclama-
> tion that you have sent me, which truly has diverted my attention, to
> come speaking of certain points that are so favorable and worthy of
> reflection and obedience. I have seen equally the pleasure that my Illus-
> trious Prelate sends to Your Reverence for the duty which we must
> carry out in explaining to the Indians the said Proclamation, and send to

Your Reverence two or three examples, writing them in two columns, one in Spanish and the other in translation.

Your Reverence knows very well that I am not entirely acquainted with this language, to translate into it the elevation of the Proclamation. Well, it is certain that while I have been given fame in it, I only know what is necessary for preaching, confessing and whatever else is conducive to my ministry. I do not feel capable of penetrating it to the degree of Your Reverence for whom it is the maternal tongue, as also Father Mariano Guzmán and other fathers in this bishopric. So I cannot help Your Reverence in this case, for I do not know yet how to write it; added to this, Dr. D. Cristóbal Ballinas is here treating me, which is the principal hindrance that impedes me from being able to give my help, my chronic illness utterly impedes me and exonerates me from such a holy thing, worthy of sacrifice in working out what it demands, so that, once my Illustrious Prelate sends you the news, having a better tongue, and mediating my grave sickness, I will feel absolved of this indispensable failing.

I see, as well, in Your Reverence's letter that you wish to retire from this parish, which certainly will cause the greatest problem; especially since you know the language of these towns completely, and Lent is approaching and there is no one to help me in confessions and because of the great harmony and brotherhood that we have maintained, both by me and by this neighborhood it will be deeply lamented if Your reverence retires from us; but I believe in the fatherly love of Your Reverence and Guardian, that they will provide you more time in these towns for my consolation, and help me in these towns for the benefit of the souls, which is of utmost importance.

I wish Your Reverence full health, and that you send whatever you please to this, your true servant, brother and captain who kisses your hand.[58]

The previous year, on June 24, this priest had informed don Ambrosio that he had had a paroxysm in church, nearly drowned in his own blood, and could not celebrate Mass. Again, on May 29, 1813, he explained that the doctor in Ciudad Real had assured him that he was gravely ill. Indeed, a month later the Vicar General relayed news of his death on June 26 to don Ambrosio.

The second letter, dated January 28, is addressed to don Ambrosio by Father de la Barrera:

My Venerable Sir in your official order of the 18th of this month I received the Proclamation of our Sovereign Regency that must be translated into the languages of this Province.

In that regard I spoke to the priest, and he excuses himself for the reasons he expresses in the accompanying letter. I, although I would like to carry out said translation in this language, my advanced age,

shortness of vision, the trips to the town of Plátanos and other
diversions impede me: I will delegate this matter to another, but I do
not know yet whether he will be able to carry out a difficult interpretation, so that I cannot promise Your Reverence that this work will
be completed.

To obey and please Your Reverence I will be here the month of
February as Your Reverence deems appropriate. And in the interim I
wish Your Reverence complete health, and may you please send whatever you please to your most humble subject who kisses the feet of
Your Reverence.[59]

The aged José de la Barrera must be the same man who, as chapter member,
was Fr. Joseph Ordóñez y Aguiar's "capital enemy," seeking to have him replaced
in Chamula. And he is surely the same "Fray Josef de la Barrera" as the Franciscan
friar who, from 1782 to 1802, sitting just outside Ciudad Real in San Felipe
Ecatepec, penned his 157-page *Libro de lengua tzotzil* that "the curious person
may see to his advantage" (de la Barrera 1806:2). Within the very same document
he also signed his name as José de la Barrera. This sophisticated grammar, written
with the aid of the sixteenth-century Tzotzil dictionary, was replete with many
sermons in that language (see Laughlin 1988).

But thoughts of Tzotzil translations may have seemed rather academic to
don Ambrosio for, Bishop Bergosa y Jordan of Oaxaca wrote him that "the rebels
here do not lose the hope of catching me, repeatedly asking travelers when I am
leaving" (Anaya y Diez de Bonilla 1934?:3,17). And on January 11 he wrote
again that despite "a furious nor'easter" and "the bloodletting inflicted on us by
the cruel mosquitoes, gnats, ticks and other insects" he had arrived safely in the
"more famous than grandiose town of Palenque" (Anaya y Diez de Bonilla
1934?:3,17). A month later, on February 12, don Ambrosio reported that he had
assumed political command of the province and that the insurrection that had
begun in Chiapa had been cut short and tranquility restored. And then, on February 19, the Interim Governor of Cuba, Julián Fernández, invited *don* Ambrosio to
join the Bishop of Cartagena as a fellow refugee, if necessary. He reported the
flight of the Bishop of Oaxaca and his attendants to Campeche. The Governor
repeated his invitation on March 8, commenting, "Since you have always been a
very good traveller it is natural that you have your mule ready to take a shortcut
when the opportunity arises."[60]

Don Ambrosio is informed by the Archdeacon of Guatemala, Antonio García,
in a letter of March 18, that Napoleon has been defeated in Russia. On the same
day, Bustamante wrote the Bishop saying:

The passions of some, personal resentments, or the intent to hide the
truth from the Chiefs very frequently are the causes for the errors we
commit, and which compromise us in the public opinion even though
we are innocent...I have tried to search for the most exact information in

> reliable sources, and considering that no one could give this to me from
> your province with greater care and prudence than Your Excellency, I
> hope you will condescend to respond to my request, for this I will live
> with eternal gratitude to Your Excellency.[61]

In this period the Intendant of Chiapa, Manuel Junguito, who was also the Military Governor of Tabasco, asked Bustamante for permission to use community funds in the defense of the province. He also asked his *Compadre* Ambrosio to transfer funds from the cathedral treasury to the royal chest of the exchequer to help pay for "the enormous costs" maintaining troops at the border.[62] Such funds were to be paid back when the circumstances permitted. The Bishop transferred 16,000 pesos to the royal chest.

At Junguito's request, Bustamante had sent General Manuel Dambrini's army to Chiapa to ensure that Morelos' forces would not advance into the Province, crossing the border from Oaxaca where they had been since December of 1811. Dambrini's forces consisted of 400 Carib *Negros,* 290 from Omoa, Honduras, and 100 dragoons from Sonsonate, Salvador. Despite Bustamante's order not to cross into Oaxaca, the army did so on February 25, killing a few insurgents in Niltepec.

Morelos' army was led by the priest General Mariano Matamoros, who had named his regiment "*Apóstol San Pedro.*" They carried a black banner with a red cross and the motto "*Inmunidad Eclesiástica.*" Matamoros in April, with 1,200 troops (700 riflemen, 200 lancers, 300 cavalrymen) and 5,000 more in the rear, prepared to attack Dambrini in Tehuantepec, but his scouts discovered that Dambrini had fled to Tonalá. On April 19, with a vanguard of only 193 of his choicest men, Matamoros spied the enemy troops encamped on a steep ridge that would be too hazardous to attack. So they fired a few shots, killing a handful of soldiers. With astonishment they watched the whole army of "two thousand two hundred men" flee, tossing their weapons over the cliff (de la Fuente 1913:48). Matamoros sent a letter to Morelos on May 8, describing how a bullet passed by his thigh, tearing his pants and burning his skin. When Dambrini's soldiers fled they shouted at their pursuers, "There are the yellow-capped Jews!" (de la Fuente 1913:100). Matamoros explained that he did not want blood to flow on Good Friday so he had waited till Saturday.

After the battle, Matamoros and his men remained in Tonalá for 10 days, trying to convince the population of their good intentions and that what Dambrini's soldiers had claimed was false—"that they were Jews, that they looted, raped, cut off women's breasts, killed children and carried them about impaled on their bayonets" (de la Fuente 1913:49).

Carrying their propaganda further, Matamoros sent a letter to the "Governor and Republic of the Natives of the Town of Ocosocoutla," telling them that the above were lies.

We are more Christian than the *gachupines* [Spaniards]. We defend the law of God, our lands, our goods, and our Creole brothers. The *gachupines* of the government…want to turn us over for their own ends to the French and the English. This is the reason for the war, my beloved sons, we defend ourselves to be free in our lands, govern ourselves, and not be the slaves of anyone…You have seen how we have defeated the army of Guatemala that they sent against us…do not be afraid. (de la Fuente 1913:49–50)

Three days later, Matamoros sent a letter to Bishop Llano reflecting his religious background, "Return to your senses Your Excellency, open your eyes, and fulfill the obligations of a good pastor, do not be the destroyer of your flock" (de la Fuente 1913:50). He informs the Bishop that there is not a priest in the whole area, that the people are dying without the sacraments, and that his chaplains must carry out all the religious duties. After describing the battle, he adds,

The American Nation is very Catholic, it defends only the rights and immunity of the Church, the liberty of its Government…everything that they say to Your Excellency and the other papers published by the Spanish government are false, to trick and seduce the unhappy towns. What I say to Your Excellency is the truth, and so I believe that persuaded by it you will speak to your flock, lead them to spiritual and temporal happiness and begin correspondence with us and adhere to the just cause that we defend, to avoid in this way the spilling of blood, the universal destruction of this Province which will surely be ours on the day we want it…We have all of North America…There are 20,000 Anglo-American warriors to give the last blow. (de la Fuente 1913:51)

On May 12 Junguito sent a letter to the Governor in Guatemala City, telling how after chasing the insurgents out of Niltepec, Dambrini's army had been defeated in Tonalá because of the insubordination of the troops, whose number was sufficient to have severely punished the enemy, and even more since it was a raw, undisciplined force, "little inclined to anything else but to be reunited with their families" (de la Fuente 1913:98). He assured the Governor that his lieutenants had seized all of Matamoros' propaganda. Junguito informed the Governor that don Ambrosio had left Ciudad Real on May 1, "caught up by the general fear" (de la Fuente 1913:98). He added that he had asked the Governor of Vera Cruz for 500 troops of those sent from Spain to defend Chiapa, Villa Hermosa and the Yucatan.

The Bishop was accompanied in his flight by his secretary, Fernando Dávila, who, one week later, was elected a deputy to represent Chiapa in the Cortes. Riding by horseback all through the night of the first day and traveling through Huixtán and Yajalón, they took 10 days to go just 33 leagues to reach their refuge in Tila. A week after their arrival, don Ambrosio sent the Governor of Guatemala his reason for abandoning Ciudad Real after he had urged his priests,

> even those most exposed to danger...to remain in the care of their parishioners until the last moment of peril...demonstrating beyond doubt my resolution not to absent myself from the Capital unless all prudent hopes had been lost...and now the designs of the cursed insurgents were known, that they were determined to penetrate through our towns until Ciudad Real.[63]

He had learned that Captain Tiburcio Farrera, instead of using Tuxtla as a last bastion of defense, had disbanded his 70 soldiers, sending them to their homes. The priest there had had to assume political and military leadership. Don Ambrosio had received "the letters from the impious" insurgents and had delivered them first to the government and then personally to his *compadre*, Junguito (Anaya y Diez de Bonilla 1934?:32). At the same time he met with Captain Farrera and persuaded him to

> place a dam to stop the unbounded torrent that menaces us...I dressed in mourning when I heard from the Intendant that none of this was possible, that there was a total lack of weapons and expedients, and that we had no help for it...Not fearing the insane furor of the vile insurgents, a death that would briefly follow my hardships, but rather the violence and abuse of my dignity that the evil insurgents would doubtless perpetrate, I left the city. (Anaya y Diez de Bonilla 1934?:32–33)

In a letter ten days later, he gave his age as his excuse for fleeing, but was consoled by the fact that "working for the good...of these, my sheep who, terrified by the enemy, had scattered in the woods, I was able, with divine favor to reunite them and in this Indian Town more than a thousand people have attended my Mass...so that they will not fall in the hands of the barbarous enemy" (Anaya y Diez de Bonilla 1934?:31). In still another letter, after reporting on Dambrini's defeat, he observes that the Indians are committed to their priests and will retreat following their instructions. "Fortunately these people are well disposed to remain loyal."[64] He reports that there are refugees in Tuxtla, and that he has chosen the town of Chiapa to be the line of defense if necessary. He adds that because the Indians are hiding their corn, Bustamante should convince Junguito to arouse the patriotism of the government of Chiapa.

But after leaving Ciudad Real, the Bishop was publicly denounced by his *compadre* for having abandoned his flock. The Bishop protested by letter to Junguito: "asking me mysteriously the reason for my departure from the City, I have answered you, writing with Castillian Clarity," since it was Junguito himself who had warned him to flee, telling him by what route, and since passports were being issued to military officers.[65] Don Ambrosio reminded his *compadre* that he had stated that the Province was lost and that he had no forces to oppose the enemy. The Bishop's companion, Dávila, thought that the towns ran the danger of "being invaded by the enemy, as well as having their in-habitants seduced by the astute politics of the chiefs of the insurgents, who win more land and follow-ers with their persuasion and perverse maxims than with arms."[66]

Indeed, after Dambrini's defeat, the Assessor, who was the political leader of Ciudad Real, suggested that delegates be named to surrender the plaza to the insurgents, causing such a scandal that he was accused before the Inquisition of having suspicious ideas, and was promptly deposed.

And though Matamoros would surely not win the Bishop over to his side, he did win a convert in a member of the Bishop's flock. Joaquín Miguel Gutiérrez was a student in the Tridentine Seminary. In 1809, while strolling in the streets of Ciudad Real with his fellow seminarians, he saw a woman being whipped by an official of Junguito. When Gutiérrez was warned by his friends not to protest, he exclaimed, "Some day slavery will end as it did in the France of the Louis."[67] Gutiérrez read Voltaire, Montesquieu and Rousseau. As an admirer of Hidalgo he was denounced and jailed by the rector for two weeks in 1810. He journeyed to the border to join Matamoros in 1813, but he was jailed in Tonalá for a month as the general had removed his troops to Oaxaca. Miguel Gutiérrez subsequently was accused of being a leader of a suspicious band of ruffians, "an anarchist, fomenting sedition...presuming to be scattering spices."[68] Later he governed the state of Chiapas from 1832 to 1835. The capital of Chiapas today, Tuxtla Gutiérrez, bears his name.

Just before his flight from Ciudad Real, don Ambrosio was sent a letter from the Capuchin Abbotess of Nueva Goatemala. Opening with, "*Mui Estimado Sr. y Tatita de mi Corazon*," and closing with, "*Maria Coleta Indigna Abadesa*," she sent passionate wishes for his safety and in a postscript advised him that "the Negro Macario" would bring him "shaving soap for the beard," which, one may hope, arrived in time for his hasty departure.[69]

While the Bishop was in the midst of his trek to Tila, the Archdeacon, Ramón de Ordóñez y Aguiar, who was left in charge, sent a letter on May 6, informing him that on the very day of his departure

> a certain priest, believing that we now had the enemy in the plaza, saddled his horse, and rushing off in flight, went through the streets, shouting repeatedly, '*What are you doing? Don't flee!*' With which the people fled into the hills, leaving their houses abandoned and that night the sluggards looted them. It was bad enough to lose the property, but upheavals followed and they even say there were deaths. Many houses remained abandoned, without anyone knowing where their owners were. (Anaya y Diez de Bonilla 1934?:36)

But even worse, the Archdeacon learned that the nuns wished to recant, so he had the convent bell rung "and those who wished to take the part of the Insurgents I declared them to be from that moment Apostates, and I promised to treat them as such" (Anaya y Diez de Bonilla 1934?:36). The Abbotess protested that she knew she had made a mistake, that she had been tricked and would not leave the faith.

But lest the Bishop feel at home in Tila, the Archdeacon advised him that in the Hospital de San Juan the poor suffer more from hunger than from sickness because "the Administrator cares nothing about the good or bad behavior of the cook and the tortilla maker, who steal a great part of the food" (Anaya y Diez de Bonilla 1934?:35).

The Archdeacon spoke with great authority, for not only was he a wealthy cattle rancher, but a pillar of *La Sociedad Económica de Amigos del País de Ciudad Real*. Learning of the ruins of Palenque in his childhood, he had later convinced his brother Joseph, "perpetual vicar of Chamula," to visit and describe the ruins, informing the *Audiencia* in 1784, so that their existence was made known to the world in 1822 by the expedition reports of Antonio del Río (Brasseur de Bourbourg 1851:4–6). In addition he was a student of both Nahuatl and "*tzendal*" (Tzeltal). As author of the *Historia de la creación del Cielo y la Tierra,* he analyzed the *Popol Vuh,* and also the *Probanza de Votán,* an historical tract in his possession that consisted of "five or six folios of common, quarto paper, written in ordinary characters in the Tzendal language, an evident proof of its having been copied from the original in hieroglyphics, shortly after the conquest" (Rio 1822:33). He concluded from these that the Americans, i.e., Maya, had come from Chaldea.

The Archdeacon's imperiousness is balanced for don Ambrosio by his right-hand man, the Vicar General, Mariano Guzmán y Solorzano, who, during the first week of his flight, sends daily missives, worrying over the effects of the tortuous journey on his health, sending him the latest military reports of the insurgents on the border, assuring him of the tranquillity in Ciudad Real, including the election of deputies on May 7, and sending him the heartfelt wishes of everyone for his health and safety. On May 9 he enclosed two letters. The first was written April 29 by the priest of Tonalá, Luciano Figueroa, who had fled down the coast to Pijijiapan: "I just learned that on the twenty-seventh Matamoros left Tonalá, saying that he was going towards Tuxtla and Ciudad Real."[70] The second, written on May 2 by Estevan Figueroa, gave the heartening news that the last enemy forces had made a very hasty withdrawal to Tehuantepec on the previous day and that none were left on the border. This news is circulated to the priests on May 6. Fr. Guzmán assures don Ambrosio on the ninth that the papers are well hidden, but because of the good news (of Morelos' withdrawal) he is ashamed to move the books. He worries about the Bishop's health and sends him French bread and ten packages of sweets.

He informs don Ambrosio that the nuns are crying and praying for him. There is no money to send deputy Dávila to Cádiz. The Indians of San Bartolomé have refused to pay the special contributions (*obvenciones*). One hundred thirteen cavalrymen have just arrived from Comitán, joining another hundred from Ciudad Real, and more still in the town of Chiapa who will travel together to aid Dambrini. *Compadre* Manuel Junguito assures don Ambrosio that all is well and that reinforcements of "many ferocious *Negros* from Omoa and Truxillo" are being sent.[71] He has heard that Napoleon's statue was burnt in the theater of Paris. Four thousand troops have arrived in Veracruz from Spain. Lamentably the "insolent Indians of Mérida are refusing to help in the churches because of the Cortes' decree."[72]

Sitting alone in his refuge in Tila, equipped perhaps with his Tyrian purple silk stockings and his Galician stockings sent to him from Nueva Goathemala by his friend Eulogio Correa at Christmastide, don Ambrosio had time to reflect about the state of the Indians who surrounded him, and the possible effect of the new Constitution on their lives. He observed that even though the towns or the parishes agreed to concede to each Indian "another piece of useful land which can be set aside for transplanting their trees, or their cornfields from one kind of seed to another that they are accustomed to plant," there would be little benefit [73]

> because without leaving the forest, [and because they are] living beyond the bell and the always devoted sight of the priest and of the political *alcalde,* who also may be devoted, there is no hope that they take advantage of the Constitution, that is, not even in fifty years will the Indian gain advantage from the honorable name of citizen nor will he know of the real profit of the name.[74]

Another view of the Constitution is provided to don Ambrosio by his loyal Vicar General, Mariano Guzmán, who wrote to him ten days later:

> The day they published in this city the edict concerning services and mandates of Indians, the Indian *alcaldes* of Chamula, Zinacantán and San Felipe rose in arms and, muttering greatly, removed the Indian servants from the monasteries, hospital, etc., beginning with the servants in the house of Your Excellency, and then they went to remove the Indians who were working in the church construction. Many of the priests are now without service and find it unsuitable. May God look upon this province with pious eyes, for the evil understanding that they give to the Constitution and the royal orders is causing great trouble and the total destruction of this Province.[75]

Just as in Mérida, the Church was in a state of alarm.

Throughout the summer Fr. Guzmán, himself suffering severe rheumatic pains, expresses concern over his beloved bishop's health and keeps him abreast on the progress of the cathedral reconstruction and all the minor details of his administration, the health of the clergy, and the military situation. He sends don Ambrosio the Guatemalan gazettes, a steady supply of bread, sweets, chocolates and hams, and arranges for a new pair of shoes. On August 8 the Capuchin abbotess writes from the capital:

> It is not easy to explain to Your Excellency the pain and concern that we have had for you since I learned that Your Excellency had left, fleeing the Insurgents, Oh how we would have wanted to bring you with us in hiding, here among your Capuchins!…May Your Excellency receive from each and every one of us a million most tender regards.[76]

On June 26, don Ambrosio issued a circular advising the Indians of the abolition of personal service, but insisting that Indians pay tithes and tariffs. He urges the priests to treat Indians with greater consideration. A month later Father Guzmán writes his bishop that the Indians are confused because they are no longer forced to offer services to priests.

Another voice speaking up about the Indians of Chiapa is that of the Rector of the Royal College of Our Lady of the Immaculate Conception in Ciudad Real. The rector observes that there are few students because of "the barbarism and poverty in which the greater part of the inhabitants of this Province have lived, abandoned. Such are the Indians who number 75,480…Occupied in the most rustic weariness," they cannot spare their children.[77] The other classes are almost "in an equally deplorable state.[78] The Constitution of the College only permits students who are "legitimate sons of Spaniards."[79] The Spaniards send their children to the University of Guatemala where they generally spend all their money and acquire "a considerable advancement in vices."[80] He argues that there should be primary schools in every town, financed by community funds that exceed 160,000 pesos, under the direction of the priest. There should be compulsory education in the rudiments of the Faith, and the pupils should learn to speak, read, and write Spanish and to count. There should be chairs of grammar in nine towns where a few Indians, too, should be taught, and also in the University—an echo of the words of the deputy of Tabasco!

Apparently there is still concern over Matamoros' troops along the border, for Governor Junguito advised his *compadre* on June 11 that the enemy had crossed the border again and kidnapped a rancher's son. The priest of Tonalá wrote don Ambrosio on July 12 that there were 140 cavalrymen on alert. Governor Junguito had 200 infantrymen in Macuilapa waiting for General Dambrini to return with his army of *Negros*. Junguito had received a copy of Morelos' *"Plan contra Callejas"*—a call to arms aginst the royalist general, urging that Spanish

Map 1. Chiapa, Nueva España.

Plate 1. Francisco Orozco y Jiménez, Bishop of Chiapas.

CAROLUS.IV.
HISPANIARVM.ET.IND.REX

Plate 2. King Carlos IV.

Plate 3. Queen María Luisa (Francisco Goya).

Plate 4. Manuel de Godoy (Francisco Goya).

Plate 5. Fernando VII (Francisco Goya).

Plate 6. King Fernando VII, his brother, Carlos, his uncle, Antonio —
"The three most innocent, the three most persecuted, the three most beloved."

FELICIDAD DE NAPOLEON Á ESPAÑA.

Præferre Patriam semetipsis.

Estos dos que aqui ves delineados
Los Matritenses son purificados,
Que por su lealtad la dura suerte
Los puso a los umbrales de la muerte.

Yo soy quien otro tiempo fue empleado
Antes que el enemigo introdujera
Las impias falanjes que han hollado
De mi florida edad la primavera:
Espectro me quedé por ser honrado,
Siempre miré al francés con saña fiera;
Que no fui partidario lo asegura
El testigo mejor, que es mi figura.

Yo fui qual ves, amigo, un artesano
Que tal qual otro tiempo lo pasaba;
Pero desde el momento que el tirano
Descubrió la perfidia que ocultaba:
Constante por la patria en un pantano
De miseria me vi, pues mendigaba
De puerta en puerta mientras los infieles
Rodeaban del intruso los doseles.

Plate 7. Cartoon of Napoleon congratulating Spain.

Plate 8. King Joseph, wearing the chain of the Order of the Golden Fleece.

Plate 9. Caricature of Napoleon, his face inscribed with
the bodies of his victims.

Plate 10. Caricature of Joseph Bonaparte,
commonly known as "Pepe Botellas,"— "Everyone has
his destiny, yours is to be drunk till death," 1814.

Plate 11. Caricature of Joseph Bonaparte— "It is not a horse,
nor a mare, nor an ass that he rides, but a cucumber," 1814.

Plate 12. Lord Wellington, El Duque de Ciudad Rodrigo.

Plate 13. Fernando VII standing on the French eagle.

Plate 14. Cádiz.

Plate 15. El Duque del Infantado.

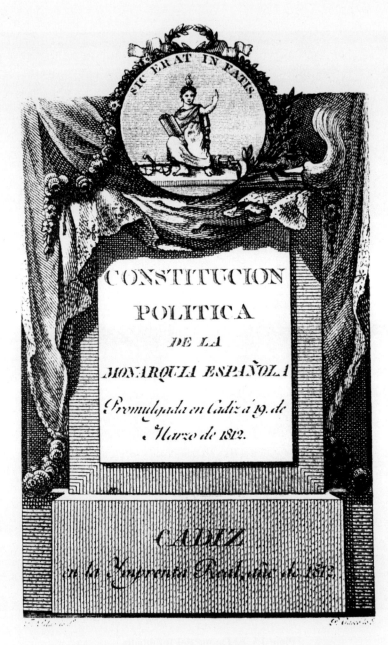

SIC ERAT IN FATIS

CONSTITUCION

POLITICA

DE LA

MONARQUIA ESPAÑOLA

Promulgada en Cadiz á 19. de
Marzo de 1812.

CADIZ
en la Ymprenta Real año de 1812.

Plate 16. The Constitution of 1812, printed in 1812.

Dr. D. Antonio Larrazábal, diputado por Guatemala
a las Cortes de Cádiz de 1811-12.

Plate 17. Antonio Larrazábal.

Plate 18. José de Bustamante.

El Exmo. é Illmo Sr. D y Mr. D. Fr. Ramon Casaus y Torres Arzobispo de Guatem.ª entró en esta Ciudad el 3o de Julio de 1811; y á la edad de 80 años, falleció en la Hab.ª el 10 de noviembre de 1845, siendo Obispo Adm.or de aquella diocesis y l'ret.ª propiet.ª de esta Su Cadav. fué sepult.ª en la Iglesia de las Relig.ª Carmel. de esta Ciudad el 1.º de julio de 1846

Plate 19. Ramon Casaus y Torres.

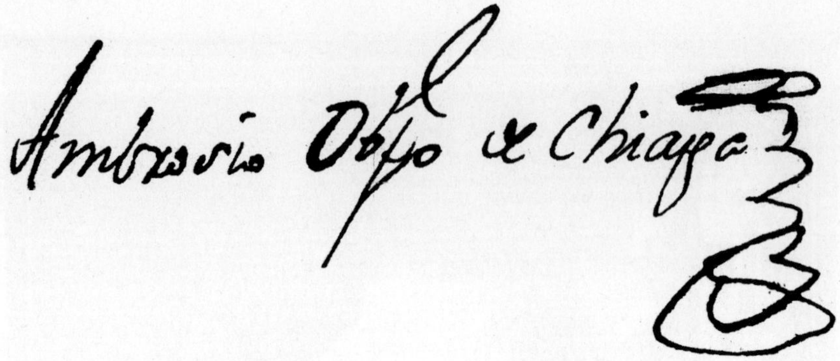

Plate 20. Signature: Ambrosio Obispo de Chiapas.

Plate 21. Seal of the Bishopric of Chiapa under Ambrosio Llano.

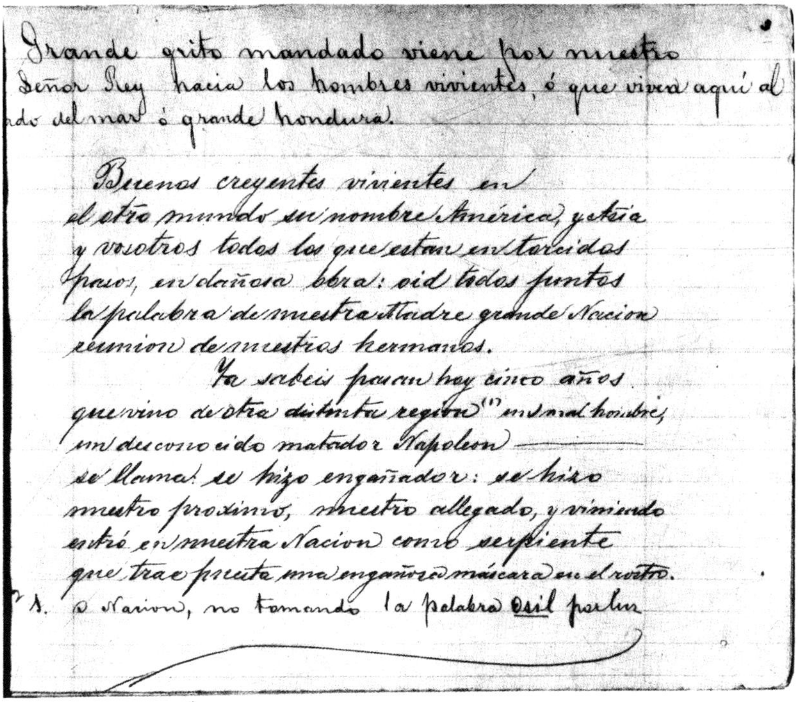

Grande grito mandado viene por nuestro
Señor Rey hacia los hombres vivientes, ó que viverá aquí al
[la]do del mar ó grande hondura.

Buenos creyentes vivientes en
el otro mundo su nombre América, y ostia
y vosotros todos los que están entorcidos
paíos, en dañosa obra: oid todos juntos
la palabra de nuestra Madre grande Nación
reunión de nuestros hermanos.
Ya sabeis pasan hoy cinco años
que vino de otra distinta región" un mal hombre,
un desconocido matador Napoleón —
se llama! se hizo engañador: se hizo
nuestro próximo, nuestro allegado, y viniendo
entró en nuestra Nación como serpiente
que trae puesta una engañosa máscara en el rostro.
1. o Nación, no tomando la palabra Ocil poslu

Plate 22. First page of the proclamation, Spanish version.

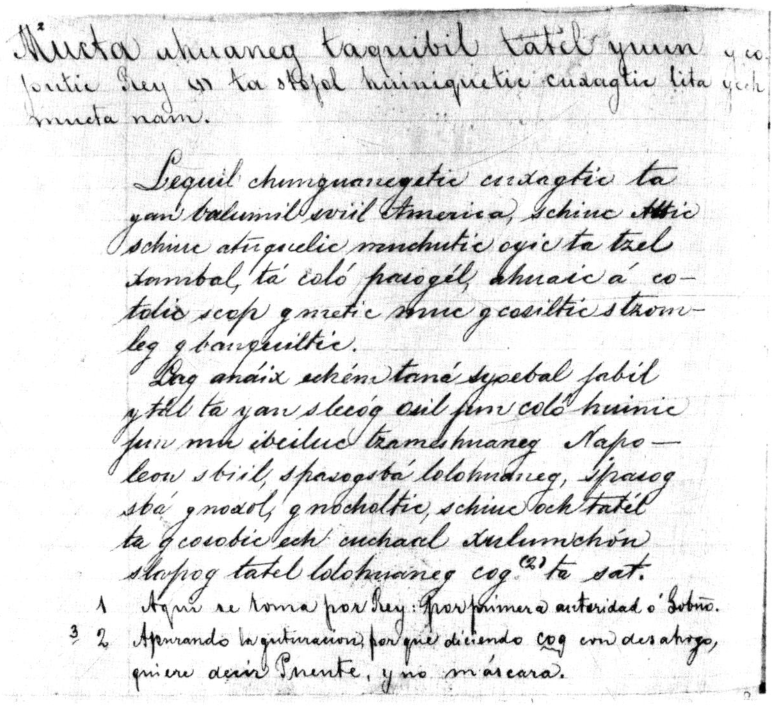

Muctay ahuaneg taquibil tatil yuun yca
puntic Rey er ta otzel huiniquetic cudagtic lita yich
mucta nam.

Leguil chinguanegetic cudagtic ta
yan balumil sviil America, schiuc Attic
schiuc atuguelic muchutic oyic ta tzel
sumbal, ta coló pasogél, ahuaic á cotolic scop gmetic smuc gcosiltic strom-
leg gbanguiltic.
Lag anáix eckén tané syebal jabil
ytil ta yan sleeóg cuil fun coló huinic
fun muk ibeiluc tzamchuaneg Napo—
leou sbiil, spasogsbá lolohuáneg, spasog
sbá gnoxol, gnocheltic, schiuc ock tatél
ta gcorobic ech cuchacl xulumchón
slapog tatél lolohuáneg cog[2] ta sat.
1 Aqui se toma por Rey: por primera autoridad ó Gobno.
3 2 Apurando la pronunciación, porque diciendo cog con desahogo,
quiere decir Puente, y no máscara.

Plate 23. First page of the proclamation, original Tzotzil version.

Plate 24. Cartoon of the Constitution—"Truth enlightens me,
justice guides me,"—facing the Persian—
"Heavens, what do I see, more useless projects," 1820.

Plate 25. Seal of the Bishopric of Chiapa under
Salvador Samartin y Cuevas (cut in Cádiz).

CONSTITUCION
politica
DE LA MONARQUIA
Española.
Promulgada en Cadiz,
á 19 de Marzo de 1812.

Rosi y Suria f.t

Plate 26. The Constitution of 1812, printed in 1820,
with a romantic view of Napoleon's bombardment of Cádiz.

ecclesiastics be confined in their monasteries, that other Spaniards be disarmed and some allowed to leave the country. On August 10, making his triumphal entry into the city of Oaxaca, Matamoros declared to the citizens that "considering less my broken health than the relief for my soldiers," he had decided to return to Oaxaca (López Sánchez 1960:2,895). For his victory in Tonalá, Morelos raised Matamoros to his second in command.

Don Ambrosio was receiving many letters in Tila expressing his colleagues' great distress over the loss of Oaxaca, and many other letters describing the insurrections in Granada, León and San Salvador, and the imprisonment of the insurgents in Guatemala City, but this was balanced by joyful, extraordinarily detailed accounts of the latest military victories in Spain and the latest defeats of the Tyrant Napoleon throughout Europe. News dated May 22 of Napoleon's withdrawal and the numbers of "*gabachos*," or "frogs," killed in battle arrived in the brigantine *Duende* that left Cádiz on May 26 and entered the port of Omoa, Honduras, on July 12. The Vicar General on June 29 had advised don Ambrosio that he would dutifully carry out the provisions of the Cortes' decree of February 16 that had just arrived, calling for a *Te Deum*, bell-ringing and illumination to celebrate the victory over Napoleon of "the Emperor of All the Russias."[81]

Probably in September the Bishop received the June 24 report of the secretary of the Constitution Commission in Cádiz declaring that they had found Governor Bustamante innocent of the charges of obstruction and despotism that had been sent to them by the Junta in Guatemala. Archbishop Casaus, on September 3, notified his bishops that the Provincial Deputations had been seated. He included a request for still another contribution for the national defense. A week later Fr. Guzmán informed don Ambrosio of this news, adding that the *Negros* of Omoa were in Quetzaltenango, returning home from their duty on the border with Oaxaca. On October 18 the Archbishop complained to don Ambrosio that the Indians as usual did not want to pay the tithes. The Archdeacon of Guatemala, Antonio García, in a letter to the Bishop despairs over the abolition of the Inquisition. He compares don Ambrosio to Job, saying, "the worst is that one cannot leave this desert as fast as one wishes."[82] In this month Bustamante gave Junguito permission to use four thousand pesos of community funds to pay troops if necessary for the defense of the Province.

Apparently the threat in 1812 of insurgents attacking from the north via Ixtacomitán was renewed a year later, for a member of that town reported to the Bishop on May 6 that they "were almost surrounded by Insurgents," and Fr. Martin Robles, on August 21, thanked the Bishop for the strength that don Ambrosio's words had given him, reporting that he was giving his service to the government for the defense of Ixtacomitán and that Captain Farrera had arrived to ensure their safety.[83]

But the situation appeared to be growing worse day by day, as reported to the Bishop on September 11 by the archconservative Ramón de Ordóñez y Aguiar, who had taken control of the Church's functions in the absence of don Ambrosio, undoing everything the Bishop had done. He announced that an insurrection in Teapa had spread like "cancer" to the priest of the town of Chiapa.[84] Furthermore, don Ramón, though complaining that he was nearly an octogenarian "with a foot in the grave…was dedicated to stopping the never ending, never corrected dissolutions of the Dominican friars" in that town.[85] On the Fiesta of Santo Domingo they had celebrated there "for 20 days a fandango, men and women dancing, and drunkenness, and the scandals that the friars cause in that town are so grave and so notorious that the people no longer want to make confession to them."[86] On October 18 he gave the further news that the priests of Tuxtla and Ixtapa were suspected of being followers of the priest of Chiapa and of an individual from Orizaba. They declared their innocence.

It was an uneasy peace, too, in Ciudad Real, from where the same Archdeacon reported on October 12:

> Suddenly the news was spread through this City that Goathemala had risen up and that the Archbishop and President were fleeing here. The spirits of the foolish people were disturbed beyond measure, but with the arrival of the mail everything has calmed down. I know from a good source that the nephew of the President has discovered the author of this news, and if, indeed, it is the one he says, this is not the first time, and Your Excellency has been affected by this to no small degree, and God willing this is the last time. I tell you clearly: He is the same one who, pretending that it is a message from Your Excellency, ordered the nuns to anticipate problems by dressing as lay people.[87]

In this same period don Ambrosio was receiving reports from Mérida, from Bishop Pedro Agustín Estéves y Ugarte, whose rough handwriting appears like that of a child, and yet whose knowledge of Latin, Greek, French, Italian and English won him the title of "the wise and virtuous Bishop Estéves" (Lanz 1905:133). The Bishop laments on May 10 that these are "bitter days, we do not see how they can become sweeter, now the priests are without their stipends, the Indians without work, nor tribute, and the Province without a *real*."[88] To this he adds reports of Napoleon's relentless advance through eastern Europe. On September 10, enclosing a brief version of the Constitution, and after mentioning Morelos' imprisonment, he remarks, "here we continue to carry out elections and do absurdities everywhere, God grant that things do not become more stirred up; certainly before we were peaceful and now we are not!"[89] A month later he laments that "the decrees of the government for a long time have produced effects contrary to what was planned."[90] On November 10 he continues disconsolately, "The anti-despots would like to be and have liked to be despots, and the monarchy cannot be preserved for long. Now the press has discredited and will discredit the past, present, and future Cortes."[91]

The only bright note that is heard for this year is the suppression of the Inquisition, as reported in a circular of September 22, and the news of November 6 that the ports of Tonalá and Tapachula are free to stimulate trade with New Spain, Guatemala, and Peru.

But the last news that don Ambrosio hears from his Vicar General is about the Belén conspirators, described in the previous chapter, who had been jailed by Bustamante and "who were found to have iniquitous papers on them, cruel plans, and the recognition of the Emperor of Guatemala for the cursed Morelos."[92]

CHIAPA IN THE CORTES OF CÁDIZ, 1812–1813

Mariano Robles was granted permission by the Church on February 10 to travel to Spain as a deputy to the Cortes. He bid adieu to don Ambrosio in Tila on March 19, 1812. He was to keep in close contact with his bishop by mail. Robles was forced to linger months in Havana, a delay, he confessed to don Ambrosio, that was lightened by the exuberance of the vegetation and the residents of the metropolis. On June 20 he admitted, "I have been struggling with my conscience over that report that I told Your Excellency I was going to make for the President of the situation in Ciudad Real, and finally I resolved to do it; God willing it will have the effect that I desire."[93] He was able to secure passage on a ship at the cost of 800 pesos, commenting, "that tastes like tobacco water because of the many expenses I am incurring, for here everything is extremely costly."[94]

After 45 days afloat, Robles reached Cádiz on September 11. A month later he described to don Ambrosio the eerie sight of 200 friars in the park "like wandering Jews, the object of mockery. The government has taken the keys to the monasteries disoccupied by the French who had used them as soldiers' quarters."[95] He pleads with the Bishop to see that he receives support "since everything is more expensive now…the Gentlemen Prefects…perhaps think that I am a chameleon, that I can live on air."[96]

He sympathizes with don Ambrosio on November 2 over how much the archdeacon has bothered him and assures him that the Guatemalan deputy, Larrazábal, returns his warmest regards.

Shortly after, he cannot refrain from expressing his opinion about "the detestable archdeacon Dr. Ramón Ordóñez," and Bustamante, "the Grand Vizier of America."[97]

Robles describes with exasperation the Cortes' efforts to suppress the Inquisition: "Twelve days of the most heated discussion have passed…there was a man…who spoke for six whole hours for three days in succession…I am certainly bored, and if I can find a pretext I will return right away."[98]

On February 26,1813, he reports the embarkation of two thousand troops sent to Vera Cruz.

Not until July 21 does the deputy's brother, Cayetano Ramón, quote to don Ambrosio from a letter of Mariano's, dated March 29:

> I am impatient, because neither the Governor, nor the Government, and what surprises me the most, the Bishop, has taken account of the publication and swearing in of the Constitution, nor have they congratulated the Cortes as has been done by other governments and corporations...Try to see these gentlemen, especially the Governor, to whom I have written, and remind him of this matter.[99]

On May 14, Fr. Guzmán made a strong request to the Bishop for his signature on a letter to accompany the priests' declarations that they had proclaimed and sworn to the Constitution in their towns. The Bishop complied with this request shortly thereafter (plates 20, 21).

Robles despaired over the Cortes, quoting Don Quixote, "'Sancho made few laws, but they were drafted well,' here, on the contrary there are many laws, but in the drafting: from God will come the remedy for you."[100] On this same day, May 19, back in Ciudad Real, the Church granted permission to Fernando Antonio Dávila to depart for Spain as a fellow deputy from Chiapa.

On May 25 was published Robles' brief but impassioned report to the President of the Cortes, *Memoria histórica de la Provincia de Chiapa, una de las de Guatemala*. Just like every other deputy, he tried to focus the Cortes' attention on his own province, striving for its advance. He sets Chiapa in its geographic context and reveals that Ciudad Real was populated by six thousand people, mostly Spanish, but that if you included the barrios and outskirts, the figure rose to over fourteen thousand. In the surrounding villages there was a population of seventy thousand Indians, thirty thousand Spanish and *Mestizos*, and a few Africans.

But not content to cite population statistics, he places in sharp contrast the behavior of the Spanish political leaders and their Indian subjects, beginning with the Conquest. The first, godchildren, servants or cronies of the Governor, are elected regardless of whether they are "inept or of wicked life and customs" (Nuñez de León 1992: 11). He describes in detail their exploitation of the Indians, who address them with such "servile and hateful fear," on bended knee, with uncovered head, referring to them as "King" (Nuñez de León 1992:12). Viewing the activities of these Spaniards "we must be filled with indignation," for in this rich land they have reduced the population to extreme poverty and virtual slavery (Nuñez de León 1992:15).

Robles tells how his colleague, Fernando Dávila, later his successor in the Cortes, came to him just before his own departure for Spain, "his eyes bathed in tears" as he described how one of his Indian parishioners had collapsed under a two hundred pound load of indigo (López Sánchez 1960:2, 871). "I myself, Sire, have been moved many times, seeing them climb those arduous slopes, naked and bathed with sweat, and hearing their pained groans of exhaustion, my spirit could only be moved and afflicted." He tells of "the barbarous inhumanity with which they are treated," sent as bearers of burdens to Vera Cruz in the hottest season (Nuñez de León 1992:13–14). If they have not died from exhaustion, thirst, hunger, from the change of climate, or from sickness after fording rivers, it is most likely that their return journey, also heavily loaded, will bring them home only to sicken and die.

> They live all their lives filled with agitation, and in continual terror and sudden dread, because they are treated with such scorn and hatred that there is not a coachman, lackey nor infamous person, not even the hangman himself, who does not consider himself authorized to mistreat them publicly, in witness of the bad example and extreme cruelty with which they are treated, especially by other people of consequence, and superior rank, whipping, slapping and clubbing them (López Sánchez 1960:2, 871).

"Is it possible that there have been those who believed [the Indians] to be lower than brutes and who even boldly denied their rationality? It is not surprising, because black envy and insatiable ambition is involved" (Nuñez de León 1992:9).

As for their education by the Spaniards:

> Although it is true that in certain towns there are those who go by the name of teacher, on salaries from the Indian community chests, they are regularly inept people so ignorant they scarcely know how to read, and what is most unfortunate, they are ill-behaved and addicted to drunkenness. They amuse themselves with three or four little Indians and use them for a variety of personal matters or domestic duties, teaching them nothing, for they scarcely learn the primer after three or four years, so their parents stop sending them to school. It happens then that the poor Spaniard and the others lack any help for the teaching of their children who go to the sepulcher with the same ignorance with which they were born. To confirm this it is enough to say that after three centuries the Indians do not speak Spanish. (Nuñez de León 1992:20)

These "true citizens" with "their natural docility and abilities" have become "the victims up until now of the very ones who ought to have labored for their happiness" (Nuñez de León 1992:23,20).

Knowing the concern of the Cortes for the loyalty of the colonists, he has shown how the most solemn and sacred votes of the entire nation [have been converted] into vain promises...[the Indians] continue to drag the same chains, without being able to leave their shameful state, and with no hope of bettering their condition, what else can be expected than the exasperation of their spirits, especially in the light of the bad example unfortunately being shown them by those with other considerations. (López Sánchez 1960:2:874–875)

Robles, after praising the Cortes' dedication to rationality and liberty, urges economic benefits and concludes with eight goals to be met for the Province of Chiapa:

(1) The need for a Provincial Deputation in Ciudad Real
(2) The need for a university in Ciudad Real
(3) Twelve scholarships for Indians
(4) That Tonalá and Tapachula be open ports
(5) Liberty for Spanish shippers
(6) A canal crossing the Isthmus of Tehuantepec
(7) Grant certain cities the title of Villa
(8) Have the friars convert the Lacandons

Robles in addition protested the abuse of the tobacco monopoly and its effects on Indians.

On August 21, he asked the Cortes for a university in Ciudad Real and the 12 scholarships for Indians. His request was approved by the Cortes on October 29, so long as the proposal was economically feasible and so long as the funds for scholarships came from the Indian communities after the establishment of primary schools. Nothing new under the sun!

Perhaps in recognition of the value of Robles' report, he was a runner up in the election for President. As a defender of the Indians, he was compared to Bishop Las Casas. For him the Indians are like "a rough diamond, which without being polished can never sparkle" (Nuñez de León 1992:25). Despairingly, he exclaimed to the President of the Cortes, "They have been declared to be true Spaniards, as a result of your wise considerations and constant vindications. Seeing that their inalienable rights are violated with scandalous infractions of the political Constitution itself...what is their liberty?" (Nuñez de León 1992:23).

Robles' encouragement of "home rule proclivities of the region helps to explain why Chiapas would be the first to break with Guatemala" (Rodríguez 1978:72).

On January 9, 1814, Robles wrote with excitement to don Ambrosio describing for him the triumphal entry of the Cortes into Madrid on December 30, 1813. There were arches, *vivas,* and acclamations.[101] On this bright note the scene is set to introduce the proclamations addressed to the colonists across the sea, and especially to "the Indians, that beautiful portion of mankind that inhabits America, favorite sons of the Motherland."

NOTES

1. Decree: Hurtado, January 2, 1788.
2. Letter: Polanco to Carlos III, May 20, 1778.
3. Letter: Polanco to Carlos III, May 20, 1778.
4. Letter: Polanco to Carlos III, May 20, 1778.
5. Letter: De las Quentas Zayas to Carlos III, May 2, 1792.
6. Letter: De las Quentas Zayas to Carlos III, May 2, 1792.
7. Archivo General del Estado: Documentos Históricos de Chiapas, 1983:9,11.
8. Within recent memory in neighboring Zinacantán the stewards royal (stewards of Lord Esquipúlas) carried shackles to the hamlet of Atz'am (Salinas) for the fiesta of La Vírgen de Rosario to punish anyone found disturbing the peace, as there was no jail there.
9. Letter: Francos to Carlos III, April 6, 1781.
10. Manuscript: de la Barrera, 1788:158. This event was considered by Friar de la Barrera to be of sufficient importance to add years later at the end of his Tzotzil dictionary.
11. Report: Ayuntamiento de Ciudad Real, January 22, 1805.
12. Report: Tosso, October 30, 1809.
13. Archivo General del Estado: Documentos Históricos de Chiapas 1983:2,104.
14. Archivo General del Estado: Documentos Históricos de Chiapas 1983:2,104.
15. Letter: Chavez to Llano, May 17, 1809.
16. Letter: Luciano Figueroa to Llano, April 18, 1809.
17. Circular: González, May 15, 1810.
18. Report: Llano, December 25, 1810.
19. Letter: Subdelegado de Simojovel to Llano, January 9, 1811. AHD
20. Circular: Bustamante, September 4, 1811.
21. Circular: Bustamante, October 22, 1811.
22. Circular: Bustamante, November 8, 1811.
23. Circular: Bustamante, November 8, 1811.
24. Circular: Bustamante, April 10, 1812.
25. Circular: Llano, November 18, 1811.
26. Regency decree: July 8, 1811.
27. Circular: Bustamante, November 25, 1811.
28. Decree: Bustamante, December 23, 1811.
29. Boletín del Archivo Histórico Diocesano 1985:II;3,19.
30. Boletín del Archivo Histórico Diocesano 1985:II;3,20.
31. Boletín del Archivo Histórico Diocesano 1985:II;3,20.
32. Boletín del Archivo Histórico Diocesano 1985:II;3,20.
33. Boletín del Archivo Histórico Diocesano, 1985:III;3,22.

34. Letter: Casaus to Llano, January 3, 1812.
35. Letter: Casaus to Llano, January 3, 1812·
36. Circular: Llano, January 13, 1812.
37. Letter: Casaus to Llano, March 3, 1812.
38. Circular: Llano, April 16, 1812.
39. Decree: Bustamante, April 10, 1812.
40. Decree: Bustamante, April 10, 1812.
41. Decree: Bustamante, April 10, 1812.
42. Letter: Priest (?) to Llano, May 24, 1812.
43. Letter: Farrera to Llano, July 18, 1812.
44. Letter: Farrera to Llano, July 20, 1812.
45. Letter: Pinto to Llano, July 30, 1812.
46. Letter: Casaus to Llano, August 3, 1812.
47. Letter: Casaus to Llano, August 3, 1812.
48. Letter: Martin Robles to Llano, September 8, 1812.
49. Report: Llano, September 17, 1812.
50. Letter: Priest of Tila (?) to Llano, September 15, 1812.
51. Letter: Bergosa to Llano, September 15, 1812.
52. Report: Dávila, October 25, 1812.
53. Letter: Estéves to Llano, October 22, 1812.
54. Letter: Three capitularies (?) to Llano, December 14, 1812.
55. Letter: Llano to three capitularies (?), December 21, 1812.
56. Regency decree: October 6, 1812.
57. Regency decree: October 6, 1812. No responses to this questionnaire are known to exist.
58. Letter: Montes de Oca to de la Barrera, January 23, 1813.
59. Letter: de la Barrera to Llano, January 26, 1813.
60. Letter: Fernández to Llano, March 8, 1813.
61. Letter: Bustamante to Llano, March 18, 1813.
62. Letter: Junguito to Llano, February 27, 1813.
63. Letter: Llano to Bustamante, May 17, 1813.
64. Letter: Llano to Bustamante, May ?, 1813.
65. Letter: Llano to Junguito, May ?, 1813.
66. López Sánchez, 1960:2;862–863.
67. López Gutiérrez, 1965:35.
68. Report (?): May 24, 1835.
69. Letter: Maria Coleta to Llano, April 26, 1813.
70. Letter: Luciano Figueroa to Llano, April 29, 1813.
71. Letter: Junguito to Llano, May 13, 1813.
72. Letter: Junguito to Llano, May 13, 1813.
73. Report: Llano, June 1, 1813.
74. Report: Llano, June 1, 1813.
75. Letter: Guzmán to Llano, June 11, 1813.
76. Letter: Maria Coleta to Llano, August 8, 1813.
77. Report: Rector del Real Colegio de Nuestra Señora de la Concepción (?), July 9, 1813.
78. Report: Rector del Real Colegio de Nuestra Señora de la Concepción (?), July 9, 1813.

79. Report: Rector del Real Colegio de Nuestra Señora de la Concepción (?), July 9, 1813.
80. Report: Rector del Real Colegio de Nuestra Señora de la Concepción (?), July 9, 1813.
81. Regency decree: February 16, 1813.
82. Letter: García to Llano, September 3, 1813.
83. Letter: Palacios to Llano, May 6, 1813.
84. Letter: Ordóñez to Llano, September 11, 1813.
85. Letter: Ordóñez to Llano, September 28, 1813.
86. Letter: Ordóñez to Llano, September 28, 1813.
87. Letter: Ordóñez to Llano, October 12, 1813.
88. Letter: Estéves to Llano, May 10, 1813.
89. Letter: Estéves to Llano, September 10, 1813.
90. Letter: Estéves to Llano, October 23, 1813.
91. Letter: Estéves to Llano, November 10, 1813.
92. Letter: Guzmán to Llano, December 28, 1813.
93. Letter: Mariano Robles to Llano, June 20, 1812.
94. Letter: Mariano Robles to Llano, June 20, 1812.
95. Letter: Mariano Robles to Llano, October 19, 1812.
96. Letter: Mariano Robles to Llano, October 19, 1812.
97. Letter: Mariano Robles to Llano, December 18, 1812.
98. Letter: Mariano Robles to Llano, January 15, 1813.
99. Letter: Cayetano Robles to Llano, July 21, 1813.
100. Letter: Mariano Robles to Llano, May 19, 1813.
101. Duque del Infantado, 30 August, 1812.

II

The Proclamations

Proclamation of
the Duque del Infantado
to the Residents Overseas

Most loyal residents of America and Asia, and those of you who have gone astray along the paths of perversity, hear all of you the voice of your Mother country (plate 22).

Now you know that more than four years ago an unknown Tyrant came from a foreign country to ingratiate himself deceitfully among us. He basely corrupted the sincere friendship with which we welcomed him.

At the head of two hundred thousand bayonets he offered us peace, decreed our banishment, and thought he was giving us happiness by presenting us with the hateful seal that would mark our perpetual slavery.

During this lengthy period his many cruel legions, always murdering and always thirsting for Spanish blood, have only achieved their own confusion and have carried this struggle to the final stage of desperation until the Spaniards, enraged and possessed with a just fury, blindly prefer death, like those followers who offered themselves to their oppressor.

The immense power of this Tyrant was turned in one blow against this poor Nation, weak and abandoned. So long enduring, she proves all too clearly her heroic determination from which she will not retreat one step. She has opposed withgreat courage the more than six hundred thousand men whom he introduced through the Pyrenees. And the greatest disasters [have been met] with great suffering.

The Spaniards were defeated a thousand times and scattered in the hills and plains so that the bulwark of Liberty seemed to have disappeared.

But a hidden hillock, a miserable village [Bailén] became the refuge and gathering place where they fought once again with zest and fury. Inch by inch the Spaniards have advanced, defending the inheritance of their forebears and their liberty.

And when the tyrant, gazing now on the Pillars of Hercules [Cádiz], believed that the conquest was over, he met up with an impregnable wall that he has been unable to scale. Sheltered by it, the Government has grown firm and resisted his threats.

It has organized respectable armies and tightened evermore the loyal and heroic alliance with England.

As related in the introduction, I discovered this proclamation in the Library of Congress (Boletín del Archivo General del Gobierno 1938, 3(3):511–515).

It has achieved the immortal fame of the whole Nation, so that all its representatives could meet in the Cortes and seal the freedom of Spain with their wise and proper decisions.

In the midst of such events the struggle continues and when the Tyrant, putting the most famous field marshals at the head of his armies, strives his utmost, the brave Spaniard still more persistently avows his liberty. And in the sad and desperate situation in which he has been placed he himself has made known the only way to acquire [his freedom]. The present generation will be followed by another, and it by another that will remind its sons and grandsons of the seven-century war sustained by our fathers. By their example Spanish blood must be avenged by the Spanish themselves, and for our consolation we must search in the bowels of France itself for our beloved Ferdinand, his brother and his uncle. And we must bear our arms to the dark prisons where these illustrious captives lie bound, groaning and weeping.

This nation offers to the world the spectacle of hunger, nakedness, and desolation. In the midst of such disaster it is a marvel of constancy in suffering and its glorious name is pronounced with respect in the farthest countries of the world.

But, oh Spaniards of America and Asia, in the midst of such cruel affliction this motherland turns its eyes to you and recalls with the greatest bitterness the sad situation whereby some conspiratorial ambitions have seduced your docile hearts, abusing the holiness of our sacred Religion.

Deeply pained by the waywardness of some of her people [the motherland] has not yet lost the comforting hope of being able to attract them and shelter them benignly on her breast so that in the future, united they may be participants in the immortal glory and happiness that is being achieved at the cost of so many bloody sacrifices. No matter how many times those who claim to be your friends repeat that Spain has lost, know that she will never put her neck in the tyrannical yoke of Napoleon.

Nor will she again become the toy of a prime minister, and even less the patrimony of a King. He must govern his people as a loving father and not a despotic Monarch. For [Spain] would resist that with arms, valor, and constancy. She is protected against arbitrariness and caprice by the wise Constitution that you have just seen sanctioned. The liberal and beneficent ideas adopted with such maturity by our Cortes disclose a delightful and pleasing field of enviable prosperity.

The free Spaniard, since now we are all [free], knows now who he is, what is his destiny, and what are his rights. He knows that his religion and his system of hereditary government are exclusively assured, and he has sworn to Ferdinand VII as his King, delimiting also his line of succession. He knows that with the annual meeting of the Cortes to which all Spaniards are equally called he cannot lack safeguards of his liberty.

He knows that he must be relieved of so many taxes which overwhelmed him and [he knows] that it is you who have been the first to enjoy their easement.

And he knows finally that his civil and criminal laws must protect his property, his honor and his individual liberty. Every judge, every minister and every office holder is held by the Constitution to the strictest responsibility.

Read [the constitution] with reflection and care so that it will provide you enlightenment capable of quieting the complaints that you have presented here, in the knowledge that so many ills that have been suffered will soon be remedied.

Consider that one of the first concerns of the Cortes has been the creation of an Overseas Ministry that must occupy itself exclusively with a profound study of the means for making you happy. By casting just a quick glance at its attributes you will conjure up the picture of your future fortune, doubtless happier than that which has been treacherously offered to the incautious by those ambitious fanatics who plan your separation.

The political and economic Government of the Provinces of America in general will be inspected by this Ministry, which will take charge of public education as the first object of its concern. This is the foundation of man's happiness in society, and the Government, recognizing its importance, believes it to be its first concern to protect, increase and convert the primary schools into a better system where the first seeds of moral virtues must be implanted in the youths. The secondary schools, the universities, academies and other establishments of science and letters will reveal a luminous field where those talents will be developed and fertilized that received the first lessons and maxims in childhood. All its efforts will be directed to the promotion of those seminaries of science where the Americans, cultivating their admirable talents, will shine among the wise men of the other nations.

Agriculture, trade and industry in all its branches, since they constitute the wealth and prosperity of a country, demand the Government's attention. The patriotic societies that have been established and those that will be established in the principal cities with the object of improving the knowledge of the products of each country, their planting and cultivation, the cotton mills that are so abundant in the Americas, the leather and tanning trade, flax, hemp, and silk, sugar, cacao and coffee, and so many other beautiful fruits that your fertile fields can produce, all are under the keeping of this Ministry so that, instructed through its channels, it may have the satisfaction and pleasure of contributing by its measures to the increase of your wealth and prosperity. Roads, bridges, canals, channels, lakes and everything that can facilitate trade between the provinces and peoples will be its particular concern.

Mining, this exclusive part of the Americas, hospitals, poor houses, hospices, and as many establishments as there are and can possibly be built to alleviate the people, reduce idleness and begging, are other such useful and worthwhile objects which the General and Extraordinary Cortes have had in sight, as a necessary consequence of your wise Constitution, so that you will be provided with a mountain of goods. If you know how to take advantage of them you will found upon them your perpetual happiness, which will be transmitted to your grandsons so that they will always bless the rich and fertile inheritance that has been left to them by their fathers.

But above all else what most merits the attention of the Government is the necessity of developing the missions in all the countries of America and Asia. The Government, far from needing stimulus for working enthusiastically in such a great enterprise, will have the greatest pleasure in dedicating itself energetically to a type of work that provides the inner satisfaction that beneficence causes in man.

The conversion of the Indians, the settlement of savage and nomadic tribes in a social environment, is the first and principal task of the missionaries. And there is nothing more commendable in the world than to see men dedicated by their profession to making other men happy and saving them from misfortunes from the time of their birth.

Finally, the Indians, that beautiful portion of humankind that inhabits America, favorite sons of the Motherland, demand precedence in the attention and scrutiny of the Government. And all its measures are designed to make them feel how aware it is of their true necessities and with what solicitude it seeks the means for their relief and happiness

For a long time it has craved [their happiness] and it weeps over the ills that they may have suffered, but a sterile sentiment would not bring any satisfaction. Their prompt relief is what can fulfill their desires and the first means for this end you now see indicated in this quick review of the concerns of the new Ministry, which are independent and separate from those of the Peninsula, so that there no longer remains the suspicion, held before, that the Overseas affairs were displaced by those of the Peninsula.

The brilliant perspective that the Government offers you, loyal Americans and inhabitants of those Kingdoms and Islands, in bringing to your notice the concerns of the new Ministry will demand your attention if you meditate on what extension they are capable of, and if you note the liberality of the ideas adopted as the principles and foundation of our Constitution. There is nothing in man's public and domestic life which could contribute to his happiness that is not included in the attentions of this Ministry. The Government confidently expects that its creation will be received by the residents overseas with all the signs of true appreciation that it deserves.

[The Government] believes at the same time that it has given evidence that it does not intend to please the Americans with vain hopes but that, being aware of their needs, it is trying seriously and vigilantly to discover the means for relieving them, establishing a single channel for receiving knowledge from all countries, no matter how distant, and for commanding the most beneficial measures which best contribute to their relief.

In this way it wishes to compensate to its utmost the firm loyalty of some, and to make known to others, whether they be seducers or innocents seduced by separation, that only by remaining united to this Country can they enjoy the peace and happiness that they will never acquire by following the perverse counsels of those who offer [peace and happiness] mixed with blood, persecution, and death. True independence will be enjoyed by he who joins forces with our glorious troops. Peace, liberty, and happiness will be enjoyed by he who, together with us, swears to and obeys the wise Constitution that our representatives have just given us. You who unfortunately have experienced the ills of a civil war that carry with it hatred and the vile desire for vengeance, even between those who most love each other, desolation, pillage, see who deceives you! Is it he who at such a price tries to dominate you to satiate his ambition, or [is it] Spain, your mother, who in the midst of her affliction works to your benefit, studies the means to make you happy, invites you with peace, and offers you the ultimate sacrifice for your happiness?

Those who have dazzled you, assuring you the protection of England in carrying forward separation, have deceived you. But he who is honorable and has a true idea of the glory of a great people must view with indignation that in this way they try to obscure and confuse the admirable virtues of a heroic people, to whom the Spanish nation owes so much for its defense, and because of whose integrity spares no sacrifice, pouring its own blood so that [Spain] may achieve her freedom. You must understand that England, far from protecting your misconduct, has manifested with the greatest clarity and sincerity that to consent to the separation of any, even the smallest part of the territory [of Spain], is not compatible with the alliance that has been contracted with Spain by such sacred and close bonds.

[England] has identified her cause with ours, and the fields of Salamanca have just given us the most recent proof of this truth. They will be eternal witnesses in history that Lord Wellington, Duke of Ciudad Rodrigo, with fifty thousand allies on the 22nd of July, 1812, has humiliated the haughty eagles of Napoleon. The enemies of the alliance of Spain and England with Portugal, try as they may, will not obscure the brilliant successes of this happy day.

The sweet echoes of liberty that resound in Madrid since the 12th of August, the joyous canticles of Cádiz, besieged for thirty months and now without enemies facing them since the 25th of the same month, the raptures of delight with which the inhabitants of Seville surrendered on the 27th, and the greater part of Spain almost free, are facts that the malign arts of Napoleon cannot distort. Nor can Spain do less than manifest forever the gratitude it owes to the pledge with which England fights for [Spanish] liberty. It would be unpardonably rash, after we see our fields drenched with the precious blood of our victorious allies, to allow even the remotest suspicion that the repeated protests of not protecting the insurrection of the Americans are insincere.

Finally, Loyal Americans, this is not the only satisfaction that the Nation, your Government, has to tell you this day. It has just received officially not only the news of peace between Russia, Sweden and England, but also [news] of the alliance of that [first] great Power with Spain. And the magnanimous Emperor Alexander recognizes our unfortunate Monarch Ferdinand VII, the General and Extraordinary Cortes of the Nation, and the Constitution sanctioned by them. This action of the finest politics offers agreeable hopes in the various and diverse effects that such a happy and fortunate event, in which this Government has taken such a part, must produce among us and in all Europe.

The Regency of the Kingdom believes it is its duty to bring this to your attention so that, having these facts in view, whose truth you cannot doubt, you will be disabused, closing your ears to the deceitful and seductive voice of those revolutionary apostles who preach peace and happiness. Those of you who have gone astray return to the breast of your Country that knows how to recompense with interest your humble repentance.

—Cádiz, 30 August, 1812.—EL DUQUE DEL INFANTADO, President.

Great Proclamation
Sent by Our Lord, The King
to People Living Here on
This Side of The Ocean

True believers living in the other world named America, and in Asia, and all of you walking in deviousness, working evil, listen everyone to the words of our great Mother Country, of our elder brothers in the Assembly (plate 23).

As you know, five years have passed now since an evil man came from another land, an unknown murderer named Napoleon. He became a deceiver, he became our neighbor, our ally, and he entered our country like a horned serpent wearing a false mask on his face.

At first his mouth showed him to be a good arbiter; he let only his good deeds be known. He showed his face to be like the faces of our elder brothers. And in the end he deceived us, he harmed us, he did not return our good deeds in kind.[1]

At the head of two hundred thousand murderers, brandishing guns in their hands, he just hurled accusations at us. "See the goodness of my heart. I do not come to hurt you," had been the words of Napoleon. But the goodness of his words was just a lie. He only wants to murder us, to pillage us. He only wants to put an end to our lives, all who believe in God, Our Lord. And he wants to become the Lord of the Universe. He thought we would believe it, he thought we would be pleased with all his deceit and evil deeds against us.

Five years ago his soldiers only wanted to drink our blood, they only wanted to kill the Spanish Christians. It was begun in vain, in vain he harmed us. Now his strength is exhausted, and the evil of his heart. Now, like a madman he just bites himself because he cannot snuff out the strength of the Spanish Christians. These Spanish Christians do not die, they do not let fear into their hearts. You see how their soul speaks:

As stated in the introduction, four copies exist of this manuscript. The handwritten copy is found in the Princeton Collection of Western Americana, Princeton University Library. Typescript copies may be found in the National Anthropological Archives, Smithsonian Institution; the Wilkinson Collection of Indian Languages, the Library of Congress; and the Biblioteca Nacional de Antropología e Historia in Mexico City.

> Even if I die, I perish, I will not let you harm my Lord, God. I do not
> want you to wound my father, my elder brother, my wife. I will not let
> you seize my father's land, my child's, my neighbor's, my ally's. Of this
> great crime I will always complain and if I die myself there are still many
> other Christians, there are still other Spaniards who will be born, who
> will mature to punish your stupidity, your error, as they are sent by God.

Beloved children, the wealth of this murderer Napoleon is so great, so great
the concealment of his heart. We cannot discern immediately how much pus he
has brought hidden in his soul. Like the flame of gunpowder, like a fatal thunderbolt, he did not wait a moment. "Let them die, let all the Christians die at one
blow," he just said with his mouth. Our elder brothers suffered, they witnessed,
they bore so much poverty, so much suffering. "I am here, I fear not. I am here, I
will not retreat a step," just said the Spanish Christians.

> Now you will see how God's power will help me. You, cursed Napo-
> leon, brought with you six hundred thousand murderers from your
> country named France. I am helpless in the face of your power. I am
> here, I fear not. My heart grows strong before the very God, the Maker,
> the Creator of the Universe.

My children, at first the Spanish Christians could not gather together. Many
were scattered, driven into the woods, into the fields. At first it seemed as if the
Spanish Christians, the guardians of our lives, were destroyed. We were nearly
destroyed, but in a small woods, in a small hamlet [our soldiers] rejoined, they
came to each other's aid. They began another fierce battle, for the evil, the madness of the murderers was nearly upon us. Our elder brothers gradually came to
each other's aid, and they did not leave, they did not abandon the land of their
fathers, their mothers in the hands of the murderers who wished to touch, who
wished to take the flowery ground, the joy of our Universe.

The murderer Napoleon, like a jaguar, wanted to put us in his mortal jaws. His
deputy settled in the great city named Madrid. [Napoleon] passed like a whirlwind and overturned Our Lord, the King. What could be done? At first he bound
him, he trampled on his holy commandments and took him to prison.

Like a lighted fire, Napoleon continues to destroy everything. In the end, he
continues to take, he continues to kill, he continues to snuff out other cities,
other towns. Appearing like the two mighty pillars of Hercules was the city of
Cádiz. "I will seize the city!" said Napoleon. "Now I am the Lord of the Universe."
So was shouted the evil, so rasped the voices of the spies, the murderers.

They all wished to enter the city of Cádiz, but there at the entrance they met
the force of the Spanish Christians who became like a high wall, and there Napoleon broke his head, there his strength was smashed, he who wished to enter to

kill the lords of the Spanish Christians living in the city. But he could not prevail, he could not knock down, he could not climb over the great wall of Christians

There in the city of Cádiz the elders, the lords, the sages had assembled, and they had prepared a well-authorized assembly. They provided for and paid visits to the great English king who had offered us great aid. In this way they bore the suffering in the brave city of Cádiz, in this way the Spanish Christians embraced the English, in this way they celebrated, rejoiced for all time, for they supported each other, they did not let their land be seized, for their hearts were not constricted before the murderer, Napoleon, and they stood firm in the midst of the mortal tornado.

Now all the wise people are blessed because they joined together, they aided us, because they unbound our prisoners and gave us the sign of our salvation.

In the midst of this great work the Spanish Christians have not tired. The murderers grind their teeth in anger, but the Spanish Christians only prayed to God in their hearts. Hear how they prayed:

> Deceiver, Napoleon, you alone wished to destroy the Spanish Christians and still the Spaniards are here. You wished to snuff out the fire of our land, and when but one ray of our fire flares up, the power of your eye is extinguished. You wished to destroy the people's faith, but you could not. The Spanish Christians will tear down your house, and smash the mortal doors of Hell. You do not wish to free Our Lord, Ferdinand. In vain you have stolen him, in vain you have taken him. So be it, so be it, Napoleon, we are here, we will break the shackles on his feet, we will loose the lashings of his hands, even if he be in prison, even if he be in blackness in the heart of the world, our arms are outstretched, the power of the Spanish Christians has risen up. We shall go to your land, we shall overturn your dominion, we shall break four hundred or eight hundred keys, and on our shoulders we shall take out Our Lord, the great Ferdinand, his younger brother, and his uncle, unjustly imprisoned in the jail. We will die, our sons will travel in the universe, others will be born, but they shall not forget this great work. It shall be blessed by all men still to be born, still to walk on the whole universe. Blessed be those who long ago chased out other murderers who settled on our land and caused our suffering seven hundred years ago.
>
> Do not weep now, Our Lord, Ferdinand. Do not constrict your heart, we beg you. We shall make compensation for your tears. We shall beg from Heaven the payment, the compensation for your suffering, and compensation for the blood of our fathers, our mothers, and our elder brothers, unjustly spilt by the murderers.

Hunger, suffering, anxiety, poverty, death, thirst, destruction, there are no longer any other riches shown to us in the world. Even so, here we are, here are the tender children[2] of the Spanish Christians, who just cry over the imprisonment of their Father, the imprisonment of their Lord.

The world falls silent at the sight of our suffering, it bears witness. May my eyes open before these great men. "Do not close the pupils of your eyes," is the message from the great land. "Bear witness," it says, too.

See how they endure, how these Spanish Christians bear so much suffering. See how they defend the belief in God and the life of Our Lord, Ferdinand. For this their name is blessed, is kissed, and will flourish forever. And no one will snuff it out, just as there is no one who can extinguish the radiance of the sun, the rays of the great star, portent of dawn.

Beloved children, this great conflict was begun unjustly by the murderer Napoleon in the land of our fathers, mothers, and elder brothers, the Spanish Christians. Now he has flown towards us, he has appeared above us. Now the evil of Napoleon has leapt at us here on this side of the ocean. That jaguar has grown weary before the Spanish Christians. For that reason he sent his visitor who just came to spy, came to hurt us, came to disrupt our spirits, came to deceive the goodness of our hearts.

This deceitful white man, these evil men, just say, "We come in God's goodness. We do you no harm. We just come to visit, to trade. You must love us because we have only come bringing peace. I believe in God, I love our Mother Mary, blessed Jesus, holy passion," they utter with their mouths. And in their hearts there is so much evil, so much pus, so much mortal madness, but it does not appear in their faces. Evil words are found in their souls, but dissimilar words are in their mouths. "We have come to bring peace to the world. We respect you. Come, believe our talk!" they just say. And deceit, evil, hatred, festering words are hidden in their hearts. Like a great horned serpent, only murder lies in their jaws, murder in their eyes, murder in their words, murder in their hands. And we cannot discern it, just as it was not discerned when they arrived in our brothers' land on the other side of the ocean.

So, now, the hearts of our fathers and elder brothers, the Spanish Christians, sorely ache, and in the midst of their suffering and their laments they turn their compassionate faces towards us lest we believe, lest we are diminished by the trickery, the evil deeds of the military men sent by the murderer, Napoleon.

May God lay hold of us, beloved children. May he support us beneath the cloak of the great protector, Mary of the Immaculate Conception. May he show us the road of life, the journey to Heaven. May he aid us, those who are pursued by the adversities of the world. This is what they are begging with tears before God, they are giving shouts for us, as many Spanish Christians as live on the other side of the ocean, and all who are living beside us. They do not discard from their hearts the hope, the coming joy of the discovery of a blessed day, a lucky hour when the night of our suffering passes and with our Spanish hearts we embrace each other, like a great father who has not been seen for years who returns home and embraces his children. "Come here, children!" he only says. "Come, feel how my soul leaps with joy. I do not wish to sleep. I do not wish to eat. Come, press against my heart. The whirlwind's cloud has passed, my poverty has passed, my captivity. Come see the great star, portent of the holy day, portent of our lives."

So speak now the Spanish Christians,

Come, younger brothers standing there on the other side of the ocean! Come, men, women, my children! Come join us in the joy, in the health that we have bought with our suffering, with blood, with persecution, with poverty, with wounds, with tears, with mortal thirst.[3] Now there is no longer an evil white man, he who did not in the past respect us beside Our Lord, the King. Now, though many times a deceitful spy, who sells himself as a friend, tells us that it no longer exists, that the land of the Spanish Christians is destroyed we must never believe him.

Our Spanish Christian elder brothers did not for a moment lower their heads, never for a moment obeyed the mandate of the mad Napoleon. So we alone, we the children following our Spanish fathers and elder brothers proceed in their footsteps, shall proceed with the strength, the deeds of the Christians forever.[4]

Following this great heavenly journey our souls will not be lost, not be wounded before God and before our true defenders who have borne great suffering so that our faith, our souls, our children, our wives, and everything in our land not be lost. See how they deliver themselves to death, others have been seized in the hands of the murderers, others are spending their money, their wealth for us, others have gathered to write and to chase out the devil's deceit.

Now the elders are gathered, sent to Cádiz by all the towns in our land. They are simply performing justice, good deeds for us. See how from their mouths comes the truth of God's commands. See how they become the saviors and advocates of our land.

Listen, open your ears to the symbol of our health. Now there is no longer stirring at the side of Our Lord, the King, an ignorant man, who merely did all that was desired by the foolishness of his heart. Now there is no one playing games in our land. Now Our Lord, the King's head is not confounded by trickery, and when he returns to his seat he will not act merely according to the desires of His Majesty. We shall see what he does. Like a great father he will favor his children who have been given by God unto his hands, in his shadow and in his care.

Now there is only at the side of Our Lord, the King, an assembly of our wise men, lest our land be spoiled again by the falseness of a single white man, a single man. And now there are other brave Spanish Christians holding guns in their hands to chase the murderers who have come from France and assaulted us.

Now this is how our great assembly speaks, seated in Cádiz. And the sovereignty of Our Lord, the King, is guarded, is manifested in a second assembly named the Regency. "Let it be done!" is the command as soon as all the good words of justice and relief have issued from the Assembly of our wise men.[5]

Now their wisdom, the thoughts of these great men are seen. The wealth of their souls is envied in the world, and it comes spilling towards us like a shower and like the goodness of sunbeams over the whole land.

Now there is no one to tell us in his wisdom that we are not Spaniards. Once those who were born on this side of the ocean were called Indians. Now we are called Spanish Christians, beloved children, for we have but one nation, but one faith, but one law, Our Lord, the King, is one, we have but one Assembly seated at the head, at the heart of our land called Spain.

Now there is no one to rub out the exaltation, the greatness of our spirits. Now there is no one to imprison us,[6] no one to hide from us the fragrance, the goodness of our name, blessed in the whole Universe. Now there is not a man who does not know how to guard his wealth that has issued from this holy name. Equally, beloved children, we touch, we sniff this flowery name.

Now the sacred faith of our holy Church, is guarded by our Assembly.[7] Now there is no insolent, heretical man to come and confound the sacred laws of Our Lord, God. Now there is no one who will come to force us to be in obedience, in fear, in respect of another man who has not brought his authority on the true road, on the right hand of Our Lord, God.

Now, at first we shall only fear, respect Our Lord, King Ferdinand brought from Heaven to our land. And afterwards we shall only fear, respect his true replacement who is born of his blood. Now there is no one to imprison, to persecute one's wisdom, one's deeds, one's spirit if he but performs God's commands, and the commands of God's substitute on earth.[8] Now we are free, we are Spanish Christians, we are the elders of our land. And if there be other evil men who unjustly harm us, there is our Assembly of wise men to aid us. And they alternate each month, each year. Now there is a surplus of our names and we are summoned to do justice, to defend our land even though once we were Indians.

Beloved children, unscreen the pupils of your eyes! Now your tribute is ended. Equally we just pay a small request, called a "Donation," for our suffering is not yet over, and in this way we obey the fourth commandment of Our Lord, God:

> Thou shalt fear, thou shalt respect thy father, thy mother. Thou shalt help them in their suffering, thou shalt aid them in their poverty, thou shalt give them their food and drink. Thou shalt wipe the tears from their eyes. Thou shalt not offend in word, deed, and in the thoughts of thy soul. For I am aggrieved in my heart by this great sin,[9]

that is what Our Lord, God, commands.

Now listen: Father is the name of that man who gave us our being, whoever serves in office, whoever is sent by God, is also called "father." Whoever shows us the road to Heaven is called "father." All the wise men who teach us the true word, the truly good deeds are called "father." Whoever is more advanced in years is called "father." And whatever man, whatever Spanish Christian helps us chase out deceit and end our suffering is also called "father."[10] And if these great men only perform good deeds for us, why do we not help them with a little donation of money? If we be the children protected by the efforts, by the poverty, by the goodness, by the strength of our Spanish Christian fathers and elder brothers, how can we not give them two or three coins to buy their food and drink, for they are engaged, they thrive in the pursuit of the murderers who spoil our land, and who unjustly wish to kill us.

Wait, wait a little, beloved children, our suffering will pass and you shall see how our land will flourish again. Now there is still suffering and in the midst of the suffering you shall discover its coming, you shall feel, you shall point to the goodness of your Spanish Christian fathers' and elder brothers' hearts that pity you.

When our persecution passes you will witness your relief. All the commands and good words of our Assembly of wise men come for the sake of your health, to protect the wealth of your homes, to respect, to favor your existence. Do not lose with your sins the goodness of this word that has come from the heart of our land.

If you have no sins, there is no officer of the law to punish your person. If there be a man of authority, an elder who unjustly harms you, unjustly torments you, he, too, will pay for his crimes before Our Lord, the King, for he did not obey the conciliatory words of our Assembly of wise men.

Just gradually consider in your souls these words of our fathers, our elder brothers written on paper. And then you will see with your eyes how soon will end our poverty, our sufferings, our laments that have long been in our hearts.

Direct your ears, direct your pupils to the goodness of this reasoning. Now they just sit here on this side of the ocean, just here beside us, others of our wise men, our lawyers are assembling a second time. We will just see them act for the relief of our suffering. Now all the goodness, the favors prepared for us cannot be discerned right away, but it is not far off, the goodness of the day given to us to measure, to see, to touch the fragrance of our souls, the flowering of our land. So, in the beginning of this year you saw the great fiesta for the proclamation of the parchment, the mandate of our land, called the "Constitution."[11]

Consider, beloved children, Napoleon's trickery does not work the same. "I favor you, I relieve your suffering, I support you," he just says, yet other mad words, other evil deeds are in his heart.

Do not put yourselves on the path of ignorance, insolence, madness and other sins followed by the murderers.[12] Indeed, close your eyes, shut your ears, lest someone befuddle your head with the pus, the evil of the great horned serpent in Hell. Just see, hear, learn the truth of this holy word sent by God and by our Spanish Christian Assembly on the other side of the ocean.[13]

Now for the second time our wise leaders will meet again nearby, here at a port, in Guatemala, and in other Spanish cities. First they are just going to serve, watch over or labor on behalf of the education of our children.

The youngsters, our children who learn from books in good schools, know the power of God's spirit, know about this great eternity or passage of time that we hear about with our ears. They know how their soul is set in their body. They know the grandeur of their being, the grandeur of their blessed name. They know, too, why we bear hardships in this world, why tears, the water of our eyes, flow in weeping, and they know how to be joyful and delight still in the everlasting life of God.

They know, too, why we must fear, respect our parents, neighbors, kinsfolk and they know why we must esteem and love them as God commands.

The apprentices in good schools know why we are together in this world,[14] why we should not take the devil's path, why we should not wound ourselves like jaguars, why the magistrates punish and admonish us, not only to rectify our actions, but also the thoughts of our souls.

Ignorance, the ferment or poison of our being, of our flesh, that we brought long ago from the belly of our mother Eve, does not enjoy repression, injunctions. Still more shall come, beloved children. At the end of the world there will be a great day when we shall talk, shall speak with our souls,

> We thank you, great God. You are blessed in all your works, because you reproved my flesh in my labors, you straightened my path in the universe.[15] We thank you, father, mother, Your Magesty, and Magistrates. May God repay you, wise Spanish Christian elder brothers. May our divine Mother Mary call you or bring you forth for this life where we are seated in the presence of the Maker, creator of the universe. May he have mercy on you while on your gloomy trails, faced with tricks of the devil, on the path to your cornfield, in the dreams of your eyes, because you baptized me, because you taught me to fear and respect God and to fear and respect the substitute of God who is on Earth.[16] We thank you because you expanded the spirit of our eyes, because you set right my thoughts, my words, my deeds, when once I was bound up in my body, and because you showed me the fragrant path, the heavenly path, forever.

That is how your souls shall speak, beloved children, when you depart from this world, and that is why all our wise lawyers are meeting now.

Now your eyes cannot discern or discover all the goodness that has been planned in their hearts. Before long you shall see, shall feel, shall hear and touch the prosperity, the joy of another nation.

Soon you shall see good teachers in the schools planting in your children's hearts all the good deeds ordered by God. Now you have just seen the boys playing games, but in just a moment our travails in the persecution of the murderers shall pass. Before long the dawn shall shine on the wise men, like a great sunbeam in the midst of the firmament, and like light rain that comes to dampen the ground of our cornfields. Then you shall see how great men, great fathers, great Spaniards are made.[17] Then you shall see how in the meeting of Christians they shine, in the meeting of the sages who are in the universe.

Only the progress of our cornfields, our trade, our markets, and the wealth of our homes is what our Spanish Christian fathers and elder brothers are envisioning, considering, preparing.

The meetings in the towns planned now by us will just reckon, will just consider in their hearts how we can discover the hiding place of the gold metal, the silver metal in the center of the world, how your poverty and your bereavement can be ended, can be remedied, what they will do to support you and your children, what they will do to fill your homes, your land, with much cattle, many horses, many pigs, many chickens, much cotton, silk, sugar, cacao and everything that will provide your wealth and your health. Neither do our assemblymen forget in their hearts the construction of your homes, the improvement of the roads to our towns, the discovery and widening of the springs of clear water and all the other good works prepared for and witnessed by us.

Now, in only a moment, men's laziness, drowsiness will end. In only a moment you will see erected the houses of refuge for the helpless, sick people. Indeed that is how the sufferings of our land will end.

Before long good teachers will come to show you the word of God,[18] writing on paper, weaving of cloth, forging of metal, carpentry, masonry, and other works which will produce the wealth of your homes and the health of your children.

So you will see that the hearts of our devoted Spanish Christians do not tire in the least. Just near here, at the entrance to the ocean, is established another Assembly which I told you has just stretched the vision of their eyes. They do not fall asleep preparing the priests, the blessed men who come to sow good works,[19] and in the land of barbarous men whose souls have not been baptized. Then you will see how they undo the bindings of their souls, how they open the shutters of their eyes, how we join them in meetings, how they themselves join us in following the path to Heaven. Then you will hear how the priests raise their voices like a great loudspeaker in the homes, in the land of the strange men, the strange heathens. Indeed you are embraced, your arms are stretched out, with your neighbors, your kinfolk. Your land is broadened, lengthened by the existence of these new Christians. Your eyes are wet with tears of joy. You shall gather together to sing with instruments, you shall scatter abroad to proclaim the goodness, the compassion of Our Lord, God.

Hear how your mouth still speaks:

> Come, come, whichever men have not in the past been baptized. Come,
> whoever once accompanied the devil, the jaguar, the tapir, the horned
> serpent at the foot of the rocks, in the woods. Come, leave the shadow
> of earth, leave the clouds in your eyes, lift your head. Come, rest in our
> arms. Come, let us raise the spirits of our voices before God. Come, let
> us also bless the goodness of our Spanish Christian Assembly.

There is indeed no other goodness, no other credible word that stands, that can
rise up beside, before these worthy deeds, so great they are spoken of everywhere.[20]

Beloved children, there are evil deeds, there are lying words on the lips, in
the mouths of the heretical murderers, but now you cannot think in your hearts
that perhaps the Spanish Christians are only playing tricks. It is not so, beloved
children. Everywhere there is evil, but there is also good; there is trickery, but
there are also true words; there is killing, but there is protection; there is false
writing, but there is true writing; there are wounds, but there are also remedies;
there is persecution, but there is support; there are muttering words, but there are
peaceful words; there are ignorant men, but there are wise men; there are heretics,
but there is also true faith in God.

Consider, beloved children, our Spanish Christian land did not lose for one
moment the commands of God that issued from the lips, the mouth of the holy
Apostle, James: If we have sins like sinful men, there are also Christian laments in
our souls. And these words, these mercies that have come to us in writing are not
false, not games. They are born, they have issued forth from the hearts of your
fathers, your elder brothers, Officers of the Law, the Spanish Christians. Hear how
the truth of their souls speaks:

> Beloved children, elder brothers, Indians, those who hold themselves in
> the power of God, those sheltered in the womb of our land, those whose
> heads have not been befuddled by the devil's falseness, and who have
> received holy water on their foreheads, the holy sign, the holy mark, the
> symbol of life under the protection of Jesus and the true Virgin, Saint
> Mary. Hear, I shall tell you two, three times, Spanish Christian Indians,
> those whose hearts do not grow weary from bearing hardship, persecu-
> tion, poverty, prison, beatings. Hear, those who have just followed the
> holy path of their fathers, their mothers, the holy path of their land, the
> strength of their Spanish Christian elder brothers, those who have cast
> off the murderers' evil and embraced God's goodness, hear the good
> words, the good deeds discovered beside you, in the heart of our land.

Your King has loved you so much, your Assembly of wise men, all their
conciliatory words come first to you Indians for you are guarded in their souls.

Your land, your holy Mother, just measures, just thinks of your life, only wishes to show you how great is her love, how she delivers herself into the hands of murderers, how she bears persecution, exhaustion, thirst and many other hardships to nourish your souls, to ensure your health, to remedy your poverty.

Many years have passed now since our Spanish Christian fathers' and elder brothers' hearts cried, their souls shrunk, for the time was short to prepare the goodness of your land. Now the time is not short. In just a moment your fathers, your Spanish elder brothers will wipe their eyes, for soon will be discovered the goodness of our land and the end of our hardship. This great work fills their souls with joy and is praised everywhere. Now the measure, the consideration of our happiness has been taken, the wise men are ready at the Christian meetings of the cities, just near us. Now we cannot say as in the past that the settlement of our disputes, the hearing of our complaints is too far away at the end of the ocean. Now the solution for your petitions is not delayed before this assembly near here.

See, beloved children, how the sunbeams shine, manifest in the writings of Our Lord, the King, our noble Assembly. You have heard all that our wise men residing in Cádiz went to do, and all that those of the second Assembly have come to do residing near here, on this side, at the entrance of the ocean.

Our hearts will leap with joy, the hearing of your ears will rejoice when you measure, when you consider in your souls the greatnesss, the goodness of these words and the goodness of the mandate named the Constitution, shouted in the proclamation, and at the fiesta that passed in our town. Everything your soul, your life desires, all the mercy, the goodness you could discover, now you can desire on the earth, all is written in the book of the Constitution and in the hearts of the Spanish Christian assemblies that will reside again here beside us.

Our Lord, the King, Our Lord, the Officers of the Law, are considering in their hearts the joy of your lives in holding, obeying, fearing, respecting what this great Assembly has told you. Indeed, the other Assembly, named the Regency, that has guarded the substitute for the power of Our Lord, the King, awaits the love of your hearts for our land.

Our Spanish Christian Assembly does not wish to deceive, it is not playing games, and the hope of so many children shall not be lost, shall not be extinguished, for it rests on these true words of justice.

Now, the heart of our Assembly just is rent apart in the preparation of the remedy of our sufferings. Even though the first great Assembly established in the city of Cádiz is far away, now we have a second Assembly beside us that only comes to do good works for us and for the Indians, for whomever guards God's laws and knows how to fear, to respect the love of God's substitute on earth.

Our Assembly wishes to make payment for the strength, the goodness of those men who assisted, who held on to our land by pursuing Napoleon's evil murderers, and it wishes also to make manifest to the eyes of the deceivers and to the ears of the ignorant men who followed the murderers, that they found nothing good on Napoleon's path, on the road to death, and in the rending, the wounding of our land.[21]

Even though another insolent man may come, another evil white man, even though he come well dressed, even though he speak as other men, the substitutes of God, speak, do not believe his deceit, do not follow behind him. He has brought evil in his heart, he only wishes to spill our blood. From where will our happiness come if they only scatter death, persecution, anxiety, hardship, heresy, poverty, hunger, confiscation, murder and other poisons of the horned serpent not seen then by us? If we are carried off to Hell, if they drag upon us the eternal punishment, the reproach of God, how can the murderers give us true happiness? Do not believe their deceit, beloved children.

If you meet some man who wishes to smear us with sin, who wishes to put evil in our souls, shut your ears, run, protest before the Officers of the Law. If you meet some man who tells you, "Come, children, here is your father, here is your defender, I will relieve your suffering," reply to him in this way:

> I know you, murderer, I have known you want to cast out my soul, you want to smash my land. I do not have two countries as you want. I have only one country together with the Spanish Christians, children of God, who have delivered themselves unto death for our sakes. Get out, get out, no one summoned you, do not come and upset my heart. Only one God, one King, the substitute of God, do I obey. I have a true father, I have Spanish Christian elder brothers. These are wise men, defenders, advocates who have shown me, who have manifested to me God's commandment, love for my neighbor, for my kinsfolk, and the path to Heaven. Do not come to take this eternal goodness from me. Do not come to give me the pursuit of death. What good is the world to me, all its objects, if I lose my soul?

You have heard, beloved children, how to return your words before the deceivers. And if they scold you, no matter; there is God, there is life for our souls in Heaven and for all time.

The land of the English people took pity on us, too. They are defending us during our persecution. Even if there be some evil man who tells us that the English are tormenting us, that they are like murderers, do not believe this slanderous talk, beloved children. The English love our country, they have delivered themselves unto death, to suffering for us, like the Spanish Christians.

The English and the Spanish Christians respect each other, equally they support each other, and they engage in a single defense. In this year that passed, on the twenty-second day of July, a great captain named Wellington came, accompanied by fifty thousand English soldiers, and these virtuous men pursued the evil murderers, undid our bindings, and exhausted Napoleon's boldness. If very truly the goodness of this deed is brought to light in the world, if the English rejoice in the defense of our souls, and if they have delivered themselves unto death, to rescue us, how can we believe the lies of the murderers who only want to sunder our country and the kindness of the English people?

Hear now another word, the city named Madrid bore great hardship until the twelfth day of August in the year that passed. The city of Cádiz was pursued, besieged by the murderers for thirty months until the twenty-fifth day of August. The city named Seville and other cities in our land witnessed the end of our suffering on the twenty-seventh day of August in the year just passed. Now they are just embracing each other with joy, they are just celebrating before God, for they have watched the end of the tornado, the destruction of the murderers who left in shameful flight.

The evil, the madness, the deceit of the murderers cannot be erased from paper. They cannot cause to be lost from the world's knowledge this great deed, this defense carried out by the Spanish Christians, the English, and another good land named Portugal. Our country prays to God for these virtuous defenders of ours, and it would be wrong ever to snuff from our hearts this virtuous deed and the strength of our English allies who have spilled their blood for our lives. So he does a great sin, whatever evil man does not believe in the virtue of our neighbors, our allies, the English people. Do not believe, beloved children, the evil stories, the evil talk that only wants to overturn the thoughts of our souls.

Now there are other countries in the world named Russia and Sweden that have joined in our defense. And the great lord named Alexander loves Our Lord, King Ferdinand. He knows and praises our wise men, our assemblies and all the just words commanded in the document of the Constitution of which I have told you. So, in one blow, the joy of our hopes cannot be lost. Before long our pursuers will retreat. In just a moment the face of the world will turn, the face of our suffering, and before long will become manifest the flowering of the land on the other side of the ocean, named Europe, in our land, named Spain, and beside us, as Our Lord, the King, has measured, prepared and awaited.

Our first Assembly, the safekeeper of authority, the replacement for Our Lord, the King, named the Regency, has thus sent, has thus transcribed on paper, so that you shall open your eyes before the virtue of this word, and so that you shall look with love on the Spanish Christians, children of God, our elder brothers, our neighbors, our kinsfolk. Do not offer yourselves to evil trickery, shut your ears to the murderers who only shout, "Life! Happiness!" and conceal death, hatred in their souls.

Ah, poor men, white men, Indians, those who have fallen on the path of evil, come back, come into the womb, into the heart of your Assembly, your Mother, your land.

Our Spanish land still loves you, supports you. It will not punish your ignorance. It will do nothing to you. It will just embrace you in its arms if you abandon murder, hatred, rage, and if you weep for all the sins that you have committed before God, before your father, your elder brother, and other men whose blood you unjustly spilled, if you broke and trod upon God's commandments, touched their land, touched the love of their hearts, but there is still a remedy for your sins. Come, do not wound your soul forever. Let them flow, let your tears issue forth. Do not wager, do not grow insolent with the strength of the Creator, the Maker of the World.

Beloved children, this blessed book is written in the city of Cádiz, on the thirtieth day of August, in this year named 1812. Its truth is made manifest by the hand of the first Governor of our Assembly, the Regency. His name or title is Duque del Infantado. Presidente.

M. .M.   9. 7. 1906

NOTES

1. That is when he served our nation ingenuously with favors, as an ally.

2. That is how they name recently born children, whose tender name is given to the beloved children of a Catholic and great nation, naming them *unetic* [*unetik*].

3. It is necessary to add this parable of the absent Son and the Father, to be able to explain the sensation of joy of which they are capable, when they stretch out their hearts and come back to see each other.

4. Those who remain firm until the end will be saved, they will give unmistakable proof of the solid principles they profess, without ever giving the lie to the nobility of such a great origin.

5. This is the way the law of the Sovereign is explained.

6. This means the true independence and liberty that consists in the peculiar rectitude and noble feeling of a great soul.

7. That is, that must be protected from all kinds of assault, schism or division: Voltaire, Rousseau and the others. Do you not remember that the earth splits open and swallows those who, like Core, broke the unity and divided the body of Jesus Christ? Saint Augustine, #29. (Book of Numbers 16–17.)

8. *It being certain that he who works against divine will or sovereign precepts cannot be a good man.*

9. *The precepts of the Decalogue are repeated, without its rules, neither flesh nor blood, nor love, nor family, nor reason, nor conquests, nor objects, nor the whole universe can give us happiness in the midst of the unfortunate insurgency.*

10. Honor your parents and you will live a long time on the earth.

11. *According to the news sent to the Government, dated February 24* [1813]. **(I cannot identify this document).**

12. As a consequence of the same ignorance. The wise man prefers the will of his creator and obedience to the laws for the greater glory and recompense.

13. Because the Eternal God is the beginning of all truth, and he communicates it to whomever he wants and by whomever he wants.

14. To carry out and not upset the laws of society and the good order established by Divine Providence, there must be those who order and those who obey; the Catholic Christian must be content with either of these two destinies. Why then, miserable insurgents, do you dispute with blood the position that God denied you by grace? Be afraid that you will be given in punishment what does not suit you.

15. *The Kings rule by the grace of God. Not only for political reasons, but in conscience they must be well-respected, and he who resists, resists God himself.*

16. Even when the Prince is not a tender father, but a cruel tyrant and oppressor it is never lawful for the vassal to shake the yoke of obedience; the only recourse is what Samuel says: Shout and cry out to the Lord, begging his aid. That is the Spanish version Chapter VIII, First Book of Kings, note 11.

17. The biggest thing is not the best, when, in following the just path, one condemns fully that which only has the appearance of greatness. David showed himself to be greater and braver by not committing treason to King Saul than when he defeated Goliath and so many armies. Folio 227 of the Book of Kings, Spanish version. *(First Book of Kings, chapter 17.)*

18. Tell us, Lord, what you wish to say; make us worthy of listening carefully to your word, that was mercifully shown to mankind for our true happiness; it gave us infinite merit and courage associating us with the Eternal Priesthood of the anointed ones. Remember, O Lord, that the bright torch of the Apostle James never was extinguished in your family. Why would we want more authentic documentation of our infallible victory?

19. Not because the precious seeds of the Gospel have not been sown among us, but because the harvest will increase and the weed be removed. We do not lack the beautiful luminaries of the firmament and the new lights will reflect a greater number of sunbeams.

20. That is: there is no other thought, word or deed that can claim primacy or a parallel with what has been.

21. Offending the result of the only reliquary or sacred deposit of our faith.

7

A Friar's Viewpoint

Well, who did it? Who assumed the difficult task of converting into Tzotzil the Regency's elevated proclamation "to the men living here on this side of the ocean," to "the Indians, that beautiful portion of mankind that inhabits America, favorite sons of the Motherland?" There is no record, no name.

As noted earlier, Fr. Montes de Oca mentioned native Tzotzil-speaking priests in the diocese, including Fr. Mariano Guzmán, the Examiner of Tzotzil and Tzeltal. But as don Ambrosio's Vicar General, Fr. Guzmán was probably too busy, in the Bishop's absence, to become involved. He makes no mention of the proclamation in his many letters to the Bishop. Another possibility was Fr. José Miguel Correa, who had authored a 102-page *Breve esplicacion de la lengua tzotzil para los pueblos de la provincia de Chiapas,* which in 1804 he had submitted to *"El Ilustrisimo Señor Doctor Don Ambrosio Llano, Dignisimo Obispo de Chiapa y Soconusco del Congreso de Su Majestad Catolica."* But a brief examination of his manuscript reveals a different alphabet and manner of spelling. While de la Barrera and Correa both employed *gh* for *j, hu* for *w,* and *z* for *s,* the proclamation translator used *g, hu,* and *s.*

Although it is possible that the translator was a diocesan priest, I think it more likely that de la Barrera, a Franciscan, would have chosen another Franciscan, especially since the friars were more intensively trained in the native languages. It would appear that the translator was not a native speaker, for he inserted Tzeltal words and occasionally Tzeltal grammar into the text, as well as attaching Tzotzil prefixes to Tzeltal roots and Tzeltal suffixes to Tzotzil roots. Even today this mix is a frequent attribute of the sermons preached by the Bishop and local priests who make an effort to communicate in an Indian language, for the diocese was then and still is so understaffed that priests must serve both Tzeltal and Tzotzil communities. Clearly, the friar believed that his translation was into Tzotzil, for not only does he head the document with *"Sotzil,"* but in his notes he contrasts a Tzotzil word to its form in the *"Zendal"* (Tzeltal) language.

The mystery deepens as one investigates the Proclamation more thoroughly, for despite the ungrammatical mix of Tzotzil and Tzeltal, in his notes to the text the translator provides keen linguistic observations, some with a remarkable degree of sophistication. There is no way of knowing whether the translator was the same individual referred to by Fr. de la Barrera in his letter to don Ambrosio: "I will delegate this matter to another, but I do not know whether he will be able to carry out a difficult interpretation." That he invokes the name of Our Lady of the Immaculate Conception as the patron saint suggests that he, like Fr. Montes de Oca, may have been resident in Huitiupán, then under Franciscan control. Though no town in Chiapas held her as its patron saint, and though Huitiupán was, indeed, Santa María de la Asunción Huitiupán, in 1813 the second most costly, i.e., most important, saint's fiesta was for Our Lady of the Immaculate Conception and today her fiesta is one of the very few still celebrated there. In addition, there are linguistic peculiarities to the text that are particular to the contemporary dialect of Huitiupán, e.g., *sy-* for third person possessive and third person marker. That Huitiupán was on the Royal Highway from Ciudad Real to Villa Hermosa may have contributed to the inclusion of many Tzeltal words in the text, for there surely were many Tzeltal travellers on this road. Possibly our friar was Fr. Montes de Oca's successor, Manuel José Solano, who, shortly after Montes de Oca's death, was himself afflicted with fierce headaches and prostrated with malaria. Whoever he was, he was well-acquainted with Indian culture and strove earnest-ly, with a considerable degree of imagination, to respond to the call to present in Tzotzil the elevation of the Spanish proclamation, while at the same time bringing home to his illiterate listeners the contents of the written document, a document inspired by the words written in the Constitution of 1812. He was so involved in the Indian language that in one instance in the Spanish text he substitutes for the paragraph-initial word, *"Ahora,"* "Now," its Tzotzil equivalent *"Taná" [tana].*

Our anonymous friar introduces his rendition with a flowery apology:

> The translation of the following Proclamation was extremely difficult, for in imitating the firmness of its spirit necessarily its gracious conciseness and literary elegance was lost.
>
> The clauses that were substituted, the notes, phrases and circumlocutions, should be taken as supplements to a limited language, so as to convey in some way the majestic National sentiments, without confusion or a mixing of a less reliable interpretation.
>
> May Heaven permit this small fiber of reality to contribute in its small way to that Catholic and majestic state, whose life is inhaled by the grafted shoots of its luxuriant grapevine. Because they are transported from a Glory that is neither measured by time nor absorbed by eternity they can never be separated from the worthy nectar of that trunk.

So unlike the baroque lines above, the Proclamation as penned by Joaquín de Mosquera y Figueroa had addressed the colonists with worldly pithiness, calling on loyalists and rebels alike to listen to Spain's appeal for unity and support, informing them that:

(1) Napoleon, promising peace and prosperity, has been a deceiver.

(2) Napoleon's war and the capture of King Ferdinand has been met by extraordinary Spanish resistance respected worldwide; the King must be rescued.

(3) Confronted with plotters at home and abroad, Spain wishes to win back the colonists.

(4) The Cortes, under the Constitution, would provide liberty, reduce taxation, protect property and assure responsible government.

(5) An Overseas Ministry has been created to promote in the colonies education, agriculture, trade, industry, patriotic societies, transportation, mining, hospitals, hospices and missions, so assuring everyone's prosperity and happiness.

(6) Indians are the favorite sons of Spain; the new ministry would establish a single channel to solve the colonists' problems and win back the loyalty of all.

(7) Despite Napoleon's claims, England has been a loyal ally. With her aid, Spain is hurling back the invader's armies and Spain has just received the support of Russia.

In conclusion, the proclamation repeats the opening plea for the colonists to listen, urging them to be disabused, and to return with the assurance that they will be forgiven for any straying from the true path.

To match the elevation of de Mosquera's Spanish prose, the translator relied on two qualities of Tzotzil formal speech. The first is the use of semantically and syntactically parallel phrases, often couplets, e.g., "he became a deceiver, he became our neighbor," where the same verb is used in adjoining phrases, or where similar verbs are paired, e.g., "even if I die, I perish," or "we will break the shackles on his feet, we will loose the lashings of his hands." Frequently the friar would abbreviate this technique by using strings of nouns, e.g., "Hunger, suffering, anxiety, poverty, death, thirst, destruction, there are no longer any other riches shown to us in this world," or "And deceit, evil, hatred, festering words are hidden in their hearts." In addition, he relied heavily on the Tzotzil use of metaphor in formal speech; "the heart of our Assembly," "the fragrant path," "the flowery ground," though many of the translator's metaphors may have been Spanish in origin.

While couplets and metaphor achieved the purpose of conveying the loftiness of the Proclamation, they meant the sacrifice of de Mosquera's conciseness, a precision rare in Spanish documents. The friar tripled the length of the Proclamation, so that when read from the pulpit it must have required the listeners' presence for a full hour!

The Spanish proclamation's primary thrust is clearly political. Aside from the espousal of missions to convert the heathen Indians there are but two references to religion: (1) how the "ambitious plotters have seduced your docile hearts, abusing our sacred religion," and (2) that the Constitution guarantees to the Spaniard "his religion and his system of hereditary government." Neither Church nor soul, neither God nor Our Lord is ever mentioned.

How then should our friar carry out his duty faithfully as a spokesperson for his religion and his system of hereditary government? How could he be true to his Spanish nation that "is blessed and always will be, because in the midst of the total darkness that covers the universe it shines like the Dawn," his "Catholic nation" that respects "the precious jewel" of its religion? How could he, so sure of the superiority of every aspect of Spanish culture, transform the dry words sent from across the ocean by white men into familiar, compelling images that would reach the hearts of his Indian congregation, convincing them to remain loyal to the state? His tactic was to create a gripping, universal moral drama, intimately personal, located not only in the political, economic, social, natural and supernatural world that enveloped his listener, but more critically in his listener's very soul. This was a contest between the forces of good and evil, a contest that was being waged on two continents and that would be waged as well in the listener's Indian soul.

The contrast with de Mosquera's moderate, secular, impersonal prose is signaled by the friar at the very start. By labeling the text "Great Proclamation Sent By Our Lord, The King," he indicates that the important words that follow are sent to the Indians by their very own king, the substitute of God on earth. The dramatis personae can be divided into the camps of good and evil (table 7.1). Some never appear on stage, but are waiting in the wings where they have been marshaled by the friar's notes. These names in the notes are recorded in italics in table 7.1. There are also places and institutions that resound positively or negatively. In the middle, between the two camps, stands the Indian listener who must decide where he or she will give allegiance.

To give a personal immediacy to the Spanish arguments brought from afar, the friar indulged in repeated references to body parts (table 7.2), to family members (table 7.3), to flora and fauna (table 7.4), to natural and supernatural phenomena (table 7.5), to morality (table 7.6), and so forth (table 7.7), frequently, but not always, in metaphorical expressions. A simple tally of these items spotlights the contrast between de Mosquera's Spanish conciseness and the friar's Tzotzil volubility.

Another device to personalize the contents of the Proclamation was the conjuring up of dialogue, often lengthy, between the human actors, and between Man and God. And so, Napoleon or his minions speak their hateful, deceitful words to the Christians in Spain and to the overseas inhabitants, who reply with Christian defiance. On the other side, God and the people's souls engage in

Table 7.1. Good and Evil

Good	Evil	Good	?	Evil
God, Our Lord, the Maker, Creator of the Universe	The Devil	Spanish Christian fathers, (elder) brothers	Spanish Christian (younger brothers), Indians	
Jesus		Father		Heretics, Ignorant men, Barbarous men
Mother Mary, the Virgin, Saint Mary	Eve	True believers		
Mary of the Immaculate Conception				
The Apostle, James		The English King		
Saint Augustine	*Rousseau*	Wellington		
Samuel	*Voltaire*	English soldiers, people		
	King Saul	Alexander of Russia		
	Core	Heaven		Hell
David	*Goliath*	Mother Country, Spain		France
King Fernando	*Napoleon*	Cádiz, the Pillars of Hercules		
Fernando's brother		Seville		
Fernando's uncle		Madrid		
El Duque del Infantado, President of the Regency	An ignorant man (Manuel de Godoy)	Portugal		
	Napoleon's deputy	Sweden		
Regency		Our Holy Church		
General and Extraordinary Cortes, Wise men of the Assembly,		The Constitution		
Overseas Ministry, Second Assembly		*Divine Providence*		
Officers of the Law, Magistrates		*The First Book of Kings*		
Spanish Christian soldiers	Napoleon's murderers, Spies	*The Decalogue*		
	Plotters, *Miserable insurgents*	*The Gospel*		

Table 7.2. Body Parts, etc.

De Mosquera		Friar	
heart	1	heart	39
		soul	27
eye	1	eye	19
hand	8		
ear	1	ear	8
mouth, jaws	8		
blood	5	blood	7
		head	7
		tears	7
		face	5
		arm	4
		body	2
		flesh	2
		lips	2
voice	1	voice	2
		womb, (entrañas)	2
		belly	1
		shoulders	1
		foot	1
		teeth	1
		shadow	1
		pus	1
breast	2		
neck	1		
bowels, (entrañas)	1		
TOTAL	13		155

Table 7.3. Family Members, etc.

De Mosquera		Friar	
father	2	father	29
		child	23
		elder brother	21
mother	1	mother	11
		neighbor	4
		kinsmen	3
		wife	2
son	2	son	1
		younger brother	1
grandson	2		
TOTAL	7		95

Table 7.4. Flora and Fauna

De Mosquera		Friar	
		horned serpent	5
		flower	4
		fragrance	4
		jaguar	3
field	2	cornfield	2
		tapir	1
eagle	1		
seed	1		
TOTAL	4		19

resolute, uplifting conversation. Spain, Spanish Christians, and the Regency emerge as father figures and elder brothers to inform, advise, and encourage the beloved children, their younger brothers across the ocean. Indeed, in several instances there is no way of determining whether the spoken words are theirs or are subsequent commentary added by the friar. Finally, he puts inviting words in the mouths of the Spanish Christian Indians whom he instructs in how to address and welcome their barbarous brothers into the Christian community.

The personal quality, not only in the dialogues, but in the entire text, is emphasized by the friar's use of possessive adjectives, "our" and "your" in Spanish,[1] and the corresponding possession markers in "Tzotzil." As seen in table 7.8, de Mosquera uses these adjectives very seldom.

But the friar wishes to convey strongly, inclusively to the Indians that they, from head to toe, from father to son, in their own country, are being defended and supported by their divine king, by their fathers and elder brothers, who are the members of the Regency and the wise members of the Cortes, and more generally

Table 7.5. Natural and Supernatural Phenomena

De Mosquera		Friar	
		God	23
		Heaven	8
		Virgin Mary	4
		sun(beam)	4
		fire	3
		Hell	3
		Devil	2
		morning star	2
		rain	2
		cloud	2
		day	2
		Jesus	1
		St. James	1
		Eve	1
		thunderbolt	1
		night	1
		hour	1
TOTAL	0		61

Table 7.7. Others

De Mosquera		Friar	
path		path, road	15
wall	1	wall	2
Pillars of		Pillars of	
Hercules	1	Hercules	1
		house	1
		door	1
		key	1
foundation	1		
channel	2		
toy	1	game	3
		cloak	1
		gunpowder	1
yoke	1		
		word	29
		deed, action	4
		thought	3
life	1	life	10
death	1	death	5
TOTAL	10		77
GRAND TOTAL	40		495

Table 7.6. Morality

De Mosquera		Friar	
		goodness	37
		evil	24
deceit, lie	2	deceit, lie	12
love	1	love	8
		sin	3
truth		truth	2
		hatred	2
TOTAL	4		88

Table 7.8. De Mosquera's Use of Possessive Adjectives

	Our	Your	TOTAL
King	2		2
Representatives, Cortes	1	1	2
Mother country, native land	3		3
Wealth, well-being, happiness, cause	1	5	6
Fields	1	1	2
Weapons	2		2
Attention, reflection	2		2
Others	8	8	16
TOTAL	17	18	35

by the loving Spaniards and by Spain's allies so that their poverty and difficulties will be replaced by prosperity. These efforts are being made for them, not only as human beings, but also as bearers of souls, dear to God and to Mother Mary. On four occasions our friar refers to God when, from the context, he clearly is invoking the King. Shifting from "our" to "your," the friar calls on their souls, their eyes, their ears, and their hearts to witness this marvelous event (table 7.9).

Table 7.9. The Friar's Use of Possessive Adjectives

	Our	Your	Total		Our	Your	Total
Assembly	8	2	10	Eyes	1	10	11
Wise men	8		8	Heart	4	4	8
Writers	1		1	Ears	1	5	6
Lawyers	1		1	Arms	3	1	4
Judges	1		1	Head		2	2
Fathers, brothers	8		8	Blood	2		2
Brothers	7	1	8	Shoulders	1		1
TOTAL	34	3	37	Throat	1		1
				Mouth		1	1
Kinsmen	2		2	Tears		1	1
Loving Spaniards	1		1	Flesh	1		1
Neighbors	2	2	4	TOTAL	14	24	38
Friends	2	1	3				
TOTAL	7	3	10	House	3	4	7
				Cornfield	1	1	2
King *(Rey)*	3		3	Wealth	1	1	2
King *(Señor Rey)*	13	1	14	Poverty *(pobresa, escasés)*	1	2	3
King *(Señor Dios)*	4		4	Difficulty *(pena, persecucion, trabajo)*	13	2	15
King *(amo Rey)*	2		2	Bonds *(prision)*	2		2
TOTAL	22	1	23	Sons	4	3	7
				Father	1	1	2
Nation	22	2	23	Behalf *(favor, defensa)*	3	1	4
Land	6	2	8	Power	2		2
Mother country	2	2	4	Sin	2	1	3
TOTAL	30	6	35	Words	3	2	5
				Mother Mary	2		2
Being *(persona, ser, existencia)*	5	3	8	Others	10	5	15
Souls	9	8	17	?tappears to be a grand total	174	79	253
Spirits	1		1				
Life	3	3	6				
Health	1	3	4				
TOTAL	19	17	36				

The intimate possessive adjective *tu* is never employed by de Mosquera and is used only 17 times by the friar: when addressing Ferdinand with compassion, "your heart"; when addressing Napoleon with anger and scorn, "your power," "your ignorance," "your error"; and when addressing the Indian in his dialogue with God, "your father and mother," "your tears," "your trials."

While de Mosquera employed the possessive adjective 35 times, our friar, who tripled the length of the proclamation, provided a grand total of 253!

Bring on the actors!

FERDINAND VII

The setting, as devised by de Mosquera, is Spain, "this poor Nation, weak and abandoned" (by none other than Ferdinand VII).

To Ferdinand, on whom as King of Spain de Mosquera had bestowed unquestioning loyalty, he awarded his one flight of fancy: "for our consolation we must search in the bowels of France itself, for our beloved Ferdinand, his brother and his uncle. And we must bear arms to the dark prisons where these illustrious captives lie bound, groaning and weeping." Was this really the nature of the illustrious captives' lives in the Palais de Chateaubriand?

But equally loyal to the Constitution, de Mosquera affirms that Spain will not again become "a toy" under the influence of an unscrupulous prime minister, nor will it become

> the patrimony of a King. He must govern his people as a loving father and not a despotic Monarch. For [Spain] would resist that with arms, valor and constancy. She is protected against arbitrariness and caprice by the wise Constitution that you have just seen sanctioned...the free Spaniard...knows that his religion and his system of hereditary government are exclusively assured, and he has sworn to Ferdinand VII as his King, delimiting also his line of succession.

De Mosquera reports further that "the magnanimous Emperor Alexander recognizes our unfortunate Monarch Ferdinand VII, the General and Extraordinary Cortes of the Nation, and the Constitution sanctioned by them." So much for Ferdinand!

But witness now in our friar's Tzotzil copy that "Our Lord, the King" is "overturned" by Napoleon's "whirlwind." Even so, there is hope— "...the Spanish Christians only prayed to God in their hearts." In the prayer that our friar put in their hearts they promise with magical power to

> smash the mortal doors of Hell...we will break the shackles on his feet, we will loose the lashings on his hands, even if he be in prison, even if he be in blackness in the heart of the world, our arms are outstretched...we shall break four hundred or eight hundred keys, and on our shoulders we shall take out our Our Lord, the great Ferdinand.

The Spanish Christians address their King in their prayer: "Do not weep now, Our Lord, Ferdinand. Do not constrict your heart, we beg you. We shall make compensation for your tears. We shall beg from Heaven the payment, the compensation for your suffering."

It is the "tender children of the Spanish Christians, who just cry over the imprisonment of their Father, the imprisonment of their Lord...See how they defend...the life of Our Lord, Ferdinand."

The friar provides the consoling news:

> Now Our Lord, the King's head is not confounded by trickery, and when he returns to his seat he will not act merely according to the desires of His Majesty. We shall see what he does. Like a great father he will favor his children who have been given by God unto his hands, in his shadow and in his care.

Now "the ignorant man" at his side has been replaced by "an assembly of our wise men" who will guard "the sovereignty of Our Lord, the King." "Our Lord, the King, is one...Now, at first we shall only fear, respect Our Lord, King Ferdinand brought from Heaven to our land. And afterwards we shall only fear, respect his replacement who is born of his blood." "If there be a man of authority...who...unjustly torments you, he, too, will pay for his crimes before Our Lord, the King." For our own rectitude "we thank you, father, mother, Your Majesty, and Magistrates." Thanks are owed also for having learned "to fear and respect the substitutes of God on earth."

The promise of special treatment for the Indians who, for de Mosquera, are "the favorite sons of the Motherland" is seconded on those same grounds by the friar, but first he tells them, "Your King has loved you so much." And the future is so bright!

> See, beloved children, how the sunbeams shine, manifest in the writings of Our Lord, the King, our noble Assembly...Our hearts will leap with joy...when you measure...the goodness of the mandate named the Constitution...Our Lord, the King, Our Lord, the Officers of the Law, are considering in their hearts the joy of your lives in holding, obeying, fearing, respecting what this great Assembly has told you...before long will become manifest the flowering of the land on the other side of the ocean, named Europe, in our land, named Spain, and beside us, as Our Lord, the King, has measured, prepared and awaited...Our first Assembly, the safekeeper of authority, the replacement for Our Lord, the King, named the Regency, has thus sent, has thus transcribed on paper, so that you shall open your eyes before the virtue of this word, and so that you shall look with love on the Spanish Christians, children of God, our elder brothers, our neighbors, our kinsmen.

The "second Assembly" (the Overseas Ministry) "only comes to do good works for us and for the Indians, for whomever...knows how to fear, to respect the love of God's substitute on earth." And if an Indian is approached by "some man who wishes to smear us with sin," the friar advises him to reply, "Only one God, one King, the substitute of God do I obey, I have a true father."

With Ferdinand, our friar has replaced de Mosquera's pale image of an "unfortunate Monarch" with a potentially powerful, loving "substitute of God." And though the friar has been able to remain true in his translation to the mandate of the Constitution by representing it as the writing of the King, he reveals his discomfort in his notes, where he avows that the divine right of a king must not be opposed. In his note 16 he states, "Even when the Prince is not a tender father, but a cruel tyrant and oppressor it is never lawful for the vassal to shake the yoke of obedience; the only recourse is what Samuel says: 'Shout and cry out to the Lord, begging his aid.'" And in note 15, "The Kings rule by the grace of God. Not only for political reasons, but in conscience they must be well-respected, and he who resists, resists God himself."

The task of converting this proclamation into Tzotzil surely provided our friar with "a difficult interpretation"!

NAPOLEON

Joaquín de Mosquera y Figueroa must have enjoyed characterizing Napoleon Bonaparte as "an unknown Tyrant" who "came from a foreign country to ingratiate himself deceitfully among us. He basely corrupted the sincere friendship with which we received him."

"At the head of two hundred thousand bayonets he offered us peace, decreed our banishment, and thought he was giving us happiness by presenting us with the hateful seal that marked our perpetual poverty...The immense power of this tyrant was turned in one blow against this poor Nation." But outside Cádiz,

> when the tyrant, gazing now on the Pillars of Hercules, believed that the conquest was over he met up with an impregnable wall that he has been unable to scale...The struggle continues and when the Tyrant, putting the most famous marshals at the head of his armies, strives his utmost, the brave Spaniard still more persistently avows his liberty...Know that [Spain] will never put her neck in the tyrannical yoke of Napoleon...The malign arts of Napoleon cannot distort [the fact that] the greater part of Spain [is now] almost free.

With very few words de Mosquera consigned Napoleon to the dust heap of history. But for our friar he is an ever present diabolical menace:

An evil man came from another land, an unknown murderer named
Napoleon...He entered our country like a horned serpent wearing
a false mask on his face. At first his mouth showed him to be a
good arbiter; he let only his good deeds be known. He showed his
face to be like the faces of our brothers...But the goodness of his
words was just a lie...He only wants to put an end to our lives, all
who believe in God, Our Lord. And he wants to become the Lord of
the Universe.

Napoleon "passed like a whirlwind and overturned Our Lord, the King...At
first he bound him, he trampled on his holy commandments and took him to
prison."

For our friar "cursed Napoleon" is an "evil white man," a "madman," whom
he likens to a "jaguar," a "flame of gunpowder," a "lighted fire," a "fatal thunderbolt," a "whirlwind," a "mortal tornado," and finally, "the great horned serpent in
Hell." This last image may have been drawn from Spanish Christian tradition by
the friar, who in his notes simply comments, "a horned animal, a serpent." Perhaps
it is the same creature as that depicted in the Book of Revelation 12:3: "...and
behold a great red dragon, having seven heads and ten horns, and seven crowns
upon his heads," and 12:9: "And the great dragon was cast out, that old serpent,
called the Devil, and Satan, which deceiveth the whole world: he was cast out
into the earth, and his angels were cast out with him." It is strange that the friar
only in Tzotzil, and never in his Spanish text, refers to a horned serpent, but
simply a serpent, as if he were afraid that this might sound too pagan. Or perhaps
the serpent as represented in the Garden of Eden seemed sufficiently evil. Today
in Zinacantán horned serpents are believed to have gouged out the ravines with
their horns and to cause earthquakes when they emerge from the underworld. "If
the sun or the moon die it is thought that animals with four horns will emerge to
kill the people" (Laughlin 1975:326).

The horned serpent is remembered still in the Zinacantec hamlet of Paste':

There is a rock with horns. It goes out on Wednesdays and Thurs-
days. A man went to see why the rock had horns. He saw the rock
move. There was a thunderbolt. The rock was struck. The rock's
horns were knocked off. The man was not struck by lightning. The
man was just scared. He returned home. He said that the rock was
called Xul Vo'. He said that there was a spring there [in] the
forest, [in] the woods. He said that there was a spring. "Let's go
look!" said the man. "Here is the spring." Five people came to look
at the spring [to see] if it was true that there was a spring where the
man said. They went to look at the rock where it was hit by lightning,
[where] the man and the rock were. The rock spoke. The rock talked

by itself. It said that its name was Xul Vo' Ton. There was a horned serpent at the rock. It dug up the ground. The people came to live there. They said that the rock was called Xulub Chon [Horned Serpent]. They went to pray. They celebrated Cross Day where the rock stood. The rock spoke, "Thank you for praying to me," said the rock. It hid the horned serpent. It didn't dig up the ground. It had wanted to kill all the people who lived there. The water couldn't be drunk then. The Earth Lord didn't want us to drink it. They appeased the Earth Lord. He was contented. He gave them permission. The people living there still drink the water. That's why the May celebration is never abandoned. (Laughlin 1977:155–156)

The storyteller described the serpent as having two horns and being as big as a bull.

Horned serpents have inhabited the Middle American cosmos for at least a millenium. Plumed serpent columns at the entrance to the Temple of Warriors in Chichen Itzá are each endowed with a pair of horns. Parsons notes the presence of horned serpents in the beliefs of the Mixe, Caddo, Mayo-Yaquis, and Pueblo Indians. They are known in Nahuatl as *mazacoatl* or 'deer snake.' Their association with water persists to this day among the Zapotecs, Totonacs, Achí, and Chorti (Parsons 1936:332–333; Ichon 1969:122; Shaw 1972:51–52; Fought 1972:82–85; Girard 1962:95–96). Like the Zinacantecs, the Chorti give offerings to the horned serpent on May 3rd for the Holy Cross Day well ceremonies. They consider the horned serpent to be the alter ego of the god of the earth's center, the lord of water, crowned at both ends with a pair of bejeweled golden horns, with which it plowed the riverbeds...it may be smitten by the gods for causing landslides. (Laughlin 1977:156)

Presumably our friar had no inkling of the positive power of horned serpents! The murderer Napoleon appears with promises of good deeds, but "so great is the concealment of his heart. We cannot discern immediately how much pus he has brought hidden in his soul...other mad words, other evil deeds are in his heart," for like a jaguar he wishes "to put us in his mortal jaws." But "that jaguar has grown weary before the Spanish Christians." "You wished to snuff out the fire of our land, and when but one ray of our fire flares up; the power of your eye is extinguished."

But one must remain vigilant, for "now the evil of Napoleon has leapt at us here on this side of the ocean."

MANUEL DE GODOY

Of Manuel de Godoy, de Mosquera writes a single line: "Nor will she [Spain] again become the toy of a prime minister."

Our friar is nearly as concise: "Now there is no longer stirring at the side of Our Lord, the King, an ignorant man, who merely did all that was desired by the foolishness of his heart. Now there is no one playing games in our land."

KING JOSEPH

For *Pepe Botellas,* de Mosquera does not waste a word, and our friar merely states that Napoleon's "deputy settled in the great city named Madrid."

LORD WELLINGTON

In one of his rare recourses to metaphor, de Mosquera records that "Lord Wellington, Duke of Ciudad Rodrigo, with fifty thousand allies on 22 July, 1812, has humiliated the haughty eagles of Napoleon."

More prosaically, our friar states that, "In this year that passed, on the twenty-second day of July, a great captain named Wellington came, accompanied by fifty thousand English soldiers, and these virtuous men pursued the evil murderers, undid our bindings, and exhausted Napoleon's boldness."

NAPOLEON'S ARMY

The "haughty eagles" are represented by de Mosquera more vividly than was his wont: Napoleon's "many cruel legions, aways murdering and always thirsty for Spanish blood." And yet they "have only achieved their own confusion and have carried this struggle to the final stage of desperation."

This description is repeated by our friar: "his soldiers only wanted to drink our blood, they only wanted to kill the Spanish Christians. It was begun in vain." But De Mosquera's record of "two hundred thousand bayonets" is converted by the friar into the same number of "murderers," just as "six hundred thousand men" becomes that tally of "murderers." "The evil, the madness of the murderers was nearly upon us."

THE SPANISH ARMY

De Mosquera:

> The Spaniard, enraged and possessed with a just fury, blindly prefers death, like those followers who offered themselves to their oppressor…The Spaniards were defeated a thousand times and scattered in the hills and plains so that the bulwark of Liberty seemed to have disappeared. But a hidden hillock, a miserable village [Bailén] became the refuge and gathering place where they fought once again with zest and fury. Inch by inch the Spaniards have advanced, defending the inheritance of their forebears and their liberty…And the greatest disasters [have been met] with great suffering.

In Cádiz, Napoleon's army "met up with an impregnable wall" of defense. And so, sheltered in Cádiz, the government "organized respectable armies." While the French soldiers strove their utmost, "the brave Spaniard still more persistently avows his liberty," reminding sons and grandsons of "the seven-century war sustained by our fathers."

The Spanish defense is given a far more personal, religious tone by the friar:

> These Spanish Christians do not die, they do not let fear into their hearts. You see how their soul speaks: "Even if I die, I perish, I will not let you harm My Lord, God. I do not want you to wound my father, my brother, my wife. I will not let you seize my father's land, my child's, my neighbor's, my ally's. Of this great crime I will always complain and if I die myself there are still many other Christians, there are still other Spaniards who will be born, who will mature to punish your stupidity, your error, as they are sent by God…Now you will see how God's power will help me…I fear not. My heart grows strong before the very God, the Maker, the Creator of the Universe."

The near defeat of the Spanish armies, "driven into the woods, into the fields," was reversed in "another fierce battle" when "our elder brothers gradually came to each other's aid, and they did not leave, they did not abandon the land of their fathers, their mothers in the hands of the murderers who wished to touch, who wished to take the flowery ground, the fragrant land."

And in Cádiz, Napoleon "could not climb over the great wall of Christians."

Now there are other brave Spanish Christians holding guns in their hands to chase the murderers who have come from France and sprung upon us...Blessed be those who long ago chased out other murderers who settled on our land and caused our suffering seven hundred years ago.

IGNORANT MEN

At the very beginning and the very end of the Proclamation de Mosquera addresses the plea to "those who have gone astray." On the one hand are the "seducers," and on the other, the "innocents seduced by separation."

The first are "those who claim to be your friends repeating that Spain has lost." "Those who have dazzled you, assuring you the protection of England in carrying forward separation, have deceived you...they try to obscure and confuse the admirable virtues of a heroic people."

The plotter is a man who fosters "the ills of a civil war that carries with it hatred and the vile desire for vengeance, even between those who most love each other, desolation, pillage, see who deceives you!" "At such a price [he] tries to dominate you to satiate his ambition." (De Mosquera's own brothers and brothers-in-law had become revolutionaries in Colombia.)

"Fortune [is] treacherously offered to the incautious by those ambitious fanatics who plan your separation." With their "perverse counsels" they offer peace and happiness "mixed with blood, persecution, and death." The Motherland, "deeply pained by the waywardness of some of her people," with the words of the Regency, "whose truth you cannot doubt," hopes to make sure that "you will be disabused, closing your ears to the deceitful and seductive voice of those revolutionary apostles who preach peace and happiness."

De Mosquera never makes mention of Napoleon's spies in America. That our friar feels they are a serious threat to his Indian listeners is not surprising, recalling the many Guatemalan edicts warning of their presence. He dramatizes the danger by inventing "the lying words on the lips, in the mouths of the heretical murderers," and he suggests to his listeners how to respond. All this in lengthy dialogues:

[Napoleon] sent his visitor who just came to spy, came to hurt us, came to disrupt our spirits, came to deceive the goodness of our hearts. This deceitful white man, these evil men, just say, "We come in God's goodness. We do you no harm. We just come to visit, to trade. You must love us because we have only come bringing peace. I believe in God, I love our Mother Mary, blessed Jesus, holy passion," they utter with their mouths. And in their hearts there is so much evil, so much pus, so much mortal madness, but it does not appear in their faces. Evil words are found in their souls, but dissimilar words are in their mouths. "We have come to bring peace to the world. We respect you. Come, believe our talk!" they just say. And deceit, evil, hatred, festering words are hidden in their hearts. Like a great horned serpent, only murder lies in their jaws, murder in their eyes, murder in their words, murder in their hands. And we cannot discern it, just as it was not discerned when they arrived in our brothers' land on the other side of the ocean.

Even though another insolent man may come, another evil white man, even though he come well dressed, even though he speak as other men, the substitutes of God, speak, do not believe his deceit, do not follow behind him. He has brought evil in his heart, he only wishes to spill our blood. From where will our happiness come if they only scatter death, persecution, anxiety, hardship, heresy, poverty, hunger, confiscation, murder and other poisons of the horned serpent not seen then by us? If we are carried off to Hell, if they drag upon us the eternal punishment, the reproach of God, how can the murderers give us true happiness? Do not believe their deceit, beloved children.

Remember the Captain General's warning to beware spies disguised as priests!

If you meet some man who wishes to smear us with sin, who wishes to put evil in our souls, shut your ears, run, protest before the Officers of the Law. If you meet some man who tells you, "Come, children, here is your father, here is your defender, I will relieve your suffering," reply to him in this way: "I know you, murderer, I have known you want to cast out my soul, you want to smash my land. I do not have two countries as you want. I have only one country together with the Spanish Christians, children of God, who have delivered themselves unto death for our sakes. Get out, get out, no one summoned you, do not come and upset my heart. Only one God, only one King, the substitute of God do I obey. I have a true father, I have Spanish Christian elder brothers. These are wise men, defenders, advocates who have shown me, who have manifested to me God's commandment, love for my neighbor, for my kinsfolk, and the path to Heaven. Do not come to take this eternal goodness from me. Do not come to give me the pursuit of death. What good is the world to me, all its objects, if I lose my soul?" You have heard, beloved children, how to return your words before the deceivers. And if they scold you, no matter, there is God, there is life for our souls in Heaven and for all time.

When Napoleon gazed on Cádiz, he shouted, "I will seize the city! I am the Lord of the Universe." "So was shouted the evil, so rasped the voices of the spies, the murderers."

> The Spanish Christians...turn their compassionate faces towards us
> lest we believe, lest we are diminished by the trickery, the evil deeds of
> the military men sent by the murderer, Napoleon....Now though many
> times a deceitful spy, who sells himself as a friend, tells us that it no
> longer exists, that the land of the Spanish Christians is destroyed we
> must never believe him.
>   So he does a great sin, whatever evil man does not believe in the
> virtue of our neighbors, our allies, the English people. Do not believe,
> beloved children, the evil stories, the evil talk that only wants to over-
> turn the thoughts of our souls...how can we believe the lies of the
> murderers who only want to smash our country and the kindness of the
> English people?

Again and again our friar urges his Indian listeners to disregard the words of
rebellion:

> Do not put yourselves on the path of ignorance, insolence, madness and
> other sins followed by the murderers. Indeed, close your eyes, shut
> your ears, lest someone befuddle your head with the pus, the evil of the
> great horned serpent in Hell. Do not offer yourselves to evil trickery,
> shut your ears to the murderers who only shout, "Life! Happiness!" and
> conceal death and hatred in their souls.

With words similar to de Mosquera's, our friar begins and ends the Proclamation's appeal to "all of you walking in deviousness, working evil...poor
men, white men, Indians, those who have fallen on the path of evil."
  While de Mosquera never mentioned Napoleonic spies, our friar never mentions the insurgents in the Proclamation. If he was located in northern Chiapas in
a parish near Simojovel or Huitiupán their proximity would have been especially
alarming. Their evil words are by implication the same as those of the Napoleonic
heretics and murderers. Only in his notes does he refer to "the unfortunate insurgency"[2] and "the miserable insurgents."[3]

> To carry out and not upset the laws of society and the good order
> established by Divine Providence, there must be those who order and
> those who obey; the Catholic Christian must be content with either of
> those two fortunes. Why then, miserable insurgents, do you dispute
> with blood the position that God denied you by grace? Be afraid that
> you will be given in punishment what does not suit you.[4]

This very obedience to authority, to the Regents' and Bishop's demand for a
true translation of the proclamation, required and permitted our friar to give his
loyalty to a liberal constitution and to those entrusted with its implementation.

And so, paradoxically for the friar, it is the regents who provide protection against heretics such as Voltaire and Rousseau,[5] who as we know inspired the revolt against the divine right of kings. In this same note our friar reminds us of the rebellions in Israel against Moses and Aaron. One was a revolt by Core and 250 malcontents against the religious leadership of Moses and Aaron. Core and his followers were punished by fire. The second rebellion was directed by Dathan and Abiram against the civil leadership of Moses alone. It was these insurgents (not Core's band, as the friar states) who were swallowed alive by an earthquake. Their actions, the friar claims, "broke the unity, and divided the body of Christ."

How difficult it must have been for our friar to endorse the Constitution, the Proclamation—he who insists that, "The Kings rule by the grace of God. Not only for political reasons, but in conscience they must be well-respected, and he who resists, resists God himself".[6] And, "Even when the Prince is not a tender father but a cruel tyrant and oppressor it is never lawful for the vassal to shake the yoke of obedience; the only recourse is what Samuel says: Shout and cry out to the Lord, begging his aid."[7]

BARBAROUS MEN

In the words of de Mosquera:

> But above all else what most merits the attention of the Government is the necessity of developing the missions in all the countries of America and Asia. The Government, far from needing stimulus for working enthusiastically in such a great enterprise, will have the greatest pleasure in dedicating itself energetically to the type of work that provides the inner satisfaction that beneficence causes in man.
>
> The conversion of the Indians, the settlement of savage and nomadic tribes in a social environment, is the first and principal task of the missionaries. And there is nothing more commendable in the world than to see men dedicated by their profession to making other men happy and saving them from misfortunes from the time of their birth.

It is not surprising that, as a friar, our translator expands rapturously on this topic! The members of the Regency

> do not fall asleep preparing the priests, the blessed men who come to sow good works, and in the land of the barbarous men whose souls

have not been baptized. Then you will see how they undo the bindings of their souls, how they open the shutters of their eyes, how we join them in meetings, how they themselves join us in following the path to Heaven. Then you will hear how the priests raise their voices like a great loudspeaker in the homes, in the land of the strange men, the strange heathens. Indeed you are embraced, your arms are stretched out, with your neighbors, your kinsmen. Your land is broadened, lengthened by the existence of these new Christians. Your eyes are wet with tears of joy. You shall gather together to sing with instruments, you shall scatter abroad to proclaim the goodness, the compassion of Our Lord, God. Hear how your mouth still speaks: "Come, come, whichever men have not in the past been baptized. Come, whoever once accompanied the devil, the jaguar, the tapir, the horned serpent at the foot of the rocks, in the woods. Come, leave the shadow of earth, leave the clouds in your eyes, lift your head. Come, rest in our arms. Come, let us raise the spirits of our voices before God."

After explaining to his beloved children how evil and good are balanced in this world, our friar assures them that "these words, these mercies that have come to us in writing are not false, not games." He urges

those whose heads have not been befuddled by the devil's falseness, [those who by baptism have come] under the protection of Jesus and the true Virgin, Saint Mary…those whose hearts do not grow weary from bearing hardship, persecution, poverty, prison, beatings…those who have just followed the holy path of their fathers, their mothers, the holy path of their land, the strength of their Spanish Christian elder brothers, those who have cast off the murderers' evil and embraced God's goodness [to] hear the good word, the good deeds discovered beside you, in the heart of our land.

Our friar shows himself to be well aware of the sufferings endured even by the Spanish Christian Indians!

SPANISH CHRISTIAN ELDER BROTHERS

Although Joaquín de Mosquera refers to the bravery and determination of Spanish soldiers, he refers only twice to the Spaniard as an individual and in the first instance the context is as a soldier: "the brave Spaniard still more persistently avows his liberty." Then, the free Spaniard, since now we are all [free], knows now who he is, what is his destiny, and what are his rights. He knows that his religion and his system of hereditary government are exclusively assured, and he is sworn to Ferdinand VII as his King, delimiting also his line of succession. He knows that with the annual meeting of the Cortes to which all Spaniards are equally called he cannot lack safeguards of his liberty. He knows that he must be relieved of so many taxes which overwhelmed him and [he knows] that it is you who have been the first to enjoy their easement. And he knows finally that his civil and criminal laws must protect his property, his honor and his individual liberty.

More frequently de Mosquera refers to the nation and the Motherland. The Proclamation opens with,

hear all of you the voice of your Mother Country...this poor Nation, weak and abandoned. So long enduring, she proves all too clearly her heroic determination, from which she will not retreat one step. She has opposed [Napoleon's army] with great courage....And the greatest disasters [have been met] with great suffering...This nation offers to the world the spectacle of hunger, nakedness, and desolation. In the midst of such disaster it is a marvel of constancy in suffering and its glorious name is pronounced with respect in the farthest countries of the world...She is protected against arbitrariness and caprice by the wise Constitution.

But, oh Spaniards of America and Asia, in the midst of such cruel affliction this motherland turns its eyes to you and recalls with the greatest bitterness the sad situation [in which you have been placed]...Deeply pained by the waywardness of some of her people [the motherland] has not yet lost the comforting hope of being able to attract them and shelter them benignly on her breast so that in the future, united they may be participants in the immortal glory and happiness that is being achieved at the cost of so many bloody sacrifices. No matter how many times those who claim to be your friends repeat that Spain has lost, know that she will never put her neck in the tyrannical yoke of Napoleon. Nor will she again become the toy of a prime minister, and even less the patrimony of a King.

In contrast to de Mosquera, only three times does our friar present the Spanish land in personal contact with the overseas inhabitants. At the very beginning he says, "listen everyone to the words of our great Mother Country." Then later,

Your land, your holy Mother, just measures, just thinks of your life, only wishes to show you how great is her love, how she delivers herself into the hands of murderers, how she bears persecution, exhaustion, thirst and many other hardships to nourish your souls, to ensure your health, to remedy your poverty.

And in conclusion:

> Our Spanish land still loves you, supports you. It will not punish your ignorance. It will do nothing to you. It will just embrace you in its arms if you abandon murder, hatred, rage, and if you weep for all the sins that you have committed before God, before your father, your elder brother, and other men whose blood you unjustly spilled, if you broke and trod upon God's commandments, touched their land, touched the love of their hearts, but there is still a remedy for your sins.

More commonly our friar refers to the inhabitants of Spain as fathers and brothers in his Spanish text; but in Tzotzil there is no general term for brother, so, in his Tzotzil translation, he always distinguishes the Spaniards as being "elder brothers."

> Our elder brothers suffered, they witnessed, they bore so much poverty, so much suffering...the hearts of our fathers and elder brothers, the Spanish Christians, sorely ache, and in the midst of their suffering and their laments they turn their compassionate faces towards us lest we [believe Napoleon's trickery]...Our Spanish Christian elder brothers did not for a moment lower their heads, never for a moment obeyed the mandate of the mad Napoleon. So we alone, we the children following our Spanish Christian fathers and elder brothers proceed in their footsteps, shall proceed with the strength, the deeds of the Christians forever.

With the freeing of Seville and other cities, "Now they are just embracing each other with joy, they are just celebrating before God."

While the Proclamation promised relief from taxation, alluding discreetly to the abolition of the tribute, "you are the first to enjoy their easement," our friar could not resist inserting an element frequent in Guatemalan decrees but unmentioned by de Mosquera—the donation:

> May [God] aid us, those who are pursued by the adversities of the world. This is what they are begging with tears before God, they are giving shouts for us, as many Spanish Christians as live on the other side of the ocean, and all who are living beside us. They do not discard from their hearts the hope, the coming joy of the discovery of a blessed day, a lucky hour when the night of our suffering passes and with our Spanish hearts we embrace each other, like a great father who has not been seen for years who returns home and embraces his children. "Come here, children!" he only says. "Come, feel how my soul leaps with joy. I do not wish to sleep. I do not wish to eat. Come, press against my heart. The whirlwind's cloud has passed, my poverty has passed,

my captivity. Come see the great star, portent of the holy day, portent of our lives."

So speak now the Spanish Christians, "Come, younger brothers standing there on the other side of the ocean! Come, men, women, my children! Come join us in the joy, in the health that we have bought with our suffering, with blood, with persecution, with poverty, with wounds, with tears, with mortal thirst."

And whatever man, whatever Spanish Christian helps us chase out deceit and end our suffering is also called "father." And if these great men only perform good deeds for us, why do we not help them with a little donation of money? If we be the children protected by the efforts, by the poverty, by the goodness, by the strength of our Spanish Christian fathers and elder brothers, how can we not give them two or three coins to buy their food and drink, for they are engaged, they thrive in the pursuit of the murderers who spoil our land, and who unjustly wish to kill us. Wait, wait a little, beloved children, our suffering will pass and you shall see how our land will flourish again. Now there is still suffering and in the midst of suffering you shall discover its coming, you shall feel, you shall point to the goodness of your Spanish Christian fathers' and elder brothers' hearts that pity you.

Many years have passed now since our Spanish Christian fathers' and elder brothers' hearts cried, their souls shrunk, for the time was short to prepare the goodness of your land...In just a moment your fathers, your Spanish elder brothers will wipe their eyes, for soon will be discovered the goodness of our land and the end of our hardship. This great work fills their souls with joy and is praised everywhere.

As our friar comments in his notes, "It is necessary to add this parable of the absent Son and the Father, to be able to explain the sensation of joy of which they are capable, when they stretch out their hearts and come back to see each other."[8]

THE WISE MEN

Just as with the Mother Country, de Mosquera assigns human emotions to the Government, the Regency, the Cortes, the Overseas Ministry:

Sheltered by [Cádiz], the Government has grown firm and resisted his threats. It has organized respectable armies and tightened evermore the loyal and heroic alliance with England...The liberal and beneficent ideas adopted with such maturity by the Cortes disclose a delightful and pleasing field of enviable prosperity...Consider that one of the first

concerns of the Cortes has been the creation of an Overseas Ministry
that must occupy itself exclusively with a profound study of the means
for making you happy...For a long time [the Government] has craved
[the Indians' happiness] and it weeps over the ills that they may have
suffered, but a sterile sentiment would not bring any satisfaction...[The
Ministry] may have the satisfaction and pleasure of contributing by its
measures to the increase of your wealth and prosperity.

Again, in reference to the necessity to develop missions: "The Government,
far from needing stimulus for working enthusiastically in such a great enterprise,
will have the greatest pleasure in dedicating itself energetically." de Mosquera
continues,

The Government confidently expects that [the Ministry's] creation will
be received by the residents overseas with all the signs of true appreciation that it deserves. It believes at the same time that it has given evidence
that it does not intend to please the Americans with vain hopes but that,
being aware of their needs, it is trying seriously and vigilantly to discover the means for relieving them, establishing a single channel for
receiving knowledge from all countries, no matter how distant, and for
commanding the most beneficial measures which best contribute to
their relief.

This concludes all the measures that the Overseas Ministry has under its
"concern," "attention," "keeping," "sight."

"Finally, Loyal Americans, this is not the only satisfaction that the Nation,
your Government, has to tell you this day," de Mosquera goes on, reporting the
alliance with Russia and Sweden. The Proclamation closes with, "The Regency
of the Kingdom believes it is its duty to bring this to your attention."

In only one instance does de Mosquera refer to the members of the Cortes:
"[The Government] has achieved the immortal fame of the whole Nation, so that
all its representatives could meet in the Cortes and seal the freedom of Spain with
their wise and proper decisions."

In sharp contrast is our friar's presentation, for seldom does he ascribe human
qualities to the Cortes, the Regency, and so forth, which he normally names the
"Spanish Christian Assembly," or simply the "Assembly" *[Junta]*. The following
are in de Mosquera's style:

Now this is how our great assembly speaks, seated in Cádiz. And the sovereignty of our Lord, the King, is guarded, is manifested in a second assembly named the Regency. "Let it be done!" is the command as soon as all
the good words of justice and relief have issued from the Assembly of

our wise men…Just see, hear, learn the truth of this holy word sent by God and by our Spanish Christian Assembly on the other side of the ocean…Our Spanish Christian Assembly does not wish to deceive, it is not playing games…Now the heart of our Assembly just is rent apart in the preparation of the remedy of our sufferings…now we have a second Assembly beside us that only comes to do good works for us and for the Indians…Our Assembly wishes to make payment for the strength, the goodness of those men who assisted, who held on to our land by pursuing Napoleon's evil murderers, and it wishes also to make manifest to the eyes of the deceivers and to the ears of the ignorant men who followed the murderers, that they found nothing good on Napoleon's path, on the road to death, and in the rending, the wounding of our land.

And finally,

Our first Assembly, the safekeeper of authority, the replacement for Our Lord, the King, named the Regency, has thus sent, has thus transcribed on paper, so that you shall open your eyes before the virtue of this word, and so that you shall look with love on the Spanish Christians, children of God, our elder brothers, our neighbors, our kinsfolk.

But the great preponderance of references made by our friar to the Assembly is not to the Assembly as such, but to "the wise men," the "fathers, elder brothers" of which it is composed. It is they, principally, who, in our friar's proclamation, address the Indians of America. And so the Proclamation begins with "listen everyone to the words of our great Mother Country, of our elder brothers in the Assembly." It continues,

There in the city of Cádiz the elders, the lords, the sages had assembled, and they had prepared a well-authorized assembly. They provided for and paid visits to the great English king who had offered us great aid. In this way they bore the suffering in the brave city of Cádiz…Now all the wise people are blessed because they joined together, they aided us, because they unbound our prisoners and gave us the sign of our salvation.

Now the elders are gathered, sent to Cádiz by all the towns in our land. They are simply performing justice, good deeds for us. See how from their mouths comes the truth of God's commands. See how they become the saviors and advocates of our land…Now their wisdom, the thoughts of these great men are seen. The wealth of their souls is envied in the world, and it comes spilling towards us like a shower and like the goodness of sunbeams over the whole land.

Now they just sit here on this side of the ocean, just here beside us, others of our wise men, our lawyers are assembling a second time. We

> will just see them act for the relief of our suffering. Now for the second
> time our wise leaders will meet again nearby, here at a port, in Guate-
> mala, and in other Spanish cities…Now the measure, the consideration
> of our happiness has been taken, the wise men are ready at the Christian
> meetings of the cities, just near us…Now the solution for your petitions
> is not delayed before this assembly near here.

This is a perplexing interpretation by our friar, who appears to seat the Overseas Ministry in America. There seems to be no justification for this statement, no
record of any such assembly seated in a port in America. Perhaps "the Christian
meetings of the cities, just near us" refers to the Provincial Deputations established by the Constitution, or perhaps the friar felt that the only way to convince
the Indians that this ministry indeed cared about them would be to move it across
the ocean!

After discussing the establishment of a new school system in America, our
friar comments optimistically,

> Before long the dawn shall shine on the wise men, like a great sun-
> beam in the midst of the firmament, and like light rain that comes to
> dampen the ground of our cornfields. Then you shall see how great
> men, great fathers, great Spaniards are made. Then you shall see how in
> the meeting of Christians they shine, in the meeting of sages who are in
> the universe.
>
> Only the progress of our cornfields, our trade, our markets, and
> the wealth of our homes is what our Spanish Christian fathers and elder
> brothers are envisioning, considering, preparing…So you will see that
> the hearts of our devoted Spanish Christians do not tire in the least.
> Just near here, at the entrance to the ocean, is established another As-
> sembly which I told you has just stretched the vision of their eyes. They
> do not fall asleep preparing the priests, the blessed men who come to
> sow good works.
>
> Your King has loved you so much, your Assembly of wise men,
> all their conciliatory words come first to you Indians for you are guarded
> in their souls…Many years have passed now since our Spanish Chris-
> tian fathers' and elder brothers' hearts cried, their souls shrunk, for the
> time was short to prepare the goodness of your land…In just a moment
> your fathers, your Spanish elder brothers will wipe their eyes, for soon
> will be discovered the goodness of our land and the end of our hardship.
> This great work fills their souls with joy and is praised everywhere…the
> wise men are ready at the Christian meetings of the cities, just near us.

Such a bright future was promised to the Indians, a future assured by the
great love held for them by their fathers and elder brothers before in Spain, and
now in America!

INDIANS

After promising support for the conversion of the heathen Indians, the Overseas Ministry provides new hope for Indians in de Mosquera's compelling words,

> The Indians, that beautiful portion of humankind that inhabits America, favorite sons of the Mother Country, demand precedence in the attention and scrutiny of the Government. And all its measures are designed to make them feel how aware it is of their true necessities and with what solicitude it seeks the means for their relief and happiness. For a long time it has craved [their happiness] and it weeps over the ills that they may have suffered, but a sterile sentiment would not bring any satisfaction. Their prompt relief is what can fulfill their desires and the first means for this end you now see indicated in this quick review of the concerns of the new Ministry which are independent and separate from those of the Peninsula, so that there no longer remains the suspicion, held before, that the Overseas affairs were displaced by those of the Peninsula.

For our friar the central character of the Proclamation is the Indian. It is he who must decide between good and evil, between loyalty and insurgency, between the road to Heaven and the road to Hell. Again and again, addressing his "beloved children," (a standard form of address in the Tzotzil sermons), he presents them with dialogues to rebuke the heretical murderers, to seek God's support in this cosmic struggle. It is not surprising that his longest additions to de Mosquera's text occur in the Overseas Ministry's concern for education and conversion. De Mosquera envisions the primary schools as a "better system where the first seeds of moral virtues must be implanted in the youths;" these lead to "establishments of science and letters." But for our friar it is all a question of moral rectitude, of asceticism, of overcoming the "ignorance, the ferment or poison of our being, of our flesh, that we brought long ago from the belly of our mother Eve," and inculcating fear and respect for our parents, neighbors and kinsfolk, for God, and for "the substitute of God who is on Earth." Here they learn to know "the power of God's spirit...why we bear hardships in this world...and how to be joyful and delight in the everlasting life of God."

De Mosquera's recondite statement, "The free Spaniard, since now we are all [free]," is made very clear by our friar:

> Now there is no one to tell us in his wisdom that we are not Spaniards. Once those who were born on this side of the ocean were called Indians. Now we are called Spanish Christians, beloved children...Equally, beloved children, we touch, we sniff this flowery name...Now we are free, we are Spanish Christians, we are the elders of our land.

Nevertheless, the non-Indian Spanish Christians are always referred to as "fathers, elder brothers." Our friar employs a paternalistic tone towards Indians that is not present in de Mosquera's text. The lack of a general term for brother in Tzotzil suits our friar well. In one instance, when referring particularly to Indians, he uses the term for younger brother, so exposing his sentiments.

CÁDIZ

For both de Mosquera and our friar, the city of Cádiz, the Pillars of Hercules, is like another actor in the mortal combat with Napoleon. While its final deliverance is reported chronologically at the end of the Proclamation, they cannot resist inserting its impregnability at the beginning, as well. For, indeed, without its extraordinary defense, through which it remained the last city of Spain not conquered by Napoleon, the Constitution, and this Proclamation, could not have been composed.

Locally, our friar and his Indian listeners knew that Ciudad Real was the center of "civilization," and so, it seems, he coined the Indian name for Ciudad Real, *Jobel*, "grass," (translated from the earlier Nahuatl name, Zacatlan), to mean "city"; e.g., *"jobel Madrid," "jobel Sevilla," "jobel Cadiz,"* i.e., "city of Madrid," city of Sevilla," and "city of Cádiz."

THE FUTURE

Our friar's rendition of the Proclamation is replete with endless instances of malevolent trickery, of possible future encounters with heretical murderers, and with warnings against the powers of evil, the great horned serpents. But the powers of good far outnumber the powers of evil: "good" and "goodness" are tallied at 36 while "evil" has only 24 references. If only we follow the path of Heaven and not the path of the Devil, our sins will be forgiven and our redemption assured. There is the promise of a bright future, the return of well-beloved Ferdinand to his throne. We know that Our Lord, the King, through his substitute, the Regency, has nothing but wise and compassionate plans for the Indians of America!

Our friar's text is undated. He does refer in his notes to a government edict of February 24, 1813. Presumably he completed his translation before Ferdinand's return to Spain on March 24, 1814, but there is no record of it ever having been proclaimed from the pulpit. This friar's interpretation, composed with such difficulty in a damp cell in the Province of Chiapa, his many written words, many holy flights of fancy, may never have been heard by a single Tzotzil or Tzeltal Indian!

NOTES

1. Nuestro, ntro., nuestros, ntros., nuestra, ntra., nuestras, ntras., vuestro, vtro., vuestros, vtros., vuestra, vtra., tu, tus.

2. Great Proclamation Sent by Our Lord, The King to People Living Here on This Side of The Ocean, note 9.

3. Great Proclamation Sent by Our Lord, The King to People Living Here on This Side of The Ocean, note 14.

4. Great Proclamation Sent by Our Lord, The King to People Living Here on This Side of The Ocean, note 14

5. Great Proclamation Sent by Our Lord, The King to People Living Here on This Side of The Ocean, note 7.

6. Great Proclamation Sent by Our Lord, The King to People Living Here on This Side of The Ocean, note 15.

7. Great Proclamation Sent by Our Lord, The King to People Living Here on This Side of The Ocean, note 16.

8. Great Proclamation Sent by Our Lord, The King to People Living Here on This Side of The Ocean, note 3.

8

The Return of Ferdinand VII

SPAIN: *YO EL REY*

On March 24, 1814, "The Well-Beloved" King of Spain and the Indies returns to Madrid, where he is received with great joy. On April 5, Napoleon, "The Horned Serpent," is imprisoned by the Senate of France as Louis XVIII is seated on the throne. "The exiled Emperor was not altogether wrong when he said mournfully that the disease which killed him was 'the Spanish ulcer'" (Broadley 1911:169).

For a little more than a month Ferdinand, feeling very unsure about himself in this new Spain, closets himself with his secret coterie of advisors, led by the King's former water boy, "*El Chamorro,*" or "Baldy," who heads the gossipers as they condemn "the King's enemies" to death. Alas, El Duque del Infantado is one of these despicable advisors. Another opinion is provided the King with a publication sent by 69 *Servile* deputies who urge him to annul the Constitution. This move is backed by the Church and the army. And so, on May 4, Ferdinand VII abolishes the Cortes and annuls the Constitution "as if those acts had never happened" (Salazar 1928:178). In Madrid a tablet commemorating the Constitution is dragged through the streets with the shout of "Death to the Liberals!" Squads of absolutist priests run through the streets, demanding severe punishment. That night a liberal deputy, is seized:

> Villanueva fainted and had to take a glass of water, asking that they lead him away politely because although he was unworthy he was a minister of God…So, we watched the night fall with liberals, and we woke up without them.
>
> Singing out, then, "Long live the King!" and "Death to the traitors!" the multitude went to hold the funeral of the monument to the Constitution. No sooner than it fell to the ground than was seen in its

place the sign, "Long Live Ferdinand VII," and [having] bound [the monument] with ropes an immense crowd pulled it through the streets. As it fell, some pieces broke off and have been distributed as relics and I have one that a guy stretched out to me, saying, "Take it, it is good for thunderbolts and flashes of lightning." Immediately the procession of Ferdinand VII came out, some with flags, others with dancing masqueraders. They adorned the streets and rang the bells. There was no disorder at all: It has all been celebration and bustle.[1]

Confidently sensing the public's mood, the King reestablished the monarchy with all its rights. A list of deputies guilty of "constitutionalism," i.e., heresy and treason, was drawn up and many were arrested. Ferdinand on the same day suppressed the newspapers and the theater. Ironically, or perhaps deliberately, the order for censorship was signed by Pedro de Macanaz, Captain General of Cádiz, who declared that all writings must be submitted for inspection and that actors must not be permitted to add verses "designed to spread confusing, irreligious, and licentious ideas."[2] "Plans were made for Liberty, the deity embellished by poets, to muzzle it, to manacle it, and finally—in the words of the Monarch himself—'to put liberty in a corral'" (Bentura 1971:266).

For America he adopted a policy of non-action. On August 7, 1814, he reestablished the Supreme Council of the Indies, following his "desire to restore the tranquility and happiness of my beloved vassals," but on September 18, 1815, he abolished the Council.[3]

On December 15 of the same year, sentences were meted out to two regents and 24 deputies (five from America). The sentences ranged from deportation to eight years' imprisonment. For the night of the 17th, carriages were to be readied and "in complete silence they would travel to the houses and hamlets where these individuals resided. They would be forced to dress and immediately be set on the road before dawn" (J. Villanueva 1820:500). Four prisoners were punished more severely according to a decree of January 10, 1816, whereby, "None of their friends may visit them; they are not permitted to write nor will any letter be delivered to them" (J. Villanueva 1820:504).

Lord Wellington protested these repressive acts, threatening to withhold support from England unless "Your Majesty promptly carries out the benevolent promises that you deigned to make to your subjects " (Menéndez Pidal 1968:535). But it was all to no avail.

Six years of increasing despotism, during which secret societies and conspiracies flourished, swept over Spain. On January 9, 1820, troops were sent to Cádiz to embark for America. A major in the Spanish army, Rafael de Rigo, supported by his troops, rebelled to restore the Constitution, his insubordination backed by the secret societies. The Constitution of 1812 was reestablished on March 9 and pusillanimous Ferdinand accepted, but freemasonry and atheism were now dominant. Lest the Constitution's reestablishment be forgotten, it was commemorated on ladies' fans, coffee services, and packs of playing cards (plate 24). Another three years of discontent followed, until Ferdinand once again annulled the Constitution, regaining his absolutist monarchy with the aid of the French army, while America was falling away. No one in Spain was cheering now! They were left with Francisco Goya's reminders of the past luxury of the monarchy, the horrors of the Inquisition, the wide-eyed people's confrontation with military subjection, and his "Disasters of the War."

CÁDIZ

One of the last acts of the constitutional government was the annual report by the Minister of the Overseas to the Cortes, presented on March 1: "In a discussion of the plight of the Indians, 'the miserable victims' of American discord…the minister got distracted and ended up complimenting the Guatemalan Economic Society for its efforts to expand weaving" (Anna 1983:111).

In honor of Ferdinand's imminent return, on March 15, the Cortes decreed that each deputy contribute one day's salary as a dowry for the first Indian woman in one of the dissident American provinces to marry a European Spaniard—"a pathetic earnest of liberal social attitudes" (Anna 1983:112).

A few days earlier, Mariano Robles wrote to don Ambrosio that he wanted to remain in Spain for Ferdinand's return, but he thought it might be more prudent to leave, writing, "Well, I fear a political revolution by the new system that does not have few enemies."[4] In a second missive to his bishop, written on April 22, Robles states, "It is believed or feared, although without reason, that [Ferdinand] does not want to swear to the Constitution. This fear is based [on the fact] that although the towns want the Constitution neither the nobility nor the friars want it. When asked about it, Ferdinand only replies that he desires 'the good of the nation.'"[5] Four days later, when the King and the infantry were in Valencia, Robles remarks to the Bishop that "the fears that he will neither swear to or sign the Constitution are increasing, and I fear some study and it appears to me that there will be some mutation."[6]

During these days a newspaper war had broken out between the liberal and conservative newspapers. An article in an absolutist periodical proclaimed, "'The name of Ferdinand is a magic or mysterious name for all good people,' thinking that this would restore imperial harmony" (Anna 1983:139).

The 69 conservative deputies who had petitioned the King to annul the Constitution became known as "*Los persas*," because their publication "began with the pedantic phrase: 'It was the custom of the ancient Persians'" (Alaman

1985:4;136). Many signed to assure themselves good employment; many did not sign until Ferdinand acted. Ten of the "Persians" were Americans, but none were from Central America (plate 25).

After the Constitution's annulment and the arrest of the deputies on May 4, "The Well-Beloved" became for the liberals *"Narizotas,"* "Schnozzola."

Fernando Dávila, more than a year after his election as deputy of Chiapa, and after five months at sea, arrived in Cádiz on May 27. With the annulment of the Cortes, he was advised to give a report on the needs of his province. This he did on July 8, urging the concentration in towns of the Indians scattered in the forests, and the necessity for them to be taught the Spanish language, as well as the fomenting of agricultural support, "especially for the most beautiful fruits of the Province" (López Sánchez 1962:2:864).

On September 14 Joaquín Mosquera and four others were appointed to a commission to judge the accused deputies. De Mosquera, who had signed the Constitution as President, and who, in a speech before the Congress on May 30, expressed the hope that "the King begin to govern the kingdom guided by the maxims of the Constitution, worthy of just princes and cultured nations," was deeply troubled (Bentura 1971:260). One of the accused was Joaquín Lorenzo Villanueva, a priest, church historian, poet, author of *Phoenician Ireland,* and an ardent defender of the Indians' cause. He had been seized and roughed up on the streets of Madrid. He protested bitterly, quoting from the Proclamation to the Overseas Inhabitants and asking the Duque del Infantado how it was possible that "these deputies so faithful to the national conscience...so beneficent, so jealous for the good of their country...be condemned by the Nation for having exceeded their powers?" (J. Villanueva 1820:338). Villanueva then addressed the man who had penned the proclamation, de Mosquera:

> And what greater triumph could be promised to the prisoners than to see their conduct presented for judicial examination with national representation? What would these persecuted men say but a repetition of the praises, the applauses, the blessings which they had received from the grandees and nobles of Spain, the Cortes, the authorities, the bishops, the town halls, the generals of the armies, the people, all for having carried out faithfully and legally the command of the Nation, for which calumny now imputes them to have been in excess? ...If you [deputies] acted in excess, it was an excess of vigils, of sweat, of eagerness, of zeal for the public cause, of love and loyalty. This is the only excess that the Nation recognizes in you; the excess of your powers is seen only by the eyes of envy, of fury, of imposture. Those who have such eyes are not Spaniards, they are the spurious sons of a noble and generous mother, who does not fail to recognize and will never fail to recognize the laws of gratitude. (J. Villanueva 1820:338–339)

Perhaps moved by Villanueva's plaint, de Mosquera, fully aware that if the deputies were guilty of crimes he was an accomplice to them, asked on July 7, 1815, to be relieved of his duty. He was joined in this request by his two fellow judges-elect. Three days later he explained his action to the Secretary of the Ministry of Justice. Although he had doubted from the beginning whether he should have accepted his appointment, he had done so because he had not known the sentiments of his fellow appointees, and had agreed "with the most blind resignation to carry out the sovereign wishes of His Majesty" (Bentura 1971:262). He deplored the "unjust and indecorous" manner in which the five regents had been dismissed (Bentura 1971:263). As these regents (including de Mosquera) "had sworn to deliver the command of the Spanish monarchy to His Majesty on his happy and desired return to the Throne," their dismissal constituted a just motive for "the alleged resentment and enmity" (Bentura 1971:263). Accordingly he requested that he be replaced by another minister not found in the same embarrassing circumstances.

For his services as a member of the Council of the Indies, de Mosquera was honored on June 28, 1817, by Ferdinand with the Great Cross of the Royal American Order of Isabel the Catholic. This award stirred de Mosquera to sign an energetic protest against the methods of "pacification" in America.

NEW SPAIN

While most news from Spain normally reached America three months later, the return of Ferdinand was learned of in little more than a month. There was a tremendous celebration in Mexico City on June 10. Viceroy Calleja ordered the Constitution and all bodies created by it annulled. "He who had seemed exaggeratedly constitutionalist became a furious detractor of it and established rigorous laws" (Nuñez y Domínguez 1950:227). This was just as Morelos had predicted.

Responding to the abolition of the Constitution, Morelos drafted the Constitution of Apatzingan. This has been called "the first Mexican constitution" (Stoetzer 1966:231). It duly copied five major points of the Constitution of Cádiz:

(1) The Catholic faith is the only one
(2) The separation of powers; legislative, executive, and judicial
(3) The division of Mexico into provinces, not states
(4) One House
(5) Electoral juntas

Morelos' Commander in Chief, Mariano Matamoros, had been captured and executed before a firing squad on February 3. It was not long before Morelos would meet the same fate. Don Ambrosio received news of the Constitution's abolition in Oaxaca in a letter dated June 7: "We are in a state of uproar with fiestas and illumination."[7]

But desire for a constitution died hard. Morelos' mentor, Carlos María de Bustamante, who had been a principal designer of the Constitution of Apatzingan, and who had been imprisoned in Vera Cruz from 1815 to 1820, was "perhaps the last liberal Mexican of his time who still believed it possible to consolidate a Spanish-American empire with a democratic base, to secure liberty and progress for the native" (Horcasitas 1969:272). So, when the Constitution was restored by Ferdinand in 1820, Bustamante published a proclamation in Spanish and Nahuatl, entitled, "La Malinche de la Constitución." Here he spoke out with these words, "Indians of this World...do you know what Constitution means? You do not and you will never know unless it is explained to you in your own language." He advises the Indians that if they are mistreated by their officials, "run to your judges and shout to them: 'Constitution, constitution!'" Referring to their new right to have elections, he says, "You are no longer the serfs of any lord...Your happiness rests in you, yourselves." He urges the Indians to have their children read, "so they can know of the great benefits they possess in the wise constitution" (Horcasitas 1969: 276–277).

Turning back to the abolition of the Constitution in 1814, the news arrived in Vera Cruz on June 26. The plaque honoring the Constitution was removed from the plaza by night at the governor's orders. In Tabasco there was a funeral procession for a copy of the Constitution that was buried in the niche of an obelisk, to the accompaniment of songs, dances, and fireworks.

Newspaper reports of the abolition of the Constitution, reached Mérida on July 23 and Campeche two days later. The Mérida city government refused to pay any attention and also refused to send troops to the plaza. While the Mérida government obeyed on July 28, Campeche demanded to see the decree itself. When copies came on August 8 and 16, the officials obeyed formally, but with no celebration.

Political agitation had been strong in the Yucatan in 1814, before Ferdinand's return. The decree of April 9, 1812, abolishing the work levies, reached Mérida on November 9 and was strongly supported by the liberal *Sanjuanistas,* but the absolutist priests and the governor influenced the Provincial Deputation to void it on January 3, 1814. The newspapers and the city government threatened to denounce the governor at the Cortes, so he retracted on February 16.

The day after the news of the Constitution's abolition arrived, the conservative *Rutineros* had their celebration. They destroyed the monument to the Constitution and proceeded to the house of the founder of the *Sanjuanista* group, Fr. Velásquez, pulling him out half-dressed. They spat on him, hoisted him into a ridiculous carriage, and paraded him about. The governor and the political officials

...took an ugly painting of Ferdinand to the cathedral where a thanks-giving *Te Deum* was offered. Then the portrait was returned to the courthouse with the same unction and ridiculous solemnity, and placed in the upper gallery on a sort of altar and under a canopy. Fragments of the Constitution were scattered on the ground as if they were the most fragrant rose petals that Yucatec loyalty could offer to the effigy of the monarch...the poor priest was forced to get down from the carriage, and though he did not offer any resistance, they shoved him up the courthouse steps, forcing him to kneel at the foot of the portrait so that he would repent all his errors and his pernicious principles. (Rubio Mañé 1969:146–147)

The bishop had fled to Campeche and was not present, but the deputy from Campeche to the Cortes joined the royalists in their merriment.

GUATEMALA

Don Ambrosio was informed by his Vicar General of the imprisonment of the members of the Belén Conspiracy: "Cleric Ruíz gave his declaration with much arrogance and with arguments appropriate to an Enemy."[8] Mariano Guzmán had heard that people were fleeing to Quetzaltenango and the provinces.

For the first five months of 1814, Guatemala received no news from Spain! On June 11 a report of Ferdinand's return was received. Such news merited an embrace of Governor Bustamante and his wife by Archbishop Casaus. On July 3 the Archdeacon of Guatemala informed don Ambrosio that, "They ran through all the streets, some places they gave them wine, in others they tossed them money, in others, rockets. Repeated artillery salutes in the old plaza made it all a pleasure and there was universal joy."[9]

When Archbishop Casaus heard of the abolition of the Constitution he was "filled with joy and hope, seeing democracy destroyed" (Salazar 1928:180). He compared Rousseau, Voltaire, Diderot and Montesquieu to "insects inflated with pride and vanity" (Salazar 1928:180). On August 19 Bustamante celebrated with military pomp the public reading of the royal decree of May 4 abolishing the Constitution. He was delighted to hear that deputy Larrazábal had been one of the five Americans jailed by the King after the deputy, who was known to have favored limitation of royal powers in the Constitution, condemned "the Persian Manifesto." Larrazábal was returned to Guatemala as a criminal and was enclosed by the Archbishop in the Belemite Monastery. On August 29 the city govern-ment pleaded for royal clemency for the highly respected deputy, but the pleas were unheard.

Bustamante's despotism was now under strong attack from the Provincial Deputation, five of whose seven members would not be silenced. The Governor asked the Archbishop on August 25 to intercede for him, since six of the members were priests. "Tell them not to fear me, I only want to defend myself." He quoted articles of the "extinguished constitution" (Boletín del Archivo del Gobierno 1938:3:523). But two days later the members of the Provincial Deputation, who seemed to believe that nothing had changed in Spain, accused Bustamante of failing to elect new deputies because he did not want witnesses of his crimes reaching Spain. After the election he refused to permit a *Te Deum* and refused to print the names of the new deputies—one more instance of the lack of freedom of the press in Guatemala!

The Archdeacon communicated once again with don Ambrosio, speaking of "the infernal constitution machine, the impious sect of liberalism."[10] He rejoiced over its abolition and the imprisonment of Larrazábal.

Don Ambrosio received a letter dated October 18 from another of the conservative Guatemalan clerics, the *Oidor*: "I am happy if things return to their old order, and if are ended such novelties as have been introduced to us by the cursed ideas of democracy." He congratulates himself, "Divine Providence and Our Mother Spain and these Americas" for conserving "the religion of our fathers."[11] The following day, as if in answer to the *Oidor's* prayers, the Provincial Deputation was abolished.

A year later Bustamante began to take his revenge on those who had attempted to limit his power. On August 22, 1815, he ordered all copies of Peynado's *"Instrucciones"* be submitted to him, while the government demanded that copies of this heretical book and all copies of the Constitution be removed from the archives. Portraits of the authors of the book were speedily removed from the main room of the Courthouse. The formerly prestigious authors were deprived from ever holding office again. The very same day as that of Bustamante's edict there was another plea for clemency for Larrazábal, signed by José Aycinena, but he was to languish in the Belemite Monastery until 1820. On December 22 Bustamante gave the order for all copies of the *"Instrucciones"* to be burned publicly by the town crier, since unfortunately there was no longer a public executioner. The only existing copy of the *"Instrucciones"* was discovered by Sofonías Salvatierra in the Archives of the Indies in Seville. It was peppered with Bustamante's condemnatory marginal notes that had served to aid in the imprisonment of Larrazábal.

In October, Bustamante received a decree from Ferdinand VII:

> I am unable to disavow that I am indebted to the great mercifulness of God, Our Lord, for my release from captivity, together with my very dear brother and uncle, the *Infantes* don Carlos and don Antonio. Nor can I disavow the joy that filled the hearts of my loyal, beloved

vassals, upon learning last year that we had stepped on Spanish territory on March 24. So, following my religious sentiments, I believe it
very proper to give in tribute to His Divine Majesty the most sincere
thanks for such an invaluable and unforeseen favor. Consequently I
order that a solemn *Te Deum* be sung in all the Churches of my
Kingdom...that a salvo of three cannonades be fired in the town squares,
and that in those places honored by my Royal presence there be a
general kissing of hands.[12]

Governor Bustamante, on October 10, "having received the above Royal
Decree, took it in his hands, kissed it, and placed it on his head, standing uncoifed,
and said: That he would obey it and obeyed it as if it were a letter from our King
and natural Lord, whom may God protect."[13] These instructions for the celebration of every March 24 were sent to don Ambrosio on November 13.

The royal tribute was restored on the first of December.

Once again the *Oidor* expresses his relief to don Ambrosio: "Thanks to God
for everything, because we are freed of the ruin that the deputies, philosophers, or
liberal innovators were preparing for us. They speak endlessly of Despotism, and
I believe that Spain and her Americas have never seen such tyranny and arbitrariness as during the time of the Cortes."[14]

There is no end to the royal efforts to extinguish liberal thought. In 1816 a
royal decree, dated March 22, arrived that forbade the use in schools and colleges
of books called *Catecismos Políticos*, which explained the Constitution.

There was also no end to the protest over Bustamante's nearly five-year
"reign of terror," but finally "Schnozzola," to placate the liberal merchants, ordered the Governor's dismissal in June 1817. News of his bad luck did not reach
him until November. For the next five months he kept this a secret in Guatemala,
until the day in March when his successor arrived to replace him! After he re-
signed on March 28,1818, he returned to Spain, where he was awarded high
honors. He later died, with poetic justice, in a shipwreck. His close companion
was mentioned in a report as "the exiled Archbishop Casaus" (Woodward 1990:64).

As the government continued to extract tributes from the Indians of Guatemala, unrest spread.

CHIAPA

Don Ambrosio receives news from his Vicar General, in a letter dated January 31,1814, that the citizens of Ciudad Real are disgusted with the new city
government and that the road from Veracruz to Mexico City has been cut. On
April 3 he reports that the priest in Tonalá has sent news of the presence of

insurgents once again in Niltepec and that they may advance into the province. The following day he tells of preparing for Holy Week. Then on April 5, he sends the good news that on March 25 the King's troops had entered Oaxaca and that on March 28 four to five thousand troops, joined by an army of 500, had settled in the city. The insurgents had fled Oaxaca and Tehuantepec, abandoning their cannons. Mass in the cathedral culminated with a procession bearing Ferdinand's portrait. On April 11, reminding don Ambrosio that Oaxaca has been reconquered, he adds that the roads are safe. He tells his bishop that it has been a year since he left his cathedral and that it is time to come back to his flock! On May 24 don Ambrosio returned to his cathedral.

The newly elected deputy to the Cortes, Juan Nepomuceno Fuero, reached Campeche only to hear that Ferdinand had dissolved the Cortes.

Despite their annulment, Governor Bustamante advised the Bishop to proceed with the Courts' decision of October 29, 1813, in support of deputy Mariano Robles' plea to convert the Lacandon Indians. The Guatemalan friars of the Merced or whoever seems most appropriate to the Bishop should be sent to convert "the unhappy Indians, called Lacandons, scattered in the jungles of Palenque."[15]

On October 27, as in one of his first acts upon arriving in the province, the Bishop declared the need for smallpox vaccinations, this time especially in Zinacantán. But on November 16 the priest of Comitán, Joseph Castillejos, reported that smallpox had spread from Teapa, Tabasco, to his region and that in Solosuchiapa and other towns the people had rebelled and refused to be vaccinated, resulting in the deaths of many natives.

Ferdinand VII's annulment on May 4 of the Constitution and of the Courts' decrees was conveyed to the clergy by don Ambrosio on September 13. After giving thanks for the return of the King to his throne, the Bishop spoke of His Royal Majesty's decisions as being "just and healthy...compelling the most enjoyable and punctual obedience over which I have no doubts."[16]

The new "Political and Military Governor of Las Chiapas," Juan Nepomuceno Batres, was confident of the people's loyalty to the beloved King Ferdinand: "The nearness of the Insurrection, its ardent seducers and even their arms penetrating as far as Tonalá had no more effect than to reinforce your love of the Sovereign...The scarcity of what is needed to exist, the havoc of plague produced by the infection of the air and the food, the corruption of customs, disorder, mutual suspicion and the other misfortunes they suffer or havesuf-fered shows you that war is not an isolated calamity."[17] On November 28 don Ambrosio directed the clergy to carry out the King's decree of May15, calling for a Mass to be celebrated on the day following the circular's receipt, in which Divine assistance was requested for the King in the execution of his royal duties.

In a letter dated December 11, sent from Campeche, the ex-deputy, Fernando Dávila, informed *don* Ambrosio that he had talked to the King before his departure. On his return trip he had been captured by the crew of an insurgent corsair from Cartagena. Most of the crew and passengers had been killed, but he had been spared, though he nearly starved as he was transferred to an American ship and was finally dumped in Matanzas.

During his absence, the efforts to keep the churches free of unseemly Indian customs continued. In 1815 the priest of Socoltenango complained that the Indians were performing the Dance of the Tiger in the church, as well as the Dance of the Principals: The first he characterized as having *"bastante deshonestidad,"* "plenty of immodesty."[18] Complaints from the other side came to the bishop in July, when the officials of San Bartolo declared that the minute the Mass was concluded, the priest locked the church door to prevent the officials' traditional dancing within the church walls.

On July 27, little more than a year after don Ambrosio returned to his episcopal seat, he died of apoplexy at the age of 67, leaving a gift of 2,000 pesos for his beloved Hospital de San Juan. Beneath his official portrait is inscribed, "He was very charitable and zealous towards his congregation, which he governed with skill, dexterity, and prudence."

As has been remarked, "Neither the Bishops Llano nor Estévez, respectively of Chiapas and Yucatan, participated in the events of our liberty" (Cuevas 1928: 93). And yet don Ambrosio won and retained the friendship and respect of so many individuals on both sides of the conflict, none of whom were the least reluctant to express to him their outrage over their opponents' beliefs and actions.

This episcopal correspondence has a universal atmosphere because it sweeps away Chiapanec and international horizons: the news of Independence in Spain arrives directly from the peninsula with the spots of Matías de Córdoba, one reads about the combats in the Caribbean as in the report of a victim of piratry; the distinguished friends of don Ambrosio (three successive archbishops of Guatemala, those of Oaxaca, Mexico City and Havana), confounded by the remote control attentions of His Excellency in Chiapas, they are relieved from their worries over their health or their pastoral duties, confiding in 'one of the finest prelates that the nation has.' In his absence of nearly a year the Juaninos tell him how the cook and the tortilla maker of the Hospital take food to the houses of the sick. The correspondence of the Spaniard Vicente Vives, architect of the Independence, together with Matías de Córdoba, minimizes the panic and terror sown by the insurgency in Tonalá; even Ordóñez y Aguiar, whose testimonies assert that the nuns are 'apostates,' followers of the 'ferment of insurrection,'...and [assert] the cowardice of the Intendant, [all this] demonstrates that San Cristóbal was on the point of defecting to the 'enemies,' and even the Indian peons rebelled, deserting the cathedral construction, just like the Indian servants of the bishop and the Hospital. (Aubry 1990:44–45)

Shortly after don Ambrosio's death, Mariano Robles, on October 13, seeing that the provincial government had all but disintegrated and that Governor Junquito had responded with despotic acts arousing public distress, reproached the Governor for his lack of judgment. Responding with insults, Junquito angrily suggested that Robles harbored suspicious sentiments and questioned his fidelity to the crown—a charge that was officially rejected two years later. Manuel Texedor, the French resident merchant of Ciudad Real, was brought to court once again on the charge of indebtedness. Now he asked for naturalization papers!

In 1816–1817 earthquakes put the cathedral in ruins again. After the position was vacant for three years, don Ambrosio's successor was Salvador Samartin y Cuevas, a former deputy from New Spain to the Cortes (plate 26). He had been one of the 10 American deputies to become a "Persian" and denounce the Con-stitution to the King, and so was awarded the episcopal seat of Chiapa! Never-theless he chose as his Vicar General the progressive deputy to the Cortes, Mariano Robles. One cannot help but wonder how Robles, who continued in this position for many years, felt about the royal decrees that arrived at the door of the cathedral, with orders for their publication throughout the parishes. There was the circular of August 25, 1815, directing the priests to read from their pulpits on the day following its receipt the edict of July 8 from the Holy Tribunal of the Inquisition of Mexico, and then to attach it to the accustomed place. It prohibited the possession and circulation of *Borroquia, ó la Victima de la Inquisicion*, and also renewed the prohibition of Rousseau's *Contrato Social ó principios del Derecho politico*.

Now in his eighties, Archdeacon Ramón Ordóñez y Aguiar continued indefatigably to uphold the old order. In a circular dated December 29, 1815, he instructed the priests "to make the Indians understand, as much from the pulpit as in informal conversations, the benefits that will be brought by the reestablishment of the Royal tributes, and the burdens that will be lifted from them by this [act], since [the tributes will be required from] all vassals in common."[19] On October 3, 1816, the Archdeacon declared that "On Wednesday, September 18, another cartoon showed itself, fixed to one of the Corners of the main Plaza, a furious and defamatory attack on the honest residents and particularly on the civil servants and their families, showing desires for Insurrection...they continue defaming [people] with their satires, and most obscene and lascivious paintings...to the prejudice of public tranquility, which, despite the disquiet, has been maintained in these Provinces."[20] Contravening all laws prohibiting such displays, the authors and their accomplices are hereby informed that if discovered they will be brought before the Holy Office of the Inquisition. At the foot of the proclamation is written, "No one may blot, erase or scratch this out, under pain of major Excommunication."[21]

In 1819 the bishop wrote a report citing the miserable poverty and lack of communication throughout the Province of Chiapa. He concludes with the words of his predecessor, Bishop Polanco, who wrote, in 1778, "Until now I have not seen a single Indian man or woman with shoes, but I have seen many naked...lacking the right to be people, without which no republic or religion can have permanence" (Aubry 1990:47). Two years later don Salvador was buried. With the confusion of independence, the bishop's seat remained vacant for a whole decade, while administration of the church affairs became the burden of Mariano Robles.

Six months after the bishop's death, independence was declared in Comitán by Fr. Matías de Córdoba on August 28, and seconded in Ciudad Real on September 3. De Córdoba's act inspired Guatemala, i.e., Central America, two weeks later to declare its independence despite the fierce opposition of Archbishop Casaus.

On September 14, 1824, the Free State of Chiapa, by popular vote, became a state of the Republic of Mexico. The event was celebrated in Ciudad Real with "a great orchestra," bell ringing, and a thanksgiving *Te Deum* sung in the cathedral. Two rows of artificial trees and four triumphal arches connected the courthouse to the cathedral, displaying in gold letters, "*Viva la religión. Viva la Unión. Viva la justa libertad, y nuestra federación*" (López Sánchez 1962:2:910).

The Constitution of 1812 had stirred the imagination of the Creoles of America. Its abolition, followed by the cruel and reactionary policy of Ferdinand, convinced the Creoles to rebel. The Constitution "operated as a transforming force. The fact of having lived as free citizens...[created] a new psychological structure—preventing them from becoming slaves again. That is why the constitution of Cádiz was one of the great causes of emancipation" (Alayza y Paz Soldán 1960:437). The love of liberty made independence a necessity. When the Constitution was annulled the reaction was identical throughout Latin America. The influence of the Constitution of 1812 on the Mexican Constitution "was as great or greater than the constitutional models of France and the United States" (Bonfil Batalla 1987:148).

But constitution or no constitution, the plight of the Tzotzil Mayan Indians, first of the Province of Chiapa, then of the Free State of Chiapa, and finally of the State of Chiapas remained for 500 years proof of their definition of history in the sixteenth century, "*ik'ti'*, *vokol*," "torment, suffering" (Laughlin 1988:492).

NOTES

1. El Correo Político y Mercantil de Sevilla, May 23, 1814.
2. Decree: de Macanaz, May 4, 1814.
3. Royal decree: Ferdinand VII, August 7, 1814.
4. Letter: Mariano Robles to Llano, March 11, 1814.

5. Letter: Mariano Robles to Llano, April 22, 1814.
6. Letter: Mariano Robles to Llano, April 26, 1814.
7. Letter: Ramírez to Llano, June 7, 1814.
8. Letter: Guzmán to Llano, January 31, 1814.
9. Letter: García to Llano, July 3, 1814.
10. Letter: García to Llano, September 3, 1814.
11. Letter: Berasueta to Llano, October 18, 1814.
12. Royal decree: Ferdinand VII, May 30, 1815.
13. Circular: Bustamante, November 13, 1815.
14. Letter: Berasueta to Llano, December 3, 1814.
15. Letter: Bustamante to Llano, July 5, 1814.
16. Circular: Llano, September 13, 1814
17. Batres: Undated report.
18. Letter: Priest of Socoltenango to Dávila, March, 16, 1815.
19. Circular: Ordóñez y Aguiar, December 29, 1815.
20. Decree: Ordóñez y Aguiar, October 3, 1816.
21. Decree: Ordóñez y Aguiar, October 3, 1816.

Appendix A

Linguistic Notes

Upon examining the linguistic vagaries of our priest's Tzotzil–Tzeltal translation there is one attribute employed consistently that seemed just plain wrong. In both Tzotzil and Tzeltal the first person possession marker is *j*- before a consonant, and *k*- before a vowel, while the third person possessive is *s*- before a consonant and *y*- before a vowel. But our priest combined *jk*- and *sy*- before all noun stems beginning with vowels. It was a great surprise to learn that in Huitiupán today *sy*- (but not *jk*-) is used accordingly. Also *sy*-, rather than *x*-, is used in the text and in Huitiupán today as a third person marker for transitive verb stems beginning with a vowel.

Unlike other Tzotzil dialects, but similar to Tzeltal, the phoneme *w* is employed in the text and in Huitiupán instead of *v*. Also, as in the text. and as in Tzeltal, what in most Tzotzil dialects is *vo'on, vo'otik,* for "I," "we," is in Huitiupán, *jo'on, jo'otik.* And again, *vun,* for "paper," is *jun; vo'ob,* for "five," is *jo'ob;* and *vo'lajuneb,* "fifteen," is *jo'lajuneb.*

The term for "also" in the Chamula dialect of Tzotzil and in Tzeltal is *ek,* while in Zinacantán, *uk,* but in this text, as in Huitiupán today, the term is *euk.*

Unique in this text is the term for "heart," *-oronton.* In Tzeltal and in several Tzotzil dialects, including Huitiupán, the term for heart is *-o'onton,* but in Huitiupán *-oronton* is used in joking contexts—perhaps it is an archaic form here.

A number of words such as *xambal,* "journey," *balumil,* "land," occurring in the text and limited to some Tzotzil dialects arc spoken today in Huitiupán.

Other expressions occurring in the text and frequent in Tzeltal are also found now in Huitiupán: *yo'lil,* "in the center of," *-utz'in,* "to bother," *swaj,* "his/her tortilla," *–olon,* "to rest."

The term *nix,* "indeed," is used in Huitiupán and in the Tzeltal dialect of Bachajón.

With some frequency our priest attached Tzotzil prefixes to Tzeltal roots, as in *ip'ijt,* "he jumped," and Tzeltal suffixes to Tzotzil roots, as in *sjabolteswanej,* "their compassionate…"

The possessed forms for instrument or place, *s-…-ibal,* as *stz'unijibal,* "planting place," are today in both Tzotzil and Tzeltal *s-…ob.*

The following 71 expressions in the text are in use in Tzeltal today (discounting the *sy*- prefix, and the *s*-...-*ibal*):

sbiil
atukelik
ana'ix
syo'ebal
swinajtes
jwinkileltik
xchamon
xlajon
xkikitay
sk'ajk'alel
skoltayon
batz'il
jch'ijteswanej
stenlejtik
syotzesotik
inajkaj
jtzakix
syajwalelon
xbulbun
muk'ul
stejk'abin
schajpanik
sjapuy
xlebloj
schukijibal
xach'bilix
wa'lanbilix
jwalk'untestik
bujtz'anbil
lijkesbil
ip'ijt
jk'uxubinex
ajk'ubal
unetik
oyukix

jmololtik
lajix
slajinik
mulanbil
malbilix
sna'ojibal
snopojibal
jocholotik
ch'aybilix
syabilal
autayel (Bachajón - ahtayel)
schanubtes
x'alot
stojobtesel
wokol awalbotik
sk'abuy
xach'tes
stz'unijibal
syajtay
smukojibal
smeltzanibal
slupojibal
ilbilix
stenojibal
smakojibal
ajch'em
jch'ultestik
k'anojibal
najkajik
cha'najkajuk
spak'taex
stunejibal
lajchaeb (Bachajón - lajchayeb)
sujtan

Twenty-five questionable terms, many with Tzeltal suffixes, also occur in the text:

jnoxol	wa'alex
syelob	ba'el
snak'bajel	snajkejibal
rojo	winajemix
jtzatzuben	chabibilix
wetzbil	syuch'umo'
ech	syilbajintesot
srojowil	sokpuk
sojkes	jo'ol
julobal	takibilix
p'olomal	syajtay
sjabolteswanej	sk'ajinel
swinajtes	syalan

Two terms, *ojow*, "king," and *-tzames*, "to murder," occurred in colonial Tzotzil, but are no longer known.

Our priest provides further insight in his notes, commenting on phonetics, grammar, semantics, and style.

While his alphabet does not mark glottalization, he notes the difference between glottalized and unglottalized consonants: "Emphasizing the throatiness, because saying *cog [koj]* with ease means bridge and not mask," and, referring to *chan*, "but if it is not pronounced violently it means snake in the Tzendal [Tzeltal] language." He also points out that "one omits the *i* [in *pleito*] to imitate the pronunciation of the Indians."

Regarding grammar, the priest points out past, present, and future tenses. He has but one additional comment that he repeats seven times, explaining how once the subject is presented in the plural, the plural form is dropped in immediately succeeding phrases: "And so for [the Indians] it is indifferent whether the following verbs or nouns are in the singular or plural, as long as at the beginning one discovers the person who is doing the action." When I first immersed myself in translation it was this loss of plurality in Tzotzil that was totally baffling. The priest justifies it in these terms: "for better pronunciation," "for better pronunciation and more intelligent," but clearly by "pronunciation" he means simply that it "sounds better."

He notes the use of repetition, as with *yepal*, "for greater clarity."

But the great majority of our priest's linguistic observations is devoted to semantics, so that his fellow priests will have a clearer understanding of the expressions he has chosen. He is particularly concerned with explaining metaphors and noting homonyms or what might be considered to be homonyms by those unfamiliar with glottalization: *"Xyac [xyak]* is not interpreted as give, submit or put *[syak],* rather for a phrase that explains something mistaken. In every case his commentary is valid today. Indeed, our priest has filled a void, for the Spanish loan word *pero* has totally replaced the Tzotzil and Tzeltal terms for "but," and in colonial dictionaries there is no record of the term, but here in his notes he explains that *stuc [stuk]* in addition to "only," also means "but." With this contribution to our knowledge I will close, wondering how this priest, so sensitive to Tzotzil speech, could have inserted so many Tzeltal expressions. Could it be that the mixture was really so deep in those times?

Appendix B

Proclamation of the Duque del Infantado to the Residents Overseas

Great Proclamation Sent by Our Lord, the King, to People Living Here on This Side of the Ocean (Combined texts)

Most loyal residents of America and Asia, and those of you who have gone astray along the paths of perversity, hear all of you the voice of your Mother Country.

True believers living in the other world named America, and in Asia, and all of you walking in deviousness, working evil, listen everyone to the words of our great Mother Country, of our elder brothers in the Assembly.

Now you know that more than four years ago an unknown Tyrant came from a foreign country to ingratiate himself deceitfully among us. He basely corrupted the sincere friendship with which we welcomed him.

As you know, five years have passed now since an evil man came from another land, an unknown murderer named Napoleon. He became a deceiver, he became our neighbor, our ally, and he entered our country like a horned serpent wearing a false mask on his face.
At first his mouth showed him to be a good arbiter; he let only his good deeds be known. He showed his face to be like the faces of our elder brothers. And in the end he deceived us, he harmed us, he did not return our good deeds in kind.

At the head of two hundred thousand bayonets he offered us peace, decreed our banishment, and thought he was giving us happiness by presenting us with the hateful seal that would mark our perpetual slavery.

At the head of two hundred thousand murderers, brandishing guns in their hands, he just hurled accusations at us. "See the goodness of my heart. I do not come to hurt you," had been the words of Napoleon. But the goodness of his words was just a lie. He only wants to murder us, to pillage us. He only wants to put an end to our lives, all who believe in God, Our Lord. And he wants to become the Lord of the Universe. He thought we would believe it, he thought we would be pleased with all his deceit and evil deeds against us.

During this lengthy period his many cruel legions, always murdering and always thirsting for Spanish blood, have only achieved their own confusion and have carried this struggle to the final stage of desperation until the Spaniards, enraged and possessed with a just fury, blindly prefer death, like those followers who offered themselves to their oppressor.

Five years ago his soldiers only wanted to drink our blood, they only wanted to kill the Spanish Christians. It was begun in vain, in vain he harmed us. Now his strength is exhausted, and the evil of his heart. Now, like a madman he just bites himself because he cannot snuff out the strength of the Spanish Christians. These Spanish Christians do not die, they do not let fear into their hearts. You see how their soul speaks:

> *Even if I die, I perish, I will not let you harm my Lord, God. I do not want you to wound my father, my elder brother, my wife. I will not let you seize my father's land, my child's, my neighbor's, my ally's. Of this great crime I will always complain and if I die myself there are still many other Christians, there are still other Spaniards who will be born, who will mature to punish your stupidity, your error, as they are sent by God.*

The immense power of this Tyrant was turned in one blow against this poor Nation, weak and abandoned. So long enduring, she proves all too clearly her heroic determination from which she will not retreat one step. She has opposed with great courage the more than six hundred thousand men whom he introduced through the Pyrenees. And the greatest disasters [have been met] with great suffering.

Beloved children, the wealth of this murderer Napoleon is so great, so great the concealment of his heart. We cannot discern immediately how much pus he has brought hidden in his soul. Like the flame of gunpowder, like a fatal thunderbolt, he did not wait a moment. "Let them die, let all the Christians die at one blow," he just said with his mouth. Our elder brothers suffered, they witnessed, they bore so much poverty, so much suffering. "I am here, I fear not. I am here, I will not retreat a step," just said the Spanish Christians.

> *Now you will see how God's power will help me. You, cursed Napoleon, brought with you six hundred thousand murderers from your*

*country named France. I am helpless in the face of your power. I am
here, I fear not. My heart grows strong before the very God, the Maker,
the Creator of the Universe.*

The Spaniards were defeated a thousand times and scattered in the hills and
plains so that the bulwark of Liberty seemed to have disappeared.

*My children, at first the Spanish Christians could not gather together. Many
were scattered, driven into the woods, into the fields. At first it seemed as if the
Spanish Christians, the guardians of our lives, were destroyed.*

But a hidden hillock, a miserable village [Bailén] became the refuge and
gathering place where they fought once again with zest and fury. Inch by inch
the Spaniards have advanced, defending the inheritance of their forebears and
their liberty.

*We were nearly destroyed, but in a small woods, in a small hamlet [our
soldiers] rejoined, they came to each other's aid. They began another fierce
battle, for the evil, the madness of the murderers was nearly upon us. Our elder
brothers gradually came to each other's aid, and they did not leave, they did
not abandon the land of their fathers, their mothers in the hands of the murderers who wished to touch, who wished to take the flowery ground, the joy of
our Universe.*
*The murderer Napoleon, like a jaguar, wanted to put us in his mortal jaws.
His deputy settled in the great city named Madrid. [Napoleon] passed like a
whirlwind and overturned Our Lord, the King. What could be done? At first he
bound him, he trampled on his holy commandments and took him to prison.*

And when the tyrant, gazing now on the Pillars of Hercules [Cádiz], believed
that the conquest was over,…

*Like a lighted fire, Napoleon continues to destroy everything. In the end, he
continues to take, he continues to kill, he continues to snuff out other cities,
other towns. Appearing like the two mighty pillars of Hercules was the city of
Cádiz. "I will seize the city!" said Napoleon. "Now I am the Lord of the Universe." So was shouted the evil, so rasped the voices of the spies, the murderers.*

…he met up with an impregnable wall that he has been unable to scale.

*They all wished to enter the city of Cádiz, but there at the entrance they met the
force of the Spanish Christians who became like a high wall, and there Napoleon
broke his head, there his strength was smashed, he who wished to enter to kill the*

lords of the Spanish Christians living in the city. But he could not prevail, he could not knock down, he could not climb over the great wall of Christians.

Sheltered by it, the Government has grown firm and resisted his threats. It has organized respectable armies and tightened evermore the loyal and heroic alliance with England.

There in the city of Cádiz the elders, the lords, the sages had assembled, and they had prepared a well-authorized assembly. They provided for and paid visits to the great English king who had offered us great aid. In this way they bore the suffering in the brave city of Cádiz, in this way the Spanish Christians embraced the English, in this way they celebrated, rejoiced for all time, for they supported each other, they did not let their land be seized, for their hearts were not constricted before the murderer, Napoleon, and they stood firm in the midst of the mortal tornado.

It has achieved the immortal fame of the whole Nation, so that all its representatives could meet in the Cortes and seal the freedom of Spain with their wise and proper decisions.

Now all the wise people are blessed because they joined together, they aided us, because they unbound our prisoners and gave us the sign of our salvation.

In the midst of such events the struggle continues and when the Tyrant, putting the most famous field marshals at the head of his armies, strives his utmost, the brave Spaniard still more persistently avows his liberty. And in the sad and desperate situation in which he has been placed he himself has made known the only way to acquire [his freedom]. The present generation will be followed by another, and it by another that will remind its sons and grandsons of the seven-century war sustained by our fathers. By their example Spanish blood must be avenged by the Spanish themselves, and for our consolation we must search in the bowels of France itself for our beloved Ferdinand, his brother and his uncle. And we must bear our arms to the dark prisons where these illustrious captives lie bound, groaning and weeping.

In the midst of this great work the Spanish Christians have not tired. The murderers grind their teeth in anger, but the Spanish Christians only prayed to God in their hearts. Hear how they prayed:

> *Deceiver, Napoleon, you alone wished to destroy the Spanish Christians and still the Spaniards are here. You wished to snuff out the fire of our land, and when but one ray of our fire flares up, the power of your*

eye is extinguished. You wished to destroy the people's faith, but you could not. The Spanish Christians will tear down your house, and smash the mortal doors of Hell. You do not wish to free Our Lord, Ferdinand. In vain you have stolen him, in vain you have taken him. So be it, so be it, Napoleon, we are here, we will break the shackles on his feet, we will loose the lashings of his hands, even if he be in prison, even if he be in blackness in the heart of the world, our arms are out-stretched, the power of the Spanish Christians has risen up. We shall go to your land, we shall overturn your dominion, we shall break four hundred or eight hundred keys, and on our shoulders we shall take out Our Lord, the great Ferdinand, his younger brother, and his uncle, un-justly imprisoned in the jail. We will die, our sons will travel in the uni-verse, others will be born, but they shall not forget this great work. It shall be blessed by all men still to be born, still to walk on the whole universe. Blessed be those who long ago chased out other murderers who settled on our land and caused our suffering seven hundred years ago.

Do not weep now, Our Lord, Ferdinand. Do not constrict your heart, we beg you. We shall make compensation for your tears. We shall beg from Heaven the payment, the compensation for your suffer-ing, and compensation for the blood of our fathers, our mothers, and our elder brothers, unjustly spilt by the murderers.

This nation offers to the world the spectacle of hunger, nakedness, and deso-lation. In the midst of such disaster it is a marvel of constancy in suffering...

Hunger, suffering, anxiety, poverty, death, thirst, destruction, there are no longer any other riches shown to us in the world. Even so, here we are, here are the tender children of the Spanish Christians, who just cry over the imprison-ment of their Father, the imprisonment of their Lord.

...and its glorious name is pronounced with respect in the farthest countries of the world.

The world falls silent at the sight of our suffering, it bears witness. May my eyes open before these great men. "Do not close the pupils of your eyes," is the message from the great land. "Bear witness," it says, too.

See how they endure, how these Spanish Christians bear so much suffering. See how they defend the belief in God and the life of Our Lord, Ferdinand. For this their name is blessed, is kissed, and will flourish forever. And no one will snuff it out, just as there is no one who can extinguish the radiance of the sun, the rays of the great star, portent of dawn.

But, oh Spaniards of America and Asia, in the midst of such cruel affliction this motherland turns its eyes to you and recalls with the greatest bitterness the sad situation whereby some conspiratorial ambitions have seduced your docile hearts, abusing the holiness of our sacred Religion.

Beloved children, this great conflict was begun unjustly by the murderer Napoleon in the land of our fathers, mothers, and elder brothers, the Spanish Christians. Now he has flown towards us, he has appeared above us. Now the evil of Napoleon has leapt at us here on this side of the ocean. That jaguar has grown weary before the Spanish Christians. For that reason he sent his visitor who just came to spy, came to hurt us, came to disrupt our spirits, came to deceive the goodness of our hearts.

This deceitful white man, these evil men, just say, "We come in God's goodness. We do you no harm. We just come to visit, to trade. You must love us because we have only come bringing peace. I believe in God, I love our Mother Mary, blessed Jesus, holy passion," they utter with their mouths. And in their hearts there is so much evil, so much pus, so much mortal madness, but it does not appear in their faces. Evil words are found in their souls, but dissimilar words are in their mouths. "We have come to bring peace to the world. We respect you. Come, believe our talk!" they just say. And deceit, evil, hatred, festering words are hidden in their hearts. Like a great horned serpent, only murder lies in their jaws, murder in their eyes, murder in their words, murder in their hands. And we cannot discern it, just as it was not discerned when they arrived in our brothers' land on the other side of the ocean.

Deeply pained by the waywardness of some of her people [the motherland] has not yet lost the comforting hope of being able to attract them and shelter them benignly on her breast so that in the future, united they may be participants in the immortal glory and happiness that is being achieved at the cost of so many bloody sacrifices. No matter how many times those who claim to be your friends repeat that Spain has lost, know that she will never put her neck in the tyrannical yoke of Napoleon.

So, now, the hearts of our fathers and elder brothers, the Spanish Christians, sorely ache, and in the midst of their suffering and their laments they turn their compassionate faces towards us lest we believe, lest we are diminished by the trickery, the evil deeds of the military men sent by the murderer, Napoleon.

May God lay hold of us, beloved children. May he support us beneath the cloak of the great protector, Mary of the Immaculate Conception. May he show us the road of life, the journey to Heaven. May he aid us, those who are pursued by the adversities of the world. This is what they are begging with tears before God, they are giving shouts for us, as many Spanish Christians as live on the other side of the ocean, and all who are living beside us. They do not discard from their hearts the hope, the coming joy of the discovery of a blessed day, a lucky hour

when the night of our suffering passes and with our Spanish hearts we embrace
each other, like a great father who has not been seen for years who returns home
and embraces his children. "Come here, children!" he only says. "Come, feel
how my soul leaps with joy. I do not wish to sleep. I do not wish to eat. Come,
press against my heart. The whirlwind's cloud has passed, my poverty has passed,
my captivity. Come see the great star, portent of the holy day, portent of our lives."
So speak now the Spanish Christians,

> *Come, younger brothers standing there on the other side of the ocean!*
> *Come, men, women, my children! Come join us in the joy, in the health*
> *that we have bought with our suffering, with blood, with persecution,*
> *with poverty, with wounds, with tears, with mortal thirst. Now there is*
> *no longer an evil white man, he who did not in the past respect us beside*
> *Our Lord, the King. Now, though many times a deceitful spy, who sells*
> *himself as a friend, tells us that it no longer exists, that the land of the*
> *Spanish Christians is destroyed we must never believe him.*
>
> *Our Spanish Christian elder brothers did not for a moment lower*
> *their heads, never for a moment obeyed the mandate of the mad Napo-*
> *leon. So we alone, we the children following our Spanish fathers and*
> *elder brothers proceed in their footsteps, shall proceed with the strength,*
> *the deeds of the Christians forever.*
>
> *Following this great heavenly journey our souls will not be lost,*
> *not be wounded before God and before our true defenders who have*
> *borne great suffering so that our faith, our souls, our children, our*
> *wives, and everything in our land not be lost. See how they deliver*
> *themselves to death, others have been seized in the hands of the mur-*
> *derers, others are spending their money, their wealth for us, others*
> *have gathered to write and to chase out the devil's deceit.*
>
> *Now the elders are gathered, sent to Cádiz by all the towns in our*
> *land. They are simply performing justice, good deeds for us. See how*
> *from their mouths comes the truth of God's commands. See how they*
> *become the saviors and advocates of our land.*
>
> *Listen, open your ears to the symbol of our health.*

Nor will she again become the toy of a prime minister, and even less the patrimony of a King. He must govern his people as a loving father and not a despotic
Monarch. For [Spain] would resist that with arms, valor, and constancy. She is
protected against arbitrariness and caprice by the wise Constitution that you have
just seen sanctioned. The liberal and beneficent ideas adopted with such maturity by our Cortes disclose a delightful and pleasing field of enviable prosperity.

> *Now there is no longer stirring at the side of Our Lord, the King, an*
> *ignorant man, who merely did all that was desired by the foolishness of*
> *his heart.*

Now there is no one playing games in our land. Now Our Lord, the King's head is not confounded by trickery, and when he returns to his seat he will not act merely according to the desires of His Majesty. We shall see what he does. Like a great father he will favor his children who have been given by God unto his hands, in his shadow and in his care.

Now there is only at the side of Our Lord, the King, an assembly of our wise men, lest our land be spoiled again by the falseness of a single white man, a single man. And now there are other brave Spanish Christians holding guns in their hands to chase the murderers who have come from France and assaulted us.

Now this is how our great assembly speaks, seated in Cádiz. And the sovereignty of Our Lord, the King, is guarded, is manifested in a second assembly named the Regency. "Let it be done!" is the command as soon as all the good words of justice and relief have issued from the Assembly of our wise men.

Now their wisdom, the thoughts of these great men are seen. The wealth of their souls is envied in the world, and it comes spilling towards us like a shower and like the goodness of sunbeams over the whole land.

The free Spaniard, since now we are all [free], knows now who he is, what is his destiny, and what are his rights. He knows that his religion and his system of hereditary government are exclusively assured, and he has sworn to Fernando VII as his King, delimiting also his line of succession. He knows that with the annual meeting of the Cortes to which all Spaniards are equally called he cannot lack safeguards of his liberty.

Now there is no one to tell us in his wisdom that we are not Spaniards. Once those who were born on this side of the ocean were called Indians. Now we are called Spanish Christians, beloved children, for we have but one nation, but one faith, but one law, Our Lord, the King, is one, we have but one Assembly seated at the head, at the heart of our land called Spain.

Now there is no one to rub out the exaltation, the greatness of our spirits. Now there is no one to imprison us, no one to hide from us the fragrance, the goodness of our name, blessed in the whole Universe. Now there is not a man who does not know how to guard his wealth that has issued from this holy name. Equally, beloved children, we touch, we sniff this flowery name.

Now the sacred faith of our holy Church, is guarded by our Assembly. Now there is no insolent, heretical man to come and confound the sacred laws of Our Lord, God. Now there is no one who will come to force us to be in obedience, in fear, in respect of another man who has not brought his authority on the true road, on the right hand of Our Lord, God.

Now, at first we shall only fear, respect Our Lord, King Ferdinand brought from Heaven to our land. And afterwards we shall only fear, respect his true replacement who is born of his blood. Now there is no one to imprison, to persecute one's wisdom, one's deeds, one's spirit if he but performs God's commands, and the commands of God's substitute on earth. Now we are free, we are Spanish Christians, we are the elders of our land. And if there be other evil men who unjustly harm us, there is our Assembly of wise men to aid us. And they alternate each month, each year. Now there is a surplus of our names and we are summoned to do justice, to defend our land even though once we were Indians.

He knows that he must be relieved of so many taxes which overwhelmed him and [he knows] that it is you who have been the first to enjoy their easement.

Beloved children, unscreen the pupils of your eyes! Now your tribute is ended. Equally we just pay a small request, called a "Donation," for our suffering is not yet over, and in this way we obey the fourth commandment of Our Lord, God:

> *Thou shalt fear, thou shalt respect thy father, thy mother. Thou shalt help them in their suffering, thou shalt aid them in their poverty, thou shalt give them their food and drink. Thou shalt wipe the tears from their eyes. Thou shalt not offend in word, deed, and in the thoughts of thy soul. For I am aggrieved in my heart by this great sin,*

that is what Our Lord, God, commands.

Now listen: Father is the name of that man who gave us our being, whoever serves in office, whoever is sent by God, is also called "father." Whoever shows us the road to Heaven is called "father." All the wise men who teach us the true word, the truly good deeds are called "father." Whoever is more advanced in years is called "father." And whatever man, whatever Spanish Christian helps us chase out deceit and end our suffering is also called "father." And if these great men only perform good deeds for us, why do we not help them with a little donation of money? If we be the children protected by the efforts, by the poverty, by the goodness, by the strength of our Spanish Christian fathers and elder brothers, how can we not give them two or three coins to buy their food and drink, for they are engaged, they thrive in the pursuit of the murderers who spoil our land, and who unjustly wish to kill us.

Wait, wait a little, beloved children, our suffering will pass and you shall see how our land will flourish again. Now there is still suffering and in the midst of the suffering you shall discover its coming, you shall feel, you shall point to the goodness of your Spanish Christian fathers' and elder brothers' hearts that pity you.

And he knows finally that his civil and criminal laws must protect his property, his honor and his individual liberty.

When our persecution passes you will witness your relief. All the commands and good words of our Assembly of wise men come for the sake of your health, to protect the wealth of your homes, to respect, to favor your existence. Do not lose with your sins the goodness of this word that has come from the heart of our land.

Every judge, every minister and every office holder is held by the Constitution to the strictest responsibility.

If you have no sins, there is no officer of the law to punish your person. If there be a man of authority, an elder who unjustly harms you, unjustly torments you, he, too, will pay for his crimes before Our Lord, the King, for he did not obey the conciliatory words of our Assembly of wise men.

Read [the constitution] with reflection and care so that it will provide you enlightenment capable of quieting the complaints that you have presented here, in the knowledge that so many ills that have been suffered will soon be remedied.

Just gradually consider in your souls these words of our fathers, our elder brothers written on paper. And then you will see with your eyes how soon will end our poverty, our sufferings, our laments that have long been in our hearts.

Consider that one of the first concerns of the Cortes has been the creation of an Overseas Ministry that must occupy itself exclusively with a profound study of the means for making you happy. By casting just a quick glance at its attributes you will conjure up the picture of your future fortune, doubtless happier than that which has been treacherously offered to the incautious by those ambitious fanatics who plan your separation.

Direct your ears, direct your pupils to the goodness of this reasoning. Now they just sit here on this side of the ocean, just here beside us, others of our wise men, our lawyers are assembling a second time. We will just see them act for the relief of our suffering. Now all the goodness, the favors prepared for us cannot be discerned right away, but it is not far off, the goodness of the day given to us to measure, to see, to touch the fragrance of our souls, the flowering of our land. So, in the beginning of this year you saw the great fiesta for the proclamation of the parchment, the mandate of our land, called the "Constitution."
Consider, beloved children, Napoleon's trickery does not work the same. "I favor you, I relieve your suffering, I support you," he just says, yet other mad words, other evil deeds are in his heart.

Do not put yourselves on the path of ignorance, insolence, madness and other sins followed by the murderers. Indeed, close your eyes, shut your ears, lest someone befuddle your head with the pus, the evil of the great horned serpent in Hell. Just see, hear, learn the truth of this holy word sent by God and by our Spanish Christian Assembly on the other side of the ocean.

The political and economic Government of the Provinces of America in general will be inspected by this Ministry, which will take charge of public education as the first object of its concern. This is the foundation of man's happiness in society, and the Government, recognizing its importance, believes it to be its first concern to protect, increase and convert the primary schools into a better system where the first seeds of moral virtues must be implanted in the youths. The secondary schools, the universities, academies and other establishments of science and letters will reveal a luminous field where those talents will be developed and fertilized that received the first lessons and maxims in childhood. All its efforts will be directed to the promotion of those seminaries of science where the Americans, cultivating their admirable talents, will shine among the wise men of the other nations.

Now for the second time our wise leaders will meet again nearby, here at a port, in Guatemala, and in other Spanish cities. First they are just going to serve, watch over or labor on behalf of the education of our children.

The youngsters, our children who learn from books in good schools, know the power of God's spirit, know about this great eternity or passage of time that we hear about with our ears. They know that their soul is set in their body. They know the grandeur of their being, the grandeur of their blessed name. They know, too, why we bear hardships in this world, why tears, the water of our eyes, flow in weeping, and they know how to be joyful and delight still in the everlasting life of God.

They know, too, why we must fear, respect our parents, neighbors, kinfolk and they know why we must esteem and love them as God commands.

The apprentices in good schools know why we are together in this world, why we should not take the devil's path, why we should not wound ourselves like jaguars, why the magistrates punish and admonish us, not only to rectify our actions, but also the thoughts of our souls.

Ignorance, the ferment or poison of our being, of our flesh, that we brought long ago from the belly of our mother Eve, does not enjoy repression, injunctions. Still more shall come, beloved children. At the end of the world there that will be a great day when we shall talk, shall speak with our souls,

We thank you, great God. You are blessed in all your works, because you reproved my flesh in my labors, you straightened my path in the universe. We thank you, father, mother, Your Magesty, and Magistrates. May God repay you, wise Spanish Christian elder brothers. May our divine Mother Mary call you or bring you forth for this life where we are seated in the presence of the Maker, creator of the universe. May he have mercy on you while on your gloomy trails, faced with tricks of the devil, on the path to your cornfield, in the dreams of your eyes, because you baptized me, because you taught me to fear and respect God and to fear and respect the substitute of God who is on Earth. We thank you because you expanded the spirit of our eyes, because you set right my thoughts, my words, my deeds, when once I was bound up in my body, and because you showed me the fragrant path, the heavenly path forever.

That is how your souls shall speak, beloved children, when you depart from this world, and that is why all our wise lawyers are meeting now.

Now your eyes cannot discern or discover all the goodness that has been planned in their hearts. Before long you shall see, shall feel, shall hear and touch the prosperity, the joy of another nation.

Soon you shall see good teachers in the schools planting in your children's hearts all the good deeds ordered by God. Now you have just seen the boys playing games, but in just a moment our travails in the persecution of the murderers shall pass. Before long the dawn shall shine on the wise men, like a great sunbeam in the midst of the firmament, and like light rain that comes to dampen the ground of our cornfields. Then you shall see how great men, great fathers, great Spaniards are made. Then you shall see how in the meeting of Christians they shine, in the meeting of the sages who are in the universe.

Agriculture, trade and industry in all its branches, since they constitute the wealth and prosperity of a country, demand the Government's attention. The patriotic societies that have been established and those that will be established in the principal cities with the object of improving the knowledge of the products of each country, their planting and cultivation, the cotton mills that are so abundant in the Americas, the leather and tanning trade, flax, hemp, and silk, sugar, cacao and coffee, and so many other beautiful fruits that your fertile fields can produce, all are under the keeping of this Ministry so that, instructed through its channels, it may have the satisfaction and pleasure of contributing by its measures to the increase of your wealth and prosperity. Roads, bridges, canals, channels, lakes and everything that can facilitate trade between the provinces and peoples will be its particular concern.

Only the progress of our cornfields, our trade, our markets, and the wealth of our homes is what our Spanish Christian fathers and elder brothers are envisioning, considering, preparing.

The meetings in the towns planned now by us will just reckon, will just consider in their hearts how we can discover the hiding place of the gold metal, the silver metal in the center of the world, how your poverty and your bereavement can be ended, can be remedied, what they will do to support you and your children, what they will do to fill your homes, your land, with much cattle, many horses, many pigs, many chickens, much cotton, silk, sugar, cacao and everything that will provide your wealth and your health. Neither do our assemblymen forget in their hearts the construction of your homes, the improvement of the roads to our towns, the discovery and widening of the springs of clear water and all the other good works prepared for and witnessed by us.

Mining, this exclusive part of the Americas, hospitals, poor houses, hospices, and as many establishments as there are and can possibly be built to alleviate the people, reduce idleness and begging, are other such useful and worthwhile objects which the General and Extraordinary Cortes have had in sight, as a necessary consequence of your wise Constitution, so that you will be provided with a mountain of goods. If you know how to take advantage of them you will found upon them your perpetual happiness, which will be transmitted to your grandsons so that they will always bless the rich and fertile inheritance that has been left to them by their fathers.

Now, in only a moment, men's laziness, drowsiness will end. In only a moment you will see erected the houses of refuge for the helpless, sick people. Indeed that is how the sufferings of our land will end.

Before long good teachers will come to show you the word of God, writing on paper, weaving of cloth, forging of metal, carpentry, masonry and other works which will produce the wealth of your homes and the health of your children.

But above all else what most merits the attention of the Government is the necessity of developing the missions in all the countries of America and Asia. The Government, far from needing stimulus for working enthusiastically in such a great enterprise, will have the greatest pleasure in dedicating itself energetically to a type of work that provides the inner satisfaction that beneficence causes in man.

So you will see that the hearts of our devoted Spanish Christians do not tire in the least. Just near here, at the entrance to the ocean, is established another Assembly which I told you has just stretched the vision of their eyes. They do not fall asleep preparing the priests, the blessed men who come to sow good works,…

The conversion of the Indians, the settlement of savage and nomadic tribes in a social environment, is the first and principal task of the missionaries. And there is nothing more commendable in the world than to see men dedicated by their profession to making other men happy and saving them from misfortunes from the time of their birth.

...and in the land of barbarous men whose souls have not been baptized. Then you will see how they undo the bindings of their souls, how they open the shutters of their eyes, how we join them in meetings, how they themselves join us in following the path to Heaven. Then you will hear how the priests raise their voices like a great loudspeaker in the homes, in the land of the strange men, the strange heathens. Indeed you are embraced, your arms are stretched out, with your neighbors, your kinfolk. Your land is broadened, lengthened by the existence of these new Christians. Your eyes are wet with tears of joy. You shall gather together to sing with instruments, you shall scatter abroad to proclaim the goodness, the compassion of Our Lord, God.
Hear how your mouth still speaks:

> *Come, come, whichever men have not in the past been baptized. Come, whoever once accompanied the devil, the jaguar, the tapir, the horned serpent at the foot of the rocks, in the woods. Come, leave the shadow of earth, leave the clouds in your eyes, lift your head. Come, rest in our arms. Come, let us raise the spirits of our voices before God. Come, let us also bless the goodness of our Spanish Christian Assembly.*

There is indeed no other goodness, no other credible word that stands, that can rise up beside, before these worthy deeds, so great they are spoken of everywhere.
Beloved children, there are evil deeds, there are lying words on the lips, in the mouths of the heretical murderers, but now you cannot think in your hearts that perhaps the Spanish Christians are only playing tricks. It is not so, beloved children. Everywhere there is evil, but there is also good; there is trickery, but there are also true words; there is killing, but there is protection; there is false writing, but there is true writing; there are wounds, but there are also remedies; there is persecution, but there is support; there are muttering words, but there are peaceful words; there are ignorant men, but there are wise men; there are heretics, but there is also true faith in God.
Consider, beloved children, our Spanish Christian land did not lose for one moment the commands of God that issued from the lips, the mouth of the holy Apostle, James: If we have sins like sinful men, there are also Christian laments in our souls. And these words, these mercies that have come to us in writing are not false, not games. They are born, they have issued forth from the hearts of your fathers, your elder brothers, Officers of the Law, the Spanish Christians. Hear how the truth of their souls speaks:

Beloved children, elder brothers, Indians, those who hold themselves in the power of God, those sheltered in the womb of our land, those whose heads have not been befuddled by the devil's falseness, and who have received holy water on their foreheads, the holy sign, the holy mark, the symbol of life under the protection of Jesus and the true Virgin, Saint Mary. Hear, I shall tell you two, three times, Spanish Christian Indians, those whose hearts do not grow weary from bearing hardship, persecution, poverty, prison, beatings. Hear, those who have just followed the holy path of their fathers, their mothers, the holy path of their land, the strength of their Spanish Christian elder brothers, those who have cast off the murderers' evil and embraced God's goodness, hear the good words, the good deeds discovered beside you, in the heart of our land.

Finally, the Indians, that beautiful portion of mankind that inhabits America, favorite sons of the Motherland, demand precedence in the attention and scrutiny of the Government. And all its measures are designed to make them feel how aware it is of their true necessities and with what solicitude it seeks the means for their relief and happiness.

Your King has loved you so much, your Assembly of wise men, all their conciliatory words come first to you Indians for you are guarded in their souls. Your land, your holy Mother, just measures, just thinks of your life, only wishes to show you how great is her love, how she delivers herself into the hands of murderers, how she bears persecution, exhaustion, thirst and many other hardships to nourish your souls, to ensure your health, to remedy your poverty.

For a long time it has craved [their happiness] and it weeps over the ills that they may have suffered, but a sterile sentiment would not bring any satisfaction. Their prompt relief is what can fulfill their desires and the first means for this end you now see indicated in this quick review of the concerns of the new Ministry, which are independent and separate from those of the Peninsula, so that there no longer remains the suspicion, held before, that the Overseas affairs were displaced by those of the Peninsula.

Many years have passed now since our Spanish Christian fathers' and elder brothers' hearts cried, their souls shrunk, for the time was short to prepare the goodness of your land. Now the time is not short. In just a moment your fathers, your Spanish elder brothers will wipe their eyes, for soon will be discovered the goodness of our land and the end of our hardship. This great work fills their souls with joy and is praised everywhere. Now the measure, the consideration of our happiness has been taken, the wise men are ready at the Christian meetings of the cities, just near us. Now we cannot say as in the past that the settlement of our disputes, the hearing of our complaints is too far away at the end of the ocean. Now the solution for your petitions is not delayed before this assembly near here.

The brilliant perspective that the Government offers you, loyal Americans and inhabitants of those Kingdoms and Islands, in bringing to your notice the concerns of the new Ministry will demand your attention if you meditate on what extension they are capable of, and if you note the liberality of the ideas adopted as the principles and foundation of our Constitution. There is nothing in man's public and domestic life which could contribute to his happiness that is not included in the attentions of this Ministry. The Government confidently expects that its creation will be received by the residents overseas with all the signs of true appreciation that it deserves.

See, beloved children, how the sunbeams shine, manifest in the writings of Our Lord, the King, our noble Assembly. You have heard all that our wise men residing in Cádiz went to do, and all that those of the second Assembly have come to do residing near here, on this side, at the entrance of the ocean.

Your hearts will leap with joy, the hearing of your ears will rejoice when you measure, when you consider in your souls the greatness, the goodness of these words and the goodness of the mandate named the Constitution, shouted in the proclamation, and at the fiesta that passed in our town. Everything your soul, your life desires, all the mercy, the goodness you could discover, now you can desire on the earth, all is written in the book of the Constitution and in the hearts of the Spanish Christian assemblies that will reside again here beside us.

Our Lord, the King, Our Lord, the Officers of the Law, are considering in their hearts the joy of your lives in holding, obeying, fearing, respecting what this great Assembly has told you. Indeed, the other Assembly, named the Regency, that has guarded the substitute for the power of Our Lord, the King, awaits the love of your hearts for our land.

[The Government] believes at the same time that it has given evidence that it does not intend to please the Americans with vain hopes but that, being aware of their needs, it is trying seriously and vigilantly to discover the means for relieving them, establishing a single channel for receiving knowledge from all countries, no matter how distant, and for commanding the most beneficial measures which best contribute to their relief.

Our Spanish Christian Assembly does not wish to deceive, it is not playing games, and the hope of so many children shall not be lost, shall not be extinguished, for it rests on these true words of justice.

Now, the heart of our Assembly just is rent apart in the preparation of the remedy of our sufferings. Even though the first great Assembly established in the city of Cádiz is far away, now we have a second Assembly beside us that only comes to do good works for us and for the Indians, for whomever guards God's laws and knows how to fear, to respect the love of God's substitute on earth.

In this way it wishes to compensate to its utmost the firm loyalty of some, and to make known to others, whether they be seducers or innocents seduced by separation, that only by remaining united to this Country can they enjoy the peace and happiness that they will never acquire by following the perverse counsels of those who offer [peace and happiness] mixed with blood, persecution, and death. True independence will be enjoyed by he who joins forces with our glorious troops. Peace, liberty, and happiness will be enjoyed by he who, together with us, swears to and obeys the wise Constitution that our representatives have just given us. You who unfortunately have experienced the ills of a civil war that carry with it hatred and the vile desire for vengeance, even between those who most love each other, desolation, pillage, see who deceives you! Is it he who at such a price tries to dominate you to satiate his ambition, or [is it] Spain, your mother, who in the midst of her affliction works to your benefit, studies the means to make you happy, invites you with peace, and offers you the ultimate sacrifice for your happiness?

Our Assembly wishes to make payment for the strength, the goodness of those men who assisted, who held on to our land by pursuing Napoleon's evil murderers, and it wishes also to make manifest to the eyes of the deceivers and to the ears of the ignorant men who followed the murderers, that they found nothing good on Napoleon's path, on the road to death, and in the rending, the wounding of our land.

Even though another insolent man may come, another evil white man, even though he come well dressed, even though he speak as other men, the substitutes of God, speak, do not believe his deceit, do not follow behind him. He has brought evil in his heart, he only wishes to spill our blood. From where will our happiness come if they only scatter death, persecution, anxiety, hardship, heresy, poverty, hunger, confiscation, murder and other poisons of the horned serpent not seen then by us? If we are carried off to Hell, if they drag upon us the eternal punishment, the reproach of God, how can the murderers give us true happiness? Do not believe their deceit, beloved children.

If you meet some man who wishes to smear us with sin, who wishes to put evil in our souls, shut your ears, run, protest before the Officers of the Law. If you meet some man who tells you, "Come, children, here is your father, here is your defender, I will relieve your suffering," reply to him in this way:

I know you, murderer, I have known you want to cast out my soul, you want to smash my land. I do not have two countries as you want. I have

only one country together with the Spanish Christians, children of God,
who have delivered themselves unto death for our sakes. Get out, get
out, no one summoned you, do not come and upset my heart. Only one
God, one King, the substitute of God, do I obey. I have a true father, I
have Spanish Christian elder brothers. These are wise men, defenders,
advocates who have shown me, who have manifested to me God's
commandment, love for my neighbor, for my kinfolk, and the path to
Heaven. Do not come to take this eternal goodness from me. Do not
come to give me the pursuit of death. What good is the world to me, all
its objects, if I lose my soul?

You have heard, beloved children, how to return your words before the
deceivers. And if they scold you, no matter; there is God, there is life for our souls
in Heaven and for all time.

Those who have dazzled you, assuring you the protection of England in
carrying forward separation, have deceived you. But he who is honorable and has
a true idea of the glory of a great people must view with indignation that in this
way they try to obscure and confuse the admirable virtues of a heroic people, to
whom the Spanish nation owes so much for its defense, and because of whose
integrity spares no sacrifice, pouring its own blood so that [Spain] may achieve
her freedom. You must understand that England, far from protecting your misconduct, has manifested with the greatest clarity and sincerity that to consent to the
separation of any, even the smallest part of the territory [of Spain), is not compatible with the alliance that has been contracted with Spain by such sacred and
close bonds.

The land of the English people took pity on us, too. They are defending us
during our persecution. Even if there be some evil man who tells us that the
English are tormenting us, that they are like murderers, do not believe this
slanderous talk, beloved children. The English love our country, they have deliv-
ered themselves unto death, to suffering for us, like the Spanish Christians.

[England] has identified her cause with ours, and the fields of Salamanca
have just given us the most recent proof of this truth. They will be eternal witnesses in history that Lord Wellington, Duke of Ciudad Rodrigo, with fifty
thousand allies on the 22nd of July, 1812, has humiliated the haughty eagles of
Napoleon. The enemies of the alliance of Spain and England with Portugal, try as
they may, will not obscure the brilliant successes of this happy day.

The English and the Spanish Christians respect each other, equally they
support each other, and they engage in a single defense. In this year that passed,
on the twenty-second day of July, a great captain named Wellington came, ac-

companied by fifty thousand English soldiers, and these virtuous men pursued the evil murderers, undid our bindings, and exhausted Napoleon's boldness. If very truly the goodness of this deed is brought to light in the world, if the English rejoice in the defense of our souls, and if they have delivered themselves unto death, to rescue us, how can we believe the lies of the murderers who only want to sunder our country and the kindness of the English people?

The sweet echoes of liberty that resound in Madrid since the 12th of August, the joyous canticles of Cádiz, besieged for thirty months and now without enemies facing them since the 25th of the same month, the raptures of delight with which the inhabitants of Seville surrendered on the 27th, and the greater part of Spain almost free,…

Hear now another word, the city named Madrid bore great hardship until the twelfth day of August in the year that passed. The city of Cádiz was pursued, besieged by the murderers for thirty months until the twenty-fifth day of August. The city named Seville and other cities in our land witnessed the end of our suffering on the twenty-seventh day of August in the year just passed. Now they are just embracing each other with joy, they are just celebrating before God, for they have watched the end of the tornado, the destruction of the murderers who left in shameful flight.

…are facts that the malign arts of Napoleon cannot distort. Nor can Spain do less than manifest forever the gratitude it owes to the pledge with which England fights for [Spanish] liberty. It would be unpardonably rash, after we see our fields drenched with the precious blood of our victorious allies, to allow even the remotest suspicion that the repeated protests of not protecting the insurrection of the Americans are insincere.

The evil, the madness, the deceit of the murderers cannot be erased from paper. They cannot cause to be lost from the world's knowledge this great deed, this defense carried out by the Spanish Christians, the English, and another good land named Portugal. Our country prays to God for these virtuous defenders of ours, and it would be wrong ever to snuff from our hearts this virtuous deed and the strength of our English allies who have spilled their blood for our lives. So he does a great sin, whatever evil man does not believe in the virtue of our neighbors, our allies, the English people. Do not believe, beloved children, the evil stories, the evil talk that only wants to overturn the thoughts of our souls.

Finally, Loyal Americans, this is not the only satisfaction that the Nation, your Government, has to tell you this day. It has just received officially not only the news of peace between Russia, Sweden and England, but also [news] of the alliance of that [first] great Power with Spain. And the magnanimous Emperor Alexander recognizes our unfortunate Monarch Fernando VII, the General and Extraordinary Cortes of the Nation, and the Constitution sanctioned by them. This action of the finest politics offers agreeable hopes in the various and diverse effects that such a happy and fortunate event, in which this Government has taken such a part, must produce among us and in all Europe.

Now there are other countries in the world named Russia and Sweden that have joined in our defense. And the great lord named Alexander loves Our Lord, King Ferdinand. He knows and praises our wise men, our assemblies and all the just words commanded in the document of the Constitution of which I have told you. So, in one blow, the joy of our hopes cannot be lost. Before long our pursuers will retreat. In just a moment the face of the world will turn, the face of our suffering, and before long will become manifest the flowering of the land on the other side of the ocean, named Europe, in our land, named Spain, and beside us, as Our Lord, the King, has measured, prepared and awaited.

The Regency of the Kingdom believes it is its duty to bring this to your attention so that, having these facts in view, whose truth you cannot doubt, you will be disabused, closing your ears to the deceitful and seductive voice of those revolutionary apostles who preach peace and happiness.

Our first Assembly, the safekeeper of authority, of the replacement for Our Lord, the King, named the Regency, has this sent, has this transcribed on paper, so that you shall open your eyes before the virtue of this word, and so that you shall look with love on the Spanish Christians, children of God, our elder brothers, our neighbors, our kinfolk. Do not offer yourselves to evil trickery, shut your ears to the murderers who only shout, "Life! Happiness!" and conceal death and hatred in their souls.

Those of you who have gone astray return to the breast of your Country that knows how to recompense with interest your humble repentance.

Ah, poor men, white men, Indians, those who have fallen on the path of evil, come back, come into the womb, into the heart of your Assembly, your Mother, your land.
Our Spanish land still loves you, supports you. It will not punish your ignorance. It will do nothing to you. It will just embrace you in its arms if you abandon murder, hatred, rage, and if you weep for all the sins that you have committed before God, before your father, your elder brother, and other men whose blood you unjustly spilled, if you broke and trod upon God's commandments, touched their land, touched the love of their hearts, but there is still a

remedy for your sins. Come, do not wound your soul forever. Let them flow, let your tears issue forth. Do not wager, do not grow insolent with the strength of the Creator, the Maker of the World.

—Cádiz, 30 August, 1812.—EL DUQUE DEL INFANTADO, President.

Beloved children, this blessed book is written in the city of Cádiz, on the thirtieth day of August, in this year named 1812. Its truth is made manifest by the hand of the first Governor of our Assembly, the Regency. His name or title is Duque del Infantado. President.

Appendix C

Proclama del Duque del Infantado a los habitantes de ultramar

(De Mosquera y Figueroa's version)

Fidelísimos habitantes de América y Asia, y vosotros los que extraviados habéis seguido las sendas de la perversidad: oid todos la voz de vuestra Madre Patria. Ya sabéis que hace más de cuatro años que de una región extraña vino un desconocido Tirano, que introduciéndose dolosamente entre nosotros corrompió vilmente a la sincera amistad con que lo recibimos: al frente de doscientos mil bayonetas nos ofreció la paz, publicó el decreto de nuestra prescripción, y creyó darnos la felicidad presentándonos el sello abominable con que se había de marcar nuestra perpetua esclavitud. En todo este dilatado tiempo sus sanguinarias y numcrosas legiones, siempre matando y siempre sedientas de la sangre española, no han sacado más fruto que su propio confusión, y haber llevado esta lucha al último grado de desesperación, en que el Español, rabioso y poseído de una justa furia, prefiere ciego su muerte como haya de darla antes a un satélite de su opresor. El inmenso poder de este Tirano convertido de un golpe contra esta Nación pobre, débil y abandonada, y por tanto tiempo resistido, prueba demasiado claramente su heróica resolución, de la que ni un paso retrocederá. A más de seiscientos mil hombres que ha introducido por los Pirineos ha opuesto valor grande, y a las mayores desgracias mayor sufrimiento. Derrotados los Españoles mil veces, y dispersos por los montes y llanuras, y parecía haber desaparecido el baluarte de la Libertad; mas un montecillo escondido, una aldea despreciable era el asilo y punto de reunión donde se volvía a pelear con entusiasmo y encarnizamiento: palmo a palmo ha ido el Español defendiendo la heredad de sus padres y su libertad; y cuando el tirano, viendo ya las Columnas de Hércules, creyó acabada la conquista, se encontró con un muro inespugnable, que no ha podido escalar, y que sirviendo de abrigo al Gobierno se ha consolidado éste, ha hecho frente a sus amenazas, ha organizado respetables ejércitos, y estrechada más y más la fiel y heróica alianza de la Inglaterra, ha conseguido la gloria inmortal de que la

Nación entera, con todos sus representantes, se reuniésen en Cortes, y sellasen con sus sabias y acertadas decisiones la libertad española.

En medio de tantos sucesos sigue la lucha, y cuando el Tirano, poniendo a la cabeza de sus ejércitos los mariscales más famosos, hace los mayores esfuerzos, el valiente Español con más empeño jura su libertad; y en la triste y desesperada situación en que le han puesto, él mismo se ha señalado el único medio de conceguirla: a la generación presente se seguirá otra, y a esta una nueva, que recordará a sus hijos y nietos la guerra de siete siglos que sostuvieron nuestros padres: a su ejemplo ha de quedar vengada la sangre de los Españoles por los Españoles mismos, y hasta en las entrañas de la misma Francia hemos de buscar para nuestro consuelo a nuestro amado Fernando, su hermano y tio y a las carceles oscuras donde gimen amarrados y derraman sus lágrimas nuestros ilustres prisioneros hemos de llevar nuestras armas. La hambre, la desnudez, y la desolación es el espectáculo que ofrece al mundo esta Nación, que en medio de tantos desastres asombra por su constancia en el padecer, y su nombre camina con gloria y es pronunciado con respeto en los países mas remotos del orbe.

Pero ¡Oh, Españoles de América y Asia! En medio de tan cruel aflicción esta madre patria convierte sus ojos hacia vosotros y no puede recordar sin la mayor amargura la triste situación en que os han puesto algunos intrigantes ambiciones, que han seducido vuestro dócil corazón, abusando de la santidad de nuestra sagrada Religión: poseída del más intenso dolor por el extravio de algunos pueblos, no pierde aun la consoladora esperanza de poder atraerlos y abrigarlos benignamente en su seno, para que a un tiempo, y unidos, sean partícipes de la gloria inmortal y de la felicidad que a costa de tantos sacrificios de sangre se labra por más veces que os repitan los que se venden por vuestros amigos que ya la España pereció: sabed que jamás rendirá su cuello al yugo tirano de Napoleón. Tampoco volverá a ser el juguete de un valido ni menos el patrimonio de un Rey, que más habrá de gobernar como padre amoroso de sus pueblos, que como Monarca despótico. Con las armas, el valor y la constancia resistiría a aquel; con la sabia Constitución que acabais de ver sancionada está a cubierto de la arbitrariedad y del capricho. Las ideas liberales y benéficas adoptadas con tanta madurez por nuestras Cortes abren un delicioso y ameno campo de envidiable prosperidad. El Español libre, supuesto que ya lo somos todos, sabe ya quien es, cual es su dignidad, y cuales son sus derechos; sabe que tiene asegurada exclusivamente su religión y sus sistemas de gobierno hereditario, y ha jurado a FERNANDO VII por su Rey, demarcando también la linea de su sucesión; sabe que no ha de faltarle el antemural de su libertad con la reunión anual de las Cortes, a que todos los Españoles son igualmente llamados; sabe que ha de ser aliviado de tantas contribuciones con que se le abrumaba, y cuyo alivio habéis sido vosotros los primeros a disfrutarlo; y sabe en fin que sus leyes civiles y criminales le han de asegurar su hacienda, su honor y su libertad individual. Todo Juez, todo ministro y todo empleado está sujeto por la Constitución a la más estrecha responsabilidad: leedla con reflexión y detenidamente, que os ministrará luces capaces de acallar las quejas que hasta aquí habéis producido con el consuelo del próximo remedio de tantos males sufridos. Fijad vuestra reflección en que una de las primeras atenciones de las Cortes ha sido la creación de un Ministerio de Ultramar, que exclusivamente se ha de emplear en el profundo estudio de los medios de haceros felices: con sólo echar una simple ojeada sobre sus atribuciones, concebiréis la idea más lisonjera, y en su bosquejo veréis trazado el cuadro de vuestra futura suerte, más feliz sin duda que la que con engaño han ofrecido a los incautos esos frenéticos ambiciosos que proyectan vuestra separación.

El gobierno político y económico de las Provincias de América en general será de la inspeccíon de este Ministerio, que como primer objeto de su atribución abrazará la educación pública. Esta es la base de la felicidad del hombre en sociedad, y el Gobierno, conociendo su importancia, cree ser de su primera atención proteger, aumentar y reducir a mejor sistema las escuelas de primeras letras, donde se han de plantar en los jóvenes las primeras semillas de las virtudes morales. Los colegios, las universidades, academias y demás establecimientos de ciencias y bellas letras abrirán un luminoso campo, donde se desarollaran y comenzaran a fecundar los talentos que recibieron las primeras lecciones y máximas de la puerilidad. Todo su conato será procurar el fomento de esos seminarios de las ciencias, donde los Americanos, cultivando sus admirables talentos, brillaran en medio de los sabios de las demas naciones.

La agricultura, el comercio y la industria en todos sus ramos, como que en ellos consiste la riqueza y prosperidad de un país, llaman toda la atención del Gobierno: las sociedades patrióticas establecidas, y las que se establecerán en las principales ciudades con el objeto de ir mejorando los conocimientos de las producciones de cada país, su plantación y cultivo, las fábricas de algodones, de que tanto abundan las Americas, el comercio de cueros y su curtido; el lino, el cañamo y la seda; el azucar, el cacao y café, y cuantos otros frutos preciosos puedan producir vuestras fértiles campiñas, todo está a cargo de este Ministerio, para que instruído por su conducto, tenga la satisfacción y el placer de contribuir con sus medidas al aumento de vuestra riqueza y prosperidad: los caminos, puentes, canales, acequías, lagunas y cuanto pueda facilitar el mutuo comercio de las provincias y pueblos entre sí, será todo de su particular atribución.

La minería, esta parte exclusiva de las Americas, los hospitales, casa de misericordia, hospicios, y cuanto establecimiento haya y sea posible edificar para aliviar a los pueblos, alejar la holgazanería y la mendicidad, son otros tantos objetos útiles y benéficos que han tenido a la vista las Cortes Generales y Extraordinarias, como consecuencia forsosa de su sabia Constitución, para proporcionaros un cúmulo de bienes, que si sabéis aprovecharlos vincularéis en ellos vuestra perpetua felicidad, que transmitida a vuestros nietos, bendeciran siempre la herencia tan rica y fecunda que les dejaron sus padres.

Pero sobre todo lo que más atención merece al Gobierno es la necesidad del fomento de las misiones en todos los países de América y Asia. Lejos de necesitar el Gobierno estímulos para trabajar con afan en tan grande empresa, tendrá la mayor complacencia en dedicarse con empeño a una clase de trabajo que le ha de proporcionar la interior satisfacción que causa en el hombre la beneficencia. La conversión de indios, y reducción de tribus salvajes y errantes a la vida social, es el primero y principal instituto de los misioneros, y nada hay en el mundo mas recomendable que ver a unos hombres dedicados por profesión a hacer felices, y sacar de las desgracias a otros hombres desde su nacimiento.

En fin, los Indios, esa preciosa porción de hombres que habita la América, hijos predilectos de la Madre Patria, llaman con preferencia todo la atención y esmero del Gobierno, y todas sus medidas se dirigen a hacerles sentir lo penetrado que se halla de sus verdaderas necesidades, y con cuanta solicitud, desea los medios de su alivio y felicidad. Mucho tiempo hace que suspira por ella, y llora los males que puedan haber sufrido; pero un estéril sentimiento no le atraería ninguna satisfacción: su pronto remedio es lo que podrá completar sus deseos, y las primeras medidas a este fin ya las véis indicadas en el lijero bosquejo de las atribuciones de el nuevo Ministerio, que como independientes y separadas del de la Peninsula, no queda ni aún el recelo que se tenía antes de que los negocios de Ultramar eran postergados a los de la península.

La brillante perspectiva que os ofrece el Gobierno, fieles Americanos y habitantes de esos Reinos e Islas al haceros presentes las atribuciones del nuevo Ministerio, llamaran vuestra atención si meditáis de cuanta extensión son capaces, y si atendéis a la liberalidad de ideas adoptadas por principios y fundamento de nuestra Constitución. No hay en la vida pública y doméstica del hombre cosa que contribuya de alguna manera a su felicidad, que no se halle comprendida en las atenciones de este Ministerio. El Gobierno se promete que será recibida su creación con todas las muestras que se merece de un verdadero aprecio de todos los habitantes de Ultramar. Cree al mismo tiempo haber dado una prueba de que no intenta lisongear con vanas esperanzas a los Americanos, sino que penetrado de sus necesidades, trata seriamente y se desvela en buscar los medios de remediarlas, estableciendo un conducto exclusivo por donde le vengan los conocimientos de todos los países, por remotos que estén y dictar las más benéficas providencias, y que más contribuyan a su remedio. Así quiere compensar del modo posible la lealtad firme de unos, y hacer conocer a otros, sean seductores o inocentes seducidos con la separación, que sólo manteniéndose unidos a esta Patria es el único modo de disfrutar la paz y la felicidad que jamás lograran siguiendo los perversos consejos de los que la ofrecen mezclada con sangre, persecución y muerte. La verdadera independencia la gozará aquel que reuna sus esfuersos con nuestras gloriosas armas: la paz, la libertad y la felicidad las disfrutará el que con nosotros jure y obedezca la sabia Constitución que nos acaban de dar nuestros representantes. Vosotros que por desgracia habéis experimentado los males de una guerra civil, que lleva consigo el odio y el vil deseo de la venganza, aun entre los que mas se aman, la desolación, el saqueo, ved quien os engaña, ¿si el qué a tanta costa por saciar su ambición intenta dominaros, o la España vuestra Madre, qué en medio de su aflicción trabaja en vuestro beneficio, estudia el modo de haceros bien, os convida con la paz, y os ofrece el último sacrificio por vuestra felicidad?

Los que os han alucinado asegurándoos la protección de Inglaterra para llevar adelante el proyecto de la separación, os han engañado; pero el que tenga honor y una verdadera idea de la gloria de un gran pueblo, ha de mirar con indignación que así se quiera obscurecer y confundir las admirables virtudes de un pueblo heróico, a quien tanto debe la Nación española, en cuya defensa, y por cuya integridad no perdona sacrificio vertiendo su propia sangre, para que consiga su libertad. La Inglaterra habéis de entender que lejos de proteger vuestros estravíos, ha manifestado con la mayor claridad y sinceridad que no es compatible la alianza, que con vinculos tan sagrados y estrechos ha contraido con la España, el consentir la separación de ninguna, ni aun de la más pequeña parte de su territorio. Su causa la ha identificado con la nuestra, y los campos de Salamanca acaban de darnos la prueba más reciente de esta verdad, de que serán en la Historia eternos testigos el Lord Wellington, Duque de Ciudad-Rodrigo, que con cincuenta mil aliados el 22 de julio de 1812 ha humillado las sobervias águilas de Napoleón. No obscureceran por más que lo pretendan los enemigos de la alianza de España y de Inglaterra con Portugal los sucesos brillantes de este día feliz: los ccos dulces de la libertad que resuenan en Madrid desde el 12 de Agosto los cánticos de alegría de Cádiz, treinta meses sitiada, y ya sin enemigos a su frente desde el 25 del mismo: los transportes de regocijo a que se entregaron los habitantes de Sevilla el 27, y la mayor parte de la España casi libre, son hechos que no alcanzarán a desfigurar las malignas artes de Napoleón; ni la España podrá menos que manifestar para siempre su agradecimiento por deberlos al empeño con que la Inglaterra pelea por su libertad: así seria imperdonable temeridad, despues que vemos nuestros campos regados con la preciosa sangre de nuestros victoriosos aliados, dar lugar aun a la más remota sospecha de que no sean sinceras las repetidas protestas de no proteger la insurrección de los Americanos.

Finalmente, Fieles Americanos, no es esta sola satisfacción con la que cuenta en día la Nación y su Gobierno que os habla. Acaba éste de recibir de oficio, no sólo la noticia de la paz de la Rusia, y Suecia con la Inglaterra, sino también la de la alianza de aquella gran Potencia con la España; y el magnánimo Emperador Alejandro reconoce a nuestro desgraciado Monarca FERNANDO VII, a las Cortes Generales y Extraordinarias de la Nacíon y a la Constitución sancionada por éstas. Este golpe de la más fina política ofrece las lisonjeras esperanzas de la variación y diversos aspectos que debe producir entre nosotros y en toda la Europa, tan feliz y afortunado suceso, en que ha tenido tanta parte este Gobierno.

La Regencia del Reino cree de su deber hacéroslo así presente, para que teniendo a la vista estos hechos, de cuya verdad no podréis dudar os desengañéis cerrando vuestros oidos a la engañosa y seductora voz de esos revolucionarios apóstoles que os predican paz y felicidad. Volved los extraviados al seno de vuestra Patria, que ella sabrá recompensar con usura vuestro humilde arrepentimiento —Cádiz 30 de Agosto de 1812.—EL DUQUE DEL INFANTADO, Presidente.

Grande Grito Mandado Viene por
Nuestro Señor Rey hacia los Hombres   *Vivientes ó que Viven*
Aquí al Lado   *del Mar ó Grande Hondura* (Friar's version)

Sotzil

MANUSCRITO
en
Lengua Sotzil
sin nombre del Autor, encontrado en la Parroquia
de Comitán (Chiapas), de los PP. Predicadores.

mandado copiar fielmente por el Ilmo. Sr. Dr. Don
Francisco Orozco y Jiménez, Obispo de Chiapas.
1906.
****

Note. *This transcript, together with two others,*
the large and important Sotzil Dictionary, and the
Soque sermons, was presented by Orozco y Jiménez to Dr. Nicolás León,
who later sold them to Paul
Wilkinson, from whose (second) sale I bought them.
The Bishop's palace was completely looted by
the Carranza-Alvarado forces, the brutal leader
of which I later encountered as Governor in Oaxaca
when I passed through there in 1918. After the
looting above, i.e. in the Spring of 1915, my agent,
F.J. Smith, was given leave to enter the former library
and "help himself." He reported "nothing left."

William Gates

    Fué tan dificil la traduccion de la siguiente Proclama, *que por imitar la solidés de su espiritu, indispensablemente se perdió el expresivo laconismo y elegancia de su letra.*

Las cláusulas substituidas, las notas, frases y rodeos se toman como suplementos de un escaso idioma para manifestar de algun modo el magestuoso concepto Nacional, sin confusion ó mexcla de alguna menos segura interpretación.

Permita el cielo que esta pequeña fibra del estado contribuya en su tanto al todo de aquel católico y augusto cuerpo, cuya vida respiran siempre los ingeridos sarmientos de su frondosa vid, por que transportados de una gloria, que ni la mensura el tiempo ni sorbe la eternidad, jamás se dividan del apreciable nectar de aquel tronco.

Grande grito mandado viene por nuestro Señor Rey hacia los hombres vivientes, ó que viven aquí al lado del mar ó grande hondura.

Buenos creyentes vivientes en el otro mundo su nombre América y Asia, y vosotros todos los que estan en torcidos pasos, en dañosa obra: oid todos juntos la palabra de nuestra Madre grande Nacion, reunion de nuestros hermanos.

Ya sabeis pasan hoy cinco años que vino de otra distinta region un mal hombre, un desconocido matador Napoleon se llama; se hizo engañador; se hizo nuestro proximo, nuestro allegado, y viniendo entró en nuestra Nacion como serpiente que trae puesta una engañosa máscara en el rostro.

En el principio solamente manifestó en su boca buena composicion ó razonamiento de palabra que lo dió en audiencia la bondad de sus obras solamente manifestó en rostro como semblante de nuestros hermanos, y despues nos engañó, nos lastimó, nos aborreció, nada bien correspondió á la bondad de nuestras obras en su favor.

Ante veinte y cinco jiquipiles de matadores, que agarran fusil en la mano, embarrador á palabra no más, nos dijo: mirad la bondad de mi corazon; no he venido á herirlos, dice solamente; la palabra de Napoleon, y esta bondad de palabra es mentira solamente; solo quiere matar, arrebatar, solamente quiere acabar nuestra existencia, toda la fé de nuestro Señor ó Amo Dios, y quiere hacerse Rey opresor ó amarrador del universo. Supuso que habiamos de creer. Supuso que por bueno habiamos de pensar toda su falsedad, malas ó dañosas obras hacia nosotros.

Cinco años ahora que los soldados suyos solamente quieren acabar á los cristianos Españoles; solamente quieren beber nuestra sangre. De valde ó injustamente comenzó: injustamente, no mas, nos aborreció. Ahora se canzó su fuerza, y la malicia de su corazón; ahora así como loco hombre, unicamente se muerde asi mismo, porque no puede borrar la fortaleza de los cristianos Españoles. Este cristiano Español no se acaba, no pone miedo en su corazón, oid de que modo habla en su espiritu:

> Aunque me muera, me acabe, no dejo ó permito qe. ofendais á mi
> amo Dios, no consiento qe. arrebateis la nacion de mi Padre, no quiero

que lastimeis á mi Padre, hermano, muger, hijo, próximo, allegado. Por este grande pecado, me enfadaré eternamente, y si me acabo yo, hay todavia otra multitud de cristianos: hay todavia otros españoles: todavia nacen: todavia criandose vienen para que reprendan tu error, tu ignorancia, asi como mandado viene por Dios.

Hijos amados: es muy alta la riqueza de este matador Napoleón: alta la ocultacion de su corazon: no se descubre á la hora por nosotros cuanta es la cantidad de podre que trae escondida en su espíritu. Asi como el fuego de la pólvora, como rayo matador, no dió un poco de hora. Que se acabe, que se acabe en un solo golpe todos los cristianos, dice solamente en su boca. Pobres de nuestros hermanos, que vieron, que cargaron tanto desamparo, tanto trabajo: aqui estoy no temo: aqui estoy: ya no se revuelvo mi paso, dice solamente el cristiano español:

> Ahora vereis como me ayuda el poder de Dios. Acompañado traes malvado Napoleon seis cientos mil matadores venidos de tu nacion Francia se nombra: consternado estoy ante tu poder, aqui estoy, yo no temo, ya se fortalece mi corazón ante el verdadero Dios, Hacedor criador del Universo.

Hijos mios: al principio no se podian juntar los cristianos españoles: se desparramaron muchas veces: empujados hácia los montes, hácia las llanuras. Pareció al principio acabador ya los cristianos españoles, los guardianes de nuestras vidas

Por poco no nos acabamos; pero en un pequeño monte en una pequeña aldea, alli fueron segunda vez á juntarse: allí se ayudaron, y comenzaron de nuevo otro esforzado, fuerte ó valiente pleito prq. no venga sobre nosotros su malicia, su locura ó rabia de los matadores. Despacio solamente se ayudaron nuestros hermanos, y no dejó no dejó la Nacion ó heredad de sus padres en las manos de los matadores que quisieron tocar, quisieron arrebatar al floreciente suelo, la alegría del Universo·

El matador Napoleon, asi como grande tigre, quiso meternos en su mortal boca se sentó su substituto en la gran ciudad Madrid se llama: asi como viento a-rrasador trastornó á nuestro amo ó Sor. Rey: con injusticia ó debalde solamente lo amarró al principio: piso sus benditos preceptos, y llamando lo llevó á la cárcel.

Asi como encendido fuego ya acaba Napoleon todas las cosas: despues ya arrebata, ya mata ya borra otras ciudades, otros pueblos divisando vino el camino, y las dos grandes columnas de Hércules se llaman como demostraciones de la ciudad de Cadiz. Ya agarré esta gran tierra dice Napoleon, ahora yo soy su dueño ó poderoso del Universo, asi grita su malicia: asi charla la boca de la espia y matadores.

Quisieron entrar todos en Cadiz, gran ciudad, pero alli en la entrada encontraron la fortaleza de los cristianos españoles que estaban sentados dentro la ciudad, pero ya no puede él derribar, no puede escalar subiendo sobre la gran muralla de los cristianos.

Alli dentro la ciudad de Cadiz se juntaron los principales, las Autoridades, los sabios, y prepararon una buena autorizada Junta, se cuidaron, acompañaron por visita doméstica ó por doméstico al grande Rey Inglés q. hizo buena defensa por nosotros ó hacia nosotros. Asi cargaron ó sufrieron la pena en la valiente ciudad de Cadiz: asi se abrazaron los cristianos españoles con los Ingleses: asi recibieron alegria, contento en la ida de la eternidad ó eternamente por que sostuvieron ó agarraron, por que no dejaron arrebatar su Nacion, por que no oprimieron sus corazones en la presencia del matador Napoleon, y que fuertemente se pararon en medio de una mortal tormenta ó huracán.

Ahora son benditos todos los ciudadanos sabios por que se reunieron, por que nos ayudaron, por que desataron nuestra prision ó amarramto., y nos dieron el indicio de nuestra vida ó salud.

En medio de esta grande obra, aun no se cansan los cristianos españoles: los matadores ya remuelen sus dientes en cólera ó malicia, pero los cristianos españoles, hablan solo á su Dios en su espiritu ó interior: Oid como hablan:

Engañador ó astuto Napoleon: tu quisisteis acabar al cristiano español y aqui todavia hay español: quisisteis apagar el fuego ó luz de ntra. nacion y cuando resplandece ó vibra un solo rayo de ntra. luz ó ardor ya se apaga la pupila ó espiritu de tus ojos: quieres exterminar la crecncia ó fé del cristianismo; mas no podeis: los cristianos españoles romperán vuestra casa, y quebrantar asi la mortal puerta del infierno: ¿No quereis soltar á nuestro Rey, amo ó Señor Fernando, injustamente no más lo ha robado, injustamente no más lo reteneis? Dejad, dejad Napoleon, aqui estamos: nosotros quebrarémos el fierro de sus pies y desatarémos la amarradura de sus manos: aunque esté en la carcel, aunque esté en el osbcuro [*sic*] corazon ó centro de la tierra, ya están ensanchados nuestros brazos, ya está parada ó dispuesta la fortaleza de los cristianos españoles: irémos á tu nacion, trastornarémos tu poder: quebrantarémos cuatro cientos ú ocho cientos llaves, y sacarémos en nuestros hombros á nuestro Rey grande Fernando, sus hermanos y su tio, injustamte. no mas aprisionados por ti en la carcel. Nos acabarémos: transitarán en el universo nuestros hijos: naciendo vendrán otros; mas no se perderá su alma esta grande obra, bendita llamada por todos los hombres que naciendo vendrán, que vendrán todavia á prisa: todo el universo. Serán benditos tambien todos los qe. hechan fuera de nuestras casas al matador Napoleon, asi como son benditos aquellos que persiguieron antiguamente á otros matadores, que se sentaron en nuestra Nacion, y nos dieron trabajos setecientos años.

Ahora no lloreis ó Rey Fernando: no oprimais tu corazón: nosotros pedirémos, sacarémos la substitucion de tus lágrimas: pediremos al cielo la paga, el resarcimiento de tus trabajos, y la sustitucion de la sangre de nuestros padres y hermanos, injustamente derramada por los matadores.

Hambre, pena, ancia, pobreza, muerte, sed, destruccion, no hay ya otra cosa ú otra riqueza nuestra manifestada por nosotros en el universo: aunque sea asi solamente, aqui estamos: aqui estan los tiernos hijos cristianos españoles, que solo lloran la prision de su Padre, la prision de su Rey.

Silencio dice solamente el universo al mirar ntros. trabajos: mirad dice solamente, que se abran mis ojos ante estos grandes hombres: no cerreis la pupila de vuestros ojos dice la palabra del grande universo: mirad vuelve á decir: mirad como carga: como sufre tanta pena este cristiano español: mirad como defiende la creencia de Dios y la vida ó la salud de ntro. Rey Fernando: por eso es bendito: por eso es fragrante reflorece, su nombre eternamente, y no hay quien lo borre, asi como no hay quien apague el resplandor del sol, el resplandor de la grande estrella precursora del dia, de la blanca luz.

Amados hijos: esta grande contienda, injustamente no más es principiada por el matador Napoleon en la nacion de nuestros padres y hermanos cristianos españoles: ahora voló viniendo, se descubrió viniendo sobre nosotros: ahora brincó viniendo la malicia de Napoleon de esta banda del mar. Se canzo aquel tigre ante el acatamiento de los cristianos españoles por eso envió su casero ó amigo que injustamente no más vino de espía: vino á dañarnos: vino á lastimarnos: vino á pertubar, á trastornar nuestros espiritus vino a engañar la bondad de nuestros corazones.

Este falso hombre blanco: estos maliciosos hombres, venimos por la bondad de Dios dicen no más: nada os hacemos: venimos no más á pasear, á contratar, nos habeis de amar; por que venimos solamente á compadecernos ó como compasivos. Creo en Dios, quiero á nuestra Madre Maria: bendito Jesus: bendita pasion, sale, ó pronuncian no más en sus bocas; mas á dentro de sus corazones tienen, ó hay mucha malicia, mucha podre, mucha locura ó rabia mortal; mas nó se descubre sobre ellos. Maliciosa palabra hallen sus espiritus, y otra palabra hay en sus bocas. Nosotros venimos á compadecernos del mundo: nosotros os estimaremos: vengan, crean nuestras palabras, dicen, no más, y engaño, malicia, aborecimiento, emponzonada palabra, solamente esconden en sus corazones: asi como grande serpiente, muerte solamente hay ó tienen en la boca: muerte en los ojos: muerte en la palabra: muerte en sus manos, y no se devisa en la hora por nosotros, asi como no se divisó venir cuando llegaron en la Nacion de nuestros hermanos, que está hacia la otra banda del mar. Por eso ahora muy mucho duele el corazon de nuestros padres y hermanos cristianos españoles, y en medio de sus trabajos y lágrimas, ya vuelven ó convierten sus compasivos rostros hacia nosotros, por que no sea que vayamos á creer, vayamos á caer en el engaño, en la dañosa obra de los militares hombres enviados por el matador Napoleon.

Que Dios nos agarre óh amados hijos: que nos proteja bajo su manto la sagrada, grande Patrona Maria de Concepcion: que nos de á mirar el camino de la vida, los pasos del cielo: que nos ayude á todos los que estamos perseguidos por la perdicion del mundo asi ante el acatamiento de Dios ya lo piden con llanto: gritos ya dan, ó hacen por nosotros todos cuantos españoles cristianos viven hacia aquella banda del mar, y todos cuantos viven junto á nuestras personas. No se pierde de sus corazones la esperanza, la venida de la alegria en descubrir un bendito dia: una bienhechora hora en que pase la noche de nuestros trabajos, y se abrazen nuestros españoles corazones, asi como un grande padre, que no visto antiguamente, llega á su casa, se abraza con sus hijos; venid tiernos hijos dice no más; venid: palpad, tocad como salta mi alma en alegria: no quiero dormir: no quiero comer: venid estrechaos con mi corazon, ya pasó la nube del torbellino: ya pasó mi pobreza, mi prision: venid á ver la magna estrella precursora del sagrado dia, pronóstico ó indicio de nuestra vida.

Asi hablan ahora los cristianos españoles:

Venid hermanos menores, que estais parados en esa banda del mar: venid hombres, mugeres, mis tiernos hijos: vengan acompañenme en alegria, en la salud que compramos con trabajo, con sangre, en aborrecimiento, con orfandad, con heridas, con llanto, con mortal sequedad, ó sed de boca. Ahora ya no hay un malicioso hombre blanco, que no nos estimó antiguamente al lado de nuestro amo Rey: ahora, aunque nos diga muchas veces un engañador emisario, ó espia que se vende por nuestro amigo, no hay ya, se acabó la Nacion de los cristianos españoles, no lo hemos de creer absolutamente.

Nuestros hermanos cristianos españoles, ni un momento bajarán sus cabezas: ni un instante creerán eternamente los preceptos del loco Napoleon: por eso nosotros que somos hijos, hacia tras la espalda de nuestros padres y hermanos españoles pisando irémos la señal de sus pies, siguiendo irémos la fortaleza, la obra de los cristianos eternamente.

En seguir este gran camino del cielo no se pierde, no se lastiman nuestras almas ante Dios y ante los verdaderos defensores nuestros, cargan alta pena por que no se pierde, no se lastiman nuestras almas, nuestros hijos, nuestras mugeres y todas la cosas que hallen nuestra tierra. Mirad como se entregan á la muerte: otros estan agarrados con las manos de los matadores: otros ya acaban su dinero, su riqueza por nosotros: otros se han juntado para escribir y para perseguir el engaño del demonio.

Ahora estan juntos los principales enviados á Cadiz por todas las ciudades que hay dentro nuestra Nacion, solo estan oficiando compositoras palabras ó buenos razonamientos, buenas obras por nosotros. Mirad como sale de sus bocas la verdad de los preceptos de Dios: mirad como se hacen ayudadores y compasivos de nuestra

Nacion. Oid, abrid vuestras orejas en la manifestacion de nuestra salud. Taná ya no hay al lado de nuestro Señor Rey, un ignorante hombre, que hizo solamente todo lo que quiso la ignorancia de su corazón: ahora no hay quien haga juguete en nuestra nacion: ahora no está sorprendida por el engaño la cabeza de nuestro Señor Rey, y cuando vuelva viniendo á su asiento, no solamente oficiará lo que quiera su autoridad, solo hemos de ver que hace ú opera asi como un grande padre que se compadece en favor de sus hijuelos entregados por Dios en sus manos, en su sombra y en su estimación.

Ahora alli no mas está allado de ntro. Sor. Rey la junta de nuestros sabios, por que no se vaya segunda vez á descontrastar nuestra Nacion por el engaño de un hombre blanco, de un solo hombre, y alli estan otros valientes españoles cristianos que tienen agarrado el fusil en sus manos, para perseguir á los matadores venidos de Francia y saltados sobre nosotros.

Asi habla ahora nuestra grande junta sentada en Cadiz y la autoridad de nuestro Señor Rey está guardada, está manifestada en otra segunda Junta Regencia se llama, hágase dice no mas, que se haga en la hora todas aquellas buenas compositoras, remediadoras palabras salidas de la reunion de nuestros sabios.

Se manifestó ahora su sabiduria, su pensar de estos grandes hombres: está envidiada su riqueza de sus almas en el universo, y se derramó viniendo hacia nosotros, asi como se derrama la menuda lluvia, y la bondad de los rayos del Sol sobre todo el Universo.

Ahora no hay quien nos diga que [no] somos Españoles: antiguamente Indios se llamaban aquellos que nacieron de esta banda del mar: ahora cristiano español nos llamamos, ó hijos queridos; una sola es nuestra tierra, una nuestra fé: una nuestra Nacion: uno nuestro precepto ó ley: uno solo nuestro amo Rey, y una solamente nuestra junta sentada en la cabeza, en la medianía de nuestra Nacion llamada España.

Ahora no hay quien borre la altura la grandeza de nuestra existencia ó espíritu: ahora no hay quien nos lo aprisione nos oculte la fragancia, la bondad dentro nombre bendito en todo el universo: ahora no hay hombre alguno que no sepa guardar en riqueza salida de este bendito nombre: iguales estamos amados hijos, en tocar, en oler este floreciente nombre.

Ahora está ya guardada por nuestra junta la sagrada fé de nuestra santa Iglesia: ahora ya no hay algun atrevido malcreyente ó hereje hombre que venga á trastornar el sagrado precepto de nuestro Señor Dios: Ahora no hay quien venga á comprimirnos llevando para creer, para tener respeto á otro hombre que no ha traido su oficio por verdadero camino, verdadera mano de nuestro Señor Dios.

Ahora solamente temerémos, respetarémos primero á ntro. Sor Rey Fernando, enviado por el cielo á nuestra Nacion, y despues solamente temeremos, respetaremos al verdadero substituto que nazca ó naciere viniendo de su sangre:

ahora ya no hay quien dé á la prision, al aborrecimiento su pensamiento, su obra, su espiritu, si solamente observa sí oficia el precepto de Dios y el precepto del substituto de Dios en la tierra. Ahora estamos desocupados, somos cristianos españoles, somos principales en nuestra nacion, y si hubiera otros maliciosos hombres, que injustamente nos hagan daño, alli esta la junta de nuestros sabios que se compadece de nosotros, y que se alternan en cada un mes en cada un año: ahora sobre salen nuestros nombres y somos llamados ó llevados para compositoras palabras para defensa de nuestra nacion, aunque hallámos sido indios antiguamente.

Amados hijos: abrid el espiritu, ó pupila de vtros. ojos ahora ya se perdonó ó está perdido vtro. tributo: solo con igualdad pagamos un pequeño pedido, Donativo se llama, por que no se han acabado nuestros trabajos, y por que asi obedecemos el cuarto precepto de nuestro Dios:

> Temerás, respeterás á tu padre y madre, te compadecerás en su trabajo, lo ayudarás en su pobreza, le dareis de comer y beber, le limpiareis las lagrimas de sus ojos en el llanto: no lo ofendereis ó aborrecereis en palabra, en obra y en el pensamiento de tu alma, por que este alto pecado, dolor me hace sentir en mi corazon,

asi habla ó preceptua nuestro Señor Dios.

Ahora vid ó atended: Padre se llama aquel hombre q. nos dió nuestro Ser: padre se llama tambien el que tiene oficio, el que tiene mision, por Dios: padre se nombra aquel ó el que nos manifestó el camino del cielo: Padres se llaman todos los sabios que nos enseñan la verdad de la palabra, la verdad de la buena obra: Padre se llama aquel á qn. no alcanzamos sus años: y padre se llama cualesquiera hombre, cualesquiera español cristiano, que nos ayuda á perseguir el engaño, y á concluir nuestros trabajos. Y si estos grandes hombres solamente ofician buenas obras en nuestro favor, ó por nosotros, ¿por qué no los ayudarémos con un poco de Donativo de plata? Si nosotros somos hijos guardados con su trabajo, con su pobreza, con su bondad, con su fortaleza de ntros. padres y hermanos cristianos españoles, ¿por qué no les hemos de dar dos ó tres especies ó figuras de plata para que compren su comida y bebida, por que se agarren se sostengan en la persecucion de los matadores, que dañan á nuestra nacion y debalde ó injustamente nos quieren matar ó nos matan?

Esperad, esperad un poco, amados hijos: pasarán nuestros trabajos, y alli vireis como reflorece ó viene refloreciendo nuestra tierra ahora, todavía hay pena, mas en medio de la misma pena ya descubres venir, ya sientes, ya señales con el dedo la bondad del corazon de tu padre, de tu hermano español cristiano que se compadece de vosotros.

Cuando pase nuestra persecucion, muy flojo ó aliviados os vereis. Todos los preceptos y bondad de palabra de la junta de nuestros sabios, vienen por vuestra salud ó felicidad para guardar la riqueza de vtra. casa: para respetar, para estimar vuestra existencia, no perdais por vuestro pecado la bondad de esta palabra, que viene saliendo del medio de nuestra nacion.

Si no teneis pecado no hay alguna Justicia que corrija ó reprenda tu persona ó existencia. Si hay algun hombre oficial ó principal que injustamente, ó debalde os haga daño que injustamente os aborresca pagará tambien su pecado ante nuestro Señor Rey por que no obedeció la compositora palabra de la junta de nuestros sabios.

Despacio solamente pensad ó considerad en vuestras almas estas palabras de nuestros padres y hermanos, escritas en el papel y allí vereis por vuestros ojos, como un poco ya falta que se acabe nuestra pobresa, nuestro trabajo, nuestras llorosas palabras ó quejas que habian antiguamente dentro vuestro corazon.

Aplicad vuestra oreja, poned el espíritu de vtro. ojo en la bondad de este razonamiento. Ahora aquí no mas junto á nuestras personas, ya segunda ves se juntan otros sabios, nuestros compositores de palabras. Solamente veremos que ofician el alivio de nuestras penas. Ahora no se puede descubrir en la hora toda aquella multitud de bienes ó bienhechoras, compasivas obras preparadas para nosotros ó en nuestro favor; pero no lejos está la bondad de un dia que nos de á medir, á mirar, á palpar la alegría de nuestras almas, el reflorecimiento de nuestra tierra. Por eso en la entrada de este año, ya habeis visto grande fiesta en gritar ó pregonar el papel de los preceptos de ntra. nacion nombrado *constitucion*.

Miraos á vosotros mismos ó refleccionad hijos amados que no es así lo que hace el engaño de Napoleon: yo os estimaré: yo aliviaré vuestra pena: yo os cuidaré, dice solamente, y otra rabiosa palabra, otra maliciosa obra hay en su corazon:

No os pongais amados hijos en el camino de la ignorancia, atrevimiento, locura y otros pecados que siguen sus matadores A la verdad cerrad vuestros ojos: tapad vuestras orejas, no vaya á trastornarse vuestra cabeza con su podre ó ponzoña, con su malicia de la grande serpiente que está en el infierno: solamente habeis de ver, habeis de oir, habeis de aprender la verdad de esta bendita palabra enviada por Dios y por la cristiana española Junta nuestra que está de la otra banda del mar.

Ahora ya segunda vez se juntan los principales sabios nuestros aquí cerca, aquí en la entrada del mar, en Guatemala, y en otras españolas ciudades: primero solamente ya van á oficiar, cuidar ó trabajar en favor de la enseñanza de nuestros hijos.

Los chicuelos, nuestros hijos que aprenden libro en buena escuela, conocen el poder ó espíritu de Dios: conocen esta grande eternidad, ó ida de los tiempos, que se dice en nuestras orejas: conocen como está su alma dentro de su carne: conocen la grandeza de su ser, la grandeza de su bendito nombre: conocen tambien por que será que cargamos penas en este mundo: por que salen lágrimas ó agua del ojo en el llanto: y conocen como se alegrarán y deleitarán todavía en la vida perdurable de Dios.

Conocen tambien, por que será que hemos de temer, de respetar á los padres, prójimos, allegados y conocen porqué será que los hemos de estimar de amar, como lo manda Dios.

Los aprendices en buena escuela, conocen por que será que estamos juntos en el mundo: por que será que no es bueno que sigamos el camino del demonio: por que será que no es bueno lastimarnos como tigres: por que será que pegan y corrigen las Justicias, no solamente por enderezar nuestras obras y los pensamientos de nuestras almas.

La ignorancia, la levadura ó ponzoña de nuestra existencia, de nuestra carne, que trajimos antiguamente del vientre de nuestra madre Eva, no siente bien en la represion, el precepto; mas vendrá todavía hijos amados, en el fin del mundo un grande dia, alli nos hablaremos y dirémos en nuestras almas:

> Os agradesemos gran Dios: eres bendito ahora en todas vuestra obras, por que reprendisteis mi carne en los trabajos: enderesasteis mi senda en el universo os agradecemos padre, madre, Señor Rey, Señores Justicias: Dios os lo pague sabios, hermanos españoles cristianos: que os llame ó traiga nuestra Madre Sagrada María á quien la vida donde estamos sentados ante el acatamiento del Hacedor criador del universo: que se compadarezca de vosotros en el nublado de la senda: en el engaño del demonio, en el camino de vuestra milpa, en el sueño de vtros. ojos por que me distes el bautismo, por que me enseñasteis á temer y respetar á Dios y á temer y respetar al sustituto de Dios, que está en la tierra: os agradecemos porque abristeis el espiritu de nuestros ojos: por que enderesasteis mi pensamiento, mi palabra, mi obra cuando amarrado estube antiguamente en mi carne, y por que me mostrasteis el camino del olor, el camino del cielo por toda la eternidad.

Asi hablarán vuestras almas, amados hijos, cuando salgais del mundo, y por eso se han juntado ahora todos los sabios abogados nuestros.

Ahora no puede señalar ó descubrir vuestro ojo toda la bondad prevenida en sus corazones; mas no lejos está la hora en que veais, en que sintais ú oigais y en que toqueis la salud, la alegría de otra nacion.

Ya poco falta que veais en la escuela buenos Maestros que siembren en el corazon de vtros. hijos todas las buenas obras mandadas por Dios. Ahora, juguete solamente veis que han hecho los muchachos, pero un momento no mas falta para que pasen nuestros trabajos en la persecucion de los matadores: ya poco falta que amanesca la luz á los Sabios, asi como el grande rayo del sol en medio del firmamento; y asi como menuda lluvia que viene á humedecer el sembrado de nuestra tierra. Alli vereis como se hacen grandes hombres, grandes padres grandes españoles. Alli vereis como resplandesen en la reunion de los cristianos, en la junta de los sabios que estan en el universo.

La bondad ó adelante de nuestras milpas: contratos ventas y la riqueza de nuestras casas, eso solamente ya dibujan, solo eso ya piensan, ya preparan nuestros padres y hermanos españoles cristianos.

Las juntas de las ciudades prevenidas ahora por nosotros solo cuentan solo piensan en sus corazones como se decubrirá por nosotros el escondridijo ó mina de oro y plata que está en el centro de la tierra: como se acabará, como se remediará vuestra pobreza y orfandad: que harán para cuidar vuestra existencia y vuestros hijos: que harán para que se llene vuestra casa, vtra. tierra de muchos ganados: muchos caballos: muchos cerdos: muchas gallinas: mucho maiz: mucho algodon: seda: azucar cacao y todo lo demás, que viniendo haga vuestra riqueza y vuestra salud. No se pierde tampoco del corazón de nuestras juntas la composicion de ntras. casas, la derechura ó composicion del camino dentros pueblos, el descubrimiento, la abertura de las vertientes ó tomaderos de verde agua, y todas las demás buenas operaciones preparadas, vistas en nuestro favor.

Ahora un momento ya falta pa. qe. se acabe la pereza, el sueño de los hombres: un instante falta para que veais paradas las compasivas casas pa. los desamparados enfermos: á la verdad asi concluir á la pena nuestra tierra. Ya poco falta que vengan buenos Maestros, que os den á ver la palabra de Dios: las letras del papel: los tejidos de paño ó lienzo: la platería: carpintería, arquitectura y otros obrages y ciencias que viniendo hagan la riqueza de vuestra casa, y la felicidad de vuestros hijos.

Asi vereis, que ni un poco se cansa el corazon de nuestros amantes cristianos españoles: aquí no más cerca, en la entrada del mar, esta ya parada le existencia de otra Junta que os dije, ensanchada solamente la vista de sus ojos, no le entre el sueño en preparar á los sacerdotes benditos hombres, que vengan á sembrar buenas obras; y tambien en la tierra de los bárbaros hombres que no tienen bautismo en el alma. Allí vereis como se desata la prision de sus almas, como se abre la ceguedad de sus ojos, como nos acompañamos en reunion, como nos acompañan ellos en seguir la senda del cielo: allí vireis como se alza la voz de los padres, como grande vozina en la casa, en la nacion de los desconocidos hombres, deconocidos gentiles: á la verdad abrazados vosotros, ensanchados vtros. brazos con tu prójimo allegado: extendida ensanchada nuestra Nacion con la existencia de estos nuevos cristianos, humedecidos vuestros ojos con el llanto de alegría, os juntareis para cantar con instrumentos, os extendereis para gritar las bondades, las compasiones del Señor.

Oid como hablara todavia vuestra boca:

> Venid, venid los hombres que no recibieron agua antiguamente: venid
> los que acompañasteis antiguamente al demonio al tigre, á la gran bestia,
> á la serpiente en el centro de las piedras, en las montañas: venid, dejad la
> sombra de la muerte: dejad la nube de vuestros ojos: levantad vuestra
> cabeza: venid, descansad en nuestros brazos: venid levantemos la voz

de nuestras gargantas ante Dios: venid, bendigamos eternamente al Hacedor, Criador del universo: venid, bendigamos tambien la bondad de la cristiana española Junta nuestra.

No hay absolutamente bondad, no hay otro crédito de palabra que se pare, que se levante al lado ó ante estas bien hechoras obras, muy grandes nombradas en todo el universo:

Amados hijos: hay maliciosa obra: hay engaños a palabra en la boca, en el diente de los malcreyentes matadores, mas ahora no podeis pensar en vuestros corazones, que solo engaño talvéz hacen los cristianos españoles: no es así, amados hijos: en todo el universo hay maldad, pero hay tambien bondad: hay engaño, pero hay verdaderas palabras, hay matanza pero hay defensa: hay engañosas letras, pero hay verdaderas letras: hay heridas, pero hay tambien curacion: hay aborrecimiento pero hay abogacía ó compasion; hay murmullosas palabras, pero hay compositoras palabras: hay hombres ignorantes; pero hay hombres sabios: hay malos creyentes ó incredulidad; pero hay tambien verdadera creencia en Dios.

Mirad con refleccion, amados hijos: ntra. cristiana española Nacion no perdió ni un momento los preceptos de Dios, salidos de la boca del sagrado Apostol Santiago: si tenemos pecados como frágiles ó pecadores hombres, hay tambien cristiano llanto en nuestras almas: y estas palabras, estas compasiones que vienen escritas en vuestro favor, no son falsas, no son juguetes: nacieron, salieron viniendo del corazon de vtro. padre, vtros. hermanos, Señores Justicias, cristianos españoles: vid como habla la verdad de sus almas.

Amados hijos, hermanos indios, aquellos que se agarran del poder ó espiritu de Dios: aquellos que estan acogidos en el vientre de ntra. Nacion: los que no tienen trastornada la cabeza con el engaño del demonio, y que tienen el bautismo en su frente, la sagda. señal, la sagrada marca, indicio de la vida, bajo la proteccion de Jesús y de la Verdadera Virgen Santa Maria. Oid, segunda, tercera vez os lo digo: oh indios españoles cristianos: los que no saben cansar sus corazones al cargar la pena; aborrecimiento, pobreza, prision y golpes: Oid: los que siguen solamente la sagrada senda de sus padres, el bendito camino de su Nacion, la fortaleza de sus hermanos cristianos españoles: los que persiguen ó rechasan la malicia de los matadores, y q. tienen abrazada la bondad de Dios, vid buena palabra, buena obra descubierta junto á vuestra existencia en medio de nuestra nacion.

Muy mucho os ama vuestro Sor. Rey, vtra. respetable Junta de los Sabios: todos los razonamientos de ellos primero ó con preferencia vienen á vosotros Indios por que estais guardados en sus almas: vuestra nacion, vuestra Madre solo mide, solo piensa vtra. vida: solo quiere mostrarnos qué tamaño es su amor:

como se entrega en las manos de los matadores, como sufre aborrecimiento, cansancio, sed, y otros muchos trabajos por cuidar vuestras almas, por preparar vuestra salud, y por remediar vuestra escasés.

Muchos años han pasado ahora, que llora el corazon, que se oprime el alma de nuestro padre y hermanos cristianos españoles, porque estrecho el tiempo miraban pa. preparar la bondad ó felicidad de vuestra tierra; ahora no está estrecho el tiempo: poco falta que se limpien los ojos de vuestro padre, de vtro. hermano español, porque de cerca ya descubre la felicidad de ntra. nacion, y la conclusion de nuestras penas.

Esta grande obra llena de alegría sus almas, y bendita se nombra en todo el universo.

Ahora esta ya tomada la medida y el pensamiento de ntra. felicidad, estan ya preparados los sabios en cristiana junta de las ciudades, aquí cerca de nuestra existencia ahora no podemos decir como antes que muy lejos está, allá al fin de los mares la composicion de nuestras palabras, la audiencia de nuestros asuntos: ahora no se detiene el remedio de nuestras peticiones ante esta cercana junta.

Mirad, hijos amados como resplandece el rayo del sol en la manifestacion de las letras de nuestro Señor Rey, y nuestra respetable junta. Ya oisteis todas las cosas que fueron á oficiar nuestros sabios sentados en Cadiz, y todas las cosas que viene á oficiar la segunda junta que se sentará aquî cerca de esta banda, en la entrada del mar.

Saltará ó salta de alegría nuestro corazón: se deleitará el oido de vtra. oreja, si mides, si consideras en vuestra alma la grandeza, la bondad de esta palabra y la bondad de lo preceptuado en la nombrada Constitucion, gritada en pregon y en fiesta que paso en nuestro pueblo. Todo lo que pida vuestra alma y vuestra vida: toda la compacion bienhechora que puedas descubrir, que puedas desear ó codiciar en el universo, todo está escrito en el libro de la constitucion, y en el corazon de las cristianas españolas juntas, que se han de sentar aquí junto á nosotros.

Nuestro Señor Rey, nuestras respetables Justicias, ya concíderan en sus corazones la alegría de vuestra vida en agarrar, en obedecer, temer y respetar esta grande Junta que os dije: á la verdad la otra junta que Regencia se llama, que guarda la sustitucion del Poder de nuestro Sor. Rey, ya espera el amor de vuestros corazones en favor de nuestra Nacion. Nuestra cristiana española Junta, no quiere hacer engaño, no hace juguete, y la esperanza de tantos hijos no se pierde no se borra, por que está parada ó descansa sobre este verdadero razonamiento ó compositoras palabras.

Ahora solo se parte el corazon de nuestra Junta en preparar el remedio de nuestras penas, aunque lejos esté la primera grande Junta sentada en la ciudad de Cadiz, hay ahora segunda junta nuestra junto de nuestra existencia que viene solamente á oficiar bienhechoras obras hacia nosotros y hacia los indios, los que guardan el precepto de Dios, y que saben temer, respetar, amar á los sustitutos de Dios en la tierra.

Nuestra Junta así quiere pagar la fortaleza, la bondad de aquellos hombres que ayudaron, á nuestra Nacion, en perseguir la malicia de los matadores de Napoleon; y así tambien quiere manifestar en el ojo de los engañadores, y en la oreja de los ignorantes hombres que siguieron á los matadores que ninguna cosa buena encontraron en la senda ó pazos de Napoleon en el camino de la muerte y en la division y en herir á nuestra Nacion.

Aunque venga otro atrevido hombre, otro malicioso hombre blanco: aunque traiga puesto buen vestido: aunque hable como hablan otros hombres sustitutos de Dios, no le creais su engaño no lo sigais hacia la espalda: trae malicia en su corazón: solo quiere derramar nuestra sangre. ¿De donde viene vida ó felicidad pa. nosotros, si solamente desparraman muerte, aborrecimiento, ansia, trabajo, incredulidad ó mala creencia, pobreza, hambre, arrebato, matanza y otras ponzoñas de la serpiente, no vista en la hora por nosotros? Si nos llaman llevando al infierno: si arrastran sobre nosotros la reprencion, el enfado ó ira de Dios por toda la eternidad, ¿cómo nos han de dar verdadera salud ó felicidad los matadores? No creais sus engaños, oh amados hijos.

Si encontrais algun hombre que quiera embarrarnos en el pecado, que quiera introducir malicia en vuestras almas, cerrad vuestros oidos, corred, dad parte ante las Justicias.

Si encontrais algun hombre que os diga venid hijos, aquí esta vuestro padre, aquí está el compasivo, yo aliviaré vuestra pena, así habeis de volver vuestra palabra ó así habeis de contestar,

> Ya os conozco matador, ya hé sabido que quereis perder mi alma: quereis partir mi nacion: no son dos mis naciones como quereis: una sola es mi tierra con los españoles cristianos hijos de Dios, que se entregan á la muerte por nosotros: salid, salid, no hay quien os halla llamado: no vengais á dislocar mi corazón: un Dios: un solo Rey sustituto de Dios obedezco: tengo verdadero padre, tengo hermanos cristianos españoles: hay sabios, defensores, abogados ó compasivos hombres, que me dieron á ver, que me manifestaron el precepto de Dios el amor á mi prójimo, allegado, y el camino del Empírio: no vengas á quitar ó arrebatarme esta bondad de la eternidad, no me vengais á dar la senda de la muerte.
>
> ¿Para qué quiero el universo y todas las cosas, si se pierde mi alma?

Ya visteis hijos amados, así volvereis vuestra palabra ante los engañadores, y si se enfada contra vosotros, no es cuidado, hay Dios, hay vida para nuestras almas en el cielo, y por toda la eternidad.

La nacion de los ingleses se compadeció tambien de nosotros, nos defiende en nuestras persecuciones aunque haya algun malicioso hombre que nos diga que nos aborrece el inglés, que esta igual con los matadores, no creais esta embarradora palabra, hijos mios. Los ingleses se duelen ó estiman a nuestra nacion, estan entregadas a la muerte, a las penas por nosotros así cómo los españoles cristianos.

El Ingles y el Español se estiman, ó cariñosamente se ven, igualmente se agarran ó sostienen y una sola defensa hacen. En este año que pasó, en veintedos dias de julio, vino un gran capitan que se llama Welington, acompañado vino con cincuenta mil soldados ingleses, y estos bienhechoras hombres persiguieron a los maliciosos matadores; desataron nuestra prision y cansaron al atrevimiento de Napoleon; si muy verdaderamente se descubre en el mundo la bondad de esta obra; si se alegran los ingleses en defender nuestras almas ó vidas, y si se han entregado a la muerte en defensa nuestra, ¿como hemos de creer el engaño de los matadores, que solo quieren dividir nuestra nacion y el amor de los ingleses?

Oid ahora otra palabra: la ciudad nombrada Madrid, sufrió muchas penas hasta doce dias de Agosto, de este otro año que pasó: la ciudad de Cadiz, perseguida, cerrada ó sitiada por los matadores treinta meses, hasta veinte y cinco dias de Agosto. La ciudad llamada Sevilla y otras ciudades de nuestra nacion vieron el fin de sus trabajos hasta veintisiete de Agosto de este año que pasó. Ahora solamente se abrazaron en alegría, solo se deleitan ó reflorecen ante Dios, por que vieron la conclusion del torbellino: el fin de los matadores salidos en vergonzosa fuga.

La malicia, la rabia, el engaño de los matadores, no puede borrar del papel: no pueden perder de los males ó sabiduria del mundo esta grande obra, esta defensa que hicieron los cristianos españoles, los ingleses, y la otra buena nacion que se llama Portugal. Nuestra Patria habla ó ruega al Señor por estos buenos defensores nuestros, y eternamente, no es bueno, ó no se debe borrar de nuestros corazones ésta bien hechora obra y la fortaleza de nuestros amigos ó aliados ingleses, que han derramado su sangre por nuestra vida ó salud. Por eso hace grande pecado cualquier malicioso hombre que no cree la bondad ó sinceridad de nuestros allegados amigos ingleses. No creais, hijos amados, la maliciosa oida, la maliciosa conversacion, que quiere solamente trastornar el pensamiento de nuestras almas.

Ahora hay en el mundo otras naciones nombradas Rusia y Suecia que nos acompañan en nuestra defensa; y el gran Señor ó Emperador que se llama Alejandro, estima á nuestro Señor Rey Fernando: lo reconoce y benditas son por él las juntas, ó cortes de nuestros sabios y todos sus razonamientos ó compositoras palabras prevenidas en el libro de la Constitucion que os dije: Así de un golpe no se pierde la alegría de nuestras esperanzas: un poco falta que se trastorne nuestra persecucion: un momento solo falta que se cambie el semblante del universo, el semblante de nuestros trabajos, y un poco falta que se descubra viniendo la floreciente de la tierra de la otra banda del mar, llamada Europa: en nuestra Nacion que se llama Españas, y al lado de nuestras personas así como lo tienen medido, prevenido y esperando nuestro Rey.

La primera junta nuestra, la conservadora de la autoridad, de la sustitucion de nuestro Señor Rey, llamada Regencia, así lo transmitió: así lo escribió en el papel para que abrais vuestros ojos ante la bondad de esta palabra, y para que amorosamente veais á los españoles cristianos hijos de Dios, nuestros hermanos, nuestros prójimos: no os vayais á poner en la malicia del engaño: cerrad vuestras orejas ante los matadores, que solo gritan vida, felicidad; y esconden muerte y odio en sus almas.

¡Ah pobres hombres, blancos, indios los que han caido en la senda de la malicia: volteaos ó regresaos, entrad viniendo á las entrañas al corazon de vuestra Junta, de vuestra Madre, de vuestra Nacion.

Nuestra cristiana española nacion todabía os ama, os cuida, no reprenderá vuestro hierro, nada os dirá: solamente os abrazará en sus manos, si dejais la matanza, el odio, el arrebato y si llorais todos vtros. pecados que hicisteis ante Dios, ante vuestro padre, vuestro hermano y otros hombres á quienes injustamente derramasteis su sangre: has quebrantado, has pisado el precepto de Dios: habeis tocado la ternura de su corazon; mas aun todavía hay remedio de vuestro pecado, venid, no lastimeis vuestras almas eternamente: salga, salga el llanto de vuestros ojos: no aposteis ó no os alliveis con la fortaleza del criador, Hacedor de Universo.

Amados hijos: este bendito libro esta escrito en la ciudad de Cádiz, á treinta dias de Agosto, de este año que pasó y se llama mil ochocientos doce. Está manifestada ó autorizada su verdad por la mano del primer Gobernador de Regencia. Su nombre ó título es el de Duque del infantado. Presidente.

M. M.   9. 7. 1906.

Appendix D

Grande Grito

Original Tzotzil Version

Mucta ahuaneg taquibil tatel yuun gcojoutic Rey ta stojol huinicetic cuxagtic lita gech mucta nam.[1]

Lequil chunguanegetic cuxagtic ta yan balumil sviil America, schiuc Astic schiuc atuquelic muchutic oyic ta tzel xambal, tá coló pasogél, ahuaic á cotolic scop gmetic muc gcosiltik stzomleg gbanquiltic.

Lag anáix echém taná syoebal jabil ytál ta yan slecóg osil jun coló huinic, hun mu ibeiluc tzamezhuaneg Napoleon sbiil, spasog sbá lolohuaneg spasog sbá gnoxol, gnocholtic, schiuc och tatél ta gcosobic ech cuchaal xulumchón slapog tatel lolohuaneg cog ta sat.

Ta bai lag noox shuinagtés ta syé lequil mel tzanhuaneg cop, lag noos yac tó ayeg syutzilal spasogel lag noox shuinagés syelob, cuchaal syelob gbanquiltic schiucta patil lag sloloyotic. Lag sylbaginotic, schiuc mu lecuc lag s sutés syutzilal gpasogeltic ta stojol.

Ta yichon joom xchahuinic ta pic tzameshuanegetic sjapuyotic tuc ta scóm, pactaeg cop noox lag yalbotic; ilahuil syutzilal gcoronton: muta xital yaigesoxuc xi noox scoplal Napoleon, schiuc alii syutzilal cop lot noox, ta nox scan milhuaneg, poghuaneg, ta noox scan slagés ghuinquileltic, scotol schunbol gcojoutic Dios, schiuc scan spas sbá ojau chuchuaneg Balumil. Xyac tá g chuuntic, xyacta lec gnoptic scotol slolohuaneg, scoló pasogél ta gtojoltic.

Syoebal jabil taná, áte soldado etic yuun, ta noox scan syuchic gchicheltic, ta noox scan slagés cristiano Españoletic. Altic noox ylic, altic noox lag yilbaginotic: taná ilumtzag syip, schiuc scoló syoronton taná cuchaal johuiel huinic, ta noox sti sba stuc yun mu xú stupés stzatzal cristiano Españoletic. Alíi cristiano Caxlan, mu xlag: mu xyac xiel ta syorontonic: ahuaic cuchaal xcopoj ta shuinquilel.

Acomé xchamón, xlajón, mu xquiquita xailbagin gcaghual Dios, mu gcan xayaigés gtot, gbanquil, gcagnil, mu g quitai xa póg syosilal gtot: gnichon, gnopol, gnochol. ja yuun li mucta mulil, xilinón ta sbatel <u>osil</u> xchiuc me xlajón gtuc, oi tó yan yepal cristianoetic, oi tó yan Españoletic ta to xhuinquilag, ta tó schitalel, yuun stzitz ábolil á jontolil ech chuchaal taquibil talel yuun Dios.

Jalal nixnab tog toyol sculejal alíi tzameshuaneg Napoleon: toyol snacbagel syoronton, mu xhuinag ta hora cuntic ech cusi yepal pojohuil smucog talel ta shuinquilel. Ech cuchaal scagcalel sibac, cuchaal milhuaneg rojon, mu ni yac jutuc hora. Aco lapic, acolapic ta junoox loquel scotol cristianoetic xi noox ta syé. Hol sba gbanquiltic, laj yilic, laj scuchic yepal meanal, yepal huocol: li hoyón, mu ta xi xiu. li hoyón, mu xa xa gsutés gtec xi noox cristiano español: tana xahuil cuchaal scoltayon syahualél Dios. A chinóg talel coló Napoleon jolaguneb xchanhuinic ta pic milhuanegetic talém ta ahuosilal Francia sbiil: Yamal hoyon ta yichon ahuaghualel, li hoyon, mu ta xi xiu, yac gtzatzuben g coronton ta yichon batzil Dios Pashuaneg, chigteshuaneg balumil.

Jalal nixnab: ta bai, mu xu stzomsbaic cristiano caxlanetic: lag spuc sbá ep ta yalél: huetzbil ta telaltic, ta stenlegtic: iguinag ta bai y lag lá ate cristiano españoletic, ate cag chabihuanég gchuleltic

Jutuc mu ilajotic; stuc ta jun biquit teltic ta jun biquit yol huacáx náte ibat scha stomsbaic, te lag scoltaisbaic, ysliquesic noox toc yan tzatzal pleito, yun tame ta luc ta cacolgtuctic scoló, sjohuiel tzameshuanegetic. Ta cumcun noox lag scoltai sbaic gbanquiltic, schiuc mu lag scomtzan mu lag yictai syosil stot, smé ta scoom milguanegetic, can spic, can spog snichimagel lum, smuibel osil.

Ate tzameshuaneg Napoleon, cuchaal muc ta Bolóm. Can syotzesotic ta schamebal stí: y nagcag sgelol ta mucul jovel Madrid sbiil ech cuchaal sutumhic lag shualcún gcohoutic Rey: altic noox, lag schuc ta bai: lag stec chul staquiob, lag yic batel ta carcel: ech cuchaal tzambil coc yac slagés Napoleon scotol cusitiabil: ta patil yac spog, yac smil yac stupés yan jovelaltic, yan teclum: lag stúun talel sbelel schiuc schibal mucta simiento ta Hércules sviil shuinagem jovel cadiz. Lag gtaquix li mucta lum xi Napoleon: taná joon syaghualel hóm, balumil, ech xhahun scotó, ech xbulbun stí il osil, tzamesguanegetic.

Can ochuc scotolic ta Cadiz mucul jovel; stuc tei ta yochebal, lag staic stzatzal cristiano españoletic, spasogsba cuchaal jun toyol simiento, schiuc te ital shuoc sjol, te ihuoc sbá yip Napoleon can ochuc smil ojohuetic, cristiano españoletic nacal hoyic ta yut jovel; stuc mu xuix yuun, mu xu syalés, mu xu stejcabin moel ta sbá mucta simiento yuun cristianoetic.

Te ta yut Jobel Cadiz lag stzoom sbaic principaletic, ojohuetic, Nahuanegetic schiuc lag schaghpanic jun lequil ojohuil tzomleg, lag smaclinsbaic lag schiinicta yuló mucul ojou Ingles, spasog utzil coltayhuaneg ta gtojoltic. Ech lag scuchic huocol ta tzatzal Jobel Cadiz: ech spetog sba cristiano caxlanetic schiuc Inglesetic ech lag yichic muibel nichimagel ta sbatel osil yuun lag sjapuy sba ic, yuun mu y yal ta pogel syosilal, yuun mu lag smich yorontonic ta yichon tzameshuaneg Napoleon, schiuc yun tzotz lag shua lansvaic ta yolil chamebal sutum ic.

Taná utzil albil scotol Jobel nahuanegetic yuun lag stzom sbaic, yuun lag scoltayotic yuun lag stitin gchuqueltic, schiuc lag yac botic shuinagem gcuxeltic.

Ta yolil li mucul pasogel, mu tó xlumtzag cristiano españoletic: ate tzameshuanetic yac sjuchic syé ta coló, stuc te cristiano caxlanetic scoponog noox Dios tas huinquilel. Ahuaic cuchaal xcopogic.

Lolohuaneg Napoleon: atuc can alagés cristiano español, schiuc litó hoy Español: can álages schuunbol cristianoetic, stuc mu xú ahun: español cristianoetic shuogés chamebál stiil catimbac. Mu xa can á colés gcohouetic Fernando altic noox ahuelcanóg, altic noox ahuicog tequé, teg ti Napoleon, lioyotic, jootic gcasbetic scoom: aco oyuc ta carcel: aco oyuc ta icubal syoronton balumil, xach bilix gcoomtic, hualanbilix stzatzal cristiano españoletic: xbotic ta ahuosilal, ghuoquestic voc me chavoc llave, schiuc gloques tic ta gnegqeltic gcojoutic mucta Fernando, smuc, xchiuc sta jún altic noox chucbil ta carcel. Xlajotic, x ech ta balumil gnichontic, xhuinquilaj talél yan tic, stuc mu xchai ta schulelic alii mucta pasogel uztil albíl ta scotol huinicetic x halaj talél, xtaltó steg scotol balumil. Utzil, ech cuchaal utzil albil muchutic lag snutz huoné yantic milhuanegetic nagcajemic ta gcosiltic, schiuc lag yacbotic huocol, voc, xchiuc holajunhuinic jabil.

Taná mu xa hoc gcohoutic Fernando, mu xa mich á huoronton: jootic g cantic, gloquestic squexol syalél á sat, g cantic ta huinagel stojol, squexol á huocol, schiuc squexol schichel gtot gmé, gbanquiltic altic noox malbil yuun tzameshuanegetic.

Huinal, huocol, icti meanal, chamebal, taquintí lagebal, mu xa oyuc cusi yan gculejaltic huinajésvil cuuntic ta balumil: manchuc echuc noox, lioyotic: lihounetic cristiano españyoletic, yax noox syóquetai schuquel stot, Schuquel Scojon.

Chan xi noox balumil, ta yilel ghocoltic: ilá huilic xi noox: acojamuc gsat ta yichon li mucta huinequetic: mu xa mutzic schulel asat xi scoplal mucta balumil: ilahui lic xi noox toc: ilahuilic cuchaal schuc, cuchaal stzic syepal huocol ali cristiano caxlan: ilahuilic cuchaal scoltai schun bol Dios schiuc scuxlegal gcojoutic Fernando: ja yuun utzilalbil: ja yuun bujtzan bil snichimaj sbiil ta sbatél osil, schitá muyuc muchu stupés s rojouil cagcal, syojohuil mucta kanal shúinagem sacúm osil.

Jalal nixnab: alii mucta pleto altic noox ligquebil yun tzameshuaneg Napoleon, ta syosilal tot, mé, gbanquiltic cristiano españoletic taná ihuiltalél, ihuinág talél scoló Napoleon lita gech mucta nám: ylumtzag alumé Bolom ta yichón cristiano espanoletic, ja yuun ylag staqui talél syuló, altic noox tal ta il osil: tal syutzinotic: tal syaigesotic; tal ssoqués guinquilaltic: tal sloloi syutzilal gcorontóntic.

Alii lolohuaneg caxlan: alí coló huiniquetic, talotic ta syutzilal Dios, xi noox; mu cusi gpasbot: talotic noox ta julubal ta polomal, xá cuxubinotic yuun talotic noox ta haboltashuaneg: gchuun Dios, gcuxubin gmetic Maria: chul Jesus: chul paxion xloc noox ta syéic, schiucta yut syorontonic, hoy tog ep scoló, tog ep spojohuil, tog ep sjohuiel chamebal, stuc mu xhuinag ta sbáic. Colóo cop oi ta shuinqui lelic, schiuc yan cop oi ta stiic. Jootic talotic noox ta ghaboltesel balumil. Jootic gen xuhuinex: laic, chunoic g coplaltic xú noox schiuc lolohuaneg, coló, hilbaginel, pojohuil noox cop smucog ta syorontonic: ech cuchaal mucta xulúm chon milhuaneg noox oi ta stí, milhuaneg ta scóm, schiuc muxhuinag ta hora cuuntic, ech cuchaal muhuinag talél calal ijulic ta syosilal gbanquiltic hoy lum ta gech mucta nam.

Ja yuun taná tog ep cux syoronton tot jbanquiltic cristiano españoletic, schiuc ta yolil shuocol, syoquebal, yac sutesic talél shaboltashuaneg sat ta gtojoltic, yuun naca me gchuntic, naca me yalucotic ta slolohuaneg, ta scoló pasogél soldado huiniquil tic tacbil talel yun tzameshuaneg Napoleon.

Aco sjapuyotic Dios jalal nixnab: aco smacli notic ta yalán scu chul mucta Patrona Concepcion: ako yac gqueltic sbelél cux leg, sxambal huinagel: aco scoltayotic muchutic nutzbilotic ta syamalel balumil ech ta yichon Dios yac scanic ta oquel: ahu tayél yac spasic ta gtojoltic, ech cusi yepal español cristianoetic cuxagtic lum ta jech muc ta nam, schiuc muchutic cuxul ta stzel ghuinquileltic. Mu xchai ta syorontonic smaligebal; stalél muibel ta shuinagesel jun chultasbil cagcal: jun utzilhuaneg hora, x ech agcabal ghuocoltic, schiuc spet sbaic español gcorontontic, ech cuchaal jun mucta tot mu ilbiluc huoné, sjul talel ta sná, spet sba schiuc snichón, laic unetic xi noox: la pica a huaic chuchaal xpigt gchulel ta muibel: mu gcan huayel: mu gcan huél: la neta abaic schiuc gcoronton, yech stocalil sutum ic: yech gmeanal; hchuquel: la ilahuilic mucta canal shuinagem chul cagcal, shuinagesem gcuxlegtic.

Ech xcopogic tana cristiano españoletic: laic banquiltac gnapalex tei ta gech mucta nam: laic huiniquetic, antzetic; ghunetic:

laic chinahuonic ta muibel, ta cuxleg, gmanogtic ta huocol, ta chichel, ta ilbajinel, ta meebál, ta yaigesel, ta oquel, ta chamebal taquintiil. Tana mu xa oyuquix jun coló caxlan, mu xcuxubinotic huoné ta stzel gcojoutic Rey: taná manchuc xyalbotic ep loquelal jun lolohuaneg quel osil yac schon sba ta gmolotic, muxa oyuquix, lagix yosilal cristiano españoletic, mu gchuuntic ta loquel noox.

Ate gbanquiltic cristiano españoletic, mu nix jutuc hora syalesic sjol: munix junuc hora schunic ta sbatel osil; staquiel johui Napoleon: ja yuun gtuctic nichonotic, ta shualapat tot, gbanquiltic cristiano españoletic, gtuntic bael shuinagem syoc, gtuntic bael stzatzal, spasogel cristianoetic ta sbatel osil.

Ta stunél alii mucta xambal huinagel, mu schai, mu xyaig gchuleltic ta yichon Dios. schiuc ta yichon vatzil coltayhuanégtic cuuntic, scuchogic toyol huocol yuun mu xchai gchumboltic, gchuleltic, gnichontic, gcagniltic, schiuc, scotol cusiticuc hoi ta glumaltic. Ilahuilic cuchaal xyacsbaic ta milel: yantic sjapuyog sba schiuc scom tzameshuanegetic: yantic yac slaginic staquin, sculejal ta gcogtic: yantic stzobogsbaic ta tzibagel, schiuc ta snutzel slolohuaneg pucug.

Taná tzobolic principaletic taquibil batel ta Cadiz, yuun scotol jobelaltic oi ta yut gcosilaltic, janoox syantelanic meltzanhuaneg cop, utzil pasogel ta gtojoltic. Ilahuilic cuchaal xloc ta syeic smelol taquihuaneg Dios: ilahuilic cuchaal spas sbaic coltayhuanej schiuc aboltaghuaneg gcosilaltic. Ahuaic jameo á chiquinic, ta shuinagejel gcuxeltic. Ahora muxa oyuquix stzel gcojoutic Rey jun bolil huinic, spasog noox scotol cusi scán sjontonil syoronton: taná muyuc muchu spás tajimól ta gcosilaltic taná mu sogquesbiluc ta lolohuaneg sjol gcojoutic Rey, schiuc calal ssut talel ta snagquegibal, mu jouc noox syantelán cusi scan syaghualel, janoox squiltic spás, ech cuchaal mucta tot, xhabolag ta stojol snix nab, acbil talél yuun Dios ta scom: ta squean, schiuc ta scuxuhuaneg.

Taná, tey noox hoi ta stzel gcojoutic Rey stzomleg nahuaneg cuuntic, yun ta me cha tzilajuc gcosilaltic ta slolohuaneg junóx caxlan, júnoox huinic; schiuc te hoi yan tzatzal españoletic cristiano, sjapuog tu ge ta scóm, ta snutzél milhuanegetic talém ta Francia, schiuc pigtém ta gcacoltic.

Ech xcopog taná mucta tzomleg cuuntic nag cagém ta Cadiz, schiuc syaghualel gcohoutic Rey, chabibil, huinagesbil ta yan cha tzomleg Regencia sbiil, pasuc xi noox acopameta hora ech cusi yepal lequil meltzanhuaneg, poxtayhuaneg cop loquem ta stzomleg nahuaneg cuuntic.

Huinagenux taná snaogibal, snopogibal alíi mucta huiniquetic: mulambil sculejal schulelic ta balumil, schiuc malbilix talel tagtojoltic, ech cuchaal xmal sba viquital hó, schiuc syutzilal srojohuil cagcal ta syagcól scotól osil.

Taná muyuc muchu snaogibal xyalbotic, mu Españoletic: huoné indioetic sbiil muchutic yhuinquilag lita gech muctanám: taná cristiano Español gbiltic jalal nixnáb, yun junoox glumaltic: junoox gcosilaltic: junoox gtaquieltic: junoox gcojoutic Rey, schiuc junoox gtzomlejtic nagcagém ta sjol, ta syolil gcosilaltic, Espana sbiil.

Taná muyuc muchu stupés stoyolil smuctical ghuinquileltic: taná muyuc muchu smucbotic sbugtzanel, syutzilal gbiiltic, utzil albil ta scotól balumil. Taná chabibilix yun gtzomlegtic, jalal chun ból gmetic Santa Iglesia: taná mu xa hoyuquix muchu toibail malchunhuaneg huinic, xtal ssogqués sjalaltaquieb gcojutic Dios. Taná muyuc muchu xtal snetotic bael ta schunél, ta xiel, squexel yantic huinic, mu yichojuc talel syantel tabatzil xambal, batzil scóm gcojoutic Dios.

Taná janoox gxi, gquextic tabay gcojoutic Rey Fernando acbil talél yun huinagel ta gcosilaltic, schiuc ta patil janoox gxi, gquestic batzil sgelol shuinquilag, talel ta schichel: taná muyuc muchu xyac ta chugquel, ta ilbaginel snaogibal; spasogel; shuinquilel, teme yac noox syan telan staquiob Dios, schiuc staquiob squexol Dios ta balumil. Taná jocholotic cristiano caxlanotic: principalotic, ta gcosilal tic, schiuc te me hoi yomtic coló huiniquetic, altic noox syutzinotic, te hoi stzomleg nahuaneg cuuntic, xhabolag ta gtojoltic, schiuc yac sgel sbaic ta jujun hu, ta jujun jabil: taná gelahuem gbiiltic, schiuc icbilotic bael ta meltzanhuaneg cop, ta coltayhuaneg gcosilaltic, manchuc indioucotic huoné.

Jalal nixnab: jamoic schulel asat: taná chaibilix á patán ja noox cool yac gtogtic yol biquit canojel, Donativo sbiil, yuun mu to xlaj ghuocoltic, schiuc yun ech ta ghchuntic schanibal taquiob gcahoutic Dios: xaxi, xaquex á tot, áme xahabolag ta shuocol, xacoltai ta smeanag, xa huacbei shuag, syuchumhó xa cusbei syalél ssat ta oquel: mu xa huilbagin ta cop, ta pasogel, schiuc ta snopogibal á chulel; yun cux ta gcai li toyol mulil ta gcoronton; ech xtaquihuán gcojoutic Dios.

Taná ahuaic: tot sbiil alumé huinic lagyacbotic ghuinquileltic: tot albil euc mucho hoi syantel, mucho yac shuinagesbotic sbelél huinagel: tot albil scotol Nahuanegetic yac schanutesbotic smelol cop, smelol utzil pasogel: tot albil muchu huinic, muchu español cristiano yac scoltayotic ta snutzel lolohuaneg, schiuc ta slagesél ghuocoltic, ¿cusi yuun mu gcoltaytic ta jutuc Donativo taquin? Te mé jootic Nixnabotic, chabibilotic ta shuocol, ta smeanal, ta syutzilal, ta stzatzal tot, ghbanquiltic cristiano españoletic, ¿cuchaal mu xacbetic chapeg, oxpeg sat taquin yun smanic shuag, syuchumhó, yun sjapui sbaic, syipan sbaic ta snutzel tzameshuanegetic yac syutzinic gcosilaltic, schiuc altic noox can snulotic?

Malilló, malilló jutuc jalal nixnab: xech tó ghoucoltic, schiuc te xa huil cuchaal snichimag talel jlumaltic: taná hoi tó huocol; schiuc ta yolil ni xhuocol yac ahuinagés talel, yac ahuai, yac acabui syutzilal syoronton á tot, abanquil español cristiano, yaxabolag ta á tojolic.

Calal xech gnutzeltic, tog chopol xa huilabaic scotol taquiel, syutzial cop yun stzomleg nahuaneg cuuntic talém ta stojol á cuxlegic: ta schabiel sculegal á ná: ta squexél, ta scuxubinél á huinquilel: mu xa chayic ta á mul syutzilal lii cop loquem ta lél ta syolil gcosilaltic.

Ate me moyuc á múl, moyuc mucho Justicia stzitz á huinquilel: te me hoy mu chu huinic oficial, principal, altic noox syutzinot, altic noox syilabgintesot, stog nix euc smul ta yichon gcohoutic Rey, yun mu lag schuun smeltzanhuaneg cop yun stzomleg nahuaneg cuuntic.

Ta cuncun noox nopaic ahuai ta á chulelic alíi scoplal tot, gbanquiltic tzibalil talel ta jun; schiuc tei xahuil ta asat cuchaal jutuc xa scan xlag gmeanaltic, ghuocoltic, oquelhuaneg cop hoi huoné ta yut gcorontontic.

Aco achiquin: aco schulel ásat ta syutzilal li alhuaneg. Taná li noox ta gech mucta nam: li noox ta stzel ghuinquileltic, yac xcha stzomsbaic yantic nahuaneg, meltzanhuaneg cop cuuntic, ja noox xquiltic syantelanic schapogibal ghuocoltic. Tana mu xi xhuinag ta hora scotol ech cusi yepal, utzilhuaneg, aboltahuaneg pasogel chagpambil ta gtojoltic; stuc mu nomuc hoi syutzilal cagcal xyacbotic ta pisél, ta ilél, ta spiquel smuibel gchuleltic, snichi magél glumaltic. Ja yuun lí ta syochebal jabil lag ahuilic mucta quin, ta ahutayel sjunal staquiel gcosilaltic, constitucion sbiil.

Ylame ahuil abá jalal nixnab, mu me echuc yac spás slolohuaneg Napoleon: joon gcuxubinot: gchopés áhuocol: joon gmaclinot xi noox, schiuc yan júhuiel cop, yan coló pasogél hoy ta syoronton:

Mamé ahuac abá jalal nixnab, ta sbelél bolil, toibal, juhuiel, schiuc yantic mulil stunog tzameshuanegetic yuun. Oquelal mutzó á sat: macó á chiquin, mu me hnu sogpuc á hol, ta spojohuil, ta scoló mucta xulúm chon hoi ta catimbac: ja noox xahuil, xahuay, xa chanutes snic lool lichul cop, taquibil talél yun Dios, schiuc yuun cristiano español tzomlegtic hoi ta gech mucta nam.

Taná yac scha stzomsbaic principal nahuaneg cuuntic, litanoch, lita syochebal mucta nam ta Guatemala, schiuc ta yan español jobelaltic: ta bay, ja noox yac xbat syantelanic, schanutesél gnichontic.

Unetic, gnixnabtic, muchutic schanutés jun ta lequil escuela, syogtaquin syag hualél Dios: syogtaquin alíi mucta sbatel osil xhalot ta gchiquintic: syocta quin cuchaal hoi schulel tal yut stacu pal: syogtaquin smuctical shuinquilel: smuctical chul sbiil: syojtaquin euc cusihuan yun gcuchtic huocol lita balumil: cusi yun xloc syalél sat ta oquelhuaneg: schiuc syogtaquin cuchaal xmuibáj snichimagic ta sbatel osil cuxél Dios.

Syojtaquin euc, cusihuan gxi, gqueltic, tot metic, gnopol, gnocholtic, schiuc syogtaquin, cusihuan yuun cuxgcaitic, johol xquiltic, cuchaal xtaquihuan Dios.

Ate chanunetic ta lequil escuela, syogtaquin cusihuan yuun tzobolotic ta ba lumil: cusi huan yuun mu lecuc g tuntic sbelél pucug: cusi huan yuun mu lecuc syagesotic cuchaal bolometic: cusi huan yuun xmaghuán stzitzhuan Justicia etic, mu gunuc noox scan syorontonic stuc ja noox yuun stojontesel gpasogeltic, schiuc snopogibal gchuleltic.

Sbolil, spojohuil ghuinquileltic, gtacupaltic gquichogtic talél huoné ta shalajebal gmetic Eva, mu lecuc xyai tzitzel, taquiel stuc xbaltó jalal nixnab ta slagebal balumil, jun mucta cagcal, tey gcopombatic schiuc xcaltic ta gchuleltic: ocola hualbotic mucta Dios: utzilhalvilot taná ta scotol pasogel, yuun lag á tzitz gtacupal ta huocol: lag á tojontés gxambal ta balumil huocol ahual tot, mé, gcohou Rey, gcohoutic Justicias: Dios stojbeot naguanegetic, gban quiltic españoletic cristiano: aco syicot talel chul gmetic Maria lita cuxleg buy nacaloyotic ta yichon Pashuaneg, chijteshuaneg balumil: aco scuxubinot ta stocalil xambal: ta slolohuaneg pucuj, ta sbelel á choom ta shuayel á sat, yuun lag á huacbon chul jhó yuun lag á chanutesón xiel, xquexel Dios, schiuc xiel, xquexel squexólil Dios hoi ta balumil ocolahualbotic, yuun lag á jam schulel jsat: yuun lag á tojontes gnopogibal, gcop, gpasogél calal chucúl hoyón huoné ta gtacupal, schiuc sbatél osil. Ech xcopogic á chulelic jalal nixnab, calal xa loc batél ta balumil, schiuc ja yuun stzoboj sbá ta ná scotol nahuaneg, aboltashuanég cuun tic. Taná mu xu scabui asat scotól syutzilal chagpanbil ta syorontonic stuc mu nomuc hoy syorail, xahuil, xahuai, xa pic scuxleg, smuibel ahuosilal.

Jutuc xa scan xa huil ta escuela lequil Maestroetic, stunic ta syoronton á nix nab, scotol lequil pasogél taquibil talel yuun Dios. Taná tagimol noox spasog ahuil queremotic, stuc ogcuc noox scan xech ghuocol tic ta snutzel tzameshuanegetic: jutuc xa scan sjam talel nichintasbil stemleg char hunetic: jutuc xa scan ssacium syosilal Nahuanegetic, ech cuchaal mucta rojohuil cag cal ta syolil huinagel, schiuc ech cuchaal victalhó, xtal xachtés stzunigibal glumaltic. Tei xá huilic cuchaal xnichimag á nix nab ta jun ta tzibajél. Tei xahuil cuchaal spasbaic mucta huiniquetic: mucta padrectic mucta caxlanetic. Tey xahuil cuchaal x lemlogic ta stzomleg cristianoetic, ta stzomleg Nahuanegetic hoy ta balumil.

Syutzilal gchoomtic: gpolomaltic: gchonbaltic: schiuc sculejal hnatic, janoox yac sac buyic, janoox yac snopilan, yac schajpan gtot, gbanquiltic Español Cristianoetic.

Stzomleg jobelaltic taquibilix taná cuun tic, janoox syagtai: janoox yac snop ta syorontonic, janoox cuchaal xhuinag cuuntic smucogibal kanal taquin, saquil taquin hoy ta yibal balumil: cuchaal xlag, cuchaal xpoxtag á meanál schiuc á mebal: cusi huan spasic ta smaclinel á huinquilel, schiuc á nixnab: cusi huan spasic yun xnog á ná, á huosilal, ta yepal huacax: yepal caballo: yepal chitom: yepal mut: yepal ixim: yepal tuxnoc: seda: azucal, cocou schiuc scotol cusiticuc spas talél á culejal, schiuc á cuxleg. Mu xhaiecuc ta syoronton g tzomlegtic smeltzangibal á ná: stojontesél sbelél glumaltic: shuinagtesél, sjamél slupogibal yoxhó schiuc scotol lequil pashuaneg chapanbilix, ilbilix ta gtojoltic.

Taná ogcuc xa scan xlag schagil, shuayel huiniquetic: ogcuc xa scan xahuilic hualanbil habolteshuaneg nanatic, yuun me báá chameletic: oquelal ech xlag shuocol glumaltic. Jutuc xá scan xtal lequil Maestroetic xyacbeot ahui scop Dios: stzibagel hun: sjolobil poc: stenogibal taquin: Carpintero, Albañil schiuc yantic antel huaneg: nahuaneg, spás talél sculejál á ná, schiuc scuxlég á nixnab.

Exch xa huil: munix jutuc xlumtzag syaronton g cuxuhuanegetic cristiano Escapoletic; lii noox ta noch, ta syochebal mucta nam hualán bilix shuinquilel yan tzomleg lag calbeoxuc xachbil noox schulél ssat, mu xoch shuayél ta schajpanél padretic, chultasbil huiniquetic xtal stzunic lequil pasogél, schiuc ta slumal jontolil huiniquetic, mu yichojuc chul jhó ta schulel. Tei xahuil cuchaal xtitin schuquebal schulelic; cuchaal xjam smacogibal s sat. cuchaal gchiintic ta tzomleg: cuchaal schinotic stuquelic ta stunél huinagél xambal: te xa huai cuchaal stoi snuc padretic, cu chaal mucta oqués ta sná, ta yosilal mu ilbiluc huiniquetic, mu ilbiluc cabelanetic: oquelal petbil aba, xachbil á cóm, schiuc á nopol; á nochol: pucbil, xachbil á huosilal schiuc shuinquilel li ach cristianoetic: agchém á sat ta oquelhuaneg muibel, xa tzobabaic ta scaginél schiuc huom, xa pucabaic ta ahutail syutz; lal shabolteshuaneg gcohoutic Dios.

Ahuaic cuchaal xcopogtó á tí: laic, laic, muchutic huiniquetic mu yichojuc joó huoné: la ic muchutic achinog huoné pucug: bolom tzenem: xulum chon, ta yibel ton, ta telaltic: laic comesoic squeahuil chamebal: comeso stogcalil asat: toyó á jol: laic, holonanic ta gcoomtic: laic gtoytic syahualel gnuctic ta yichón Dios: laic gchultestic ta sbatel osil ate Pashuaneg Chigteshuanég balumil: laic gchultastic: euc syutzilal cristiano Español tzomlegtic. muyuc ta loquel noox yan utzilal: yan chunhuaneg cop, shulán sba, stoysbá ta stzel, ta yichon líi meltzanhuaneg pasogel tog muc albil ta scotól osil.

Jalal nixnab: hoi coló pasogel: hoi lothuaneg cop ta sti, ta syé malchuunhuaneg tzames huanegetic; stuc taná, muxú xa nop ta ahuorontonic, lolohuaneg nooxhuan yac spás cristiano españoletic: muechuc jalal nixnab: ta scotol balumil hoi malhuaneg; stuc hoi euc utzilhuaneg: hoi lothuaneg: stuc hoy coltay huaneg: hoi lothuaneg tzibagel; stuc hoi me lelhuaneg tzibagel: hoi yaigesél; stuc hoi euc poxtaghuaneg: hoi ilbaginél; stuc hoi habolteshuaneg, hoi bulbunél cop; stuc hoi meltzan huaneg cop: hoy bolil huiniquetic: stuc hoy nahuaneg huiniquetic: hoy malchunhuaneg etic; stuc hoy euc melel chunból Dios.

Ylamé ahuil jalal nixnab: gcosilaltic cristiano español, mu lag schai junuc hora staqui huaneg Dios loquem talél ta sti, ta syé chul Apostol Santiago: me hoy gmultic cuchaal mulahuil huiniquetic; hoy euc cristiano oquelhuaneg ta gchuleltic: schiuc liicop: lii habolteshuaneg ta tzibagel talém ta atojolic, mulothuanejúc, muta jimoluc: huinquilagem loquem talél ta syoronton á tot, á banquil, á huag Justicia cristiano españoletic: Lahuaic cuchaal xcopog smelol schulelic.

Jalal nixnab: banquiltic: indioetic, até muchu sjapuyog sba ta syahualél Dios: muchutic ghutzul hoy ta shalagebal gcosiltic: muchutic mu sogpernuc sjol ta slolohuaneg pucug: schiuc yichog ta stibá chul jhó: chul yetal, chul marca, shuinagtesél cuxlég, ta syalán ha bolteshuaneg Jesús, schiuc batzil tzeum Santa Maria. Ahuaic, chaloquél, oxloquel xcalbeoxuc indio español cristianoetic: muchutic musná shuntzag syorontonic ta scuchél huocol: ilbaginél: meanál: chuquanég: magel:

Ahuaic: muchutic stunog noox chul xambal smé, chul xambal syosilal, stzatzal sbanquilal cristiano españoletic: muchutic snutzog scoló tzamehuanegetic schiuc spetogic syutzilal Dios: ahuaic lequil cop, lequil pasogel huanagem ta stzel áhuinquilél, ta syolil gcosilaltic.

Tog ep scuxobinot ahuag Rey: ahuag tzomleg nahuanegetic scotol meltzanhuaneg cop yuunic, ta bai yac xtalic ta atojolic indioetic yun chabibilot ta schulelic: ahuosilal, á chulmé, ja noox yac spis, yac snop á cuxleg: ja noox can yacbeot ahuil cuchaal smuctical cuxubinhuaneg yuun: cuchaal xyac sba ta scoom milhuaneg, cu chaal súch ilbaginél, lumtzagél, taquintiil, schiun yan yepal huocol, ta smaclinel á chulelic ta schagpanél á cuxlég, schiuc ta spoxtayél á meanál.

Yepal habil jech taná xhoc syorontón, xmich schulel tot, gbanquiltic cristiano espanoletic yun chucul osil yac yil ta schagpanel syutzilal á lumalic: taná mu chuculuc osil: ogeuc scan, scussba ssat á tot, á banquil español, yun ta noch yac shuinagés syutzilal gcosilaltic, schiuc slagebal ghuocoltic.

Alii mucul pasogel, yac snogés ta muibel schulelic, schiuc utzil albil ta scotol osil: taná ich bilix spisol, snopogibal gcuxlegitic: hualanbilix nahuanegetic ta stzomleg cristiano jobeltic: linoox ta stzel ghuinquileltic: tana mu xú xcaltic, cuchaal huoné, tog nom hoy ta slagebal mucta nam, meltzanhuaneg cop cuuntic ayegibal parta: taná muxjalag spoxil canogibal ta yichon lii nochol tzomleg.

Ilahuil jalal nixnabcuchaal xlemlog sxoojohuil cagcal ta shuinagesém stzibajel gcojoutic tzomleg. Lag ahuaic cusitic ibat syantelanic nahuaneg cuuntic nagcagic ta Cadiz, schiucscotol cusitituc xtal syantelan cha tzomleg, xnagcag li ta noch, li ta gech, ta yochebal mucta nam.

Xpigt ta muibel ahuorontón: xnichimag s ayegibal á chiquin, me xa pis, me xa nop ta á chulel, smuctical, syutzilal li cop, schiuc syutzilal taquihuaneg Constitucion sbiil ahutabilix ta pregon, schiuc ta quin yech ta glumaltic. Scotol cusi scan á chulel á cuxlég: scotol habolteshuaneg, utzilhuaneg xxa huinagtés, xú xa cupin ta balumil, scotol tzibabil ta sjunal Constitucion, schiuc ta syoronton cristiano español tzomlegtic, yac cha nagcapic li ta stzel ghuinquileltic.

Gcohoutic Rey, gcohoutic Justicias, yac snop tá syorontonic smuibagél á cuxlegic ta sjapuel, ta schunel, xiel, xquexél allii mucta

tzomleg lag calbeoxuc: oquelal ate yan tzomleg Regencia sbiil, ate schabiog squexol, syaghualél gcojoutic Rey, yac smalii scuxubinél áhuorontonic ta stojol gcosilaltic.

Ate cristiano español tzomleg, muscán spás lolohuaneg, mu tagimoluc yac spás schiuc smaligebal yepal nixnab, mu xchai mu xtup, yuun hualanbilix ta sbá lii me lol meltzanhuaneg cop.

Taná yac noox sjat sbá syorontón gtzomlegtic ta schagpanel spoxil ghuocoltic manchuc nom hoyuc sbá mucta tzomleg nagcagém ta sjobelal Cadiz, hoy taná chatzom leg cuuntic ta stzel ghuinquileltic, xtal noox syantelán utzilal pashuaneg ta g tojoltic, schiuc ta stojoll indioetic, muchutic schabi staquiel Dios, schiuc snaic xiel, squexél, cuxubinél squexolil Dios ta balumil.

Gtzomlegtic ech can stoj stzatzalél, syutzilal muchutic huiniquetic lag scoltaic, lag sjapuic gcosilaltic ta snutzel coló tzameshuaneg Napoleon schiuc ech nix can shuinagtés ta ssat lolohuaneg, schiuc ta schiquin bolil huiniquetic lag tun tzameshuanegetic, mu nix cuxi le cuc lag staicta sxambalil Napoleon, ta sbelel chamebal, schiuc ta sjatél, ta yaijesél, gcosilaltic.

Manchuc xtál yan toibaíl huinic, yan coló caxlan: manchuc slap talel lequil Sku: manchuc xcopog cuchaal xcopogic yantic huiniquetic squexolil Dios, mu xa chunbeic slolohuaneg: mu me xatunic ta shualapat: yichog talél coló ta syoronton: ja noox scan smal gchicheltic. ¿Bu xtal cuxleg cuuntic, te me ja noox ta spuqij chamebal: hilbaginél: icti: huocol; malchunhuaneg: meanal: vuinal: poghuaneg: milhuaneg, schiuc yantic poghou xulunchon, mu ilbiluc ta hom cuuntic? ¿Teme yac yicotic bael ta catinbac: teme yac stasbotic talel ta gcacoltic stzitzhuaneg, silinteshuaneg Dios ta sbatel osil, ¿Cuchaal xyacbotic batzil cuxleg tzameshuanegetic? Mu xa chun slolohuaneg jalal nixnab.

A te me hoy xa taic muchu huinic can spactaex ta mulil: can syotzés coló ta á chulelic, macó á chiquin anilajanic accic parte ta yichón Justicia etic. Me hoy xa ta muchu huinic xyalbeot: la nixnab: li hoy á tot: li hoy ábolteshuaneg: joon gchopés á huocol, ech xasutesbeic á cop.

Yac gcojtaquinot tzameshuaneg, jnaix can á chai gchulel: can ahuoc gcosilal: mu chibuc gcosilal, cuchaal xacan: junoox glumal schiuc español cristiano etic snixnab Dios, syacog sbaiíc ta milél ta gtojoltic: locan, locan: muyuc muchu yicot talél: mu xtal á scop gcoronton: jun noox Dios: junoox Rey squexolil Dios yac gchuum: hoy batzilgtot: hoy gbanquil cristiano españoletic: hoy nahuanegtic, coltaihuanegtic, habolteshuanegtic lág yacboonic gquil, lag shuinagtesbonic staquiel Dios: scuxubinel gnopol, gnochol schiuc sbelél huinagel: mu me xtal apoghbon líi syutzilal sbatel osil: mu me xtal á huacbon stunegibal chamebal ¿Cusi stuc cuun balumil, schiuc scotol cusiticuc, me xchai gchulel? Lag ahuaic jalal nixnab, ech xa sutesic á cop ta syichon lolohuanegtic, xchiuc teme xilin ta á tojolic, mu cusi, hoy Dios, hoy scuxleg gchuleltic ta huinagel schiuc ta sbatel osil.

Ate syosilal inglesetic, yabolag euc tá gtojoltic: yac scoltayotic ta gnutleltic manchuc oyuc muchu coló huinic X yalbotic yac yilbaginotic ingles cool schiuc tzameshuanegtic, mu xa chuunic lii pacta cop jalal nixnab: Ate inglesetic yac scuxubin gcosilaltic, yacog sbá ta milel, ta huocol ta gcogtic, cuchaal español cristianoetic.

Inglés, xchiuc español cristiano, johol x yil sbaic, cool yac sjapui sbaic, xchiuc junoox coltaihuaneg yac spasic. Li ta jun jabil yech, ta cim sxchahuinic scagcalel Julio, i tal mucul capitan sbiil Welington, schinogtalel huac pic, xchiuc joom ta voc ingles soldadoetic, schiuc líi utzilhuaneg huiniquetic lag s nutzi bael ate coló tzameshuanegtic: lag stitinic gchuqueltic, schiuc lag slumtzaic s toibail Napoleon: ¿te me tog melel xhuinag ta balumill syutzilal lii pasogel: te me yac xmuibaginglesetic ta scoltayel gchuleltic, schiuc te me s yacog sbaic ta milel, ta coltaihuaneg cuuntic, cuchaal gchuuntic slot tzameshuanegtic can noox shuoc gcosilaltic, schiuc scuxubinel inglesetic?

Ahuaic taná yan cop: ate jobel sbiil Madrid, lag scuch yepal huocol, calal ta lagchaeb scagcalél Agosto, li ta yan jabil iech: ate jobél Cadiz, nutzibil, macbil ta tzameshuanegtic, lajunim schahuinic hú; calal tá joom schahuinic scagcalél Agosto. Ate jobél sbiil Sevilla, schiuc yantic jóbel, yuun gcosilaltic, lag yilic slagebal huocol calal ta jucum xchahuinic scagcalél Agosto, litó ta jabil y ech. Taná yac noox spet sbaic ta muibél: yac noox xnichi magic ta yichón Dios, yuun lag squelic slagebal sutum hic: slagebal tzameshuanegtic loquemic bael ta quexlal jatan.

Até scoló, sjoui, slolohuaneg tzameshuanegtic, mu xu stupés ta jun: mu xu schayic ta snaogibal balumil; a líi mucta pasogél: alii coltaihuaneg lag spasic cristiano españoletic, inglesetic, schiuc yan lequil osil sbiil Portugal. Ate gcosilaltic yac scopon Dios, ta stojol lii utzil coltaihuanegtic, cuuntic, schiuc ta gcorontontic alii utzil pashuaneg, schiuc stzatzalél gmololtic inglesetic, smalog schichel yuun gcuxlegtic. Ja yuun yac spás mucta mulil muchu coló huinic mu schuun sy utzilal gnopoltic, gmolotic inglesetic. Mu xa chuun jalal nixnab ate coló ayeg, coló cophuaneg can noox s hualcun snopogibal gchuleltic.

Taná hoy tá balumil yantic osilaltic sbiil Rusia, schiuc Suecia, gchinogtic ta coltaihuaneg; schiuc ate mucul ojohu S vil Alejandro, yac scuxubin gcohoutic Rey Fernando: syogtaquin, schiuc utzil albil yuun gnahuanegtic, gtzomlegtic, schiuc scotol meltzanhuaneg cop taquibil talel ta s junál constitucion lag cal beoxuc. Ech ta junoox loquel, mu x chai smuibel gmaligebaltic: jutuc xa scan x hualcun sbá gnutzeltic: ogcuc noox scan s gel sbá syelób balumil, syelob ghuocoltic, schiuc jutuc scan shuinag talel snichimagél lum, ta gech mucta nam, sbiil Europa: ta gcosilaltic sbiil Españas, schiuc ta stzel ghuinquileltic, cuchaal spisog, schagpanog, smaliog gcohoutic Rey.

Ate s bá tzomleg cuuntic, ate chabihuaneg syaghualel, squexolil g cohoutic Rey, Regencia sbiil, ech lag staqui talel: ech lag stzibai ta jun, yuun xa jam á sat ta yichon syutzilal lii cop; schiuc yun johol xa huilic español cristianoetic snichonic Dios: gbanquiltic: gnopol, gnocholtic: mu me sa huac abaic ta coló lolohuaneg: macó á chiquinic ta yichon tzameshuanegetic, yac noox X autayic cuxleg, cuxleg; schiuc s niucogic chamebal, hilmaginel ta schulelic.

¡ Ah pobre huiniquetic: caxlanetic: indioetic, muchutic yalemic ta coló xambal: sugtán abaic: ochanic talél ta shalagebal, ta syorontón _á tzomleg, á mé, á huosilal.

Ate cristiano español gcosilaltic, yacto s cuxubinot, smaclinot, mu stztitzá bolil, mu cusi xyalbeot: yac noox s petot ta scóm, teme xa comtzan milhuaneg: hilbaginél: polhuanég, schiuc te me xa huoquetai scotol á mul lag apasic ta yichón Dios, ta yichón á tot, á banquil, schiuc yantic huiniquetic, altic noox lag á malbeic schichel: lag á huoc, lag á tec s taquiel Dios: lag á piebeic Syosilal: lag á piebeic scuxibinhu neg syoronton: stuc hoi t_ó spoxil á mul: laic, mu me xa yaigés á chulele ic ta sbatel osil: aco locuc, locucsyalel á sat: mu me xa pis á baic mu me xa toi abaic schiuc stzatzal chigteshuaneg, pashuaneg, balumil.

Jalal nixnab: alii chultasbil jun tzibabil ta Jobel Cádiz, ta lajunim x chahuinic scagcalel Agosto, alii jabil yech S biil 1812. Huinagesbil smelol tascoom sbá Gobernador y gtzomlegtic Regencia, sbiil.

El Duque del infantado. Presidente.

NOTES

1. The friar's notes to this text, when referring to the "Tzotzil" language have been placed in appendix E, when they provide the friar's world view, they are found in the "Great Proclamation Sent by Our Lord, The King to People Living Here on This Side of The Ocean."

Appendix E

Grande Grito

Revised Tzotzil Version

Muk'ta awanej takibil talel yu'un kojowtik Rey ta stojol winiketik kuxajtik li' ta jech muk'ta nab. [1]
Lekil jch'unwanejetik kuxajtik ta yan balumil sbiil Amerika, schi'uk Asia schi'uk atukelik much'utik oyik ta tzel xambal, ta kolo' pasojel, awa'ik akotolik sk'op jme'tik muk' jkosiltik stzoblej jbankiltik.[2]
Laj ana'ix ech'em tana syo'ebal jabil ital ta yan slekoj osil[3] jun kolo' winik, jun mu ilbiluk jtzameswanej Napoleon sbiil, spasoj sba lo'lowanej spasoj sba jnoxol, jnocholtik, schi'uk och talel ta jkosiltik ech k'u cha'al xulub chon slapoj talel jlo'lowanej k'oj[4] ta sat.
Ta ba'i laj no'ox swinajtes ta sye[5] lekil meltzanwanej k'op, laj no'ox yak' to a'yej[6] syutzilal spasojel laj no'ox swinajes syelob, k'u cha'al syelob jbankiltik schi'uk ta patil[7] laj slo'loyotik. Laj syilbajinotik, schi'uk mu lekuk laj sutes syutzilal jpasojeltik ta stojol.
Ta yichon jo'ob xcha'winik ta pik'[8] jtzameswanejetik sjapuyotik tuk' ta sk'ob, pak'taej k'op no'ox laj yalbotik; il awil syutzilal jkoronton; mu ta xital yayijesoxuk xi no'ox sk'oplal Napoleon, schi'uk a li syutzilal k'op lot no'ox, ta nox sk'an milwanej, pojwanej, ta no'ox sk'an slajes jwinkileltik, skotol sch'unbol jkojowtik Dios, schi'uk sk'an spas sba ojow jkuchwanej Balumil. Xyak[9] ta jch'untik, xyak ta lek jnoptik skotol slo'lowanej, skolo' pasojel ta jtojoltik.
Syo'ebal jabil tana, a te soldadoetik yu'un, ta no'ox sk'an syuch'ik jch'ich'eltik, ta no'ox sk'an slajes kristyano Espanyoletik. Altik no'ox ilik, altik no'ox laj yilbajinotik, tana ilubtzaj syip, schi'uk skolo' syoronton tana k'u cha'al jowiel[10] winik, ta no'ox sti' sba stuk yu'n mu xu' stup'es stzatzal kristyano Espanyoletik[11]. A li kristyano kaxlan, mu xlaj, mu xyak' xi'el ta syoronton awa'iik k'u cha'al xk'opoj ta swinkilel.
Ak'o me xchamon, xlajon, mu xkikitay xa'ilbajin jkajwal Dios, mu jk'an xayayijes jtot, jbankil, jkajnil, mu jkikitay xapoj syosilal jtot; jnich'on, jnopol,

jnochol; ja' yu'un li muk'ta mulil, x'ilinon ta sbatel osil[12] xchi'uk te me xlajon jtuk, oy to yan yepal kristyanoetik, oy to yan Espanyoletik ta to xwinkilaj, ta to xch'i talel, yu'un stzitz abolil ajontolil ech k'u cha'al takibil talel yu'un Dyos.

Jalal nich'nab, toj toyol[13] sk'ulejal a li jtzameswanej Napoleon; toyol snak'bajel syoronton; mu xwinaj ta ora ku'untik ech k'usi yepal pojowil smukoj talel ta swinkilel. Ech k'u cha'al sk'ajk'alel sibak',[14] k'u cha'al milwanej rojo, mu'nix yak' jutuk ora. Ak'o lajuk, ak'o lajuk ta jun no'ox lok'el skotol Kristianoetik xi no'ox ta sye.[15] Abol sba jbankiltik, laj yilik, laj skuchik yepal me'anal, yepal wokol; li' oyon mu ta xixi' o; li' oyon mu xa xajsutes jtek' xi no'ox kristyano espanyol; tana xawil k'u cha'al skoltayon syajwalel Dyos. Achi'inoj talel kolo' Napoleon jo'lajuneb xchanwinik ta pik'[16] jmilwanejetik talem ta awosilal Fransia sbiil yamal[17] oyon ta yichon awajwalel, li' oyon, mu ta xixi' o, yak jtzatzuben jkoronton ta yichon batz'il Dios jPaswanej, jCh'ijteswanej balumil.

Jalal nich'nab; ta ba'i, mu xu' stzob sbaik kristyano kaxlanetik; laj spuk' sba ep ta yalel; wetzbil[18] ta te'laltik, ta stenlejtik; iwinaj ta ba'i ilaj a te kristyano espanyoletik, a te kajchabiwanej jch'uleltik.[19]

Jutuk mu lilajotik, stuk[20] ta jun bik'it te'eltik ta jun bik'it yol wakax na[21] te ibat scha'tzob sbaik, te laj skoltay sbaik, islijkesik no'oxtok yan tzatzal pleto, yu'n ta me taluk ta kak'ol jtuktik skolo', sjowiel jtzameswanejetik. Ta k'unk'un no'ox laj skoltay sbaik jbankiltik, schi'uk mu laj skomtzan mu laj yikitay syosil stot, sme' ta sk'ob jmilwanejetik, sk'an spik, sk'an spoj snichimajel lum, smuibel osil.[22]

A te jtzameswanej Napoleon, k'u cha'al muk'ta Bolom. Sk'an syotzesotik ta schamebal sti'; inajkaj sjelol ta muk'ul jobel Madrid sbiil ech k'u cha'al sutum ik' laj swalk'un jkojowtik Rey; altik no'ox, laj schuk ta ba'i; laj stek' ch'ul stakiob, schi'uk laj yik' batel ta karsel.

Ech k'u cha'al tzanbil k'ok' yak slajes Napoleon skotol k'usitik awil; ta patil yak spoj, yak smil yak stup'es yan jobelaltik, yan tek lum; laj stuch' talel[23] sbelel schi'uk schibal muk'ta simyento ta Erkules sbiil[24], swinajeb jobel Kadis. Laj jtzakix[25] li muk'ta lum xi Napoleon; tana jo'on syajwalelon balumil, ech x'a'un skolo', ech xbulbun sti' j'il osil,[26] jtzameswanejetik.

Sk'an ochuk skotolik ta Kadis muk'ul jobel, stuk tey ta yochebal, laj staik stzatzal kristyano espanyoletik, spasoj sba k'u cha'al jun toyol simyento, schi'uk te ital swok' sjol, te iwok' sba yip Napoleon sk'an ochuk smil ojowetik kristyano espanyoletik nakal oyik ta yut jobel; stuk mu xnik yu'un, mu xu' syales, mu xu' stejk'abin muyel ta sba muk'ta simyento yu'un kristyanoetik.

Te ta yut jobel Kadis laj stzob sbaik prinsipaletik, ojowetik, jNa'wanejetik, schi'uk laj schajpanik jun lekil ojowil tzoblej, laj smak'lin sbaik laj schi'inik ta yulo' muk'ul ojow Ingles, spasoj utzil koltaywanej ta jtojoltik. Ech laj skuchik wokol ta tzatzal jobel Kadis; ech spetoj sba kristyano kaxlanetik schi'uk[27] Inglesetik ech laj yich'ik muibel nichimajel[28] ta sbatel osil[29] yu'un laj sjapuy sbaik, yu'un mu iyak' ta pojel syosilal, yu'un mu laj smich'[30] syorontonik ta yichon jtzameswanej Napoleon, schi'uk yu'n tzotz laj swa'lan sbaik ta yo'lil chamebal sutub ik'.

Tana utzil albil[31] skotol jobel jna'wanejetik, yu'un laj stzob sbaik, yu'un laj skoltay sbaik, yu'un laj stitin jchukeltik, schi'uk laj yak'botik svinajeb jkuxeltik.

Ta yo'lil muk'ul pasojel, mu to xlubtzaj kristyano espanyoletik a te jtzameswanejetik yak sjuch'ik sye ta kolo', stuk te kristyano kaxlanetik sk'oponoj no'ox Dyos ta swinkilel. Awa'iik k'u cha'al xk'opojik.

Jlo'lowanej Napoleon: atuk sk'an alajes kristyano espanyol, schi'uk li' to oy espanyol; sk'an atup'es sk'ajk'alel jkosiltik, schi'uk k'alal xlebloj jun no'ox sxojobil jk'ajk'aleltik, yak xtup' syajvalel asat: sk'an alajes sch'unbol kristyanoetik; stuk mu xu' awu'un: espanyol kristyanoetik swok'es ana, schi'uk swok'es chamebal sti'il k'atin bak. Mu xak'an akoles jkojowtik Fernando altik[32] no'ox awelk'anoj, altik no'ox awik'oj teke, tek' ti'[33] Napoleon, li'oyotik, jo'otik jk'asbetik stak'inal syok; jtitinbetik schukijibal sk'ob; ak'o oyuk ta karsel; ak'o oyuk ta ik'ubal syoronton balumil, xach'bilix jk'obtik, wa'lanbilix stzatzal kristyano espanyoletik xbatik ta awosilal jwalk'untestik awajwalel, jwok'estik jbok' me cha'bok' yave schi'uk jlok'estik ta jnekebtik jkojowtik muk'ta Fernando, smuk xchi'uk stajun altik no'ox chukbil ta karsel. Xlajotik x'ech' ta balumil jnich'ontik, xwinkilaj talel yantik, stuk mu xch'ay[34] ta sch'ulelik a li muk'ta pasojel utzil albil ta skotol winiketik x'alaj talel,[35] xtal to[36] stek' skotol balumil. Utzil albil euk much'utik snutz lok'el ta jnatik a te jtzameswanej Napoleon, ech k'u cha'al utzil albil much'utik laj snutz wo'ne yantik jmilwanejetik najkajemik ta jkosiltik, schi'uk laj yak'botik wokol jbok', schi'uk jo'lajun winik jabil,[37]

Tana mu xa'ok' jkojowtik Fernando, mu xamich' aworonton jo'otik jk'antik, jlok'estik sk'exol sya'lel asat, jk'antik ta winajel[38] stojol, sk'exol awokol, schi'uk sk'exol sch'ich'el jtot jme', jbankiltik[39] altik no'ox malbil yu'un jtzameswanejetik.[40]

Wi'nal, wokol, ik'ti'[41], me'anal, chamebal, takin ti'[42] lajebal, mu xa oyuk k'usi van jk'ulejaltik winajesbil ku'untik ta balumil; manchuk echuk no'ox, li' oyotik, li' oy unetik kristyano espanyoletik, yak no'ox syok'etal schukel stot, schukel syojow.

Ch'an[43] xi no'ox balumil, ta yilel jwokoltik; il awilik xi no'ox; ak'o jamuk jsat ta yichon li muk'ta winiketik; mu xamutz'ik[44] sch'ulel asat[45] xi sk'oplal muk'ta balumil; il awilik xi no'oxtok; il awilik k'u cha'al skuch, k'u cha'al stzik' syepal wokol a li kristyano kaxlan; il awilik k'u cha'al skoltay sch'unbol Dyos, schi'uk skuxlejal jkojowtik Fernando; ja' yu'un utzil albil; ja' yu'un bujtz'anbil snichimaj sbiil ta sbatel osil schi'uk mu'yuk much'u stup'es, ech k'u cha'al mu'yuk much'u stup'es srojowil k'ajk'al, srojowil muk'ta k'anal swinajeb sakub osil.

Jalal nich'nab a li muk'ta pleto[46] altik no'ox lijkesbil yu'n jtzameswanej Napoleon, ta syosilal jtot, jme', jbankiltik[47] kristyano espanyoletik; tana iwil talel, iwinaj talel ta jkak'oltik; tana ip'ijt talel[48] skolo' Napoleon li' ta jech muk'ta nab; ilubtzaj alume Bolom ta yichon kristyano espanyoletik; ja' yu'un ilaj staki talel syulo', altik no'ox ta il osil; tal syutz'inotik; tal syayijesotik; tal sojkes jwinkileltik; tal sjowi yutzilal jkorontontik.

A li jlo'lowanej kaxlan; a li kolo' winiketik talotik ta syutzilal Dyos, xi no'ox, mu k'usi jpasbot; talotik no'ox ta julobal ta p'olomal, xak'uxubinotik yu'n talotik no'ox ta abolteswanej; jch'un Dyos, jk'uxubin jme'tik Maria; ch'ul Jesus; ch'ul paxyon xlok' no'ox ta syeik; schi'uk ta yut syorontonik, oy toj ep skolo', spojowil, toj ep jowiel chamebal, stuk mu xwinaj ta sbaik; kolo' k'op vi ta swinkilelik, schi'uk yan k'op vi ta sti'ik. Jo'otik talotik no'ox ta aboltasel balumil. Jo'otik jk'uxubinex: la'ik, ch'unoik jk'oplaltik xi no'ox schi'uk lo'lowanej, kolo', ilbajinel, pojowil no'ox k'op[49] smukoj ta syorontonik; ech k'u cha'al muk'ta xulub chon milwanej no'ox vi ta sti', milwanej ta sk'ob,[50] schi'uk mu xwinaj ta ora ku'untik, ech k'u cha'al mu winaj talel k'alal ijulik ta syosilal jbankiltik oy lum ta jech muk'ta nab.

Ja' yu'un tana toj ep k'ux syoronton jtot jbankiltik kristyano espanyoletik, schi'uk ta yo'lil swokol syok'ebal, yak sutesik talel sjabolteswanej sat[51] ta jtojoltik, yu'un naka me jch'untik, naka me yalukotik ta slo'lowanej, ta skolo' pasojel soldado winikiltik takbil talel yu'un jtzameswanej Napoleon.

Ak'o sjapuyotik Dyos jalal nich'nab; ak'o smak'linotik ta yalan skuchul muk'ta Patrona Maria Konsepsyon; ak'o skoltayotik much'utik nutzbilotik ta syamalel balumil[52] ech ta yichon Dyos yak sk'anik ta ok'el; autayel yak spasik ta jtojoltik, ech k'usi yepal espanyol kristyanoetik kuxajtik lum ta jech muk'ta nab, schi'uk much'utik kuxul ta stz'el jwinkileltik. Mu sch'ay ta syorontonik smalijebal, stalel muibel ta swinajesel jun ch'ultasbil[53] k'ajk'al jun utzilwanej ora x'ech' ajk'ubal jwokoltik, schi'uk spet sbaik espanyol jkorontontik, ech k'u cha'al jun muk'ta tot mu ilbiluk wo'ne, xjul talel ta sna, spet sba schi'uk snich'on, la'ik unetik xi no'ox; la' pik awa'iik k'u cha'al xp'ijt jch'ulel ta muibel; mu jk'an wayel; mu jk'an we'el; la' net' abaik schi'uk jkoronton, i'ech' stokalil sutub ik' i'ech' jme'anal, jchukel; la' il awilik muk'ta k'anal swinajeseb ch'ul k'ajk'al, swinajtes jkuxlejtik.

Ech xk'opojik tana kristyano espanyoletik; la'ik jbankiltak wa'alex tey ta jech muk'ta nab; la'ik winiketik, antzetik, kunetik; la'ik chi'in awu'unik ta muibel, ta kuxlej, jmanojtik ta wokol, ta ch'ich'el, ta ilbajinel, ta me'ebal, ta yayijesel, ta ok'el, ta chamebal takin ti'il. Tana mu xa oyukix jun kolo' kaxlan, mu xk'uxubinotik wo'ne ta stz'el jkojowtik Rey; tana manchuk xyalbotik ep lok'elal jun lo'lowanej jk'el osil yak schon ta jmololtik, mu xa oyukix, lajix syosilal kristyano espanyoletikk mu jch'untik ta lok'el no'ox.

A te jbankiltik kristyano espanyoletik, mu'nix jutuk ora syalesik sjol; mu'nix junuk ora sch'unik ta sbatel osil, stakiel jowi Napoleon; ja' yu'un jtuktik nich'onotik, ta swalapat jtot, jbankiltik kristyano espanyoletik, jtuntik ba'el swinajeb syok, jtuntik ba'el stzatzal, spasojel kristyanoetik ta sbatel osil.

Ta stunel a li muk'ta xanbal winajel, mu xch'ay, mu syayijes jch'uleltik ta yichon Dyos, schi'uk ta yichon batz'il koltaywanejetik ku'untik, skuchojik toyol wokol yu'un mu sch'ay jch'unboltik, jch'uleltik, jnich'ontik, jkajniltik, schi'uk skotol k'usitikuk oy ta jlumaltik. Il awilik k'u cha'al xyak' sbaik ta milel; yantik sjapuyoj sba schi'uk sk'ob jtzameswanejetik,[54],yantik yak slajinik stak'in, sk'ulejal ta jk'ojtik; yantik stzoboj sbaik ta tz'ibajel, schi'uk ta snutzel slo'lowanej pukuj.

Tana tzobolik prinsipaletik takibil batel ta Kadis, yu'un skotol jobelaltik oy ta yut jkosilaltik, ja' no'ox syabtelanik meltzanwanej k'op, utzil pasojel ta jtojoltik. Il awilik k'u cha'al xlok' ta syeik smelol stakiwanej Dyos; il awilik k'u cha'al spas sbaik koltaywanej schi'uk abolteswanej jkosilaltik. Awa'iik jamo achikinik, ta swinajelal jkuxeltik. Tana mu xa oyukix ta stz'el jkojowtik Rey jun bolil winik, spasoj no'ox skotol k'usi sk'an sjontolil syoronton; tana mu'yuk much'u spas tajimol ta jkosilaltik, tana mu sojkesbiluk[55] ta lo'lowanej sjol jkojowtik Rey, schi'uk k'alal sut talel ta snajkejibal, mu oyuk no'ox syabtelan k'usi sk'an syajwalel,[56] ja' no'ox xkiltik spas, ech k'u cha'al muk'ta tot, x'abolaj ta stojol snich'nab, ak'bil talel yu'un Dyos ta sk'ob, ta sk'ean, schi'uk ta sk'uxuwanej.

Tana tey no'ox oy ta stz'el jkojowtik Rey stzoblej na'wanej ku'untik, yu'n ta me cha'tz'ilajuk jkosilaltik ta slo'lowanej jun no'ox kaxlan, jun no'ox winik; schi'uk ta oy yan tzatzal espanyoletik kristyano, sjapuoj tuk'e ta sk'ob, ta snutzel jmilwanejetik talem ta Fransia, schi'uk p'ijtem ta jkak'oltik.

Ech xk'opoj tana muk'ta tzoblej ku'untik najkajem ta Kadis, schi'uk syajwalel[57] jkojowtik Rey, chabibil, winajesbil ta yan cha'tzoblej Rejensya sbiil, pasuk xi no'ox ak'o pasuk ta ora ech k'usi yepal lekil meltzanwanej, poxtaywanej k'op lok'em ta stzoblej jna'wanej ku'untik.

Winajemix tana sna'ojibal, snopojibal a li muk'ta winiketik; mulanbil sk'ulejal sch'ulelik ta balumil; schi'uk malbilix talel ta jtojoltik, ech k'u cha'al smal sba bik'ital jo', schi'uk syutzilal srojowil k'ajk'al ta syak'ol skotol osil.

Tana mu'yuk much'u sna'ojibal xyalbotik, mu Espanyoletik; wo'ne Indioetik sbiil much'utik iwinkilaj li' ta jech muk'ta nab; tana kristyano Espanyol jbiiltik jalal nich'nab, yu'n jun no'ox jlumaltik, jun no'ox jch'unboltik, jun no'ox jkosilaltik; jun no'ox jkojowtik Rey, schi'uk jun no'ox jtzoblejtik najkaem ta sjol, ta syolil jkosilaltik, Espanya sbiil.

Tana mu'yuk much'u stup'es stoyolil, smuk'tikal jwinkileltik; tana mu'yuk much'u schukbotik; mu'yuk much'u smukbotik sbujtz'anel, syutzilal jbiiltik, utzil albil ta skotol balumil; tana mu'yuk much'u winik mu sna' schabi sk'ulejal, lok'em li' ta ch'ul biil; ko'ol oyotik jalal nich'nab ta spikel, ta sbujtz'anel li nichimajem biil.

Tana chabibilix yu'n jtzoblejtik, jalal ch'unbol jme'tik Santa Iglesia, tana mu xa oyukix much'u toy bail malch'unwanej winik, xtal sojkes sjalal takieb jkojowtik Dyos. Tana mu'yuk much'u xtal snet'otik ba'el[58] ta sch'unel, ta xi'el, sk'exel yantik winik, mu yich'ojuk talel syabtel ta batz'il xambal, batz'il sk'ob jkojowtik Dios.[59]

Tana ja' no'ox jxi', jk'extik ta ba'i jkojowtik Rey Fernando ak'bil talel yu'n winajel ta jkosilaltik, schi'uk ta patil ja' no'ox jxi', jk'extik batz'il sjelol xwinkilaj, talel ta sch'ich'el; tana mu'yuk much'u xyak' ta chukel, ta ilbajinel sna'ojibal, spasojel; swinkilel, te me yak no'ox syabtelan stakiob Dyos, schi'uk stakiob sk'exol Dyos ta balumil[60]. Tana jocholotik kristyano kaxlanotik, prinsipalotik ta jkosilaltik, schi'uk te me oy yantik kolo' winiketik, altik no'ox syutz'inotik, te oy stzoblej jna'wanej ku'untik x'abolaj ta jtojoltik, schi'uk yak sjel sbaik ta jujun u, ta jujun jabil. Tana jelavem jbiiltik, schi'uk ik'bilotik ba'el ta meltzanwanej k'op, ta koltaywanej jkosilaltik manchuk Indiokotik wo'ne.

Jalal nich'nab: jamoik sch'ulel asat, tana ch'aybilix apatan; ja' no'ox ko'ol yak jtojtik yol bik'it k'anojel,[61] Donativo sbiil, yu'un mu to xlaj jwokoltik, schi'uk yu'n ech ta jch'untik schanibal takiob jkojowtik Dyos: xaxi', xak'ex atot, ame'; xa'abolaj ta swokol, xakoltay ta sme'anal xawak'be swaj, syuch'umo', xakusbe sya'lel sat ta ok'el; mu xawilbajin ta k'op, ta pasojel, schi'uk ta snopojibal ach'ulel, yu'n k'ux ta jka'i li toyol mulil ta jkoronton; ech xtakiwan jkojowtik Dyos.

Tana awa'iik; tot sbiil alume winik laj yak'botik jwinkileltik; tot albil euk much'u oy syabtel, much'u oy stakiel yu'n Dyos; tot albil much'u yak schanubtesbotik smelol k'op, smelol utzil pasojel; tot albil much'u mu jtabetik syabilal; schi'uk tot albil much'u winik, much'u espanyol kristyano yak skoltayotik ta nutzel lo'lowanej, schi'uk ta slajesel jwokoltik. Schi'uk te me li muk'ta winiketik ja' no'ox syabtelanik utzil paswanej ta jtojoltik. ¿K'usi yu'un mu jkoltaytik ta jutuk Donativo tak'in?[62] Te me jo'otik snich'nabotik, chabibilotik ta swokol, ta sme'anal, ta syutzilal, ta stzatzal jtot, jbankiltik kristyano espanyoletik, ¿K'u cha'al mu xkak'betik cha'p'ej, oxp'ej sat[63] tak'in yu'n smanik swaj, syuch'umo', yu'n sjapuy sbaik, syipan sbaik ta snutzel jtzameswanejetik yak syutz'inik jkosilaltik, schi'uk altik no'ox sk'an smilotik?

Malayo, malayo jutuk jalal nich'nab; x'ech' to jwokoltik, schi'uk te xawil k'u cha'al xnichimaj talel jlumaltik; tana oy to jwokol; schi'uk ta yo'lil nix wokol yak awinajes talel, yak awa'i, yak ak'abuy syutzilal syoronton atot, abankil espanyol kristyano, ja' x'abolaj ta atojolik.

K'alal x'ech' jnutzeltik, toj chopol[64] xawil abaik, skotol takiel, syutzilal k'op yu'n stzoblej jna'wanej ku'untik, talem ta stojol akuxlejik; ta schabiel sk'ulejal ana, ta sk'exel, ta sk'uxubinel awinkilel; mu xach'ayik ta amul syutzilal li k'op lok'em talel ta syo'lil jkosilaltik.

A te me mu'yuk amul, mu'yuk much'u justisya stzitz awinkilel; te me oy much'u winik ofisyal, prinsipal, altik no'ox syutz'inot, altik no'ox syilbajintesot, stoj nix euk smul ta yichon jkojowtik Rey, yu'n mu laj sch'un smeltzanwanej k'op yu'n stzomlej jna'wanej ku'untik.

Ta k'unk'un no'ox nopoik awa'i ta ach'ulelik a li sk'oplal jtot, jbankiltik tz'ibabil talel ta jun; schi'uk tey xawil ta asat k'u cha'al jutuk xa sk'an xlaj jme'analtik, jwokoltik, ok'elwanej k'op oy vo'ne ta yut jkorontontik.

Ak'o achikin, ak'o sch'ulel asat ta syutzilal li alwanej. Tana li' no'ox ta jech muk'ta nab; li' no'ox ta stz'el jwinkileltik, yak xcha'tzob sbaik yantik jna'wanej, meltzanwanej k'op ku'untik, ja' no'ox xkiltik syabtelanik schapojibal jwokoltik. Tana mu xa xwinaj ta ora skotol ech k'usi yepal utzilwanej, abolteswanej pasojel chajpanbil ta jtojoltik; stuk mu nomuk oy syutzilal k'ajk'al xyak'botik ta p'isel, ta ilel ta spikel smuibel jch'uleltik, snichimajel jlumaltik. Ja' yu'un li' ta syochebal jabil laj awilix muk'ta k'in, ta autayel sjunal, stakiel jkosilaltik, Konstitusyon sbiil.

Ilo me awil aba jalal nich'nab, mu me echuk yak spas slo'lowanej Napoleon; jo'on jk'uxubinot; jo'on jchopes awokol; jo'on jmak'linot xi no'ox; schi'uk yan jowiel k'op, yan kolo' pasojel oy ta syoronton.

Mu me awak' aba, jalal nich'nab, ta sbelel bolil, toy bail, jowiel, schi'uk yantik mulil stunoj jtzameswanejetik yu'un. Ok'elal mutz'o asat; mako achikin, mu me k'usi sokpuk ajol, ta spojowil, ta skolo' muk'ta xulub chon, oy ta k'atin bak; ja' no'ox xawil, xawa'i, xachanubtes smelol li ch'ul k'op, takibil talel yu'n Dyos, schi'uk yu'un kristyano espanyol jtzoblejtik oy ta jech muk'ta nab.

Tana yak scha'tzob sbaik prinsipal jna'wanej ku'untik, li' ta noch, li' ta syochebal muk'ta nab, ta Guatemala, schi'uk ta yan espanyol jobelaltik; ta ba'i, ja' no'ox yak xbat syabtelanik, schanubtesel jnich'ontik.

Unetik, jnich'nabtik, much'utik schanubtes jun ta lekil eskwela, syojtakin[65] syajwalel Dyos; syojtakin a li muk'ta sbatel osil x'alot ta jchikintik; syojtakin k'u cha'al oy sch'ulel[66] ta yut stakupal; syojtakin smuk'tikal swinkilel: smuk'tikal ch'ul sbiil: syojtakin euk k'usi wan jkuchtik wokol li' ta balumil: k'usi yu'n xlok' sya'lel sat ta ok'elwanej: schi'uk syojtakin k'u cha'al xmuilaj snichimajik ta sbatel osil kuxel Dyos.

Syojtakin euk, k'usi wan yu'un jxi', jk'extik, jtot, jme'tik, jnopol, jnocholtik, schi'uk syojtakin, k'usi wan yu'un k'u xka'itik , jo'ol xkiltik k'u cha'al xtakiwan Dyos.

A te jchan junetik ta lekil eskwela, syojtakin k'usi wan yu'un tzobolotik ta balumil; k'usi wan yu'un mu lekuk jtuntik sbelel pukuj; k'usi wan yu'un mu lekuk syayijesotik k'u cha'al bolometik; k'usi wan yu'un xmajwan stzitzwan justisyaetik, mu yu'nuk no'ox sk'an syorontonik stuk ja' no'ox yu'un stojobtesel jpasojeltik, schi'uk snopojibal jch'uletik.

Sbolil, spojowil jvinkileltik, jtakupaltik jkich'ojtik talel wo'ne ta yalajebal[67] jme'tik Eva, mu lekuk xa'i tzitzel, takiel stuk xtal to, jalal nich'nab ta slajebal balumil, jun muk'ta k'ajk'al, tey jk'opon jbatik schi'uk xkaltik ta jch'uleltik, wokol awalbotik muk'ta Dyos; utzil albilot tana ta skotol pasojel, yu'un laj atzitz jtakupal ta wokol; laj atojobtes jxanbal ta balumil wokol awal jtot, jme', jkojow Rey, jkojowtik Justisyas, Dyos stojbeot jna'wanejetik, jbankiltik espanyoletik kristyano; ak'o syik'ot talel ch'ul jme'tik Maria li' ta kuxlej buy nakal oyotik ta yichon jpaswanej, jch'ijteswanej balumil; ak'o sk'uxubinot ta stokalil xanbal; ta slo'lowanej pukuj, ta sbelel achob ta swayel asat, yu'un laj awak'bon ch'ul jo' yu'un laj achanubteson xi'el xk'exel Dyos, schi'uk xi'el sk'exel sk'exolil Dyos oy ta balumil wokol awalbotik, yu'un laj ajam sch'ulel jsat; yu'un laj atojobtes jnopojibal, jk'op, jpasojel k'alal chukul oyon wo'ne ta jtakupal, schi'uk yu'un laj awinajtesbon sbelel

bujtz'anijel, sbelel winajel ta sbatel osil. Ech xk'opojik ach'ulelik, jalal nich'nab, k'alal xalok' batel ta balumil, schi'uk ja' yu'un stzoboj sba tana skotol jna'wanej, j'aboltawanej ku'untik. Tana mu xu' sk'abuy asat skotol syutzilal chajpanbil ta syorontonik stuk mu nomuk oy syorail, xawil, xawa'i, xapik skuxlej, smuibel awosilal.

Jutuk xa sk'an xawil ta eskwela lekil Maystroetik, stz'unik ta syoronton anich'nab, skotol lekil pasojel takibil talel yu'un Dyos. Tana tajimol no'ox spasoj awil keremetik; stuk j'ok'uk[68] no'ox sk'an x'ech' jwokoltik ta snutzel jtzameswanejetik; jutuk xa sk'an xjam talel nichimtasbil stenlej jchan junetik; jutuk xa sk'an sakub syosilal jna'wanejetik, ech k'u cha'al muk'ta rojowil k'ajk'al ta syo'lil winajel, schi'uk ech k'u cha'al bik'tal jo', xtal xach'tes stz'unijibal jlumaltik. Tey xa k'u cha'al xnichimaj anich'nab ta jun ta tz'ibajel. Tey xawil k'u cha'al spas sbaik muk'ta winiketik; muk'ta padreetik, muk'ta kaxlanetik. Tey xawil k'u cha'al xleblojik ta stzoblej jna'wanejetik oy ta balumil.

Syutzilal, jchobtik, jp'olomaltik, jchonbaltik; schi'uk sk'ulejal jnatik, ja' no'ox yak sk'abuyik, ja' no'ox yak snopilan, yak schajpan jtot, jbankiltik espanyol kristyanoetik.

Stzoblej jobelaltik takibilix tana ku'untik ja' no'ox syajtay; ja' no'ox yak snop ta syorontonik k'u cha'al xwinaj, ku'untik smukojibal k'anal tak'in, sakil tak'in oy ta yibel balumil, k'u cha'al xlaj, k'u cha'al xpoxtaj, ame'anal schi'uk ame'ebal, k'usi wan spasik yu'n xnoj ana, awosilal, ta yepal wakax, yepal kabayo, yepal[69] chitom, yepal mut, yepal ixim, yepal tuxnok', seda, asukal, kokow, schi'uk skotol k'usitikuk spas talel ak'ulejal, schi'uk akuxlej, mu xa'i euk ta syoronton jtzoblejtik smeltzanibal ana; stojobtesel sbelel jlumaltik; swinajtesel sjamel slupojibal[70] yoxo'[71] schi'uk skotol lekil paswanej chajpanbilix, ilbilix ta jtojoltik.

Tana j'ok'uk xa sk'an xlaj sch'ajil, swayel winiketik; j'ok'uk xa sk'an xawilik wa'lanbil abolteswanej nanatik, yu'un me'balal jchameletik; ok'elal ech xlaj swokol jlumaltik. Jutuk xa sk'an xtal lekil Maystroetik xyak'beot awil sk'op Dyos; stz'ibajel jun; sjolobil pok'; stenojibal tak'in, karpintero, albanyil, schi'uk yantik abtelwanej; na'wanej, spas talel sk'ulejal ana, schi'uk skuxlej anich'nab.

Ech xawil; mu'nix jutuk xlubtzaj syoronton jk'uxuwanejetik kristyano espanyoletik; li' nox ta noch, ta syochebal muk'ta nab wa'lanbilix swinkilel yan tzoblej laj kalbeoxuk xach'bil no'ox sch'ulel sat, mu x'och swayel ta schajpanel padreetik, ch'ultasbil winiketik xtal stz'unik lekil pasojel, schi'uk ta slumal jontolil winiketik, mu yich'ojuk ch'ul jo' ta sch'ulel. Tey xawil k'u cha'al xtitin schukebal sch'ulelik; k'u cha'al xjam smakojibal sat,[72] k'u cha'al jchi'intik ta tzoblej; k'u cha'al schi'inotik stukelik ta stunel Winajel xanbal; te xawa'i k'u cha'al stoy snuk'[73] padreetik, k'u cha'al muk'ta ok'es ta sna, ta syosilal mu ilbiluk winiketik, mi ilbiluk kabenaletik; ok'elal petbil aba, xach'bil ak'ob, schi'uk anopol, anochol; puk'bil, xach'bil awosilal schi'uk swinkilel li ach' kristyanoetik; ajch'em asat ta ok'elwanej muibel, xatzob abaik ta sk'ajinel schi'uk wob, xapuk' abaik ta autayel syutzilal syabolteswanej jkojowtik Dyos.

Awa'iik k'u cha'al xk'opoj to ati'; la'ik, la'ik, much'utik winiketik mu yich'ojuk jo' wo'ne; la'ik much'utik achi'inoj wo'ne pukuj, bolom, tzemen, xulub chon,[74] ta yibel ton, ta te'laltik; la'ik, komesoik sk'eawil chamebal; komeso stokalil asat; toyo ajol; la'ik, olonanik ta jk'obtik; la'ik jtoytik syajwalel[75] jnuk'tik ta yichon Dyos; la'ik jch'ultestik ta sbatel osil a te jPaswanej, jCh'ijteswanej balumil; la'ik jch'ultestik euk syutzilal kristyano jtzoblejtik, mu'yuk ta lok'el no'ox yan utzilal; yan ch'unwanej k'op, swa'lan sba stoy sba ta stz'el, ta yichon li meltzanwanej pasojel toj muk' albil ta skotol osil.[76]

Jalal nich'nab, oy kolo' pasojel; oy lotwanej k'op ta sti', ta sye malch'unwanej jtzameswanejetik; stuk tana, mu xu' xanop ta aworontonik, lo'lowanej no'ox wan yak spas kristyano espanyoletik; mu echuk, jalal nich'nab; ta skotol balumil oy malwanej, stuk oy euk utzilwanej; oy lotwanej, stuk oy koltaywanej; oy lotwanej tz'ibajel, stuk oy melelwanej tz'ibajel; oy yayijesel, stuk oy euk poxtawanej; oy ilbajinel, stuk oy abolteswanej; oy bulbunel k'op, stuk oy meltzanwanej k'op; oy bolil winiketik, stuk oy na'wanej winiketik; oy jmalch'unwanejetik, stuk oy euk melel ch'unbol Dyos.

Ilo me awil, jalal nich'nab, jkosilaltik kristyano espanyol, mu laj sch'ay junuk ora stakiwanej Dios lok'em talel ta sti', ta sye ch'ul Apostol Santiago; me oy jmultik k'u cha'al mulawil winiketik; oy euk kristyano ok'elwanej ta jch'uleltik; schi'uk li k'op, li abolteswanej ta tz'ibajel talem ta atojolik, mu lotwanejuk, mu tajimoluk; winkilajem lok'em talel ta atojolik, mu lotwanejuk, mu tajimoluk; winkilajem lok'em talel ta syoronton atot, abankil, awajustisya, kristyano espanyoletik;[77] awa'iik k'u cha'al xk'opoj smelol sch'ulelik.

Jalal nich'nab: jbankiltik, indioetik, a te much'u sjapuyoj sba ta syajwalel Dyos: much'utik jutzul oy ta yalajebal jkosiltik; much'utik mu sokemuk sjol ta slo'lowanej pukuj; schi'uk yich'oj ta sti' ba ch'ul jo'; ch'ul yetal, ch'ul marka swinajtesel kuxlej, ta syalan j'abolteswanej Jesus, schi'uk batz'il tzeub Santa Maria. Awa'iik, cha'lok'el, oxlok'el xkalbeoxuk indio espanyol kristyanoetik; much'utik mu sna' xlubtzaj syorontonik ta skuchel wokol; ilbajinel, me'anal, chukwanej; majel; awa'iik, much'utik stunoj no'ox ch'ul xanbal sme', ch'ul xanbal syosilal, stzatzal sbankilal kristyano espanyoletik; much'utik snutzoj skolo' jtzameswanejetik, schi'uk spetojik syutzilal Dios; awa'iik lekil k'op, lekil pasojel winajem ta stz'el awinkilel, ta syo'lil jkosilaltik.

Toj ep sk'uxubinot awajRey, awajtzoblej jna'wanejetik; skotol meltzanwanej k'op yu'unik, ta ba'i yak xtalik ta stojolik indioetik, yu'n chabibilot ta sch'ulelik;

awosilal, ach'ul me', ja' no'ox yak sp'is, yak snop akuxlej; ja' no'ox sk'an yak'beot awil k'u cha'al smuk'tikal k'uxubinwanej yu'un; k'u cha'al xyak' sba ta sk'ob jmilwanej; k'u cha'al skuch ilbajinel, lubtzajel, takin ti'il, schi'uk yan yepal wokol, ta smak'linel ach'ulelik ta schajpanel akuxlej, schi'uk ta spoxtayel ame'anal.

Yepal jabil i'ech' tana x'ok' syoronton, smich' sch'ulel jtot, jbankiltik kristyano espanyoletik yu'n chukul osil yak yil ta schajpanel syutzilal alumalik; tana mu chukuluk osil; j'ok'uk no'ox sk'an, skus sba sat atot, abankil espanyol, yu'n ta noch yak swinajes syutzilal jkosilaltik, schi'uk utzil albil ta skotol osil; tana ich'bilix sp'isol, snopojibal jkuxlejtik, wa'lanbilix jna'wanejetik ta stzoblej kristyano jobeltik; li' no'ox ta stz'el jwinkileltik; tana mu xu' xkaltik, k'u cha'al wo'ne, toj nom oy ta slajebal muk'ta nab, meltzanej k'op ku'untik a'yejibal parte ku'untik; tana mu xjalaj spoxil k'anojibal ta yichon li nochol tzoblej.

Il awil jalal nich'nab k'u cha'al xlebloj sxojowil k'ajk'al ta swinajeseb stz'ibajel jkojowtik Rey, jkojowtik tzoblej. Laj awa'iik k'usitik ibat syabtelanik jna'wanej ku'untik najkajik ta Kadis, schi'uk skotol k'usitikuk xtal syabtelan cha'tzoblej, xnajkaj li' ta noch, li' ta jech, ta yochebal muk'ta nab.

Xp'ijt ta muibel aworonton; xnichimaj sya'yejibal achikin, me xap'is, me xanop ta ach'ulel, smuk'tikal, syutzilal li k'op, schi'uk syutzilal takiwanej konstitusyon sbiil, autabilix ta pregon, schi'uk ta k'in i'ech' ta jlumaltik. Skotol k'usi sk'an ach'ulel akuxlej; skotol abolteswanej, utzilwanej xawinajtes, xu' xak'upin ta balumil, skotol tz'ibil ta sjunal Konstitusyon, schi'uk ta syoronton kristyano espanyol jtzoblejtik, yak cha'najkajuk li' ta stz'el jwinkileltik.

Jkojowtik Rey, jkojowtik Justisias, yak snop ta syorontonik smuibajel akuxlejik ta sjapuel, ta sch'unel, xi'el xk'exel a li Rejensya sbiil, a te schabioj sk'exol, syajwalel jkojowtik Rey, yak smaliik sk'uxubinel aworontonik ta stojol jkosilaltik.

A te kristyano espanyol tzoblej mu sk'an spas lo'lowanej, mu tajimoluk yak spas schi'uk smalijebal yepal nich'nab, mu xch'ay, mu xtup', yu'un wa'lanbilix ta sba li melol meltzanwanej k'op.

Tana yak no'ox sjat sba syoronton jtzoblejtik ta schajpanel spoxil jwokoltik, manchuk nom oyuk sba muk'ta tzoblej najkajem ta sjobelal Kadis, oy tana cha'tzoblej ku'untik ta stz'el jwinkileltik, xtal no'ox syabtelan utzilal paswanej ta jtojoltik, schi'uk ta stojol indioetik, much'utik schabi stakiel Dyos, schi'uk sna'ik xi'el sk'exel k'uxubinel sk'exolil Dyos ta balumil.

Jtzoblejtik ech sk'an stoj stzatzalel, syutzilal much'utik winiketik laj skoltaik, laj sjapuik jkosilaltik ta snutzel kolo' jtzameswanej Napoleon, schi'uk ech nix sk'an swinajtes ta sat lo'lowanej, schi'uk ta schikin bolil winiketik laj stun jtzameswanejetik, mu'nix k'usi lekuk laj staik ta sxanbalil Napoleon, ta sbelel chamebal, schi'uk ta sjatel ta yayijesel, jkosilaltik.

Manchuk xtal yan toy bail winik, yan kolo' kaxlan; manchuk slap talel lekil sk'u'; manchuk xk'opoj k'u cha'al xk'opojik yantik winiketik sk'exolil Dyos, mu xach'unbeik slo'lowanej; mu me xatunik ta swalapat; yich'oj talel kolo' ta syoronton; ja' no'ox sk'an smal jch'ich'eltik. ¿Bu xtal kuxlej ku'untik, te me ja' no'ox xpukij chamebal, ilbajinel, ik'ti', wokol, malch'unwanej, me'anal, wi'nal, pojwanej, milwanej, schi'uk yantik pojow xulub chon, mu ilbiluk ta ora ku'untik? ¿Te me yak yik'otik ba'el ta k'atin bak; te me yak stasbotik talel ta jkak'oltik stzitzwanej, syilinteswanej Dyos ta sbatel osil? ¿K'u cha'al xyak'botik batz'il kuxlej jtzameswanejetik? Mu xach'un slo'lowanej, jalal nich'nab.

A te me oy xataik much'u winik sk'an spak'taex[78] ta mulil, sk'an syotes kolo' ta ach'ulelik, mako achikin anilajanik, ak'oik parte ta yichon Justisyaetik. Me oy xata much'u winik xyalbeot: la' jnich'nab, li' oy atot, li' oy abolteswanej, jo'on jchopes awokoll, ech xasutesbeik ak'op:

Yak jkojtakinot jtzameswanej, jna'ix sk'an ach'ay jch'ulel; sk'an awok' jkosilal, mu chibuk jkosilal, k'u cha'al xak'an; jun no'ox jlumal schi'uk espanyol kristyanoetik snich'nab Dyos, syak'oj sbaik ta milel ta jtojoltik; lok'an, lok'an; mu'yuk much'u yik'ot talel; mu xtal asok jkoronton; jun no'ox Dyos; hun no'ox Rey sk'exolil Dyos yak jch'un; oy batz'il jtot; oy jbankil kristyano espanyoletik; oy jna'wanejetik, jkoltaywanejetik, j'abolteswanejetik laj yak'bonik jkil, laj swinajtesbonik stakiel Dyos; sk'uxubinel jnopol, jnochol schi'uk sbelel winajel; mu me xtal apojbon li syutzilal sbatel osil; mu me xtal awak'bon stunejibal chamebal. ¿K'usi stu ku'un balumil, schi'uk skotol k'usitikuk, me xch'ay jch'ulel? Laj awa'iik, jalal nich'nab, ech xasutesik ak'op ta yichon jlo'lowanejetik, xchi'uk te me x'ilin ta atojolik, mu k'usi, oy Dyos, oy skuxlej jch'uleltik ta winajel schi'uk ta sbatel osil.

A te syosilal Inglesetik, i'abolaj euk ta jtojoltik; yak skoltayotik ta jnutzeltik; manchuk oyuk much'u kolo' winik xyalbotik yak yilbajinotik Ingles ko'ol schi'uk jtzameswanejetik; mu xach'unik li pak'ta k'op, jalal nich'nab. A te Inglesetik yak sk'uxubin jkosilaltik yak'oj sba ta milel, ta wokol, ta jk'ojtik, k'u cha'al espanyol kristyanoetik.

Ingles schi'uk Espanyol kristyano, ko'ol xil sbaik, ko'ol yak sjapuy sbaik, xchi'uk jun no'ox koltaywanej yak spasik. Li' ta jun jabil i'ech', ta chib xcha'winik sk'ajk'alel Julyo, ital muk'ul kapitan sbiil Welington, schi'inoj talel wakpik', xchi'uk jo'ob ta bok'[79] ingles soldadoetik, schi'uk li utzilwanej winiketik laj snutzi ba'el a te kolo' jtzameswanejetik; laj stitinik jchukeltik schi'uk laj xlubtzajik stoy bail Napoleon; te me toj melel xwinaj ta balumil syutzilal a li pasojel; te me yak xmuibaj inglesetik ta skoltayel jch'uleltik, schi'uk te me syak'oj sbaik ta milel, ta koltaywanej ku'untik, ¿K'u cha'al jch'untik slot jtzameswanejetik sk'an no'ox swok' jkosilaltik, schi'uk sk'uxubinel inglesetik?

Awai'ik tana yan k'op; a te jobel sbiil Madrid laj skuch yepal wokol k'alal ta lajchaeb sk'ajk'alel Agosto; li ta yan jabil i'ech'. A te jobel Kadis, nutzibil, makbil ta jtzameswanejetik, lajuneb scha'winik u; k'alal ta jo'ob scha'winik sk'ajk'alel Agosto, li' to ta jabil i'ech'. Tana yak no'ox spet sbaik ta muibel; yak no'ox xnichimajik ta yichon Dyos, yu'un laj sk'elik slajebal sutub ik'; slajebal jtzameswanejetik lok'emik ba'el ta k'exlal jataw.

A te skolo', sjowi, slo'lowanej jtzameswanejetik, mu xu' stup'es ta jun; mu xu' sch'ayik ta sna'ojibal balumil a li muk'ta pasojel; a li koltaywanej laj spasik kristyano espanyoletik, inglesetik, schi'uk yan lekil osil sbiil Portugal. A te jkosilaltik yak sk'opon Dyos, ta stojol li utzil jkoltaywanejetik ku'untik, schi'uk ta sbatel osil mu lekuk xtup' ta jkorontontik a li utzil paswanej, schi'uk stzatzalel jmololtik inglesetik, smaloj sch'ich'el yu'un jkuxlejtik. Ja' yu'un yak spas muk'ta mulil much'u kolo' winik mu sch'un syutzilal jnopoltik, jmololtik inglesetik. Mu xach'un, jalal nich'nab, a te kolo' a'yej, kolo' k'opwanej sk'an no'ox swalk'un snopojibal jch'uleltik.

Tana oy ta balumil yantik osilaltik sbiil Rusia schi'uk Swesia, jchi'inotik ta koltaywanej; schi'uk a te muk'ul ojow sbiil Alejandro, yak sk'uxubin jkojowtik Rey Fernando; syojtakin, schi'uk utzil albil yu'un jna'wanejetik, jtzoblejtik, schi'uk skotol meltzanwanej k'op takibil talel ta sjunal Konstitusyon laj kalbeoxuk. Ech jun no'ox lok'el, mu xch'ay smuibel jmalijebaltik; jutuk xa sk'an xwalk'un sba jnutzeltik; j'ok'uk no'ox sk'an sjel sba syelow balumil, syelow jwokoltik, schi'uk jutuk sk'an xwinaj talel snichimajel lum, ta jech muk'ta nab, sbiil Yuropa, ta jkosilaltik sbiil Espanyas, schi'uk ta stz'el jwinkileltik, k'u cha'al sp'isoj, schajpanoj, smalioj jkojowtik Rey.

A te sba tzoblej ku'untik, a te chabiwanej syajwalel, sk'exolil jkojowtik Rey, Rejensya sbiil, ech laj staki talel; ech laj tz'ibay ta jun, yu'un xajam asat ta yichon syutzilal li k'op; schi'uk yu'n ko'ol xawilik espanyol kristyanoetik snich'onik Dyos; jbankiltik, jnopol, jnocholtik; mu me xawak' abaik ta kolo' lo'lowanej; mako achikinik ta yichon jtzameswanejetik, yak no'ox xautayik kuxlej, kuxlej; schi'uk smukojik chamebal, ilbajinel ta sch'ulelik.

¡A pobre winiketik, kaxlanetik, indioetik, much'utik yalemik ta kolo' xanbal; sujtan abaik; ochanik talel ta syalajebal, ta syoronton atzoblej, ame', awosilal!

A te kristyano espanyol jkosilaltik, yak ta sk'uxubinot, smak'linot, mu stzitz abolil, mu k'usi xyalbeot; yak no'ox spetot ta sk'ob, te me xakomtzan milwanej; ilbajinel; polwanej, schi'uk te me xawok'etay skotol amul laj apasik ta yichon Dyos, ta yichon atot, abankil, schi'uk yantik winiketik, altik no'ox laj amalbeik sch'ich'el, laj apikbeik sk'uxubinwanej syoronton; stuk oy to spoxil amul; la'ik, mu me xayayijes ach'ulelik ta sbatel osil; ak'o lok'uk, lok'uk sya'lel asat; mu me xap'is abaik, mu me xatoy abaik, schi'uk stzatzal jch'ijteswanej jpaswanej balumil.

Jalal nich'nab: a li ch'ultasbil jun tz'ibabil ta jobel Kadis, ta lajuneb xcha'winik sk'ajk'alel Agosto, a li jabil i'ech' sbiil 1812. Winajesbil smelol ta sk'ob sba Gobernador jtzoblejtik Rejensya, sbiil.

El Duque del infantado. Presidente.

NOTES

1. I have placed the friar's notes that comment primarily on the "Tzotzil" language here, while those that reflect his worldview are placed following the "Great Proclamation Sent by Our Lord, The King to People Living Here on This Side of The Ocean". The friar annotated both the "Tzotzil" and his Spanish translation. I have italicized here the notes occurring in the Spanish column. When the friar attached his notes to a particular word within the sentence, I have done so also.

2. This means King, supreme authority, or Government.

3. *Or Nation, not interpreting the word <u>osil</u> as light.*

4. Emphasizing the throatiness, because saying <u>cog</u> [koj] with ease means bridge and not mask.

5. *Or tooth, not interpreting the word <u>osil</u> as light.*

6. *Or vague conversation that is heard.*

7. *And behind or towards the back.*

8. This means 25 *jiquipiles*, each *jiquipil* is 20 *zontles*, each *zontle* is 400 grains, which would be 200,000 grains or soldiers.

9. <u>Xyac</u> [xyak] is not interpreted as give, submit or put, rather for a phrase that explains something mistaken.

10. *Or rabid.*

11. One does not say caxlan or Spaniard alone, rather, Christian Spaniard, because the I Indians do not understand that one is referring to all white men.

12. <u>Osil</u> means eternity here.

13. This means whatever height or elevation.

14. *Or pus or something that looks like soot.*

15. *Tooth means mouth.*

16. Seventy-five *jiquipiles* of murderers in the terms explained before, adding afterwards that to count 20 one says <u>tom</u>; [jtob] but reaching two twenties one says <u>chahuinic</u> [cha'winik] three twenties, <u>oxhuinic</u> [oxwinik]: <u>jolahuneb</u> [jo'lajuneb] is fifteen,which added to the three twenties makes seventy five; and so <u>joluneb xchanhuinic ta pic</u> [jo'lajuneb xchanwinik ta pik'] means fifteen counted by four twenties in *jiquipiles.* *One does not count by jiquipiles until the numbering reaches 20 zontles, nor by zontles until the figure is composed of four hundred grains, men, pesos, etc.* <u>Hohuinic</u> [vo'winik] *are 5 twenties*; <u>lahunhuinic</u> [lajunwinik], *10 twenties,* <u>jolahunhuinic</u> [jo'lajunwinik], *15 twenties;* <u>Voc</u> [jbok'], *20 twenties, which is 400, or a zontle*; *in this way one continues counting up to 20 zontles that makes a jiquipil that is 8,000 pesos, which is what the word* <u>pic</u> [jpik'] *means.*

17. This is an expression to explain the adverse.

18. *That is, crowded, pushed by others.*

19. Souls here mean lives.

20. This word means "but;" and not "only" as elsewhere.

21. This is the way to indicate a hamlet, a mean hut, as a cattle shed or that looks like a bull.

22. This means "nation."

23. *As one who follows in the footsteps of another.*

24. This is the way to denote what is a column or rampart.

25. *As a violent impulse.*

26. *Meaning a voice that speaks with a disconcerting and turbulent pronunciation.*
27. This does not mean here "and," but "with."
28. Here it does not mean a flowering, but contentedness.
29. In the passage of time, of light or eternity.
30. *As when squeezing with the hands.*
31. *Or "called good."*
32. A word that is used to mean injustice or futility.
33. An expression that denotes compensation or just revenge. *This means just vengeance, when it is uttered or spoken with menace.*
34. *Or it will not be erased or forgotten.*
35. *That is, they will be born.*
36. *Here the verb is the determinant, i.e.* xtal, *come,* ytal *[ital], came,* xtalto *[xtal to], he or they will come.*
37. A *zontle* and fifteen twenties of years.
38. Huinagel [Winajel] is what is descried at a distance, and that is how they name the sky.
39. Here the plural is assumed for the two preceding nouns put in the singular, for better pronunciation. (i.e. the plural termination is only added here to the last of the three words, but meant to apply—so we are told—to all of them.)
40. With the term, quexol [k'exol] is meant the substitution, that is that the blood and tears may flourish. *He has the recompense to demand justice and public good.*
41. It is an expression that they use to mean difficulty in breathing, or excessive anxiety, which they call "air of the mouth." (icti, [ik'ti'] sigh).
42. This means dryness of the mouth, or thirst.
43. This is another expression that means he who is silent because of humiliation or admiration; but if it is not pronounced violently, it means "snake," in the Zendal (Tzeltal) language.
44. Close one's eyes with fear.
45. *The spirit, soul, or sight of your eyes.*
46. One omits the "i" (in *pleito*) to imitate the pronunciation of the Indians.
47. Here the preceding singular elements are plural. (See note 39.)
48. *This verb is repeated many times, because it is indispensable.*
49. Pussy words, which mean venom or poison.
50. *This means the death of the soul and the body.*
51. Here the singular means the plural.
52. Yamal means the adverse, the bad, the impassible.
53. This does not mean purely fire or sun, rather, a sunny day.
54. That is, not that they are holding each other affectionately, but rather in struggle, according to the meaning of that which they are about to say. Sjapujog sbá [sjapujoj sba] should be translated in the plural for better speech.
55. *Or dislocated, a term that means the perturbation of ideas.*
56. This has the legitimate meaning: not only will he not serve, which is what it arbitrarily means, and that is the way the Indians understand it in the way they speak their language.
57. This means not only spirit, but also authority, indicating the third person with s.
58. Constrained or pushed.
59. This is how you understand what is…

60. It being certain that he who works against divine will or sovereign precepts cannot be a good man.

61. *This is what they call the contribution of the Donation.*

62. *It equals any amount of silver or coin of whatever value or size.*

63. This is for whatever silver piece or coin of any value or size.

64. *This term does not mean cowardliness or laziness, but rather something at rest or not tied up, with this expression is understood what is alleviation or alleviated.*

65. Here the singular means plural for sounding better and more intelligent.

66. *This and other words placed in the singular are denoted by the plural in which the sentence begins this way: The kids, our children. This is the common usage of the Indians, and so for them it is indifferent whether the following verbs or nouns are in the singular or the plural, so long as at the beginning one discovers the person who is doing the action.*

67. Because you gave me blessed water, or you baptised me.

68. This is an expression that denotes a small period of time.

69. This term is repeated many times in similar cases for greater clarity.

70. The source of water, being fluid material that is received in the corresponding receptacles, because if it is solid, there is another term to designate similar places.

71. This is what they call clear, cristalline water.

72. Using the singular for the plural: one should say S Satic [satik]: but then they could think one had said 'eye of air [sat ik'],' black eyes, and not 'their eyes,' or from their eyes.'

73. This means the voice of the throat, according to the meaning of the words that follow.

74. Animal with horns, or serpent.

75. This means a spirit that resounds in the throat.

76. That is, that there is no other thought, word, or deed that can claim to better or equal what has been. *That is: there is no other thought, word, or deed that can claim primacy or a parallel with what has been.*

77. Here the plural refers to the preceding cases placed in the singular.

78. What wishes to confound us or make us accomplices.

79. See note in the folio. (Note 37.)

References Cited

MANUSCRIPTS, OFFICIAL DOCUMENTS

AG—Archivo General del Gobierno, (now the Archivo General de Centro América), Guatemala City.
AGE—Archivo General del Estado, Tuxtla Gutiérrez, Chiapas.
AGI—Archivo General de las Indias, Seville.
AGN—Archivo General de la Nación, Mexico City.
AHD—Archivo Histórico Diocesano de San Cristóbal de Las Casas, Chiapas.
INAH—Instituto Nacional de Antropología e História, Mexico City.
LC—Library of Congress, Washington, D.C.

de la Barrera, Josef,
   1788. Libro de lengua tzotzil en que se hablara la doctrina christiana con preguntas y explicacion, administracion de los sacramentos, dos artes, barios sermones, y otras cosas que el curioso puede ver para su aprovechamiento. 157 pages. Washington, D.C.: LC.
Correa, José, Miguel,
   1804. Breve esplicacion de la lengua tzotzil para los pueblos de la provincia de Chiapas. 102 pages. AHD; III, B5.

PROCLAMATIONS

"Castellanos," Joaquín Mosquera y Figueroa, Cadiz, ? January, 1812, AHD.
"Extremeños," Joaquín Mosquera y Figueroa, Cadiz, ? February, 1812, AHD.
"Manuscrito en Lengua Sotzil," typescript copy of translation of proclamation signed by the Duque del Infantado, by William E. Gates, 1930 (?), Archives of the Bureau of American Ethnology, Smithsonian Institution, 3168:IV, National Anthropological Archives.
"Proclama a los españoles americanos," Los Sevillanos, 1808?, Biblioteca del Senado, Madrid; 041478.
"Proclama a los españoles europeos," El Duque del Infantado, Cadiz, 28 August, 1812, AGN; Impresos Oficiales, 30:80.
"Proclama a la Suprema Junta Central," Antonio de Aguirre Arza y Sanpelayo, Havana, 16 December 1808, AGI; leg. 51B:205.
"Proclama a los habitantes de ultramar," El Duque del Infantado, 30 August, 1812, Cadiz, AGN; Reales Cedulas 207:93, AHD.

"Proclama a los habitantes de ultramar," translated into Cehchi (Q'eqchi') by Padre Fr. Francisco Abella, del Orden de Predicadores, AGI; *leg.* Guatemala, 943.

"Proclama a los habitantes de ultramar," translated into Ixil by Padre FR. Francisco Abella, del Orden de Predicadores, AGI; *leg.* Guatemala, 943.

"Proclama a los habitantes de ultramar," translated into Quechua, AGI; *leg.* Indiferente General, 1525.

"Proclama a los habitantes de ultramar," translated into Zeefe (Xinca) by Don Hermenegildo Morales, Presbitero Indio, AGI; *leg.* Guatemala, 943.

"Proclama de la Madre España a sus hijos americanos," Filopatro de orden superior, Mexico City, 1811, AHD.

"Proclama de un cura indio del obispado de Valladolid, a todos los padres curas y vicarios indios, y a nuestros hijos los caziques gobernadores y demas indios de esta America," Mexico City?,1811?, Bancroft Library; Papeles varios 12:31.

"Proclama de Veracruz a los españoles americanos," la Viuda de Don Manuel Comes Esquinas de Porriño, Cadiz, n.d., The Lilly Library, Indiana University.

"Proclama del Arzobispo Virey de México, contra los engaños pérfidos de los Bonapartes," Mexico City, 24 April, 1810, AGN; Impresos Oficiales 30:53–63, LC.

"Proclama del Arzobispo Virey de Nueva España a los fieles vasallos de Fernando VII," Mexico City, 23 January, 1810, LC.

"Sotzil," Princeton University Library, the Garrett Collection of Middle American Mss., 254.

For additional published copies of "Proclama a los habitantes de ultramar" see Duque del Infantado and Rivet.

CIRCULARS, DECREES, AND REPORTS

Circular, José de Bustamante Guerra de la Vega, Rueda, Cobo, Estrada, y Zorlado, 3 September, 1811, INAH; TII, *doc.* 45.

4 September, 1811, AHD.

22 October, 1811, AHD.

8 November, 1811, AGE; Serie Chiapas, *rollo* 90.

18 November, 1811, AHD.

25 November, 1811, AHD.

10 April, 1812, AHD.

13 November, 1814, AHD; San Cristóbal, VIII, F1.

Circular, Ramón Casaus y Torres, 20 April, 1812, 1–11, AHD.

2 June, 1812, AHD.

Circular, Antonio González Mollinedo y Saravia, 15 May, 1810, AHD.

Circular, Mariano Guzmán y Solorzano, 6 May, 1813, AHD.

25 August, 1815, AHD.

Circular, Ambrosio Llano, 19 October, 1808, AHD.

17 January, 1811, AHD; San Cristóbal, II, A4.

10 July, 1811, AHD; San Cristóbal, X, C3.

13 January, 1812, AGE; Serie Chiapas, *rollo* 90.

16 April, 1812, AHD.
19 May, 1812, AHD; San Cristóbal, II, A4, AGE; Serie Chiapas, *rollo* 90.
16 October, 1812, AHD; San Cristóbal, II, A4, AGE; Serie Chiapas, *rollo* 90.
19 October 1812, AHD.
18 November, 1812, AHD; San Cristóbal, X, C3.
26 June, 1813, AHD.
22 September, 1813, AHD.
13 September, 1814, AHD.
27 October, 1814, AHD.
28 November, 1814, AHD.
Circular, Ramón Ordóñez y Aguiar,
29 December, 1815, AHD.
Circular que el Señor Gobernador de la Sagrada Mitra dirige a los Parrocos y Eclesiasticos del Arzobispado de Mexico, recordando la obediencia y fidelidad a Dios y a Nuestro Cautivo Rey Fernando VII, Mexico City, 26 April, 1810, AGN; Impresos Oficiales, 30.
Decree, José de Bustamante, 25 November, 1811, AHD.
23 December, 1811, AHD.
16 March, 1812, INAH; TII, *doc.* 48.
10 April, 1812, AHD.
12 October, 1812, AHD; X, C4.
12 July, 1813, INAH; TII, *doc.* 51.
1 December, 1815, INAH; TII, *doc.* 52.
Decree, Fernando VII, 5 September, 1809, INAH; TII, *doc.* 43.7.
5 December, 1809, INAH; TII, *doc.* 42.
7 August, 1814, AHD; San Cristóbal, X, C3.
30 May, 1815, AHD.
Decree, Antonio González, 25 January, 1805, AHD.
30 June, 1808, AHD.
Decree, Juan Hurtado, 2 January, 1788, Tulane University Library; T1, 2.
Decree, Francisco Javier de Lizana, 25 April, 1810, AGN; Impresos Oficiales, 30, 77–78.
Decree, Pedro de Macanaz, 4 May, 1814, AHD; San Cristóbal, VIII, F1.
Decree, Ramón Ordóñez y Aguiar, 3 October, 1816, AHD.
Decree of the Regency, 5 May, 1810, AGI; 1145, *est.* 88, C1, *leg.*1
15 October, 1810, AG; A1.1, *exp.* 803, *leg.* 28.
9 February, 1811, AHD.
10 February, 1811, AG, A.1.1, *exp.* 805, *leg.* 28, AGN; Reales Cedulas, 204:53, AGE, Serie Chiapas, *rollo* 90.
22 April, 1811, AG; A1.23, *leg.* 2595, *fol.* 198.
30 May, 1811, AHD; San Cristóbal, X, C3.
6 July, 1811, AHD; San Cristóbal, X, C3.
8 July, 1811, AGN; Reales Cedulas, 204, 228.
7 January, 1812, AHD.
22 January, 1812, AHD.
23 January, 1812, AHD.
24 January, 1812, AG; B1.5, *exp.* 206, *leg.* 6.
31 January, 1812, AHD.
? January, 1812, AHD.

? February, 1812, AHD.
16 April, 1812, AHD; San Cristóbal, VIII, F1.
2 June, 1812, AHD.
8 June, 1812, AG; B1.5, *exp*. 291. *leg*. 7.
14 August, 1812, AG; B1.5, *exp*. 281, *leg*. 7.
6 October, 1812, AHD.
9 November, 1812, AHD.
13 November, 1812, AHD.
16 February, 1813, AHD.
8 September, 1813, AG; B1.5, *exp*. 344, *leg*. 8.
Decree, Santo Oficio, Mexico City, 22 April, 1810, AHD.
Libro de Cordilleras 1810–1814, AHD.
Libro de Gobierno 1799–1816, AHD.
Manifiesto que el Asesor General del Reino, dirigió a los Justicias Indígenas del Reino de Guatemala, José Yañez, 5 September, 1809, Tulane University Library; II, 43.
Relación de los Meritos, Grados, y Exercicios Literarios del Lienc. D. Ambrosio Llano, Presbitero, Provisor y Vicario General de la Diocesis de Guatemala, Madrid, October 6, 1781, AHD; II,B1.
Report (?), May 24, 1835, Tulane University Library, IV, 183.
Report, Ayuntamiento de Ciudad Real, 22 January, 1805, INAH; TII, *doc*. 13.
Report, Comisión de Constitución, 24 June, 1813, AHD.
Report, Juan Nepomuceno Batres Arribillaga, Naxera, y Mencos, Ciudad Real, n.d., AG; *leg*. 2596, A1 21275.
Report, Fernando Dávila, 25 October, 1812, AHD.
Report, Martin de Garay, Junta Suprema de Sevilla, January ?, 1809, AHD.
Report, Ambrosio Llano, 14 October, 1809, AG; B2.7, *exp*. 768, *leg*. 31.
25 December, 1810, AHD.
17 September, 1812, AHD.
27 May, 1813, AHD.
1 June, 1813, AHD.
Report, Ramón Ordóñez y Aguiar, 6 May, 1813, AHD.
Report, Rector del Real Colegio de Nuestra Señora de la Concepción, 9 July, 1813, AHD.
Report, Regency, 2 June, 1812, AHD.
Report, Manuel José Solano, Quadrante de Gueyteupan 1813–1816, Huitiupán, 25 September, 1817, AHD; Huitiupán IV, C1.
Report, Juan Bartolomé Tosso, Tuxtla, 30 October, 1809, AHD.

LETTERS

Aguilera, Urbano, to Ambrosio Llano, 29 July, 1812, AHD.
Bergosa y Jordan, Antonio to Ambrosio Llano, 15 September, 1812, AHD.
de la Barrera, José, to Ambrosio Llano, 26 January, 1813, AHD.
de Berasueta, José Ignacio, to Ambrosio Llano, 18 October, 1814,AHD.
to Ambrosio Llano, 3 December, 1814, AHD.
de Bustamante Guerra de la Vega, José, to Ambrosio Llano, 29 March,1811, AHD.

to Ambrosio Llano, 3 July, 1811, AHD.
to Ambrosio Llano, 18 March, 1813, AHD.
to Ambrosio Llano, 13 September, 1814, AHD.
Capitularies to Ambrosio Llano, 14 December, 1812, AHD.
Casaus y Torres, Ramón, to Ambrosio Llano, 3 January, 1812, AHD.
to Ambrosio Llano, 3 March, 1812, AHD.
to Ambrosio Llano, 3 August, 1812, AHD.
to Ministro de la Gobernación de Ultramar, ?, 1813, AHD.
to Ministro de la Gobernación de Ultramar, 3 December, 1813, AGI; *leg.* Guatemala, 943.
Castillejos, Joseph, to Ambrosio Llano, 16 November, 1814, AHD.
Chávez, Juan Nepomuceno, to Ambrosio Llano, 17 May, 1809, AHD.
Coleta, Maria, to Ambrosio Llano, 26 April, 1813, AHD.
to Ambrosio Llano, 8 August, 1813, AHD.
de Córdova, Matías, to Ambrosio Llano, 6 August, 1811, AHD.
to José de Bustamante, 20 July, 1811, AHD.
Correa, Eulogio, to Ambrosio Llano, 18 December, 1813, AHD; Guatemala, IV, B1.
Estéves y Ugarte, Pedro Agustín, to Ambrosio Llano, 10 May, 1813, AHD.
to Ambrosio Llano, 10 September, 1813, AHD.
to Ambrosio Llano, 22 October, 1813, AHD.
to Ambrosio Llano, 23 October, 1813, AHD.
to Ambrosio Llano, 10 November, 1813, AHD.
Farrera, Tiburcio José, to Ambrosio Llano, 18 July, 1812, AHD.
to Ambrosio Llano, 20 July, 1812, AHD.
Fernández, Julian, to Ambrosio Llano, 8 March, 1813, AHD.
Figueroa, Estevan, to Ambrosio Llano, 2 May, 1813, AHD.
Figueroa, Luciano, to Ambrosio Llano, 18 April, 1809, AHD.
to Ambrosio Llano, 29 April, 1813, AHD.
to Ambrosio Llano, 12 July, 1813, AHD.
Francos y Monroy, Cayetano, to Carlos III, 6 April, 1781, AHD; San Cristóbal; IIB,1.
García, Antonio, to Ambrosio Llano, 3 September, 1813, AHD.
to Ambrosio Llano, 3 July, 1814, AHD.
to Ambrosio Llano, 3 September, 1814, AHD.
Gates, William, memorandum list #7 to Carles Bowditch, 1915
(?), Princeton University Library, The Garrett Collection of Middle American Mss., 254.
Guzmán y Solorzano, Mariano, to Ambrosio Llano, 7 May, 1813, AHD.
to Ambrosio Llano, 9 May, 1813, AHD.
to Ambrosio Llano, 14 May, 1813, AHD.
to Ambrosio Llano, 1 June, 1813, AHD.
to Ambrosio Llano, 11 June, 1813, AHD.
to Ambrosio Llano, 26 June, 1813, AHD.
to Ambrosio Llano, 29 June, 1813, AHD.
to Ambrosio Llano, 9 July, 1813, AHD.
to Ambrosio Llano, 11 September, 1813, AHD.
to Ambrosio Llano, 22 September, 1813, AHD.
to Ambrosio Llano, 28 December, 1813, AHD.
to Ambrosio Llano, 31 January, 1814, AHD.
to Ambrosio Llano, 3 April, 1814, AHD.

to Ambrosio Llano, 4 April, 1814, AHD.
to Ambrosio Llano, 5 April, 1814, AHD.
to Ambrosio Llano, 11 April, 1814, AHD.
to Ambrosio Llano, 3 July, 1814, AHD.
Junguito, Manuel, to Ambrosio Llano, 27 February, 1813, AHD.
to Ambrosio Llano, 13 May, 1813, AHD.
to Ambrosio Llano, 11 June, 1813, AHD.
to Ambrosio Llano, 26 March, 1814, AHD.
de Loma, Enrique, to Ambrosio Llano, 3 June, 1814, AHD.
Llano, Ambrosio to José de Bustamante, ? May, 1813, AHD.
to José de Bustamante, 17 May, 1813, AHD
to Capitularies, 21 December, 1812, AHD.
to Matias de Córdova, 30 July, 1811, AHD.
to Manuel Junguito, ? May, 1813, AHD.
Marciot y Ortega, José, to Ambrosio Llano, 25 July, 1813, AHD; Huitiupán, IV, C2.
de Moneda, Tomás, to Ambrosio Llano, 18 January, 1813, AHD.
Montes de Oca, Marcos, to Ambrosio Llano, 24 June, 1812, AHD; San Cristóbal, II.11.b.
to Ambrosio Llano, 29 May, 1813, AHD; Huitiupán, IV, B2.
to José de la Barrera, 23 January, 1813, AHD.
Ordóñez y Aguiar, Ramón, to Ambrosio Llano, 6 May, 1813, AHD.
to Ambrosio Llano, 11 September, 1813, AHD.
to Ambrosio Llano, 28 September, 1813, AHD.
to Ambrosio Llano, 12 October, 1813, AHD.
Palacios, Guillermo, to Ambrosio Llano, 6 May, 1813, AHD; Ixtacomitán.
Pinto, José, to Ambrosio Llano, 30 July, 1812, AHD.
Polanco, Francisco, to Carlos III, 20 May, 1778, AGE; Serie Chiapas, *rollo* 69.
to Carlos III, 28 November, 1778, AGE; Serie Chiapas, *rollo* 69.
Priest of Ixtapa to Ambrosio Llano, 10 February, 1809, AHD.
Priest of Palenque to Ambrosio Llano, 21 January, 1813, AHD.
Priest of Socoltenango to Dávila, March, 16, 1815, AHD.
Priest of Tila to Ambrosio Llano, 15 September, 1812, AHD.
Priest of ? to Ambrosio Llano, 24 May, 1812, AGE; Serie Chiapas, *rollo* 90.
Priests of Tuxtla, Ixtapa to Ambrosio Llano, 13 January, 1813, AHD.
De las Quentas Zayas, Agustín, to Carlos III, 2 May, 1792, INAH; T1:7–34*ff.*
Ramírez, Francisco Javier, to Ambrosio Llano, 7 June, 1814, AHD.
Robles, Cayetano, to Ambrosio Llano, 21 July, 1812, AHD.
Robles, Mariano, to Ambrosio Llano, 20 June, 1812, AHD.
to Ambrosio Llano, 19 October, 1812, AHD.
to Ambrosio Llano, 2 November, 1812, AHD.
to Ambrosio Llano, 18 December, 1812, AHD.
to Ambrosio Llano, 19 May, 1812, AHD.
to Ambrosio Llano, 15 January, 1813, AHD.
to Ambrosio Llano, 9 January, 1814, AHD.
to Ambrosio Llano, 11 March, 1814, AHD.
to Ambrosio Llano, 22 April, 1814, AHD.
to Ambrosio Llano, 26 April, 1814, AHD.

Robles, Martin, to Ambrosio Llano, 21 August, 1812, AHD; Ixtacomitán, VIII, B4, 3.
to Ambrosio Llano, 8 September, 1812, AHD; Ixtacomitán, VIII, B3.
Rueda, Manuel Isidro, to Ambrosio Llano, 9 November, 1814, AHD.
Sala Capitular de Guatemala to Ministro de la Gobernación de Ultramar, 19 February, 1813, AG; B1.5, *exp.* 278, *leg.* 7.
Subdelegado de Simojovel to Ambrosio Llano, 4 September, 1811, AGE; Serie Chiapas, *rollo* 69.

PUBLICATIONS

Abennumeya Rasis
1808 *Proclama a los españoles y a la Europa entera del africano numida Abennumeya Rasis...sobre el verdadero carácter de la revolucion francesa, y de su xefe Napoleon, y sobre la conducta que deben guardar todos los gobiernos en hacer causa comun con los españoles para destruir el de una gente enemiga por sistéma y necesidad de todas las instituticiones sociales. Obra traducida del arabe vulgar al castellano por D.M.S.G.S..* J. Niel, Cádiz.

Alaman, D. Lucas
1985 *Historia de Méjico desde los primero movimientos que prepararon su independencia en el año de 1808, hasta la época presente.* Vol. 4. Impr. de J.M. Lara, Mexico City.

Alayza y Paz Soldán, Luis
1960 Las Cortes de Cádiz como causa de la emancipación. In *Simposio sobre la causa de la emancipación del Peru: Testimonios de la época precursora 1780–1820*, pp. 435–437.

de Alba, Rafael (ed.)
1912–1913 *La constitución de 1812 en la Nueva España.* 2 vols. Tipografia Guerrero hnos, Mexico City.

Anaya y Diez de Bonilla, Gerardo
1934? *Compilación de datos relativos a los obispos de la Santa Iglesia de Chiapas.* 3 vols unedited. Archivo Histórico Diocesano, San Cristóbal de Las Casas.

Anderson, W. Woodward
1966 Reform as a Means to Quell Rebellion. In *Mexico and the Spanish Cortes, 1810–1822*, edited by Nettie Lee Benson, pp. 185–207. Institute of Latin American Studies, Latin American Monographs no. 5. University of Texas Press, Austin.

Anna, Timothy E.
1983 *Spain and the Loss of America.* University of Nebraska Press, Lincoln.

Arendt, Hannah (ed.)
1968 *Illuminations*, by Walter Benjamin. Harcourt, Brace & World, New York.

de Argüelles, Agustín
1835 *Examen histórico de la reforma constitucional que hicieron las Córtes generales y estraordinarias desde que se instalaron en la isla de Leon, el dia 24 de setiembre de 1810, hasta que cerraron en Cadiz sus sesiones en 14 del propio mes de 1813.* Impr. de C. Wood e hijo, London.

Armellada, Fray Cesareo de
1959 *La causa indígena americana en las cortes de Cádiz.* Ediciones Cultura Hispánica, Madrid.

Arrangoiz y Berzábal, D. Francisco de Paula de
1871–1872 *México desde 1808 hasta l867: Relación de los principales acontecimientos políticos.* 4 vols. Impr. A. Perez Dubrull, Madrid.

Aubry, Andrés
1990 *Los obispos de Chiapas.* Instituto de Asesoría Antropológica para la Región Maya, A.C. San Cristóbal de Las Casas, Mexico

Aznar Barbechano, Tomás and Juan Carbó
1861 *Memoria sobre la conveniencia, utilidad y necesidad de erigir constitucionalmente en estado de la confederación mexicana el antiguo distrito de Campeche.* Impr. de I. Cumplido, Mexico City.

Batres Jáuregui, Antonio
1920 *La América Central ante la historia.* Vol. 2. Impr. Marroquín hermanos, "Casa colorada," Guatemala City.

Benitez Porta, Oscar Rodolfo
1973 *Secesión pacífica de Guatemala de España.* Universidad de San Carlos de Guatemala, Facultad de Ciencias Jurídicas y Sociales, Guatemala City.

Benson, Nettie Lee
1966 *Mexico and the Spanish Cortes, 1810–1822: Eight Essays.* Latin American Monographs no. 5. Institute of Latin American Studies, University of Texas Press, Austin.

Bentura, Benjamín
1971 *El hidalgo payanés: Don Joaquín de Mosquera y Figueroa.* Ediciones Cultura Hispánica, Madrid.

Bermejo, Vladimiro
1960 El Iltmo. Señor Luis Gonzaga de la Encina XVIII obispo de Arequipa y el fidelisimo del clero arequipeño. In *La causa de la emancipación del Peru: testimonios de la época precursora 1780–1820; actas del Simposio organizado por el Seminario de Historia del Instituto Riva-Agüero.* pp. 355–416. Publicaciones del Instituto Riva-Agüero, no. 26. Pontificia Universidad Católica del Perú, Lima.

Berruezo, María Teresa
1986 *La participación americana en las Cortes de Cádiz 1810–1814.* Centro de Estudios Constitucionales, Madrid.

Berry, Charles R.
1966 The Election of the Mexican Deputies to the Spanish Cortes. In *Mexico and the Spanish Cortes,* 1810–1822, edited by Nettie Lee Benson, pp. 10–42. Latin American Monographs no. 5. Institute of Latin American Studies University of Texas Press, Austin.

Boletín del Archivo General del Gobierno
1938 3(2,3,4), 4(1), Guatemala City.

Bonfil Batalla, Guillermo
1987 *México profundo: Una civilización negada.* Secretaría de Educación Pública. Mexico City.

Brasseur de Bourbourg, Charles Etienne
1851 *Lettres pour servir d'introduction a l'histoire primitive des nations civilisées de l'Amérique septentrional—Cartas para servir de introducción a la historia primitiva de las naciones civilizadas de la América setentrional: Adressées a Monsieur le Duc de Valmy.* M. Murgía, Mexico City.

Breedlove, James M.
1966 . Effect of the Cortes, 1810–1822, on Church Reform in Spain and Mexico. In *Mexico and the Spanish Cortes, 1810–1822: Eight Essays*, edited by Nettie Lee Benson, pp. 113–133. Institute of Latin American Studies, Latin American Monographs no. 5. University of Texas Press. Austin.

Bricker, Victoria
1981 *The Indian Christ, The Indian King: The Substrate of Mayan Myth and Ritual.* University of Texas Press, Austin.

Broadley, A.M.
1911 *Napoleon in Caricature.* John Lane Company. New York.

de Cárdenas, José Eduardo
1985 Memoria a favor de la provincia de Tabasco. In *Tabasco: Textos de su historia*, vol. 1, edited by María Eugenia Arias G, Ana. Lau J., and Ximena Sepúlveda O., pp. 71–107. Gobierno del Estado de Tabasco/Instituto Mora, Mexico City.

Carr, Raymond
1966 *Spain 1808–1939.*: Clarendon Press, Oxford.

Casasola, Gustavo
1980 *Hechos y hombres de México: Anales gráficos de la historia militar de México 1810–1980.* 6 vols..Editorial G. Casasola, Mexico City.

de Castro y Rossi
1862 *Cádiz en la guerra de la independencia.* Cuadro histórico, Revista médica, Cádiz.

Chinchilla, Perla
1985 *Mariano Matamoros.* Comisión Nacional para las Celebraciones del 175 Aniversario de la Independencia Nacional y 75 Aniversario de la Revolución Mexicana, Mexico City.

Collins, Adele Yarbro
1976 *The Combat Myth in the Book of Revelation.* Scholars Press for Harvard Theological Review, Missoula, Montana.

Comenge y Dalmau, Rafael
1909 *Antología de las Cortes de Cádiz.* Hijos de J.A. Garcia, Madrid.

Connelly, Owen (ed.)
1985 *Historical Dictionary of Napoleonic France 1799–1815.* Greenwood Press, Westport, Connecticut.

Cuevas, P. Mariano
1921–1928 *Historia de la iglesia en México.* 5 vols. Impr. del asilo, Patricio Sanz, Tlalpam, Mexico.

Dávila Garibi, José Ignacio Paulino
1913 *Datos biográficos del Ilmo. y Rmo. Sr. Dr. y Mtro. D. Francisco Orozco y Jiménez actual Dignísimo Metropolitano de Guadalajara y Administrador Apostólico de Chiapas.* El Regional, Guadalajara.

De Vos, Jan
1985 *Catálogo de los Documentos Históricos que se conservan en el Fondo llamado "Provincia de Chiapas" del Archivo General de Centro América, Guatemala,* 3 vols. Centro de Estudios Indígenas, UNACH, Centro de Investigaciones Ecológicas del Sureste, San Cristóbal de Las Casas.

1994 *Vivir en frontera: La experiencia de los indios de Chiapas.* Historia de los pueblos indígenas de México. Centro de Investigaciones y Estudios Superiores en

278 REFERENCES CITED

Antropología Social, Instituto Nacional Indigenista, Mexico City .

Du Greco a Goya: chefs-d'oevre du Prado et de collections
1989   *espagnoles: 50è anniversaire de la sauvegarde du patrimonie artistique espagnol, 1939–1989: Musée d'art et d'histoire, Genève, 16 juin–24 septembre.* Le Musée, Geneva.

Echánove Trujillo, Carlos A. (ed.)
1947   *Enciclopedia Yucatanense, conmemorativa del IV centenario de Mérida y Valladolid (Yucatán).* Vol. 5. Edición Oficial del Gobierno de Yucatán, Mexico City.

El Correo Político y Mercantil de Sevilla,
1814   Seville.

El Duque del Infantado
1938   Proclama del Duque del Infantado a los habitantes de ultramar. *Boletín del Archivo General del Gobierno,* 3(3):511–515.

El sueño del Tio José, que quisó ser primero, y quedó cola
1808   Madrid.

Encyclopaedia Britannica
1910   s.v. "Bonaparte" 4:192–197. University Press, Cambridge, England.

Farriss, Nancy M.
1984   *Maya Society under Colonial Rule: The Collective Enterprise of Survival.* Princeton University Press, Princeton.

Fernández Almagro, Melchor
1944   *La emancipación de América y su reflejo en la conciencia española.* Instituto de Estudios Políticos, Madrid.

Fernández Guardía, Ricardo
1941   *Costa Rica: La independencia.* Librería Lehmann y cía, San José.

Fernández Hall, Francisco
1928   Las Cortes de Cádiz y la actuación del diputado de Guatemala en ellas. *Anales de la Sociedad de Geografía e Historia,* 5(2):119–135.

Fisher, Lillian Estelle
1934   *The Background of the Revolution for Mexican Independence.* The Christopher Publishing House, Boston.

Fought, John G.
1972   *Chorti (Mayan) Texts (1).* University of Philadelphia Press, Philadelphia.

de Gandia, Enrique
1928   La colonia y la independencia. *Anales de la Sociedad de Geografía e Historia,* 26(1):3–1.

García Laguardia, Jorge Mario
1971   *Orígenes de la democracia constitucional en Centroamérica.* Editorial Universitaria, San José.

Garcia Rosell, César
1960   Las lenguas indígenas en las campañas de la independencia. In *Simposio sobre la causa de la emancipación del Peru: Testimonios de la época precursora 1780–1820,* pp. 491–494.

Garza, David T.
1966   Mexican Constitutional Expression in the Cortes of Cádiz, In *Mexico and the Spanish Cortes, 1810–1822: Eight Essays,* edited by Nettie Lee Benson, pp. 43–58. Latin American Monographs no. 5. Institute of Latin American Studies, University of

Texas Press, Austin.

Gazeta de Guatemala

1810   vol. XIV, Guatemala City.

Gerhard, Peter

1982   *The Southeast Frontier of New Spain.* Princeton University Press, Princeton.

Gil y Sáenz, Manuel

1985   Epoca de Fernando VII (última del período colonial). In *Tabasco: Textos de su Historia,* vol. 1, edited by María Eugenia Arias G, Ana. Lau J., and Ximena Sepúlveda O. pp. 69–70. Gobierno del Estado de Tabasco/Instituto Mora, Mexico City.

Girard, Rafael

1962   *Los mayas eternos.* Libro Mex, Mexico City.

Glover, Michael

1971   *Legacy of Glory: The Bonaparte Kingdom of Spain 1808–1813.* Scribner, New York.

Gómez Carrillo, Agustín

1879–1905 *Historia de la América Central, desde el descubrimiento del país por los españoles (1502) hasta su independencia de la España (1821).* Estab. Tip. de El Progreso, Guatemala City.

Goya y la constitución de 1812

1982   *Goya y la constitución de 1812,* [exposición] diciembre 1982–enero 1983. Museo Municipal. Ayuntamiento de Madrid, Delegación de la Cultura, Madrid.

Guillén, Flavio

1981   *Un fraile prócer y una fábula poema: Estudio acerca de Fray Matías de Córdova.* Talleres Gráficos del Estado, Tuxtla Gutiérrez.

Gurevich, Aaron

1992   *Historical Anthropology of the Middle Ages.* University of Chicago Press, Chicago.

Gurría Lacroix, Jorge

1985   La Protesta de un Cunduacanense. In *Tabasco: Textos de su historia,* vol. 1, edited by María Eugenia Arias G, Ana. Lau J., and Ximena Sepúlveda O., p. 70. Gobierno del Estado de Tabasco/Instituto Mora, Mexico City.

Hamill, Hugh M., Jr.

1966   *The Hidalgo Revolt, Prelude to Mexican Independence.* University of Florida Press, Gainesville.

Hernández y Dávalos, Juan

1877   *Colección de documentos para la historia de la guerra de independencia de México de1808 a 1821.* Vol. 2. Impr. J.M. Sandoval, Mexico City.

Horcasitas, Fernando

1969   Proclama en náhuatl de don Carlos María de Bustamante a los indígenas mexicanos. *Estudios de Cultura Nahuatl* 8:271–278.

Ichon, Alain

1969   *La Religion des Totonaques de la Sierra.* Centre National de la Recherche Scientifique, Paris.

Kaufmann, William W.

1951   *British Policy and the Independence of Latin America 1804–1828.* Yale University Press, New Haven

Kern, Robert W.

1990   *Historical Dictionary of Modern Spain, 1700–1988.* Greenwood Press, New York.

Knight, Franklin W. and Peggy K. Liss (eds.)
1994   Atlantic Empires: The Network of Trade and Economy, Culture, and Society in the Atlantic World, 1650–1850. University of Tennessee Press, Knoxville.

de La Fuente, José M.
1913   Matamoros: Apuntes biográficos. Imp. del Museo Nacional de Arqueología, Historia, y Etnología. Mexico City.

Lacroix, Jorge Gurría
1985   La Protesta de un Cunduacanense. In Tabasco: Textos de su história, vol 1 edited by María Eugenia Arias G, Ana. Lau J., and Ximena Sepúlveda O., pp. 70–107. Gobierno del Estado de Tabasco/Instituto Mora, Mexico City.

Ladd, Doris M.
1976   The Mexican Nobility at Independence 1780–1826. Institute of Latin American Studies, Latin American Monographs no. 40. University of Texas Press, Austin.

Lafuente y Zamalloa, Modesto
1869   Historia general de España. Vol. 17. Impr.Chaulie, Madrid.

Lanz, Manuel A.
1905   Compendio de historia de Campeche. El Fenix, Campeche.

Laughlin, Robert M.
1975   The Great Tzotzil Dictionary of San Lorenzo Zinacantán. Smithsonian Contributions to Anthropology, 19. Smithsonian Institution Press, Washington D. C.
1977   Of Cabbages and Kings: Tales from Zinacantán. Smithsonian Contributions to Anthropology, 23. Smithsonian Institution Press, Washington., D. C.
1988   The Great Tzotzil Dictionary of Santo Domingo Zinacantán. Smithsonian Contributions to Anthropology, 31. Smithsonian Institution Press, Washington, D. C.

Lemmon, Alfred E. (comp.)
1987 Royal Music of the Moxos. New Orleans Musica de Camera, New Orleans.

Lemoine Villicaña, Ernesto
1965   Morelos: Su vida revolucionaria a través de sus escritos y de otros testimonios de la época. Universidad Nacional Autónoma de México, Mexico City.

Lerdo de Tejada, Miguel
1988   El regreso de Fernando VII y la constitución de Cádiz. In Veracruz, textos de su historia, edited by Carmen Blázquez Domínguez, pp. 174–182. Gobierno del Estado de Veracruz, Instituto Veracruzano de Cultura, Mexico City.

Liss, Peggy K.
1983   Atlantic Empires: The Network of Trade and Revolution 1713–1826. The John Hopkins University Press. Baltimore.
1992   Isabel the Queen. Oxford University Press, New York.

López Gutiérrez, Gustavo
1957   Chiapas y sus epopeyas libertarias, 3 vols. Talleres tip. del gobierno del estado, Tuxtla Gutiérrez.
1965   Gutiérrez coloso federalista chiapaneco. Tuxtla Gutiérrez, Chiapas.

López Reyes, Diógenes
1980   Historia de Tabasco. Consejo Editorial del Gobierno del Estado de Tabasco, Mexico City.

López Sánchez, Hermilo
1960   Apuntes históricos de San Cristóbal de las Casas, Chiapas, México, 2 vols. Mexico City.

Lynch, John
  1973   *The Spanish American Revolutionaries 1808–1826.* Norton, New York.
Lynch, John (ed.)
  1994   *Latin American Revolutions, 1808–1826.* University of Oklahoma Press, Norman
Malaspina, Alessandro
  1885   *Viaje político-scientífico alrededor del mundo por las corbetas Descubierta y Atrevida al mando de los capitanes de návio D. Alejandro Malaspina y Don José de Bustamante y Guerra desde 1789 a 1794.* Impr. de la viuda e hijos de Abienzo, Madrid.
Manifesto of the Spanish Nation, to the Other Nations of Europe
  1909?   G. Sidney, printer, London.
Marroquin Rojas, Clemente
  1971   *Historia de Guatemala.* Tipografia Nacional, Guatemala City.
Medina, José Toribio
  1930   Bibliografía de las lenguas quechua y aymará. *Contributions from the Museum of the American Indian Heye Foundation* 7:7.
Menendez Pidal, Ramón
  1968   *Historia de España: La España de Fernando VII.* Espasa Calpe, 26. Madrid.
de Mier Noriega y Guerra, Servando Teresa
  1922   *Historia de la revolución de Nueva España antiguamente Anahuac o verdadero origen y causas de ella en la relación de sus progresos hasta el presente año de 1813,* 2 vols. Impr. de la Cámara de Diputados, Mexico City.
Moreno, Laudelino
  1926?   *Guatemala y la invasión napoleonica en España,* 7(1):3–17. Talleres poligráficos, Madrid.
  1927   *Independencia de la Capitanía General de Guatemala,* 8:3–32. Talleres poligráficos, Madrid.
Nuñez de León, Rodrigo
  1992   *Memoria Histórica de la provincia de Chiapa, una de las de Guatemala.* Rodrigo Nuñez, Editores, Tuxtla Gutiérrez.
Nuñez y Dominguez, José de J.
  1950   *La virreina mexicana: Doña María Francisca de la Gándara de Calleja.* Impr. Universitaria, Mexico City.
Ordóñez y Aguiar, Ramón
  1907   *Historia de la creación del Cielo y de la Tierra, conforme al sistema de la gentilidad mexicana.* Mexico City.
Parsons, Elsie Clews
  1936   *Mitla: Town of the Souls.* University of Chicago Press. Chicago.
Pérez Castro, Ana Bella
  1989   *Entre montañas y cafetales Luchas agrarias en el norte de Chiapas.* Universidad Nacional Autónoma de México, Mexico City.
Pike, Fredrick B. (ed.)
  1969   *Latin American History: Select Problems; identity, integration, and nationhood.* Harcourt Brace and World, New York.
Porrúa, Miguel Angel, (ed.)
  1992   *Autos seguidos por algunos de los naturales del pueblo de Chamula en contra de su cura don José Ordóñez y Aguiar por varios excesos que le suponían 1779.* Gobierno

del Estado de Chiapas, Universidad Autónoma de Chiapas, Facultad de Derecho, UNAM. Mexico City.

Rio, Antonio del
1822 *Description of the ruins of an ancient city, discovered near Palenque, in the kingdom of Guatemala...translated from the original manuscript report of Captain Antonio del Rio: followed by Teatro critico americano: or, A critical investigation and research into the history of the Americans, by Doctor Paul Felix Cabrera.* Henry Berthoud, and Suttoby, Evance and Fox, London.

Rivet, Paul, and Georges de Créqui-Montfort
1951 *Bibliographie des langues aymará et kichua,* vol. 1. Institut d'ethnologie, Université de Paris, Travaux V51.. et mémoires de l'Institut d'ethnologie, Paris.

Robertson, William Spence
1939 *France and Latin American Independence.* The Johns Hopkins Press, Baltimore.

Robles Dominguez de Mazariegos, Mariano
1813 *Memoria histórica de la provincia de Chiapa una de las de Guatemala.* Cádiz.

Rodríguez, Mario
1978 *The Cadiz Experiment in Central America, 1808–1826.* University of California Press, Berkeley.

Rosenthal, Mario
1962 *Guatemala: The Story of an Emergent Latin-American Democracy.* Twayne Publishers, New York.

Rubio Mañé, J. Ignacio
1968 Los Sanjuanistas de Yucatán: I-Manuel Jiménez Solís, el padre Justis. *Boletín del Archivo General de la Nación,* 9(3–4):401–508, Mexico City.

Rydjord, John
1972 *Foreign Interest in the Independence of New Spain: An Introduction to the War for Independence.* Russell and Russell, New York.

Salazar, Ramón
1928 *Historia de veintiun años: La independencia de* Guatemala. Tipografia Nacional. Guatemala City.

Salvatierra, Sofonías
1939 *Contribución a la historia de Centroamérica.* Tipografia Progreso, Managua.

Saviñon, Antonio
1812 *Roma libre: Tragedia en cinco actos.* Imprenta Tormentaria, Managua.

Schickel, Richard, and the Editors of Time-Life Books
1968 *The World of Goya 1746–1828.* Time-Life Books, New York.

Shaw, Mary (editor)
1972 *Según nuestros antepasados: textos folkloricos de Guatemala y Honduras.* Instituto Linguistico de Verano, Guatemala City.

Solis, Ramón,
1969 *El Cádiz de la cortes: La vida en la ciudad en los años de 1810 a 1813.* Alianza Editorial, Madrid.

Sotelo Regil, Luis Fernando
1963 *Campeche en la historia,* 2 vols. Mexico City.

Stanhope, Philip Henry, 5th Earl of
1888 *Notes of Conversations with the Duke of Wellington, 1831–1851.* John Murray,

London.

Stoetzer, O. Carlos

1966   *El pensamiento político en la América española durante el período de la emancipación (1789–1825), las bases hispánicas y las corrientes europeas.* Vol. .2. Instituto de Estudios Póliticos, Madrid.

Timmons, Wilbert H.

1963   *Morelos of Mexico: Priest, Soldier, Statesman of Mexico.* Texas Western College Press, El Paso.

Trens, Manuel Bartolomé

1947   *Historia de Veracruz.* Impr. Enríquez, Jalapa.

1957   *Historia de Chiapas: desde los tiempos más remotos hasta la caida del segundo imperio.* Mexico City.

de Vadillo, José Manuel

1836   *Apuntes sobre los principales sucesos que han influido en el actual estado de la América del Sud.* Librería de Feros. Cádiz.

Vela, David

1956   *Barrundia ante el espejo de su tiempo.* Editorial Universitaria, Guatemala City

Vidal, Manuel

1935   *Nociones de historia de Centro América (especial de El Salvador).* Talleres gráficos cisneros, San Salvador.

Villacorta Calderón, José Antonio

1941   Guatemala en las Cortes de Cádiz. *Anales de la Sociedad de Geografía e Historia* 7(1):3–6.

1942   *Historia de la Capitanía General de Guatemala.* Tipografía Nacional, Guatemala City.

Villanueva, Carlos A.

1911   *Napoleon y la independencia de América.* Ed. Garnier, Paris.

Villanueva, Joaquín Lorenzo

1820   *Apuntes sobre el arresto de los vocales de cortes egecutado en mayo de 1814. Escritos en la carcel de La Corona por el diputado Villanueva, uno de los presos.* D. Garcia y Campoy, Madrid.

Villanueva U., Horacio

1960   La jura de la constitución de 1812 en Cajamarca. In *Simposio sobre la causa de la emancipación del Peru: Testimonios de la época precursora 1780–1820,* pp. 438–439.

Walton, William

1814   *Exposé on the Dissentions of Spanish America.* Booth, London.

1837   *The Revolution of Spain from 1808 to the end of 1836*: *With biographical sketches of the most distinguished personages, and a narrative of the war in the peninsula down to the present time, from the most authentic sources,* 2 vols. R. Bentley, London.

1993   *Weekly News Update on Nicaragua and the Americas.* Nicaragua Solidarity Network of Greater New York, #196, October 31, 1993.

Wilson, Carter

1972   *A Green Tree and a Dry Tree.* The Macmillan Company, New York.

Woodward, Ralph Lee, Jr.
1965a Economic and Social Origins of the Guatemalan Political Parties. *Hispanic American Historical Review* 45(4):544–566.
1965b The Guatemalan Merchants and National Defense: 1810. *Hispanic American Historical Review* 45(3):452–462.
1990 Changes in the Nineteenth Century Guatemalan State and its Indian Policies. In *Guatemalan Indians and the State:1540 to 1988*, edited by Carol A. Smith, pp. 52–71. University of Texas Press,. Austin.
Wortman, Miles L.
1982 *Government and Society in Central America, 1680–1840*. Columbia University Press. New York.
Zamora Castellanos, Pedro
1935 *El grito de independenci*a, *por el general de división Pedro Zamora Castellanos; publicación hecha bajo los auspicios del gobierno de la república, con motivo de la inauguración del monumento a los próceres de la independencia, el 15 de septiembre de 1935*. Tipografía Nacional, Guatemala City.

Index